Freedom's Debtors

ɘⱲɘ

THE LEWIS WALPOLE SERIES
IN EIGHTEENTH-CENTURY CULTURE AND HISTORY

The Lewis Walpole Series, published by Yale University
Press with the aid of the Annie Burr Lewis Fund, is dedicated
to the culture and history of the long eighteenth century (from
the Glorious Revolution to the accession of Queen Victoria). It
welcomes work in a variety of fields, including literature and
history, the visual arts, political philosophy, music, legal history,
and the history of science. In addition to original scholarly work,
the series publishes new editions and translations of writing from
the period, as well as reprints of major books that are currently
unavailable. Though the majority of books in the series will
probably concentrate on Great Britain and the Continent, the
range of our geographical interests is as wide as
Horace Walpole's.

Freedom's Debtors

British Antislavery in Sierra Leone
in the Age of Revolution

Padraic X. Scanlan

Yale
UNIVERSITY PRESS
NEW HAVEN AND LONDON

Published with assistance from the Annie Burr Lewis Fund.

Yale University Press books may be purchased in quantity for educational, business, or promotional use. For information, please e-mail sales.press@yale.edu (U.S. office) or sales@yaleup.co.uk (U.K. office).

Set in Fournier MT type by IDS Infotech Ltd.
Printed in the United States of America.

Library of Congress Control Number: 2017935589
ISBN 978-0-300-21744-5 (hardcover : alk. paper)

A catalogue record for this book is available from the British Library.

This paper meets the requirements of ANSI/NISO Z39.48–1992 (Permanence of Paper).

10 9 8 7 6 5 4 3 2 1

For Catherine

[The slave trade] has now become, in this country at least, the object of universal execration . . . how was this extraordinary revolution effected? By examination, inquiry, evidence.
—Zachary Macaulay, *East and West India Sugar* (London, 1823)

As for stopping the Slave Trade, I see it must be done partly by force.
—John Kizell to Governor Edward Columbine, Sierra Leone, 15 November 1810

Contents

Acknowledgments

This book began in the History Department at Princeton University. My first thanks are to Linda Colley. Her command of British culture and politics in the long eighteenth century, and her incisive criticism and editorial instincts, made this book, and the dissertation from which it emerged, sharper, clearer, and more serious. I hope her influence is obvious; her work is a model of scholarship and writing which I try to emulate. Jeremy Adelman, Lauren Benton, Christopher Leslie Brown, and Emmanuel Kreike helped me to find threads in my dissertation that might eventually hold together as a book. I hope that this looks something like what they imagined. Mariana Candido, David Cannadine, Michael Gordin, Dirk Hartog, Bhavani Raman, and Wendy Warren also generously offered their time and expertise at various stages of the project. I started thinking about the contradictions of British radicalism and reform in the age of Atlantic revolutions long before I met Charles MacCarthy in the archive. As an undergraduate at McGill, I read E. P. Thompson on "miners, potters and cutlers reading *Rights of Man*" and was mesmerized by the possibilities of a radical British politics cut down by Tory reaction, and buried under the starchy reforms of the Victorians. That lost world of the 1790s, although it may well be a fantasy, still nourishes me. But it would never have occurred to me that I might be able to think and write about the past for a living had it not been for the encouragement of Brian Cowan and Elizabeth Elbourne, who remain mentors, colleagues, and friends.

I wrote this book while I spent two good years as a Prize Fellow in Economics, History and Politics at Harvard University. Emma Rothschild has been a stalwart supporter, and her unparalleled understanding of the commercial world of the eighteenth century has changed the way I think about the economic history of everyday life. The Senior Fellows, and especially Sunil Amrith and Walter Johnson, provided good counsel when I needed it. I am also grateful to my colleagues in the fellowship, and especially to

Fahad Bishara, Diana Kim, Anne O'Donnell, Brandon Terry, Kirsty Walker, and Alexia Yates. I am very pleased to be able to stay on as a Research Associate at the Joint Centre for History and Economics at Cambridge and Harvard to continue the conversations I started as a Fellow.

My research was made possible by the support of the History Department, the Program in Canadian Studies, and the University Center for Human Values at Princeton University, and by the Program in Economics, History and Politics and the Center for History and Economics at Harvard University. The Department of International History at the London School of Economics generously supported the finishing touches of my research and writing. I am grateful to the librarians and archivists at the University of Illinois at Chicago Special Collections, the Nova Scotia Archives, and the Templer Study Centre at the National Army Museum for helping me to navigate their fascinating collections. Abu Koroma at the Sierra Leone Public Archives in Freetown helped me to understand the records of one of Britain's most interesting and overlooked colonial experiments. Phil Misevich guided me through the logistics of getting to Sierra Leone, and put me in touch with the indomitable Momoh Taziff Koroma, who opened his home in Freetown to me.

I was invited to present versions of the arguments in this book to the History and Economics Seminar at Cambridge University, the History Department at the University of Georgia, the British History Seminar at McGill University, the Eighteenth-Century Seminar at Princeton University, and the Harriet Tubman Institute for Research on Africa and its Diasporas at York University. I am grateful to those audiences for comments and suggestions. Early versions of the arguments of this book have appeared in other forms: "The Rewards of Their Exertions: Prize Money and British Abolitionism in Sierra Leone, 1808–1823" (*Past & Present* 225:1 [2014]), and "The Colonial Rebirth of British Anti-Slavery: The Liberated African Villages of Sierra Leone, 1815–1823" (*American Historical Review* 121:4 [2016]). I am grateful to the editors of these journals for their permission to print some of the material from those articles here, and for their insights into the project as a whole. Thanks also to several anonymous reviewers for comments that helped to clarify both the more narrow historiographic points of the articles, and the wider thrust of this book.

I am also grateful to an extended family of historians whose friendship, support, and solidarity have helped me to navigate a peripatetic, often unstable professional life. I first got to know Bronwen Everill and Richard Anderson in the Freetown archives; they helped me to understand the history of early Sierra Leone and the world of the Liberated Africans, and have saved me from all kinds of unforced errors. Christopher M. Florio has been a probing critic and boundless source of insight into the history of slavery and emancipation in the nineteenth-century United States. Greg Childs, Henry Cowles, Rohit De, Will Deringer, Zack Kagan-Guthrie, Jamie Kreiner, Kyrill Kunakhovich, Sarah Milov, Julie Stephens, Melissa Teixeira and Nurfadzilah Yahaya also provided suggestions, encouragement, and advice on the manuscript. Thanks also to Laura Davulis (now at the Naval Institute Press) and Jaya Chatterjee at Yale University Press for their confidence in this project, to Jeff Schier for careful copyediting, and to two anonymous readers for their thoughtful comments.

My family in Montréal have been a constant source of support; thanks to my parents, Elizabeth Therrien Scanlan and Larry Scanlan, my father- and mother-in-law, Alan Evans and Karen Evans, and my brother Sean Scanlan and his partner, Patty Chan. The purity of Elspeth and Ike's animal nature kept me sane through hours of reading and writing, and has kept homes in New Jersey, Massachusetts, and Cambridgeshire mostly vermin-free. Rafe arrived just in time for copyediting: his kicking and screaming and consciousness-building is beautiful. Finally, Catherine Evans read this book before it was a book, before it was a dissertation, before it was anything but a mess of vignettes, characters, errors, and intuitions. The clarity of her historical insight, her sense of argument, her deep understanding of British imperial history and the common law, and her rigorous editorial skills made this book better. Her love made this book possible.

Freedom's Debtors

Introduction

On 21 January 1824, in what is now Ghana, near the banks of the Pra River, between the British fort at Cape Coast Castle and the bivouacked Asante army at Asemkow, Sir Charles MacCarthy and a party of soldiers under his command were surprised by an Asante detachment. MacCarthy, governor-in-chief of Britain's West African possessions, was shot twice in the firefight and bled out. His private secretary, J. T. Williams, was knocked unconscious and taken prisoner. Williams came to in the Asante camp, next to MacCarthy's headless corpse.[1] A few years later, when British fortunes in the First Anglo-Asante War improved, a skull, resting on tiger skin and silk and "enveloped in paper covered with Arabic characters," was seized as part of a hoard of Asante jewelry, ivory, and weapons. The British officer who found it believed that it was MacCarthy's skull.[2]

In 1807, Britain passed the Slave Trade Act and became the first major European slave-trading power to abolish its slave trade. Many nineteenth-century Britons were enormously proud of their government for what they took to be the sacrifice of a lucrative branch of British commerce on the altar of Christian national virtue (fig. 1). In Britain, antislavery proved to be a persuasive justification for domestic reform and imperial expansion. Since 1807, many scholars have taken a deep interest in the origins of British antislavery and in the campaign for the abolition of the slave trade. And yet, many of those histories have been histories of the white conscience, of how antislavery went from an unthinkable fantasy to an urgent national priority. *Freedom's Debtors* is a different kind of history. This book is a history of putting laws against the slave trade into force: a history of severed heads and

Figure 1. "Britannia Implored by Slaves." From *Poems on the Abolition of the Slave Trade* (London, 1809). Britannia, the mythic personification of Britain, hears the pleas of enslaved Africans while the figure of Justice presides. The abolition of the slave trade was a source of patriotic pride for many Britons, particularly during the Napoleonic wars. (Courtesy of the John Carter Brown Library at Brown University)

everyday commerce, of people in pain and in motion, of improvisation and miscommunication. Before Charles MacCarthy lost his head, he served for ten years as governor of Sierra Leone, a small British colony on the coast of West Africa. His success in Sierra Leone led to his being appointed to the command of all British forces in the region; antislavery made MacCarthy's career and eventually put him in the sights of Asante riflemen. In 1807, there were no slaves in Britain to emancipate, and the end of the slave trade was a far cry from the end of slavery in the sugar colonies of the West Indies. Antislavery activists painted the Slave Trade Act as a moment of atonement, a charter for further reform, and a confirmation of British superiority. When the Act passed, many Britons felt a sense of collective guilt relieved and national virtue affirmed—profound symbolic achievements, but symbols nonetheless. In Sierra Leone, British antislavery was not a triumph of good over evil, but a practical and difficult problem of governance. The history of British antislavery looks very different from West Africa.

First, *Freedom's Debtors* is a history of the ideology of British antislavery in practice. From 1807 through the 1820s, Sierra Leone was the headquarters of British slave-trade interdiction. Among all of Britain's colonies, only Sierra Leone had been founded with an explicit antislavery mandate. In 1787, the colony was established as the "Province of Freedom," a short-lived experiment that collapsed under the pressures of starvation and attacks from local peoples. The settlers dispersed to nearby villages and trading forts. In 1792, the colony was refounded as a new settlement, Freetown, a pilot plant intended to prove that free workers could produce cash crops as profitably as slaves could. After 1807, most of the people rescued from slave ships captured by the Royal Navy off the Atlantic coast of Africa were put ashore and resettled in Sierra Leone—at least 81,745 people over the course of the nineteenth century.[3] These people were given a number of names by the colonial government, including "recaptives" and "prize Negroes." However, until about 1820 they were most frequently referred to as "captured Negroes" and, from roughly 1820 through the rest of the nineteenth century, as "Liberated Africans." Sierra Leone was not the only place where Liberated Africans were repatriated by British officers and courts. The category appears in the records of the Cape Colony and in Barbados, Trinidad, Mauritius, Zanzibar, and elsewhere.[4] However, far more Liberated Africans were repatriated in Sierra Leone than anywhere else in the empire, and the colony was unique in the degree to which its governance was defined by institutions designed for their emancipation and management. In Britain, antislavery ideology was often illustrated using motifs of debt and credit, and often reckoned in speculative financial terms. What was freedom worth? What had the end of the slave trade cost Britain and what credit had Britain earned? Britain, many antislavery activists felt, was in moral debt because of the transatlantic slave trade. By abolishing the trade, Britain seemed to have made a financial sacrifice for national atonement. But what if Britain had overpaid? Converting moral into financial debt and credit posed a new question: What did former captives owe in exchange for their freedom? After 1807, colonial officials in Sierra Leone and their antislavery patrons in London set about answering this question. Former slaves were treated as a source of flexible, fungible labour. They grew crops, cut roads, built and maintained buildings, worked on ships or as stevedores, fought under British command, were assigned to live in purpose-built villages—all according to official perceptions of the "needs" of the colony. In the age of revolution, Liberated Africans were freedom's debtors; no longer enslaved, but bound to the British empire by the rhetoric and practices of antislavery.

Freedom's Debtors is also a history of the beginning of a new kind of British empire in West Africa. The fifty-odd years between MacCarthy's death and the beginning of the violent, greedy land grab by the European powers that historians usually call the "Scramble for Africa" was a period of vast economic change and incrementally increasing European presence on the African continent. In eighteenth-century West Africa, the most common model of European settlement had been the trading fort, strongly associated with slave dealing. In this kind of trade, European states and private companies established forts at key points along the coast, under the protection of local kings and chiefs. Oceangoing European ships brought trade goods to the forts, to be exchanged for commodities and enslaved people brought by African merchants traveling overland by caravan or by sea in smaller coast-hugging vessels. The forts were warehouses for goods, and prisons for enslaved people about to make the Middle Passage. The forts survived through the protection of their landlords and the profits to be made selling people. In contrast, Sierra Leone was founded to change Africa. The great antislavery campaigner Thomas Clarkson declared that the end of the British slave trade had scrubbed out "the stain of the blood of Africa."[5] With hands washed clean of the "blood of Africa," many British Evangelicals and missionaries were eager to wash Africa in the Blood of the Lamb. Merchants hoped to open new markets for their goods. Military officials hoped to recruit African soldiers. The end of the slave trade in Sierra Leone became an invitation to imagine a new kind of empire in Africa, based on commerce in African commodities rather than enslaved people, and firmly rooted in the righteous rhetoric of antislavery. The colony allowed a generation of antislavery campaigners to write and rehearse the scripts for later colonial experiments in "civilization."

Finally, *Freedom's Debtors* is a history of everyday economic life in a British colony devoted to the end of the slave trade. The commercial projects set in motion in Sierra Leone had at least two profound consequences for British colonial governance in West Africa and antislavery in the wider

British empire. First, in Sierra Leone after the end of the slave trade, British antislavery transformed into colonialism. Economic reform was the thin end of the wedge. The elite group of parliamentarians, financiers, and orators who guided colonial Sierra Leone believed that British commerce was the most evolved way of doing business. Traditions of exchange that did not include cash, wage work, regular hours, savings, interest, credit, underwritten insurance, capital accumulation, individual and transferable ownership of land, clear pricing, and the consumption of manufactured consumer goods seemed like inferior deviations from a self-evident norm. However, the economic practices of the slave trade on the West African coast were not "primitive" precapitalist practices, a way station on the way to "modernity," but part of a robust political economy connected to, but independent of, British capitalism. Replacing barter with cash commerce required changing not only a means of exchange, but an entire commercial culture. This might seem obvious. And yet, the commercial expectations of early nineteenth-century Britons are far closer to the norms of economic life in the globalized, capitalist twenty-first century than were the barter practices of precolonial West Africa. It is easy to see commerce in West Africa through the eyes of colonial officials, to treat the reform of commerce under colonial rule as natural, or at least inevitable. It wasn't. It might take a deliberate effort to remember, but contemporary capitalism is as much a contingent cultural tradition as "traditional" barter commerce is. To try to emphasize this point, I occasionally refer to the package of economic practices which colonial officials hoped to impose in West Africa as "economic folkways." I use this turn of phrase as a reminder—and to remind myself—that British capitalism was itself a culture, and not a blank space from which to assay and transform other cultures. Economic reform was inherently a kind of colonialism.

In addition to British plans to replace "traditional" barter with British economic folkways, the laws against the slave trade allowed colonial officials and their backers in London to put into place financial incentives for capturing slave ships. These incentives shaped colonial governance in profound ways, and helped to attract the British armed forces' interest in West Africa. By managing this new source of income on their behalf, elite activists in London could guide—if not exactly control—officers and colonial officials in West Africa. Under the Slave Trade Act, antislavery was profitable. In London, the financial transactions associated with interdiction were a new source of cash and capital, while privileged information from military officers about West

African conditions gave merchants associated with antislavery a competitive edge. In Freetown, military officers and colonial officials made money from captured slave ships, and built a post-emancipation society around the labor of former captives. Recent histories of capitalism and slavery emphasize the way the two vast, complex phenomena grew together, and how the global economy of the eighteenth and nineteenth centuries was made on the backs of enslaved people. Historians of an earlier generation were preoccupied with finding the connection between capitalism and antislavery.[6] *Freedom's Debtors* shows how the acquisitive values of capitalism underwrote both slavery and antislavery. In Sierra Leone, the bright lines of antislavery principle faded into the ambiguities of colonial practice.

British Antislavery in the Age of Revolution

The transatlantic slave trade was grotesque. On the Middle Passage from Africa to the Americas, captives were locked below the decks of slave ships, sometimes packed in like cordwood, sometimes shackled to the damp timbers of the hull, with blood, shit, and vomit sloshing around their ankles. The slaves "danced" for exercise, kept in time by the armed crew. Violence saturated the fug of the hold and the salt breeze on deck. Many voyages ended in revolt. Many slaves died of disease or suicide. Dead and near-dead people were thrown overboard and gulped down in ragged mouthfuls by the sharks following the wake.[7] When the ships finally arrived in the Americas, most survivors began a life of miserable work, planting, cutting, and processing sugarcane, cotton, or tobacco.

By the late eighteenth century, most Britons understood in the abstract that there was something unsavory about their sweets. "We, unthinkingly, sacrifice whole crowds of human beings every year to a paltry gratification," wrote one mournful activist, calling for a boycott on sugar.[8] The colonies of the West Indies, where most of the sugar consumed in Britain was produced, had a seedy reputation. Jamaica, the largest sugar colony, was considered to be a morbid, dangerous place where unscrupulous men went to get rich or die trying. Sailors in the slave trade were reviled both by Royal Navy hands and by other merchant seamen.[9] However, the average British consumer never met an enslaved plantation worker, or had enough capital or credit to gamble as a planter. Although many Britons were uncomfortable with the slave trade, they rarely had to see it. The physical torments of slavery were mostly invisible, and sugar was cheap.

In the mid-eighteenth century, Quaker communities on both sides of the Atlantic began to organize against slavery, expelling slave owners and slave traders from their communion. In London in 1772, James Somerset, an enslaved man, sued his erstwhile master for attempting to take him by force from England to the West Indies. A leading judge, Lord Mansfield, refused to allow Somerset to be taken, making Somerset de facto a free man. Somerset's case technically did not change the status of any other enslaved people residing in Britain. However, interpretations of *Somerset*, particularly among the general public, ran far ahead of the jurisprudence of the case, and the decision was widely understood formally to have abolished slavery in Britain. The turbulent decades of the American and French Revolutions helped to connect this growing culture of antislavery to more immediate, visceral issues in British politics. In 1776, thirteen of Britain's colonies in the Americas rose in revolt. In 1783, the end of the American War of Independence made it easier to imagine a British empire without slavery. The West Indian colonies were disreputable slave societies, embarrassing and intransigent; the American slave colonies had seemed valuable, even respectable, to many Britons, and losing them made it easier to oppose slave trading.[10]

In 1787, it became even more difficult for Britons to ignore the physical horrors of the slave trade. An image of a shackled African man in a loincloth, with the caption "Am I Not a Man, and a Brother," appeared everywhere—on prints and plates, on badges and brooches—even on sugar bowls. Josiah Wedgwood, a member of the newly founded Society for Effecting the Abolition of the Slave Trade and a pioneer in the industrial manufacture of pottery, had commissioned the image, and ordered his factories to stamp it onto dozens of different products. In the same year, a popular print of a cross section of the slave ship *Brookes*—full of bodies lying end to end—showed just how many people might be crammed into the hold of a slave ship. Activists gave speeches across Britain, gathering thousands of signatures from ordinary people on long petitions against the slave trade and submitted them to Parliament. British abolitionism had come of age.

And yet, the Britons who signed petitions, boycotted sugar, or bought and displayed antislavery prints were not declaring that people freed from slavery ought to be "citizens." In this book, I use British "antislavery" and "abolitionism" nearly interchangeably; in Britain and the British empire, there was little that divided the concepts until well into the 1820s. By contrast, the "abolitionism" coming of age in the United States was more radical. American abolitionism called not only for emancipation but also for the rights of American citizenship to be granted to freedpeople. By this standard, even William Wilberforce—Britain's most famous abolitionist—would not be considered part of the movement. Anglo-American abolitionism was not a single movement, but a series of discrete and overlapping movements, with different objectives, tactics, and bases of support. "Abolitionism" meant different things in different times to different people. British abolitionism was much more conservative and much more imperial in its geography and its ambitions. Enslaved people in the British empire lived, for the most part, far from most Britons. Moreover, even Britons in Britain were not "citizens" in the sense of the word as it was used by the French or the Americans. "Freedom" for former slaves in the British empire, and "antislavery" in Britain itself, were concepts intertwined with careful reconsiderations of the meaning and limits of a vague but beloved "British liberty." To many Britons, "liberty" was defined against French *liberté*. The former was disciplined and wholesome, the latter wild and licentious.[11] And soon after "Am I Not a Man and a Brother" became ubiquitous in British homes and shops, Britain was at war with the French Republic.

Fears of *liberté* were compounded by fears of slave insurrection. In 1791, a revolution led by enslaved people in the French colony of Saint-Domingue, the single most valuable colony in the West Indies, confirmed for many British abolitionists the advantages of teaching "British liberty" to slaves before emancipation, of "training" enslaved people for freedom. The revolt, which led to the founding of the Republic of Haiti in 1804, seemed to show both that the slave colonies of the West Indies would need to improve living conditions for slaves or risk revolution, and that black freedom was dangerous, and emancipation ought to be slow and incremental.[12] The first step, though, was to end the slave trade. Revolutionary France had abolished slavery in 1794. When the new First Consul and future emperor, Napoleon Bonaparte, reestablished slavery in the French West Indies in 1802, activists in Britain seized the advantage and made the end of the slave trade part of the war effort. Antislavery reformers' inclinations toward gradual, heavily regulated emancipation had been sharpened by the Haitian Revolution. Moreover, the war caused fluctuations in the price of sugar that produced bonanza windfalls and sudden bankruptcies in the sugar islands. The representatives of the West Indian "interest" in the British Parliament were skilled in political persuasion, but vulnerable to the economic and political crises of wartime.[13]

Robert Charles Dallas, a Jamaican-born lawyer and historian, stood in awe at the global convulsions of the early nineteenth century. He described a world where "the revolution of empires, the destruction of states, the extinction of whole classes of men . . . [and] the sacrifice of millions of lives" had made people accustomed "to gigantic contemplations."[14] When the 1807 Slave Trade Act passed, it was shaped in at least three important ways by these "gigantic contemplations." First, it was planned, written, and passed as part of the global war against France. The abolition of the trade was intended to be permanent, but it was pushed through Parliament as a patriotic expedient. Second, the Act affirmed a kind of "liberty" committed to the preservation of the social order. The Act presumed that people released from the slave trade would remain under the control of their liberators. After all, the kneeling slave in Wedgwood's famous cameo did not ask, "Am I not an equal?" Third, although the Act clearly expressed revulsion at the physical pain endured by people on the Middle Passage, it offered only vague instructions for how to relieve that suffering. The Act proposed to reform the supply side of the transatlantic slave trade by encouraging the interdiction of slave ships sailing from Africa.

That was British antislavery on paper—and on commemorative mugs, jugs, and dinner plates. In 1814, twenty-seven years after Wedgwood's "kneeling slave" became famous in Britain, a more obscure image was struck onto a copper coin intended for circulation in West Africa. The caption on the newly minted piece read, in answer to the question "Am I Not a Man and Brother"?: "We are all Brethren: Slave Trade Abolished by Great Britain, 1807." In the foreground, a slim British officer in full regalia shakes the hand of an African king in a flowing robe. In the background, farmers till fields, while people dance around a tree near a row of tidy huts. On the back of the coin, in Arabic, an inscription read, "The abolition of the sale of slaves in England in 1807 of the Christian calendar, in the reign of Sultan George III" (fig. 2). Like Wedgwood's image, the penny was a mass-produced object depicting the aspirations of British abolitionists. The coin was minted at the order of Zachary Macaulay, senior partner in the firm of Macaulay & Babington, to circulate as a trade token, a kind of commercial calling card, in Sierra Leone and beyond. Muslim merchants, many of whom were literate in Arabic, were among the colony's most important trading partners. In theory, as they took the tokens, the merchants would be persuaded that the end of the British slave trade would not be rolled back, and would be inspired by the picturesque

Figure 2. Front and back of copper trade token, known as the "Macaulay & Babington Penny," struck for circulation in West Africa. It was designed for a leading antislavery businessman and depicted the fantasies of elite anti-slavery for West Africa after the abolition of the slave trade. The token was struck in 1814 at the Soho Mint, Handsworth, East Midlands. (Photo © Birmingham Museums Trust)

image of a future without slavery. In 1815, 40,000 of the coins arrived in Freetown, the colonial capital, as part of the cargo of the warship H.M.S. *Ariel*. It was rumoured that the copper used to mint the coins came from the melted-down boilers of slave ships captured by Royal Navy cruisers.[15] The stakes were high for Sierra Leone, in the estimation of a writer of a piece published in the popular digest *The Gentleman's Magazine*. "Although the Continent of Africa," he wrote, "is of great extent, yet the civilization of its rude and uncivilized parts will probably be effected from this small Colony."[16]

The history of Josiah Wedgwood's image is the history of British slave-trade *abolitionism*: of how Britain, after centuries of perpetuating and profiting from the slave trade, came to be the first major slave-trading power in Europe to make it illegal. That history took place in Quaker churches on both sides of the Atlantic, in crowded meeting halls in British provincial cities, in the consciences of renegade West Indian planters, in the warrens of offices where Members of Parliament met to trade favours and votes. The copper penny hints at the history of *abolition*, the history of putting into force the ban on the slave trade. Where the kneeling slave extolled the sensitivity of the British public to the pain of African captives, the copper piece depicted a stylized fantasy of bringing "civilization" to Africa after the slave trade.

Sierra Leone and British Antislavery

Today, Sierra Leone is a small country, about the size of West Virginia, located a few hundred miles north of the equator, between Guinea and Liberia. For much of the nineteenth century the British colony in Sierra Leone was much smaller, restricted roughly to what is now called the Western Area, a peninsula of about two hundred and twenty square miles, about the size of greater Columbus, Ohio. Sierra Leone is mostly known in the West as a setting for humanitarian tragedy: a horrific civil war in the 1990s, the deadly 2014–15 Ebola epidemic. When Sierra Leone, a British colony from 1792 to 1961, isn't a stage for the heroism of peacekeepers or medical adventurers, it is overlooked. Even in the nineteenth century, most Britons, if they thought of Sierra Leone at all, thought of it as a "white man's grave," a place where heat, exotic disease, and hostile fauna conspired to kill Europeans. As early as the 1830s, even travelers friendly to the colony admitted, "The beautiful peninsula has, hitherto, received the rough treatment commonly accorded to the forlorn."[17] But before Sierra Leone became the white man's grave, it represented the hopes of a generation of leading British opponents of slavery.

In 1787, the colony was settled by a group of indigent black soldiers and sailors, called the "Black Poor," recruited in London. Granville Sharp, a leading advocate for abolition, organized this first colony, called the "Province of Freedom." When it collapsed, the colonists dispersed to hardscrabble makeshift villages or to the factories of local European and Euro-African slave traders.[18] Despite this early failure, Sierra Leone attracted the attention of a group of prominent Evangelical businessmen, who formed a joint-stock company, the Sierra Leone Company, and resolved to try again. Antislavery was a big tent in Britain, including pamphleteers, local reform societies, and the many tens of thousands of ordinary Britons who signed antislavery petitions to Parliament and bought antislavery memorabilia.[19] However, a relatively small clique of mostly male, mostly wealthy, and mostly Anglican politicians and businessmen, which included famous figures like William Wilberforce, Zachary Macaulay, Henry Thornton, and Thomas Clarkson, represented the movement to the powerful and to Parliament. Many members of this group, often called the "Clapham Sect" (many lived in the village of Clapham, in greater London, and most were ostentatiously pious), served as directors of the Company. The directors reasoned that if their colony prospered, it would be easier to convince Parliament to abolish the slave trade. Sierra Leone would show skeptics that West Africa could produce commodities other than human flesh, and that former slaves could be wage workers, growing cash crops as profitably and efficiently as slaves. As a bonus, when the slave trade did end, the directors would be on the ground floor of a new market.

In 1792, Freetown was founded, settled by self-emancipated and free-born "Black Loyalists" from North America and administered by a group of white Company employees. The Black Loyalist community included African Americans who had escaped behind British lines during the American Revolutionary War. Some had been resettled in Nova Scotia and New Brunswick, where they were assigned the worst agricultural land in a famously rugged place. When rumours of a West African colony circulated in Nova Scotia, more than 1,500 people volunteered to emigrate. In 1800, they were joined by more than 500 Maroons in exile from Jamaica, members of a community that had lived in an uneasy truce with white planters, until an armed revolt in 1795.[20]

To the Company, the end of the slave trade would be a humanitarian triumph and a commercial opportunity. However, the directors knew relatively little about plantation agriculture and still less about African trade. Slave traders and slave owners often knew detailed information about the ethnic origins of individual slaves, information widely considered valuable for making divisions of labour.[21] Out of arrogance or ignorance, or to make a rhetorical point about Britain's complicity in the slave trade, British abolitionists ignored the diversity of West African trade, economics, and politics in favor of the idea that the abolition of the slave trade had broken "the chain which bound Africa to the dust."[22] To the Clapham Sect, "legitimate trade"— that is, selling goods, not human bodies—was a panacea. Once the slave trade stopped, wars among African "tribes" would stop, and Africa would be more open to British "civilization" and Christian missionaries. In the first years of the Company's experiment, this rhetorical strategy translated into a set of policies that denied the connection between slave labour in Africa and the production and transportation of "legitimate goods." The idea of "legitimate goods" blended political economy with religion, and put a theological gloss on capitalism. To many of the directors, beyond the physical horrors of the Middle Passage, slavery was unfair because it denied an enslaved person the right to test his or her spiritual value on an open "market."[23] Wage labour, some prominent Evangelicals assumed, was so obviously the best, most natural way of organising production that once it was introduced, it would immediately overwhelm other, inferior systems. As Zachary Macaulay put it, "The influence of want and wages is infallible."[24]

And yet, cash crops failed to thrive in the reddish soil of Sierra Leone. Ants, termites, and cockroaches devoured young sugar, coffee, and cotton plants. The Company's directors abandoned the idea of turning Sierra Leone into a wage-labour plantation, and began to buy other goods from local traders for export. Increased demand for "legitimate" trade pushed villages that grew produce for the market to acquire more slaves to meet demand. Rather than restructuring trade after abolition, traders based in Sierra Leone used the same coastal shipping routes and systems of exchange and value as slave traders; they became tacit participants in a political economy where slave labour was a primary mode of production.[25] Meanwhile, Freetown foundered. In 1794, marauding French sailors sacked the town, taking tens of thousands of pounds worth of merchandise, and razing Company buildings. Mende and Temne warriors from villages near the colony attacked Freetown several times between 1800 and 1804. In 1800, a group of frustrated African American settlers rose in armed revolt. The Company expected loyalty, service, and subordination. The settlers, having escaped the plantation, were disinclined to cut cane in West Africa. Most preferred to compete with the Company's European staff and try their hand as traders, buying and selling rice, camwood, palm oil, gold, and ivory in the forts and factories near Freetown.

Hemorrhaging money, the Company tried to divest itself of its colony. By as early as 1801, the Company's directors had petitioned to make Sierra Leone a Crown Colony, with a Governor appointed directly by the Crown, and a budget supplied by the Treasury. The Company began actively to solicit government contracts to shore up its trade. Ironically, these contracts ensured that as the Company failed, its directors, and especially Zachary Macaulay, the young former Governor of Sierra Leone, acquired more and more influence over British policy in West Africa. In 1807, the Company dissolved, and on 1 January 1808 Sierra Leone became Britain's first West African Crown Colony. Sierra Leone passed to the Crown at roughly the same time as the abolition of the slave trade by coincidence. Still, the end of the trade transformed the colony. The former directors of the defunct Company restyled themselves as the "friends of Africa" and formed a new pressure group, the African Institution. The leaders of the Institution helped to design the Slave Trade Act as a condominium between elite antislavery and the British military. The Act, in the midst of the Napoleonic wars, declared slave ships to be another kind of contraband eligible for capture. Soon, the Royal Navy brought slave ships back to Freetown, where a special Vice-Admiralty Court condemned them and turned over former captives to the care of the colonial government. Military officers were rewarded for their efforts with prize money. Colonial trade boomed as goods seized from slave ships flooded the market in Freetown.

However, by framing abolition in the policy idiom of the global war against France, the Slave Trade Act had a built-in time limit. While Britain was at war, slave ships owned by enemies, allies, and neutral parties could be seized with impunity. In peacetime the practices of slave-trade interdiction were effectively piracy. After 1815, several shipowners successfully sued in British courts for compensation and damages for their lost vessels and slaves.[26] The Vice-Admiralty Court at Sierra Leone was replaced, in 1819, by a bilateral system of new Courts of Mixed Commission, with British and international judges. The end of the wars forced colonial officials to think of new ways to make antislavery profitable. In practice, that entailed an expanded civilizing mission, and new ways of making former slaves work at the kinds of tasks that made the most money for the colony. Sierra Leone's transformations track the growing ambitions of British antislavery, from a commercial experiment to the dramatic vision of an empire governed on humanitarian principles for the ostensible benefit, but without the consent, of millions of nonwhite subjects.

The Political Economy of Atlantic Slavery

For even the most antislavery British merchant working in the Atlantic world of the early nineteenth century, slavery was impossible to avoid. Britain's economy was too closely connected to its sugar islands in the Caribbean and to the cotton fields of the American South, its consumers too reliant on the products made by slave labour in the Americas, its stock markets and insurance companies too deeply invested in slave ships and plantations. As the historian Edward Rugemer observes, slavery "transcended the political boundaries of nation-states . . . and the movement to abolish slavery developed on the same transatlantic stage."[27] Colonial Sierra Leone found its niche within this Atlantic political economy. In the West Indies and the Americas, that meant navigating the economic heft of the sugar colonies and the growing value of cotton production. In West Africa, it meant integrating the colony into a complex African commercial world where slavery and the slave trade were imbricated in the production and trade of virtually every commodity available for sale, from ivory to palm oil.

When they spoke to Europeans in the common trading pidgin of Atlantic Africa, many kings and chiefs referred to negotiating and settling disputes as "making palaver" or "talking palaver." The governors of Sierra Leone were accustomed to palaver with local rulers; the survival of the colony depended upon it. Sierra Leone was small, and relatively weak. In a regional context, Sierra Leone was "British" only "by virtue of the small body of British and British West Indian administrators and European missionaries who claimed to direct its life."[28] *Freedom's Debtors* is a history of a British experiment *in* West Africa: most of the principals are white Europeans, or African Americans, or Liberated Africans from other parts of the continent. But the rice and palm oil the colony ate, the hardwood it offered wholesale, and the ivory and gold it sold to European and American traders would not have entered Sierra Leone without the colony's participation in the regional caravan and "coasting" trades (fig. 3). The "Peninsula" was officially British territory from the 1790s, but the majority of its population, for nearly the entire span of time covered in this book, were not British subjects. In the period from 1818 to 1834, for example, the annual average numbers of white Europeans resident in the Freetown Peninsula were 84 men and 13 women, and the far larger African American, Maroon, and Liberated African populations were also outnumbered by "native" Africans.[29]

The human geography of the Peninsula shaped the early history of the colony in profound ways. In the late eighteenth century, the area of the West African coast near Freetown, a region Walter Rodney called "the Upper Guinea Coast" and which European slave traders sometimes called the "Windward Coast," was politically fractured, and ethnically diverse—in contrast to other regions of West Africa dominated by big, powerful states like the Asante empire or the kingdom of Dahomey.[30] This meant that local chiefs and kings could exercise considerable independence and autonomy in dealing with British officials, yet the kings' options for both adapting to and resisting the demands of the colony were relatively limited. In the hinterland of Freetown, the Temne people predominated. According to a Sierra Leone Company employee writing in 1803, the Temne had, at some point in the relatively recent past, driven down from the interior toward the coast, displacing the Bullom people. A large Temne town in the Peninsula, Rokelle, became

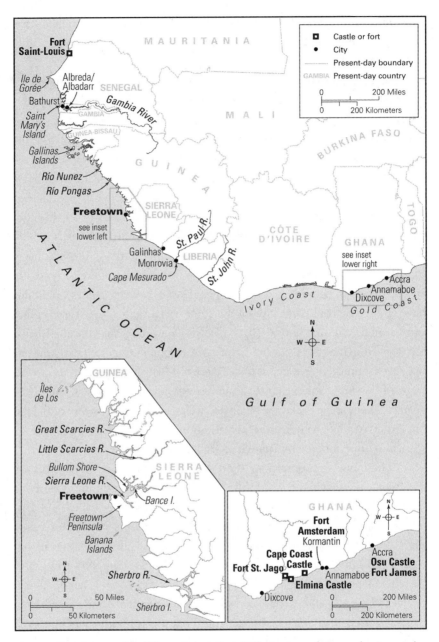

Figure 3. Sierra Leone and the "Upper Guinea Coast." The inset map shows nearby rivers and trading factories significant to colonial trade.

an important point of contact between the British at Sierra Leone and the interior—as well as an important place of refuge for accused criminals and runaways from the colony. On the other side of the wide Sierra Leone River was the Bullom Shore, the southern frontier of a territory occupied mostly by the Bullom people, running as far north as the Scarcies Rivers a few hundred miles away. North of the Scarcies, in the region around what colonists called the "Northern Rivers," the Rio Pongas and the Rio Nuñez, an important centre of trade for colonial merchants, the Susu people predominated. In Freetown itself, migrant, nearly exclusively male labourers from the Kru people, native to the coasts of present-day Liberia, came by the hundreds to work as longshoremen in the coastal shipping trade.[31] Sierra Leone's immediate neighbours, coastal trading partners, and largest labour force were all "native" Africans.

Another ethnic group which exerted a strong influence on early Sierra Leone were the Mende, sometimes called "Mandingos" (or, more infrequently, "Bookmen"). "Mandingo" is a confusing term, because it was applied universally to converts to Islam, whether they belonged to the Mande-speaking Mende or Mandinka peoples or not. Some colonial officials also folded the Mande-speaking Bambara people into the category.[32] When I use the term "Mandingo" in this book, I use it in this very broad sense, since it is often impossible to determine in the archives whether a convert to Islam was actually Mende or Mandinka; the issue is made still more complicated by the fact that many Mende were not Muslims, while many Temne, Bullom, and Susu were. The term points to the prominence of Islam in the region near Sierra Leone, and to the place occupied by Muslims in the colonial imagination. Animists were pitied as "uncivilized." Muslims were treated with both more respect and more trepidation. The encounter with West African Islam presented colonial officials with an enticing chance to access valuable trade networks, but it also posed a threat as an alternative "civilization" and as a competitor for the souls of colonial subjects.

The most powerful state in the region near Sierra Leone was the Muslim Fula empire of Futa Djallon, based in the highlands of what is now Guinea. In the mid-eighteenth century, a jihad, led by the Alimami (or Caliph) of Futa Djallon, drove down to the coast, reconfiguring local trade and politics. At the turn of the nineteenth century, Sierra Leone Company officials remarked that locals had "no tradition by which we can learn at what period this event took place," but generations of historians of West Africa have carefully reconstructed the history of the religious war on the coast.[33] The Fula, with a long-standing stake in both the trans-Saharan and coastal trade, were British Sierra Leone's most desired trading partners, and the colony's relationship with Futa Djallon shaped its overall economic life.

Although Sierra Leone was deeply integrated into this complex political economy, British officials' correspondence with London included overwhelmingly more about affairs within the colony, and about the colony's relationship with a relatively small circle of long-distance caravan traders, than about the Africans who shared the Peninsula with colonial settlers. From the perspective of the colonial merchants, most of the colony's trading partnerships with African traders were informal, and merchants in Sierra Leone tended to keep few records. Furthermore, the perspective of colonial officials required the preservation of an official fiction that the colony and its leaders were free to act unconstrained by the local politics of "uncivilized" Africans. And yet, the influence of local kings and chiefs on the colony weighed heavily on colonial officials.

British Antislavery in Practice and Theory

Historians of Sierra Leonean nationalism dig for the roots of contemporary Sierra Leonean politics in the colony's early history. Historians of the American Revolution and early republic read the early history of the colony as an echo of the American War of Independence.[34] A few legal scholars identify the colonial slave-trade Courts as the ancestors of contemporary courts of human rights, a claim which is difficult to square with the fundamentally commercial character of the courts.[35] This book is not a national history, a coda to the American Revolution, or a hymn to British values. Instead, it asks what the larger histories of British slavery and emancipation in the age of revolution looked like from West Africa.

Coerced labour and violence against emancipated people follow emancipation like an evil twin. Laurent Dubois, adapting the work of the sociologist Jean Casimir, identifies a peasant ideology in post-emancipation Haiti which he calls the "counter-plantation" "a steadfast resistance to plantation labor in all its forms."[36] The "counter-plantation" prevailed in Haiti partly because the Republic's leaders in Cap-Haïtien and Port-au-Prince did not have the administrative capacity to impose their will on peasants. Everywhere but Haiti, post-emancipation societies in the Atlantic world were defined by the anxious desire of both opponents of slavery and former slave owners to get free people back to work producing cash crops. Thomas Holt, writing about Jamaica, calls this phenomenon "the problem of freedom," of how "thoroughly [to reform] the ex-slaves' culture so as to make them receptive to the discipline of free labour."[37] Or, as Laurent Dubois asks, "How do you get from slavery to freedom?"[38] Recent work on the history of slavery in the Americas shows the fragility of freedom in slave states, the continuities between slaveholding societies and post-emancipation societies, and the deep connections between the expansion of slavery and the growth of industrial capitalism.[39] Indeed, as Ada Ferrer shows, even as Haiti became a symbol of black freedom in the Atlantic, emancipation in the new republic happened in tandem with a rapid, violent increase in the slave production of sugar in nearby Cuba, driven by a planter elite conjuring "images of racial apocalypse" to bolster its position within the Caribbean and the wider Spanish empire.[40] In all these histories, the limits of emancipation hide in plain sight, in the daily lives of people living at the edges of slavery. Until 1833, when Britain abolished slavery in its colonies, Sierra Leone was the largest post-emancipation society in the British empire. Just as the transition from slavery to freedom in the United States shows the ambiguities and limitations of American freedom, the practices of abolishing the slave trade in Sierra Leone expose the logic of British liberty.

That is not to say that antislavery in Sierra Leone was a coherent policy. Miscommunications and misunderstandings were common, and colonial officials responded to the challenge of abolition with whatever resources were at hand: mechanisms from older institutions, personal experiences, half-understood and outdated dispatches, rumors, and spur-of-the-moment inventions. "Every Governor has been left to follow his own plans," one colonial official complained, "however crude and undigested; and no two succeeding Governors have ever pursued the same course."[41] A visitor to the colony in the 1830s offered the eccentric architecture of the colonial Anglican church, St. George's (which still stands), as a metaphor for colonial policy. The church, a hodgepodge of new and old construction, was "many years in progress . . . the choir-windows had originally been Gothic, but a fastidious governor preferring the circular to the pointed, the walls were pulled in pieces to allow of the change."[42] And yet, despite generations of architectural changes, it remained a church. Likewise, despite the variation from one colonial administration to the next, at least three overlapping characteristics of British antislavery as put into practice in Sierra Leone persisted, no matter who lived in Government House. In Sierra Leone, abolitionism was *acquisitive*, it was *gradualist*, and it was *militarized*.

First, in practice British abolitionism was acquisitive. It was not selfless, or self-sacrificing, except in its rhetoric. Whatever replaced slave trading and slavery was expected to be profitable. For several generations, historians' questions about the relationship between abolitionism and capitalism in the British empire hinged on measuring the profitability of slavery. Eric Williams, in the essential *Capitalism & Slavery*, attributed the emergence of abolitionism to the rise of industrial capitalism and concomitant decline of the West Indian plantation economy. In the 1970s, David Brion Davis's *Problem of Slavery in the Age of Revolution* offered a compelling account of the intellectual origins of antislavery in Enlightenment political economy and in Evangelical and Quaker theology and commerce.[43] Davis's and Williams's work shows that slave ownership and abolitionism were not like Hell and Heaven, eternally in opposition. Instead, free labour and slave labour were connected to one another by their relationship to capital accumulation, labour discipline, and ideas about the "improvement" of human societies. The same Enlightened concept of the perfectibility of human institutions that pushed antislavery thinkers and campaigners to reject slavery as violent and economically backward also pushed slave owners and plantation managers in the West Indies to experiment with new crops, new machines, and new ways of terrorising and controlling enslaved people.[44]

In the late 1970s and 1980s, Seymour Drescher attacked the "Williams thesis" by revisiting the statistical evidence Williams had used to make his point. Drescher and his allies aimed to rehabilitate British abolitionists by proving that slavery had been profitable after all at the time of abolition. To paraphrase Thomas Holt's clever gloss on the debate, although Eric Williams got the math wrong, he was unassailably correct that the movement to end slavery *was* a function of the growth of capitalism. In the 1980s, David Eltis's work emphasized that slavery and industrialism evolved concurrently, in both Britain and West Africa. In the twenty-first century, Christopher Leslie Brown's *Moral Capital* revivified a stale field. Brown showed that the legislative achievement of abolition was at least as much a function of the consequence of imperial politics and transatlantic networks of activists as of Atlantic economics.[45] Despite the tonic of *Moral Capital*, historians of Britain have been posing the same question over and over again, asking *why* and not *how* Britain abolished the slave trade.

The campaign to end the slave trade was always expected to earn money for its champions. Implicit in the plans for the colony in Sierra Leone were plans for legitimate trade, and for the large-scale cultivation of cash crops like sugar and cotton. Many colonial traders prospered as exporters of legitimate goods. However, capturing and processing slave ships was even more important to the colonial economy. The Vice-Admiralty Court generated cash and cheap trade goods and created demand for ancillary services, from surveying captured ships to creating contracts for gear and provisions. After peace broke out, formerly enslaved people became the focus of an elaborate system of labour control. By 1815, Liberated Africans were the colony's most numerous and least-expensive workers. Their labour both helped to shore up colonial prosperity and to attract block grants and free goods from Britain.

Second, British abolitionism emphasized the gradual end of slavery. The British and American versions of abolitionism have common origins. And yet, historians have tended to treat British and American versions of emancipation as divergent, if not mutually exclusive. Britain itself did not experience the same anxiety that the United States did concerning mass emancipation. For white American opponents of slavery, worries about black freedom were raw and immediate. Historians of the United States notice that gradual emancipation was built into mainstream white abolitionism in the United States from the very beginning. Even in the North, virtually every scheme for emancipation presumed that whites would continue to exercise significant control over black former slaves after emancipation. As James Gigantino notes, in former slave states people may have had their status as "slaves" removed, but they "never participated in a true *emancipation*," and white abolitionists "embraced the term *abolition* by supporting a program that mediated black freedom with white supervision."[46] By the 1860s, many American abolitionists had abandoned their commitment to gradual emancipation in favour of much more radical plans for immediate emancipation and full citizenship for freedpeople. However, in the 1790s, British and American legislators opposed to slavery shared a commitment to the idea that emancipated black people posed a threat to social order, and ought to "earn" their freedom by proving that they were reconciled to the continuation of white supremacy. In general, British officials called this period of continued forced labour after emancipation "apprenticeship," adapting an ancient British legal instrument and institution to a new colonial purpose. In

Britain, while under a contract of apprenticeship, the apprentice learned a trade. In exchange, he (it was virtually always "he") gave up many of his rights to his master. British statute books and case reports are thick with "master and servant" law, defining and explaining the various responsibilities of both parties, and the limits of masters' rights over their servants, including apprentices. Consequently, the idea of freedom as the beginning of an apprenticeship was seductive to the authors of British laws against the slave trade and slavery. In Sierra Leone, the British empire confronted mass emancipation for the first time by devising elaborate systems for attenuating and controlling the transition from slavery to freedom.

New and celebrated global histories of slavery and commodity production put the lie to the idea that slavery was somehow at arm's length from Britain.[47] And as Alexander X. Byrd reminds readers, "As far as the transatlantic movement of people was concerned, the late eighteenth-century British empire was overwhelmingly black."[48] Millions made the Middle Passage to British colonies in British ships, but by 1807 there was no slavery in Britain. Despite (or because of) this fact, the logic of gradual emancipation suffused British antislavery. British Sierra Leone was never a slave society, but its leaders were gradualists. In the 1820s, as the abolition movement in Britain recommitted itself to the end of colonial slavery, most activists rejected the idea that the end of slavery was anything other than the first step in the "civilization" of former slaves. Tellingly, the abolition of slavery in the West Indies in 1833 was contingent on former slaves continuing to serve as apprentices for up to five more years, in order to learn the folkways of wage labour. The Emancipation Act of 1833 also offered £20 million in compensation to slave owners; in gradualist style, slave owners and not enslaved people received reparations for their "losses." However, neither compensation nor apprenticeship was a novelty in 1833. Apprenticeship of former slaves was a well-established (although unofficial) practice in Sierra Leone decades *before* 1807. The idea of formally ending a person's status as a slave by measuring the monetary value of their labour, and treating that price as a debt they owed to their liberator, was policy for generations of colonial officials. That does not necessarily mean that the policies developed in Sierra Leone after 1807 were exported to the West Indies after 1833. Rather, a basic principle of British antislavery appeared in both West Africa and the West Indies: gradual emancipation was necessary in order to show appropriate respect for the "property" rights of slave owners, and to force freedpeople to show the same respect for property by reminding them of the debt their freedom had incurred.

Moreover, British antislavery, by emphasizing "civilization" and by compromising with European and Euro-African slave traders and African dealers in slave-produced goods, helped to frame the category of "domestic" slavery. In British reckoning, the "traditional" forms of slavery practiced by more "primitive" people were to be abolished not with legislation, but with a long, slow process of cultural transformation. As Zachary Macaulay wrote in the 1820s, defending the purchase of slave-produced sugar from the East Indies, "In the East, whatever slavery exists, we found there; we did not ourselves create it: it was the fruit of Pagan, Mahometan, or Portuguese rule, and will, I trust, soon disappear before the superior benignity of our paternal and Christian institutions."[49] In the meantime, it would be unconscionable not to profit from it. Christian institutions might be necessary to end slavery, but their action was gradual, and in the meantime domestic slavery was tolerable. This was echoed in the instructions to the antislavery Royal Navy squadron, published in 1844 and 1866, which "recognized the distinction between the export of slaves . . . and the system of Domestic Slavery."[50] In Sierra Leone, gradualism was a feature of colonial governance and was essential to British imperial expansion in West Africa.

Third, abolitionism was militarized. From as early as 1800, the British armed forces maintained an official presence in Sierra Leone, and soldiers and officers were present in the colony from its very beginning. The work of ending the slave trade relied on the energy and initiative of military officers willing to pursue and capture slave ships in the hope of receiving prize money. From 1808 until the 1830s and beyond, the Governors of Sierra Leone were exclusively recruited from the Royal Navy or from British army regiments, and military officers filled many other colonial offices. From 1807 to 1815, many former slaves arriving in Sierra Leone were simply conscripted as soldiers for lifetime service in either West Africa or the West Indies. In the 1810s and 1820s, the Governors of Sierra Leone launched a series of campaigns in West Africa, attacking slave forts in order to seize valuable goods and bring enslaved people back to Sierra Leone as Liberated Africans. Military officers adapted quickly to the acquisitive and gradualist character of abolitionism, extended it, and entrenched it.

The swashbuckling image of Royal Navy ships seizing slavers and freeing slaves is undeniably appealing, and several historians have dramatized the Senior Service's role in ending the slave trade.[51] The prize money from slave ships, the sale of goods and services for equipping and feeding

British soldiers and sailors, and the influx of cheap labourers freed from the Middle Passage made Freetown a boomtown for contractors and profiteers. Military and civilian rule became virtually indistinguishable. The Royal African Corps, a unit composed of former slaves and white deserters from other regiments, raided slave forts and garrisoned British outposts, forming a network for transporting supplies and people up and down the coast.

These three characteristics of British abolitionism in practice—its acquisitiveness, its gradualism, and its militarism—transformed the domestic campaign against the slave trade into an imperial project of expansion and colonialism. But the practices of antislavery were not a wild departure from the ideology of antislavery as developed by elite activists in Britain. On the one hand, since former slaves were assumed to be both savage and grateful to their liberators, it was obvious to colonial officials that people released from the Middle Passage and brought to Sierra Leone ought to work and live according to a plan established by "civilized" white Britons. On the other hand, the structure of pay and prizes in the armed forces pushed British officers and ships further and further from Freetown. The relationship between military expansion and imperial expansion is obvious, but antislavery itself proved to be expansionist and profit-hungry.[52] Sierra Leone collapses the superficial contradiction between military-aristocratic despotism and free-trade freedom. Military officers with extensive arbitrary power—archetypal "proconsular despots" (to borrow the late C. A. Bayly's term)—governed Sierra Leone under the auspices of the abolition of the slave trade.[53]

All of these characteristics of British antislavery in practice were evident in Sierra Leone, intensified and refined by the daily routine of governance. The documents produced by the colonial government emphasize that former slaves in the colony were there to work as directed, to fight as ordered, and to accept white tuition as commanded. The Governors from 1807 to 1824 used the "captured Negroes" in a wide variety of ways: as soldiers, as pioneers, as manual labourers, as Christian converts. When they passed through the King's Yard off Water Street in Freetown, where they were measured, described, and renamed by colonial officials, former slaves were ritually denatured. In 1802, James Stephen, a leading jurist and opponent of the slave trade, commented, "There are no proper and peculiar names to distinguish the state of the negro in bondage, from his enfranchised condition."[54] In 1807, in Sierra Leone, colonial officials set to work making the distinction.

The pathologies of the slave trade and the campaign to end it have a common root in the logic of capitalism—not a carefully theorized or calibrated version of capitalism, but a blunter system of money and power dictating "who worked where, on what terms, and to whose benefit."[55] When leading antislavery activists like Zachary Macaulay and William Wilberforce imagined an empire without slavery, they imagined conflict-free commerce and capital accumulation regulated by the natural respect of former slaves for their liberators.[56] Thomas Clarkson, the preacher, activist, and publicist of abolitionism, proclaimed the Slave Trade Act "a Magna Charta for Africa in Britain."[57] Just as the Great Charter was the root of the tradition of English liberty, the Slave Trade Act would push the seeds of English civilization deep into African soil. Clarkson imagined that roots of the slave trade were shallow, that the ground could be harrowed and replanted. But the slave trade was more robust than Clarkson imagined, and, in practice, antislavery had more in common with slavery than Clarkson would have wanted to admit. What grew in Sierra Leone was an authentic fruit of "British liberty."

This book is organized into five chapters. The argument is shaped by the archives used to research and write it, archives that have accumulated around the careers of individual colonial officials, and that are scattered across three continents, from Chicago to London to Freetown. Chapter One, "Antislavery on a Slave Coast," follows John Clarkson and Zachary Macaulay, both Governors of Sierra Leone appointed by the Sierra Leone Company. Under Clarkson, the colony nearly starved. Macaulay, his replacement, learned how to compromise with slave traders and mastered the structures of the local slave trade. Despite his successes, it was clear by 1800 that the Company's project was close to collapse. The directors reached out to the British armed forces and arranged for the emigration of 500 exiled Maroons from Nova Scotia to Sierra Leone. The colony soon enjoyed access to valuable government contracts and began to integrate British officers into its government. In 1808, thanks to the foundation laid by Macaulay in Freetown and London, Sierra Leone became a Crown Colony.

Chapter Two, "Let That Heart Be English," follows the mercurial first Crown Governor, Thomas Perronet Thompson. By 1808, the lineaments of British antislavery in practice were already in place in Sierra Leone. Colonial officials, through the Company's local trade, and through schemes for the apprenticeship of emancipated slaves, had already established a vernacular for explaining what it meant, both for Britain and for emancipated people, for a British court to have legally released someone from the Middle Passage. Former slaves were still expected to work at command and still "belonged" to masters. Thompson, groomed in London to follow the instructions of the Company, rejected what he saw as the casuistry of the Clapham Sect, and was swiftly recalled. But while in office, he attempted to recruit former slaves as pioneers, soldiers, and settlers. In his reaction to Company rule, he invented a new way of "using" former slaves.

Chapter Three, "The Vice-Admiralty Court," anatomizes the slave-trade Court and its impact on the colony. The Vice-Admiralty Court was a judicial instrument that expressed the ambitions and priorities of the colony, and of the London-based leaders of the antislavery lobby. It was fundamentally commercial, it relied upon and benefited British military officers, and it turned over "captured Negroes" to the control of the colonial government. This chapter explains how the Court functioned and how it both represented and advanced the aspirations of British antislavery. The chapter also explores the formation of the Royal African Corps, the military regiment headquartered in West Africa, which depended on the slave-trade Courts for recruits.

Chapter Four, "The Absolute Disposal of the Crown," explores the consequences of the system of incentives established by the Court of Vice-Admiralty. The chapter follows the conflict between two Governors, Edward Columbine and Charles Maxwell, over access to prize money and explains how Maxwell came most acutely to grasp the military logic of imperial anti-slave-trade laws. Maxwell took over a West India Regiment recruiting station in the colony on the grounds that he ought to have the right to determine what happened to former slaves, and then launched a series of campaigns to seize slave forts in order to generate prize money, and to release more people who might prove to be potential recruits.

Chapter Five, "The Liberated African Department," follows Charles MacCarthy's attempts to compensate for the economic shock caused by the end of the Napoleonic wars by formalizing and reinforcing regimes of control over people released from the slave trade, and by expanding Sierra Leone's footprint in West Africa. Where the military aspects of abolitionism were emphasized before 1815, the postwar focus of the colonial government turned to the management of the lives and labour of the people whom MacCarthy renamed "Liberated Africans." MacCarthy organized a formal civilizing mission, with the joint purpose of both improving social and economic life in the colony and attracting attention, money, and goods from London. He coped with postwar austerity and increased regulation of trade by establishing his own empire-in-miniature in West Africa. The Epilogue, "MacCarthy's Skull," follows MacCarthy into war with Asante, and follows British antislavery into the high noon of the Victorian British empire.

1. Antislavery on a Slave Coast

John Clarkson lay unconscious in a puddle of bilge. Clarkson had fallen ill in late December 1791, on the voyage from Halifax to Sierra Leone. His older brother, Thomas, his friend William Wilberforce, and several other members of the Clapham Sect had established a new business venture, the Sierra Leone Company. The younger Clarkson shared their antislavery convictions and volunteered his years of experience as a Royal Navy officer to the Company. In Nova Scotia and New Brunswick, Clarkson recruited more than a thousand Black Loyalist settlers, former slaves, and freeborn people from the United States living under British protection, and coordinated the hire of a convoy of transport ships. The settlers were to sail across the Atlantic to Sierra Leone and found a new town, accompanied by dozens of white employees of the Company. It was exhausting work: merchants in Nova Scotia gouged, settlers conspired, white artisans brawled and sulked, food spoiled, water soured, ships blew off course. As the days passed at sea, Clarkson became feverish. His head ached. On 21 January 1792, he collapsed.[1] Soon, other passengers and crew fell sick. On 29 January, while the ship tossed at anchor in a storm, Clarkson was found pitching and rolling with the ship on the floor of his cabin, "covered with blood & water and very much bruised."[2] By mid-February, he had regained his feet, but lost his memory.

While in Sierra Leone, Clarkson kept a diary. The diary, preserved in pieces in archives on three continents, was not a private document. As a Royal Navy officer, Clarkson was accustomed to keeping a log. An officer's log included not only the origin, destination, location, and direction of his ship and the vital statistics of his crew, but also notes on daily life and on mundane and unusual encounters with other vessels. As the historian Greg Dening writes, every officer knew what "sort of a public history a log might be, and how different it was from other private histories."[3] Clarkson's employers had their own traditions of journal keeping. Writing and reading confessional diaries were a part of daily devotions for Clapham Sect members like Zachary Macaulay and Henry Thornton.[4] A diarist laid bare his sins as though alone with God, but then circulated his confessions among his fellow Christians in a ritual self-criticism.

The tensions between the secular and devotional purposes of Clarkson's diary were set aside when he arrived in Africa, because Clarkson's memory deteriorated to a point where he claimed to have "not the least recollection of any thing I did yesterday, or an hour ago."[5] Clarkson's journal became his memory. He sent the Company's chaplain back to London to report on his mission; he worried that if he made the voyage himself, he might forget everything that had happened in the first months of the settlement.[6] Clarkson came to Sierra Leone with a vision of himself as the white "father" of the black settlers, entitled to exercise a benign but firm paternal authority. He was also expected to turn a profit in "legitimate trade," growing tropical crops and buying the gold, ivory, and other commodities traded alongside human beings in the forts of West Africa. Clarkson chose to return to England to recover his health in late 1792 and never returned to Freetown, but his journal remains an essential record of the Company's ambitions. Clarkson's desire for obedience and gratitude from people emancipated from slavery hinted at the expectations of generations of colonial officials. His triple role as military officer, merchant, and abolitionist would be reproduced again and again by the Governors of Sierra Leone, under both the Company and the British Crown.

The earliest colonists and colonial officials in Sierra Leone struggled under a double burden of heavy expectations and limited resources. Many of the directors of the Sierra Leone Company, and Henry Thornton in particular, were innovators in the management of financial markets, and experts in the manipulation of currency, credit, and debt.[7] They also had grand ambitions for their colony. "Should this Experiment fail," the Company's directors wrote, "it may be long if ever before a similar one may be again attempted." If the colony was successful, the directors declared in an open letter to the colonists, "Millions as yet unborn may have reason to look up to you as being under heaven the instruments of rescuing them from a state of darkness, oppression, & disorder and of imparting to these the light of religious truth & the security & comforts of civilized society."[8]

And yet, for all of the directors' grandiosity and economic sophistication, the Sierra Leone Company had an impoverished understanding of the political economy of West Africa, and a crude plan for its transformation from an economy based on barter to one based on currency. The Company tried to prove that free labour could turn a sweeter profit than slave labour. They planned to trade exclusively in goods, not slaves, and to employ free black workers to grow cash crops. However, the Company's agents in Africa could not hold the line between slavery and freedom drawn in London. Slaves carried the commodities that the Company eventually purchased; slave traders sold the rice the colony needed to survive. To many Company directors, paying people wages was assumed to be both evidence of, and a catalyst for, the development of British civilization. A bundle of other practices was assumed self-evidently to follow from accepting a wage: working according to a schedule and a system of discipline set by employers; becoming a consumer of other goods, purchased with wages; understanding and respecting debt and credit. However, the directors of the Company never acknowledged the tension between their ideological commitment to wages and their commercial dependence on slavery. The tension could be written off in the present against civilization in the future.

Sierra Leone, founded to prove the economic efficiency of wage labour and the potential of the West African market for non-slave goods, became a clearinghouse for goods made by slaves. The African American settlers clashed with the Company over land promised but never delivered. In 1800, some rose against the Company and were swiftly suppressed. Even as the Company faltered, Zachary Macaulay, Governor for most of the years from 1793 to 1799, learned the physical plant of the slave trade from local slave traders. Facing bankruptcy and unrest, the directors of the Company began to search for a way to devolve responsibility for the colony onto the British Crown. In 1797, after a nearly yearlong uprising, the Trelawny Maroons of Jamaica, a community of free blacks who lived in relative safety in the rugged jungles of northeast Jamaica, were defeated and sent into exile. The Company volunteered to take them in, and in 1800 they arrived in Freetown in time to assist in tracking and capturing several of leaders of the settlers' revolt.[9] The arrival of the Maroons was more than a military boon. Their alleged ferocity gave the directors in London standing to request a Royal

Navy warship to maintain order, and set a precedent for an enduring rela-
tionship between the armed forces in Africa and the abolitionists in London.
The presence of troops and ships in Freetown created a market for supplying
British armed forces with logistical support, gear, and provisions. Once
Sierra Leone was a military outpost as well as a trading post, the ongoing war
with France made plausible its transfer to the Crown.

In its early days, colonial Sierra Leone represented the ambitions of
British antislavery in an empire where slavery remained not only acceptable
but profitable. Under Company rule, the practices of British antislavery reflected the desire of both colonial officials and their London-based backers to
prove that free labour was more profitable than slave labour, and that African
commodities were more valuable than enslaved African people in Atlantic
markets. The Sierra Leone Company bet its capital on these two dearly held
hypotheses, and lost. As the Company's trade began to fail, officials in Sierra
Leone gave up on uprooting the slave trade and committed themselves to
carving out a place for the colony in an environment where both slaves and
slave labour were ubiquitous. Concurrently, the Company began to reach
out to the British government, both for direct financial support and for contracts. The Company dissolved in 1808 as a government contractor and a
player in a trade network constructed around slavery. Sierra Leone began as
a privately owned trading post but became Britain's first Crown Colony in
West Africa.

Civilization, Trade, and Free Labour

In the region around the colony, the cultural scripts for marketing goods,
the uses of currencies and traditions of barter, and the routes taken by ships
had been refined over centuries. The reforms proposed by the Sierra Leone
Company sluiced easily into the channels carved by local riverine and transatlantic trade. The Company's directors did not understand the societies that
produced African commodities, or the role of slaves in producing and carrying them, but many saw the commodities themselves and were intoxicated.
While the colony was in the planning stages, Thomas Clarkson brought a
box full of samples of African goods, including rice, dried peppers, cinna-
mon, rich tropical woods, and the pungent musk gland of a civet cat, to a
meeting of the directors. From this cornucopia, the directors conjured an
idea of their colony as a market for African exotica, dotted with fields of

sugar, cotton, tobacco, and coffee. Thomas Clarkson suggested three ways of collecting these treasures: first, by cultivation by the natives and by the settlers; second, by making the colony "the centre of cruizing northward & southward"; and third, by making the colony a magnet for the caravan trade from Futa Djallon.[10] Slave traders knew that West African states and polities produced a wide variety of commodities for export along with slaves, but also that the commodities were always sold *with* slaves as part of an assortment. The Company fantasized that the effects of the transatlantic slave trade could be quickly reversed, that removing slaves from the coastal trade would not affect trade in any other commodity.[11]

Europeans had been trading in West Africa long before the Clapham Sect tried their luck. The slave trade was brutal, but it could be a precise ethnographer. Many popular books were published in London and elsewhere in the 1780s and 1790s with accounts of the cultures and customs of African peoples involved in the slave trade, some with an abolitionist slant, some callously pro-slavery. The slave trade, with its hunger for information and its far-flung networks of credit, was important to the consolidation of transatlantic trading networks in the eighteenth century.[12] Centuries of contact between European slave traders, Afro-European and European middlemen and the slave-dealing peoples of the African littoral and interior built up a complex political economy, which the Sierra Leone Company believed it could replace at a stroke. As Jane Guyer shows, the economic life of Atlantic Africa in the late eighteenth century was complex and variegated on its own terms, and was also part of the European money economy, "shaped by its demands and its indifferences."[13] And yet, the Sierra Leone Company officials were convinced that local commerce could be converted to a cash economy, just as easily as they imagined Africans could be converted to Christianity. The Company devised a new currency for the purpose, the Sierra Leone Company dollar. The Company's directorate was seduced by the idea that cash-based commerce and Christian belief were continuous, mutually reinforcing, and intrinsically compelling. To use the Company's dollar was ineluctably to step toward accepting the Company's savior.

At the same time, an understanding of "freedom" as indexed to "civilization" reinforced the Company's flattened understanding of trade in Africa. As the antislavery jurist James Stephen explained, "In the negro, the self-dependency of a rational being, the close connection between his conduct and his natural, or social welfare, are ideas perfectly new."[14] Africans in general, and former slaves in particular were by definition not "ready" to discharge or even to understand the responsibilities that "civilization" imposed upon white Europeans. The Company's leaders thought not that emancipation restored lost dignity to a person formerly enslaved, but that it granted it for the first time. Consequently, the act of emancipation was an implicit license to civilize. To earn a Company dollar was a wage and a lesson. The Company was willing to accept more modest profits from its own trade, and sales and purchase taxes on goods traded in the colony, as opportunity costs of its high-minded mission.[15]

The colony was not the first British venture in West Africa to propose replacing the slave trade with "legitimate" trade. No one in Britain assumed the end of the slave trade would mean the closing of African markets to British merchants. Rather, abolitionists imagined that the end of slave trading would expand European trade to and from Africa.[16] The slave trade was profitable; trade in legitimate goods would be more profitable. Consequently, projects like the Sierra Leone Company were acquisitive and capital-intensive, but also experimental. Profit and growth were the ultimate aims for the Company, but at the same time commercial success would prove that ending the slave trade could be "worth it" for Britain. Commerce and morality were yoked to one another. As Thomas Holt observes of emancipation-era Jamaica, "One finds the commercial terminology of the contract invoked to express all manner of human relations."[17] It is hard to overstate how deeply ingrained was the language and logic of finance in schemes for abolition and emancipation.

In the 1790s, the directors of the Sierra Leone Company were convinced that African societies were easy to read and understand, and that judicious European intervention would reform and regularize the vernacular of African commerce.[18] First, the Company assumed that there was a bright line separating the coast and the interior, and that the gradient of "civilization" climbed as a traveler moved inland away from the "debased" coast and toward the capitals of the kingdoms and caliphates of the interior. The colony's neighbours kept slaves, and lived in a world shaped by the threat of enslavement. The Sierra Leone Company surgeon, Thomas Winterbottom, noticed that villages near Freetown were built so as to be impossible to surprise. In his experience, Temne and Bullom villages were accessible only by one or two narrow footpaths, often leading through thick jungle or tangled mangrove swamp. Susu and Mende towns were built on open ground, but hidden behind "a lofty palisade of bamboos, or by a wall built of bricks hardened in the sun."[19] Winterbottom also noted that this caution extended beyond physical defenses to a deep distrust of strangers, especially Europeans. He complained that his attempts to understand the "native Africans" were stymied by their habit of answering "yes" to every question he asked, "merely to avoid trouble . . . they are apt to suspect that the curiosity of the European has some sinister end in view."[20]

But the Sierra Leone Company had little interest in trading with its immediate neighbours. Temne and Bullom homes and villages were small, and made to be easily rebuilt or even moved in case of emergency, whereas the villages built by the Susu and Mende were more permanent, with as many as 3,000 residents. The capital of Futa Djallon, Timbo, had at least 8,000 residents.[21] To the Company, permanence and the concentration of population signaled greater civilization and commercial sophistication. As Company officials looked for trading partners in Africa, they turned, in the immediate vicinity of the colony, to the Muslim "Mandingos" and to the caliphs of Futa Djallon. They assumed that the Fula and "Mandingo" stood apart from the "debased" coast. However, Futa Djallon was well integrated with the coast. Itinerant Muslim clerics, for example, regularly traveled from the highlands to coastal polities, and there were converts scattered all along the coast.[22]

Another misapprehension the Company treasured was the idea that the coastal political economy was entirely the creation of European slave traders. And yet, as historians of sub-Saharan West Africa recognize, the slave trade and "legitimate" trade were entangled.[23] Futa Djallon was the dominant force in local trade. Timbo was a hub connecting the transatlantic and trans-Saharan trading networks. The Fula bought and sold all kinds of goods, but they were especially well known as gold traders, transporting "country rings" of standardized sizes around their wrists and around the wrists of their slaves.[24] Meanwhile, many of the coastal villages produced labour-intensive commodities like salt and rice, usually with slave labour, to trade with both Europeans and Fula caravans. Other local traders sold goods in assortments, which almost always included slaves. Within many of these societies, slaves were both a kind of kin and a symbol of status in a political economy where the European idea of land ownership by deed was alien. Moreover, the trade routes and infrastructure—factories, forts, and wharfs— of the coast were oriented toward supplying slave ships.[25] Slave dealers in

West Africa sold a great deal of merchandise other than slaves, and the consolidated trade in slaves and goods dominated the coastal trading routes used by Europeans. The Sierra Leone Company did not have the resources to break these long-established patterns.

Trade in "legitimate" goods was one-half of the Company program, although the Company had an incomplete and naïve view of West African trade. Free labour was the other. The Company did not intend Sierra Leone to be a test case for mass emancipation. Rather, the colony was intended to show British lawmakers and consumers that emancipated people could be productive, pious, and docile enough in a small settlement to scale up the project, and begin the long process of ending the slave trade, and eventually slavery in the West Indies. In this, the Company was very much in the mainstream of Anglo-American antislavery. British abolitionists drew strength from Quaker antislavery activism and from new ideas about market economies: both taproots of inspiration emphasized a painstaking path to economic and personal autonomy for former slaves. For example, Anthony Benezet, one of the leaders of Quaker antislavery in the mid-eighteenth century, proposed that former slaves work to pay off the cost of their manumission, and that they be bound to designated farms and closely supervised even after they had purchased their own freedom. The *philosophes* of the French Enlightenment endorsed similar forms of surveillance and control.[26] In the 1780s and 1790s, after years of agitation by leading Quakers, many of the northern states in the United States formally abolished slavery, but virtually all replaced it with programs of gradual emancipation and bonded labour for former slaves. Gradualism allowed Northerners in the new republic to embrace antislavery as a sentimental, spiritual, and gentle process of education, rather than a revolutionary act of liberation and an economic shock. It was easier to be against slavery when all it required was a spiritual commitment, a chance to scrub out "the stain of sin and the fear of just reprisal but retain the control."[27] By focusing on the slave trade as a target for immediate abolition, abolitionists on both sides of the Atlantic could put off the difficult question of what post-emancipation society would be like, preserve plantation economies, and coddle politically powerful planters.[28] The Sierra Leone Company's leaders did not need to worry about the effects of immediate emancipation in their colony, but they remained committed to the idea that the end of slavery was only the first step toward full membership in society and economic life.

Pidgin and Creole Commerce and the "Bar" Trade

The very first purchase of land on the Freetown Peninsula on behalf of British abolitionists shows the gulf between the antislavery vision of African trade and the status quo of trade between European slave traders and African chiefs and kings. In 1787, before the Company re-founded the colony as Sierra Leone, Granville Sharp arranged for the emigration of several hundred former soldiers and sailors from among the "Black Poor" of London.[29] On 22 August 1788, Captain John Taylor, on Sharp's behalf, "bought" Sierra Leone from King Naimbanna, "for the sole benefit of the free community of settlers, their Heirs & Successors." Captain Taylor believed that the terms of the transaction transferred ownership of the Peninsula to the settlers he had brought with him. Naimbanna, according to the treaty, had sworn allegiance to King George and had vowed to protect "the said Free Settlers, his subjects, to the utmost." In exchange for surrendering ownership of the land, the king received the right to charge ships that called at Sierra Leone fifteen "'bars," nominal units of currency equivalent to the value of a bar of iron. Naimbanna also received an array of European luxury goods and trinkets: some satin waistcoats, a "mock Diamond ring," pistols, a telescope, rum, pipes, fine cotton, cases of wine, barrels of salt pork, and several giant wheels of cheese.[30] Sierra Leone had been purchased for Britain.

And yet, on the same day, at the same time, Naimbanna, a king of the Koya Temne, accepted gifts commensurate with his status from a group of European "strangers." He could not sell the land to the Europeans, because land was not the sort of property that could be sold, but he pledged himself as their "landlord."[31] In exchange for the tribute, he agreed to permit the Europeans to establish a town and trading post in his territory. British Sierra Leone, then, began with a misapprehension. Joseph Miller remarks that "one can only speculate at the extent of the working misunderstandings that facilitated transactions that Europeans understood as individually contracted, re-payable debt, but that Africans interpreted . . . as the largesse of patron-like figures investing in relationships of obligation."[32] The Europeans thought they were purchasing land; Naimbanna thought he was accepting gifts in exchange for recognizing a right to trade. To a slave trader, this lack of a common system of value was inconsequential. Traders bought slaves to amass capital; kings bought the European goods they wanted, and enhanced their prestige by selling the rights they held in people. These disparate models of wealth and property did not trouble the parties to the slave trade, but they mattered to colonial administrators.

Linguists distinguish between "pidgin" and "creole" languages: a pidgin is a trade language, a way of getting business done without a language or culture in common. Creole languages are made when children grow up speaking a pidgin as their first language—they are complete languages, with fully articulated grammars.[33] European and African traders in the Upper Guinea Coast spoke pidgin languages with one another, and the transactions of the transatlantic slave trade in Africa can be understood as pidgin transactions. To African slave owners, slaves were subordinate kin and markers of social prestige; to Europeans they were saleable commodities. Through pidgin exchanges, Europeans bought slaves for American markets. The Sierra Leone Company, however, demanded a naturalized, creole commerce in African goods. Because they had no colonial ambitions, slave traders did not have to confront the gulf between imaginary and real African societies.[34]

Before the arrival of the Company's agents, the bar was the pidgin currency of the Upper Guinea Coast near Sierra Leone. Bars were a barter currency whose value was different for both parties in any given transaction. A bar, Winterbottom explained, was "like our pound sterling, merely nominal, but much less precise in its value, and subject to great irregularities." In one town, cloth might be worth six bars, and ten bars in another. Traders tried to average out the value of their goods, accepting that some goods would be sold at a lower bar value than others, while constantly hunting for high-bar transactions.[35] Bars, in the view of the Company, threatened both the stability of prices and the availability of trade goods. First, the bar trade made it difficult to know what goods were worth, since bar values fluctuated according to a system of value that was effectively invisible to Europeans. Second, bar trade encouraged African traders to hop from one market to the next, looking for a bargain, rather than reliably buying and selling their goods in the same market. Consequently, one of the first proposals made by the Sierra Leone Company was the end of the bar. "The present rude methods of . . . making a sort of standard of *iron bars* of no determinate quality or weight must greatly obstruct the currency of Transactions," the Company's agents wrote, arguing that not only did the bar make their own bookkeeping more difficult, it also interfered with "the free circulation of Commerce." The pidgin transactions of the era of the slave trade would be replaced by "regular habits of Industry & Traffic" as soon as dollars and pounds became the principal means of exchange on the coast.[36]

And at first, the Company seemed to have succeeded. From 1792 to 1794, the Company offered African merchants specially minted Company silver dollar and half-dollar coins and copper pennies, which most accepted as payment. After an attack on the colony by French privateers in 1794, when thousands of pounds' worth of specie were taken as loot, the Company offered paper money to African traders, which was also accepted. But the Company's "success" was principally an aesthetic achievement. Traders continued to treat silver and paper money as convertible into bars. "The natives," Winterbottom wrote, were "as capable of computing by dollars, and probably by any other European coin, as by their usual mode of bars."[37] African traders recognized that gathering European currency was useful (particularly in trade with Europeans), but the bar remained their standard of value. Company money did not destroy the bar economy; it was assimilated into it.

Just as the Company reckoned that the bar represented instability, which might expose the Company to being shorted, they also feared being cheated. Consequently, the Company sought African partners "uncorrupted" by the slave trade. John Gray, a Company employee, described one potential trading partner, "Furry [Fouré] Cannaba," a local Muslim chief. Fouré, Gray remarked, only "pretends to be a Mahometan himself . . . I take it as a corroborating proof of with the Gin bottle that his pretence to Religion is merely to make a shew, to gratify his own pride & to dazzle the eyes of his people." The people led by Fouré, the Company reassured themselves, were not vulnerable to the schemes of the slave traders. Unlike their chief, Fouré's people had apparently not converted to Islam. "Uncorrupted by European vices," Gray concluded, "& apparently not [having] their minds much clogged by any prejudices of their own (& especially not being under the bias of the Mahometan faith) there is a firm basis to build upon."[38] Societies that seemed "primitive" were good raw material for trade, Gray reasoned, since the slave trade created perverse incentives for African traders, making them unable to see the advantages of trade in "legitimate" goods. But the distinction between legitimate and illegitimate trades existed in Europe only as a slogan invented for the consumption of the British public.[39] There were at least three different slave trades in West Africa: the trans-Saharan, the transatlantic, and the coastal. There were no clean lines between "legitimate" and "illegitimate" trade in the Atlantic world. Slaves cultivated most commodities, and the greater the demand, the more slave labour was required to produce them.[40]

The Company's written orders to their employees in Freetown echoed Thomas Clarkson's prospectus for African trade. It hoped for both an internal trade, "by light Vessels sailing up the Rivers, or by communication with Caravans that may be drawn from the interior country," as well as "a Trade along the Coasts, by means of which a large quantity of scattered produce may be collected in their Stores." At the same time, the Company advised its staff that villagers should become farmers (as though local villages did not grow their own food already). "Cultivation," they continued, "naturally implies the civilization of those among whom it is to be introduced, for without this no great degree of effective industry is to be expected. Civilization is therefore even in this commercial view a fundamental point."[41] And so, when the Company's ships arrived in 1792 they sailed low in the water, full of settlers, trade goods, and building materials, and also a heavy burden of pious optimism, misinformation about African trade, gradualist ideas of freedom, and grandiose plans for cultivation.

Learning the Slave Trade

John Clarkson returned to England late in 1792, where he learned that he had been sacked. Clarkson had not, in the eyes of the majority of the directors, acted quickly enough to trade on the Company's behalf. The man who replaced him as Governor, Zachary Macaulay, experimented with all three models of commerce originally proposed in the Company's orders, and discovered flaws in each. The caravan trade proved tricky to maintain, slave traders refused to give up the coastal trade, and the Nova Scotian settlers were more interested in trade for their own benefit than in doing agricultural work for a pittance under white supervision. Despite Macaulay's instincts and flinty loyalty to his superiors, the Company's trading schemes began to fail. Soon, Macaulay relied on the friendship of local slave traders for information and access to local trade routes. By the time he left Sierra Leone in 1799, although the Company did not buy or sell slaves, it exported goods made and carried by slaves in Africa and imported goods made by slaves in the Americas.

European slave traders had used the Sierra Leone River for centuries, and although the river's slave trade was at relatively low ebb in 1792, there were still a number of European traders who either lived at factories built on its several small islands or who made regular use of them. The most famous was Bance (or Bense, or Bunce) Island, a famous slave-trading fort in the Sierra Leone River, owned in the 1790s by the Anderson brothers of London (fig. 4). John Clarkson had been suspicious of the slave traders who lived near Freetown. He was cordial with them out of necessity, although he thought the "white Clerks, Doctors, &c." were "all ghastly looking creatures."[42] European traders tried to invite Clarkson into the networks that supported their businesses in West Africa. Shortly after Clarkson arrived, a slave trader named Bolland, based in the Banana Islands, off the coast south of Freetown, tried to convince Clarkson to enter into a partnership with his landlord, a trader named Cleveland, the descendent of a European trader and an African woman. Bolland, Clarkson wrote, "strongly urged me, to establish a Plantation with Cleveland's permission on these Islands, or on the Continent, highly praising the fitness of the soil."[43] If Clarkson and the Sierra Leone Company became just another "stranger" on the coast, Bolland may have reasoned, then they would be unable to take any kind of action against the slave trade.

Bolland was not the only slave trader to sweet-talk the Governor. "All the Captains of the Slave vessels, which we found in the Roads shew me great attention," he wrote. When Clarkson, feverish, collapsed on board the *America*, a slave ship captained by a man named Connolly, he woke up to find that "two female Slaves [were] . . . sent to fan me while I slept," which "prevented me from enjoying that repose."[44] Connolly also sent goats and provisions to one of the Company vessels, the *Felicity*, and refused to accept payment for them.[45] Finally, Connolly insisted that King Jimmy, Naimbanna's successor, was only "pretending to be our friend, was not so, that he, & all his people,

Figure 4. Eighteenth-century depiction of Bance Island, which was the nearest significant slave-trading fort to Freetown, and a point of contact between the Sierra Leone Company and European slave traders before 1807. (Reprinted from William Smith, *Thirty Different Drafts of Guinea* [London, 1727]; courtesy of Harvard Map Collection, Pusey Library, Harvard University)

had lately assembled at the Devils House, making sacrifices . . . in order to secure his interest to help us out of the Country."[46] Local slave traders used rumors, gifts, threats, and appeals to European solidarity to try to defuse the ambitions of the Company by putting the Company in their debt.

Traders like Connolly were enmeshed with many local chiefs in a web of mutual expectations and responsibilities. The Cleveland family were ostensibly the "strangers" of King Naimbanna, but they had been masters of the Banana Islands for several generations, and enjoyed significant power and autonomy. "They have always carried on a great Slave Trade," one Company official noted, "& the present Cleveland is said to expend annually 50 puncheons of Rum in drams treating his Negroe acquaintance."[47] Bolland, in exchange for the right to a factory on the Bananas, agreed not to interfere with the slave trade in the Sherbro' River to the south, which was Cleveland's preferred territory. Bolland and Connolly urged the Company to establish a settlement on the Bananas. "Several Slave Captains have concurred in this advice, which good as it may be cannot proceed from benignity towards us," James Strand wrote, "but perhaps they wish to see our strength divided."[48]

After a short period when the former Royal Marine officer William Dawes acted as interim Governor, Zachary Macaulay replaced Clarkson. Clarkson's loyalties were divided between the settlers, whom he admired and respected (albeit in a paternal, condescending way), and the Company. Zachary Macaulay, by contrast, was Henry Thornton's man. Zachary Macaulay was born, blind in one eye, at Inverary on 2 May 1768, the third son of the Reverend John Macaulay and his wife, Margaret Campbell.[49] Macaulay went to Glasgow at 14 to work as a clerk in a counting house.[50] At 16, a relative secured a job for him in Jamaica, as the bookkeeper of a sugar plantation, where he watched enslaved people cut and boil cane. While Macaulay was in the West Indies, his sister Jean married Thomas Babington, a wealthy Evangelical merchant and philanthropist and member of the Clapham Sect. Macaulay was introduced to Babington and his friends, including William Wilberforce and Henry Thornton, at Babington's estate in Leicestershire. Macaulay became an enthusiastic Evangelical.[51] His brother-in-law became his friend and his spiritual and professional godfather.[52] Macaulay was invited by Henry Thornton to join the Sierra Leone Company as a clerk. In 1793, he was sent as a Member of Council to Sierra Leone, and was soon promoted to Governor. He wrote to his future wife, Selina Mills, "I feel on my mind a secret and involuntary dread that God will require me in Africa."[53]

Suzanne Miers and Martin Klein have observed that the relative weakness of European officials in Africa pushed even the staunchest opponents of slavery to accept local institutions of forced labour.[54] For his part, Macaulay was a zealot in his loyalty to the Company. In his view, the Sierra Leone Company would eventually be the Christian redeemer of Africa; compromises with slave traders were a small price to pay. In 1793, the colony was short of food and risked starvation. The demand for rice, the colony's staple, was enormous. Macaulay wrote, "All of our exertions scarce keep us supplied with that article and there is a necessity for having a stock on hand if we wish to avoid the famine which would follow the loss or detention of our craft."[55] In September and October of 1793, Macaulay bought fifty tons of rice from a slave dealer named Aspinall, resident in the Little Scarcies River, and another fifty tons from Cleveland.[56] Macaulay also bought a half-ton of ivory for the Company's warehouse from a slave trader named Jackson, who had a factory at the Iles-de-Los, along with another fifty tons of rice. In September 1793, Macaulay contacted Mr. Tilley, the manager of the slave factory at Bance Island, to buy nearly four more tons.[57]

Records of Macaulay's conversations with the slave traders do not survive, but it is safe to assume they talked about more than rice. Macaulay may have been interested to know at what forts or towns the factors bought their own supplies and at what price, as well as what routes they followed to get to them. And he must have gained some valuable information, because soon after making his purchases Macaulay deployed the Company's vessels along traditional coastal routes. In October 1793, the Sierra Leone Company's schooner, the *Ocean,* was sent to cruise from Bissau to Cape Mesurado. The ship collected African commodities from forts along the coast and then returned to Freetown, where the goods were warehoused for future export.[58] In April 1794, other ships in the Company fleet followed suit. The *Domingo* was sent to buy wax, ivory, and redwood in the River Gabon. The *Thornton* was sent to the Gold Coast to trade in gold and ivory. The *James & William* was packed with rum and rice and sent to the Gold Coast. The *Amy* was sent to St. Thomas (São Tomé), to collect "useful plants and seeds," and the *Duke of Clarence* was dispatched to act as a factory vessel in the Rio Pongas. Finally, a smaller ship was assigned to packet duty, supporting the trade ships by cruising the coast as far as Cape Palmas, relaying goods and letters back to Freetown between visits from the merchant vessels.[59] All of these stations were slave ports, and the routes between the stations were regular channels for the distribution of slaves and other commodities before the Middle Passage: doing business *with* slave traders led the Company to do business *like* slave traders.

However, access to shipping routes was valuable only in conjunction with specialized knowledge about the rituals of coastal trade. As Macaulay admitted, slave traders had "superior skill" in making up assortments for their cargo to appeal to African merchants.[60] Macaulay's compromises with the slave trade may have helped him to understand better the expectations of African traders and the rhythms of trade in the region. Slave traders intervened on the Company's behalf in disputes with local kings and chiefs. When the Temne chiefs from whom the Company had obtained the rights to the Freetown Peninsula demanded the return of the land, Tilley of Bance Island and another slave trader, a Frenchman named Renaud, the proprietor of a fort on Gambia Island (an island near Bance in the Sierra Leone River), helped to protect the colony by defending the Company at a palaver with the Company's landlords. Palavering effectively required experience, as well as diplomatic sensibilities and linguistic skills. Macaulay wrote in his journal, "It would be uncharitable to suppose that Tilley means to use his present good offices as a foil on some future occasion."[61] Macaulay recognized that until he was able to master the vernacular of African trade, he would need men like Tilley.

The Company also bought supplies from the many American slave-trading ships that stopped in Freetown to sell off their cargo before sailing south to buy slaves and begin the Middle Passage. The Company bought rice from Americans, but they were especially interested in rum, tobacco, and sugar—all products in demand in the markets of the Upper Guinea Coast (and most produced with slave labour in North America or the Caribbean).[62] In 1799, the Company turned down an offer to buy rum and tobacco from exporters in Nova Scotia, since "the articles could not be obtained . . . on such eligible terms as we are in the habit of getting them from the more southern parts of America."[63] The Company fed its settlers, who had fled slavery in the United States, rice grown by slaves in Africa and the Carolinas. They traded commodities like rum and tobacco, distilled and grown by slaves in the Americas, for legitimate goods grown and carried by slaves in Africa. The Company built this commercial circuit to advance the cause of the abolition of the slave trade.

After normalizing the colony's relationship with local slave traders, Macaulay's next goal was to build up the Company's trade with Futa Djallon.

Since the sixteenth century, caravan traders followed established routes from inland marts to trading towns like Forekaria, Kambia, and Port Loko on the Kissi, Great Scarcies, and Port Loko Rivers, respectively, to sell their slaves and goods to African and European merchants. Futa Djallon, which rose to prominence in the 1730s, was only the most recent master of the caravan trade.[64] The Fula *Alimami,* Sadu, sent an envoy to Freetown in 1793, after the outbreak of war in Europe drastically reduced the number of European traders calling at the factories on the banks of the Rio Nuñez.[65] In 1794, the Company sent James Watt, a former sugar-plantation manager from Dominica, to Timbo to solicit the caravan trade. Watt was captivated by the landscape. Everywhere he looked he saw money to be made: "It is inconceivable how much good might be done," he wrote, reiterating the Company's preference for European-style cultivation, "by the introduction of the plough into this country and of a few English ploughmen to teach the use of it."[66]

The Fula had been at war with the coastal Susu intermittently in the eighteenth century, and Susu hostility remained an obstacle. Watt and Sadu had different reasons for working to end the war. For the Fula, a European ally could help them to pry open trade routes; the Company, for its part, believed that ending "tribal" war was an important step towards ending the trade in slaves. Watt was told by the King of Labé, a province of Futa Djallon, that "the Soosoo people were bad people." Watt replied that "the Sierra Leone Company had some thoughts of placing a factory there [in Susu territory], and in that case they would make it their business by presents to the Soosoo chiefs to make and keep peace between them and the Foulahs."[67] In May 1794, a Fula ambassador, Mahommado, arrived in Freetown. At a meeting of the Governor and Council, the governing body of Sierra Leone under Company rule, the envoy and his hosts discussed likely locations for the factory. The ambassador rejected the Nuñez and Kissi Rivers as potential sites, the former because of the "evil, ferocious disposition of the natives who occupy that river," and the latter because it passed through territory controlled by the Susu.[68] The Sierra Leone Company took its lead from Futa Djallon, and made plans to build its factory in the Rio Pongas. War with France stalled the Company's plans. In 1792, the delegates of the French National Convention had considered founding their own company to collaborate with the Sierra Leone Company and trade in Senegal.[69] However, war broke out in 1793, and in 1794 French sailors sacked Freetown. The attack cost the colony £40,000 in goods and stores, and caused an additional £15,000 in damage; it was now doubly important that the new factory thrive.[70] In 1795, the Company's commercial agent, Robert Buckle, sailed to the Rio Pongas. The Council immediately sent a message to Sadu to request that he send down "a confidential person" to open trade.[71]

A colonial official complained thirty years later, "Between Sierra Leone and the Rio Pongas there has been a long and decided conflict of principle."[72] The conflict began in 1795, when "Freeport" Factory was founded with the grudging consent of the local chiefs, and in the face of violent protest from European slave dealers. The Company's agent, Mr. Cooper, was grateful to see the Company's ship *Providence* drop anchor at the factory's wharf. One local European had tried to bribe the Company's landlord, and another had called a palaver of traders and chiefs, held at a slave factory at Bangalan, upriver from Freeport. "A thousand lies were told," Cooper wrote to Macaulay and the Council, "about the treatment the head men had met with at Sierra Leone by all the Company's officers, and that it would not be long before they would do the same here."[73] In late May 1795 Buckle reported that very little had been done to actually build the factory, because other traders "had jointly been using every means to misrepresent us & by presents of Rum & among the lower class to stir them up to do mischief." When Buckle confronted one European trader, he snarled that the Company "*should spoil the River.*"[74]

In the Sierra Leone River, European slave traders had responded to the arrival of the Company with solicitude. The Rio Pongas European traders boycotted African traders willing to sell ivory or gold to the Sierra Leone Company.[75] The Fula, friendly and well disposed after James Watt's embassy, sent a caravan bound for Freeport at the beginning of 1796. However, a revival in the slave trade flooded local markets with European goods, weakening the Company's position in the market just as European slave traders and their African landlords arranged for the murder of a Fula caravan leader in February or March of 1796.[76] In addition to poisoning the Company's relationship with Fula wholesalers, Rio Pongas slave traders also used the perceived honesty of the Company to bolster their own profits. Traders, Macaulay reported, would mark the guns they sold "SLC," to sell them more quickly and at twice the price. Macaulay commented, "The cloths marked SLC are also in such repute in that river that the traders will probably have recourse to a similar expedient with respect to them."[77]

To the Company, the factory on the banks of the Rio Pongas was a staging area for a campaign to "civilize" African trade. The coastal Susu were degenerate, but they were open to trade with both Europeans and Muslim caravan traders and so were potentially open to "improvement." The Fula were Muslims, and the Fula elites were literate, cultured, and sophisticated long-distance traders. When James Watt visited Timbo, he felt himself to be negotiating with a near equal: the Alimami was alien but rich and powerful in a way comprehensible to a European. One traveler wrote, "I never visited a town in this part of Africa where I did not find a Mandingo man as prime minister, by the name of *bookman*, without whose advice nothing was transacted."[78] The Company and its successors maintained a certain respectful caution around Muslims, holding them in both higher esteem and greater suspicion. Animists were bracketed as pagans, and considered nearly as empty vessels, ready to be filled with the good news of Christianity.

The Company felt that trade in the Rio Pongas might tip the majority of the Susu away from Islam and toward Christianity. In September 1795, Macaulay toured Freeport. He saw in the factory an opportunity to emphasize the connection between commerce and Christianity. He recommended a missionary named Grieg to Fantimani, the Company's landlord in the Rio Pongas. He visited other local chiefs, "preparing [their] minds for the expected abolition," and explained that the scarcity of European trade goods at the factories in the river was not the fault of the Company, despite the claims of local slave traders. He also urged the chiefs to send their children to Freetown or England for education. "In these objects," he told himself, "I pretty well succeeded."[79] Macaulay returned from a brief leave in England in October 1797, on board the Sierra Leone Company's vessel, the *Calypso,* along with six missionaries—two each from the London, Edinburgh, and Glasgow Missionary Societies. The two Edinburgh missionaries, Brunton and Grieg, were sent to Freeport Factory.[80] The missionaries were intended to convert nearby villagers, but were soon slotted into the same niche filled by itinerant Muslim *marabout* scholar-priests; they were valued for the prestige they brought to a village and for their literacy and other special skills, but they were marginal; "they, like Muslim teachers . . . represented a cost rather than an income."[81]

When conversion to Christianity failed, the Company offered European education, an incentive also touted by slave traders, to secure allies and cement friendships in West Africa.[82] As one visitor to the colony in its infancy noted, "They seem desirous to give education to their children or in their own way of expressing it, 'Read book, and learn to be *rogue* as well as white man'; for they say that if white men could not read or wanted education, they would be no better rogues than *black gentlemen*."[83] Macaulay tried to offer the prestige of European education to foster trade relationships. In February 1795, James Watt informed one chief that "it was Mr. M[acaulay]'s wish if they could agree about terms to open trade . . . for Camwood, Ivory, Bullocks . . . that Mr. M. would be glad to see [him] send children to Sierra Leone to learn book."[84] In Freeport, Henry Brunton wrote a series of books in "Susoo," including a grammar, an abecedarium, and a catechism.[85] When Macaulay returned to London in 1799, he brought some twenty-five African children with him. The children lived in a rented home known as the "African Academy," in Clapham.[86] He hoped that even the recalcitrant Nova Scotians could be made "docile" by the education of their children.[87]

Macaulay learned the routines of the European coastal trade from the local slave traders who sold him rice and ivory. He and his fellow colonial officials and merchants learned the routines and idiosyncrasies of commerce with local Africans from their experiences trading with Fula caravan leaders and "Mandingo" petty traders. For example, trade with the Fula required elaborate hospitality before negotiation could begin. The would-be purchaser of Fula goods was required to invite the entire party of traders to stay in his home or, at the very least, at his expense, and to give the leader of the caravan a gift of kola nuts, tobacco, rice, and other goods at both the beginning and the end of the negotiation. "Days may elapse," Winterbottom reported, "before the business-palaver is opened." Once the palaver began, the Fula expected to negotiate on the price of each individual item in their inventory separately, causing negotiations to last for days, even weeks.[88] The Company's officials needed to learn the commercial and diplomatic skills required not just to profit in African trade, but to even begin to trade at all. Local merchants had the advantage; if the Company did not conform to their expectations, or if their traders breached etiquette, there were plenty of other places to bring their goods.

In the hope of colonial prosperity, Macaulay set aside the plans of the Company in London to transform the coastal trade at a stroke, in favor of a commercial strategy cobbled together from the advice of European slave traders and the ambassadors of an African empire. He learned the folkways of coastal trade. However, Macaulay maintained a capacity to conduct himself with canny pragmatism in his dealings with the colony's neighbours while acting to protect an austere hierarchy of civilization, with Europeans at the top and animist Africans at the bottom. Macaulay could deal amiably with slave traders while remaining rigidly antislavery; he could palaver with the Alimami while remaining suspicious of Futa Djallon. And yet, Macaulay's willingness to be flexible with local slave traders made him stricter in his dealings with the Company's settlers. The young Scot had mastered an important trick for a colonial official: to say one thing and do another, to compromise with people outside the scope of British control and to dominate people within it.

The Company and the Settlers

In 1826–27, two Commissioners of Inquiry sent to Sierra Leone were puzzled to find that the surviving Nova Scotian settlers were devoted to maintaining legal possession over farms they owned outside of Freetown, even though they generally did not cultivate them, or even consider them to be particularly valuable in monetary terms. The Commissioners recommended that the settlers lose their title to the land unless they agreed to put it under the plow.[89] In 1827 as in 1792, British officials in West Africa were convinced that British colonies ought to be built on a sturdy base of agriculture, ideally organized into owner-occupied farms. However, the Freetown Peninsula was not particularly good farmland for the kind of intensive cultivation the Company expected. The African American settlers from Nova Scotia were caught between the assumption that the colony would not prosper without farmers and the reality that farming in the colony was unlikely to prosper. Zachary Macaulay was willing to be taught the rhythms of the West African coastal trade, but he was not willing to change his mind about the place of the settlers in the colony.

The odyssey of the Nova Scotian settlers from the United States to Sierra Leone is justifiably famous. The millwright Thomas Peters, a formerly enslaved man who joined the British ranks and became a leader of the Black Loyalist community in Nova Scotia and New Brunswick, was as much the founder of Freetown as was John Clarkson. It was Peters who, by sailing to London to meet with Company leaders, attracted the attention of the Company to his people as a potential source of settlers. Peters was also an enthusiastic recruiter in Nova Scotia, and his example inspired Clarkson to agree to act as Governor. Peters felt that, given his prominent role in the establishment of the colony, he ought to share power.[90] However, the two men quarreled on the voyage over, and Clarkson feared Peters's influence among the settlers. Peters died soon after the settlers arrived, but his spirit remained in Freetown. Vincent Brown calls colonial Jamaica "a theater of ghosts," a place where the dead were unusually politically active.[91] Freetown, too, was a theater of ghosts: several settlers reported that Thomas Peters had risen from the dead to seek vengeance on the Company; others said that Peters had a guilty conscience for embezzling from the Company, and that his spirit had returned to confess.[92] Peters's ghost haunted his friends and rivals, and the memory of Peters's challenge to Clarkson's authority haunted the Company. Clarkson met Peters's demand to share in the government of the colony by casting the Nova Scotians and himself in a pantomime of naughty children and their disappointed but indulgent father. He blamed their opposition to the Company on "the bad example set by the Europeans when they first landed, the unfeeling manner in which they are often addressed, the promiscuous intercourse with so many dissatisfied sailors."[93] He would nudge the settlers toward his views by threatening to leave the colony. "This fear," his friend James Strand wrote, "has often been a check upon them."[94] Many of the settlers respected Clarkson; when he returned to England, some continued to write to him about events in the colony.

Clarkson felt the settlers had been offered a raw deal in British North America. In Nova Scotia the Black Loyalists lived in oppressed, impoverished communities. They were pushed off of scant arable land in a relatively unfertile province and worked as labourers instead, pushing down the cost of labour and infuriating poor whites, including many recently demobilized British soldiers. In the cold of the Maritimes, religion kept them warm and preserved their solidarity. The itinerant preacher William Jessop, who visited Birchtown, a settlement in remote Shelburne County, Nova Scotia, wrote in his diary that he had "tarried all night with the black-people, but the house being smoky, I found it disagreeable, but why should I complain? It was better lodging than my dear Master had."[95] Later in the week he preached at the future settler Boston King's congregation. Then Jessop held a prayer meeting where, after hours of song and prayer, "the power of the Lord came down upon us & a general shout of thanksgiving ascended to heaven for the space of an hour."[96]

In Nova Scotia, the Black Loyalists were expected to farm. Many refused, and for good reason. Nothing worth eating seemed to grow in the rocky soil of Shelburne County. Many preferred to fish for a living if they had enough money ("yellow and white earth") to pay for a boat and gear. If they couldn't fish, they hired themselves out.[97] In Nova Scotia, the deal offered by the Company seemed like a good one: the Company wanted cash crops, and the settlers wanted more and better land than they had been given in the Canadian Maritimes. The Company promised that Sierra Leone had rich soil and good water. In exchange for agreeing to relocate to the colony, the head of every household would receive both a "town" and a "country" lot, the former for a residence in Freetown, the latter for a farm. However, the country lots proved to be no easier to farm than the rocky fields of Nova Scotia.

African farmers in the rice-growing regions near the colony relied on crop rotation and controlled fires and floods to squeeze as much yield as they could from the soggy, nutrient-poor soil.[98] Planting was relatively simple. Farmers used sharp hoes to cut short furrows in the earth, and scattered seeds across them. However, bringing a crop to maturity required significant manpower, sophistication, and vigilance. Older people and children would often be conscripted to build and live in lean-tos in the fields, to "drive away the prodigious flocks of rice birds" and other pests.[99] Farmers also needed to be mindful of the bush, which always threatened to reclaim farmland. One visitor to the colony in 1811, the African American merchant Paul Cuffe, went to a farm that had been left untended for just a few years and noted "it has got so that it Looks as tho it had never been Cleared."[100] Because farming required constant attention, most of this activity in the region near the colony was done by enslaved people, often in large numbers.

The Nova Scotian settlers had not agreed to be reenslaved in West Africa. And since local villages produced staples like rice and palm oil and were willing to sell their crops to the colony, agriculture was not a do-or-die proposition. Many of the settlers decided that they would prefer to trade, like the Company's employees. The settlers argued they should nonetheless be allowed to keep the farmland they had been promised, since the Company had misled them about its arability. The Company's officials disagreed. When the settlers did not work their country lots, their grants of land were reduced to 20 percent of the agreed acreage, on the pretense that restricting access to land would protect the colony from attack by keeping the population of the settlers relatively dense and concentrated.[101] Moreover, the Company intermittently taxed the settlers by demanding quitrents against the value of the land they had been granted. Meanwhile, as Freetown's connections with the coastal trade expanded, the town lots, particularly those with access to the water, became much more valuable.[102]

One settler many years later claimed that he had been a cotton and coffee farmer in the American South. He was not telling the whole truth, even if he had been a free farmer before the American Revolution. In 1776, cotton was a relatively minor crop in the United States. The cotton gin, which made growing cotton outrageously profitable, was still nearly two decades away. Coffee does not grow well enough for commercial cultivation anywhere in the continental United States. Despite the embellishment, the settler's sense of betrayal was real and profound. "I had given up three hundred acres," he told a visitor to the colony, "which my father has possessed before me, in the service of the King, and obtained fifty for them in Nova Scotia." He gave up his 50 Canadian acres for "a grant of thirty-five in Sierra Leone free of tax, and with difficulty obtained seven of wilderness; and, now that it began to be productive, an annual charge was fixed upon it."[103] The settlers felt cheated. They were charged for land they could not cultivate, and threatened when they tried to trade instead of farm.

As the Company's trade became more organized, its plans for growing crops in the colony became more capricious. In 1794 Acting Governor William Dawes ordered the settlers to grow cotton, indigo, pepper, and ginger.[104] When Zachary Macaulay returned to the colony, he opened his own plantation of coffee, sugarcane, plantains, grains of paradise, and other crops and demanded that the settlers follow suit.[105] Each succeeding Company official had a new plan for what Sierra Leone should grow. As the settler John Kizell explained, "Macaulay went away, and John Gray succeeded him, than we brought our Cotton, peper and ginger and other articles of cultivation . . . then Thomas Ludlam came, he strove very much to begin the cultivation, but the people was disappointed and taken in so very often that they paid no much heed to what he said."[106] The settlers who did farm struggled. George Carroll complained that he couldn't find enough pickers to harvest his coffee, and when he did manage to bring a crop to market, he was undercut on price by coffee grown in nearby villages, harvested by slaves.[107] The Company interpreted the settlers' frustration as defiant laziness. Ignoring the gardens the settlers planted with food for their own consumption, the Company's *Reports* complained that the settlers "prefer eating cassava, in a miserable way, to climbing the hill, where they may enrich themselves by exertion."[108] Cassava became shorthand for sloth, a commonplace in descriptions of West African agriculture. As the traveler John Matthews wrote, "To save labour, which the natives studiously avoid as much as possible, they plant their cassada."[109] This racist judgment was also false: cassava is relatively easy to plant, but difficult to process. The crop requires extensive soaking and cooking to remove toxins from the roots and leaves, and careful pounding and drying to prepare for long-term preservation. Moreover, cassava was reliable insurance against starvation; the Maroon settlers, who arrived in 1800, soon learned that although bugs destroyed their yams and corn, "they did not attack the Cassada."[110] However, to European eyes, cassava cultivation was cause and consequence of "idleness."

The settlers correctly perceived that since they couldn't prosper as farmers, and since they were making headway in trade, the Company was beginning to see them as a nuisance. The Company store began to accept trade goods in preference even to its own dollars. The settler Nathaniel Wansey, one of the leaders of the revolt against the Company in 1800, wrote, "We settlers will take our money and go to the store and we will be turned away with our paper money that they make in our hands . . . At the same time the slave traders can come be supplied whenever they think proper."[111] Luke Jordan wrote to John Clarkson after the French burned the town, "In your being here we wance did call it Free Town but since your Absence We have A Reason to call it A Town of Slavery." The French attack, Jordan hoped, was divine punishment of the Company, a "Message of his Power to attack the Barbarous Task Masters."[112]

Macaulay had little patience for these grievances. As Luke Jordan and Isaac Anderson wrote to John Clarkson in 1794, "the times [is] as not as it was when you left us." Macaulay, they reported, "allows the Slave Traders to come here and abuse us" and fired any settlers working for the Company if they complained.[113] In June 1794, several men whom he had fired from the Sierra Leone Company's service confronted Macaulay and threatened him. Macaulay sent the town marshal, a loyal settler named Richard Crankepone, to arrest the men. Crankepone was beaten up in the street. Macaulay acted decisively. He vowed to cancel all employment for all settlers in the case of any violence, had all of the arms in the colony put aboard the Company's ships, and assembled a militia of loyal settlers under the Baptist preacher David George and the Company employee Richard Pepys.[114] Tensions with the Nova Scotians continued through 1794–95. Finally, in March 1795 Macaulay harangued the settlers in a speech preserved in the colony's Council minutes. "By the Company," Macaulay began, "have I been intrusted with the Management of their property, & to them alone will I account of it. They are my only Judges. Are you free," he asked the settlers. "So am I." Macaulay insisted that he worked for the Company, not for the settlers. "I feel myself," he concluded, "independent either of the approbation or censure of the inhabitants of *Freetown* . . . I shall act regardless of these, & with a single eye to my employer's views."[115] The slave trade had not yet been abolished in the British empire, and mass emancipation was a long way away. In Macaulay's tirade, the settlers got a preview of the expectations colonial officials held for former slaves, and for the descendants of slaves. The settlers, consistent with their place in the hierarchy, were expected to listen to European commands and grow cash crops for the market. And as Macaulay made clear, if they refused they would forfeit European patronage.

The Maroons and the Militarisation of Antislavery

John Clarkson condescended to the settlers but still considered them to be the backbone of the colony. After Clarkson was sacked, Zachary Macaulay took over and began to make inroads with European and African traders living near Sierra Leone. He aggressively censured the settlers for their unwillingness to farm according to Company specifications. And yet, despite Macaulay's best efforts, Sierra Leone did not prosper. The French attack on the colony in 1794 was a major setback. The settlers' commitment to trade over agriculture stifled Company plans for plantation agriculture. And although the settlers' rebellion and attacks from the Temne in 1800 and 1801 did not destroy Freetown, they did make it all but impossible for the Company to break even, much less turn a profit.[116] The Company turned to the British government for support, and it had enough supporters among antislavery Members of Parliament to make a persuasive case. Although the French attack had nearly ruined the Company in 1794, it proved useful six years later. In the midst of war, Parliament was spendthrift with British colonies, even commercial colonies only unofficially connected to Britain, if it seemed possible that they might fall to France. And so, in 1800, with the Company's trade in dire straits, Parliament voted to support the colony with an annual grant of £7,000. Macaulay wrote to his fiancée, Selina Mills, "Thornton was overjoyed when I told him of it three days ago. He ran to his wife, 'Marianne, do you not wish me joy? I have seven thousand a year given to me.'"[117] The grants weren't enough: a year later, the Company told a Parliamentary Select Committee, "Unless additional Funds are granted, the colony must be relinquished."[118]

The Company recognized that Sierra Leone needed money and better defenses. In the midst of the Napoleonic wars, the British military was armed to the teeth and flush with cash. Stephen Saunders Webb's assessment of the early modern English empire—"Colonization was at least as much military as it was commercial"—was just as true of the British empire in the late eighteenth and early nineteenth centuries.[119] The Sierra Leone Company based its colony on the principles of "Christianity, commerce and civilization," but by 1800 it was clear to the directors that, without military support, their trinity would be a dumb idol. The colony was under regular threat of attack. The Company recognized that the armed forces were skilled record-keepers; Royal Navy ships in particular could be critical infrastructure, as useful for communication and transportation as for cannon, carronades, and armed Royal Marines.[120] Finally, and especially relevant to a failing trading concern, the British armed forces were a rich source of contracts. Soldiers and sailors needed food, supplies, and support. The advantages of having a permanent military presence were obvious; the question was how to get one.

In 1800, the Company admitted some 500 Jamaican Maroons as settlers to the colony on condition that the Jamaican legislature would pay the cost of settling them. When they arrived in Freetown as settlers, the Maroons, like the Nova Scotians, were expected to work for wages under the supervision of white employers. But to the Company the Maroon community was less important as a labour force than as a beacon for attracting the British armed forces and the lucrative contracts for food, support, and supplies they brought with them to West Africa. The Company was beginning to lose faith in its colony, and its directors hoped to preserve its trading business and concomitantly to convince Parliament to make the government of the colony the Crown's responsibility. The Maroons helped to give the Company leverage in these negotiations; Jamaica was exponentially more valuable to Britain than Sierra Leone.

When the Company accepted the Maroons as settlers, they opened connections with all of the government departments interested in Jamaican affairs, especially the War Office. Between the arrival of the Maroons in 1800 and the abolition of the slave trade in 1807, the number of connections between the Sierra Leone Company and the apparatus of British government multiplied. The Maroons' arrival created opportunities to fulfill government contracts for transportation, provisions, and lodging. Soon after, the colony received grants to build fortifications. In 1800, a detachment of the Royal

African Corps, a British convict regiment based at Gorée and composed of white deserters and other soldiers convicted of crimes by courts-martial, was posted to Freetown as an official colonial garrison. In 1804, the Company named a Royal Navy captain Governor of Sierra Leone. Historians of New South Wales argue that the French blockade of the first decade of the nineteenth century made outposts like Sydney critically important; the British government grabbed any outposts it could, both to deny them to the French on principle, and to secure alternative supply chains to evade French blockades.[121] This logic applied to West Africa as much as to Australia. The Sierra Leone Company was finessing its retreat from Government House.

Notwithstanding a vague sense that the Company were doing good work for a good cause under the threat of French attack, there were few strategic reasons for the Crown to take over Sierra Leone. It had other possessions in West Africa, including the forts of the Gold Coast and the island of Gorée; Britain did not need a foothold on a coast where British merchants had been in business for centuries. Since they were Loyalists, the Nova Scotian settlers had some claim on the protection of the Crown, but they could have been uprooted and moved to another settlement if necessary. The colony did not produce any goods that could not be obtained elsewhere, usually at a better price. So why did the Crown take over Sierra Leone in 1808? Reginald Coupland suggests that the handover happened because "the pioneer work [had] been done, and the experiment justified."[122] Coupland's hypothesis cannot be true: considering the miserable balance sheet of the Company and the unrest among the settlers, the results of the "experiment" were unimpressive. Instead, the Company succeeded in making the colony appealing to the Crown by pushing, as trade faltered and the settlers rebelled, for a permanent military presence at Sierra Leone. The Maroons connected British antislavery, at last, with the war effort.

In 1796, the Governor of Nova Scotia, John Wentworth, received a surprising dispatch from the Earl of Portland. Portland discussed a recent rebellion by the Trelawny Maroons against the Jamaican Legislature. The Maroons, a community of free people who lived in the densely forested "cockpit country" in the mountains of central Jamaica, went to war after the Legislature violated a treaty from the 1730s that guaranteed them their freedom in exchange for certain obligations, including the promise that they would capture runaway enslaved people from sugar plantations in the lowlands. Portland informed

Wentworth that the Governor of Jamaica, the Earl of Balcarres, "may have directed [the Maroons] to be conveyed to Halifax . . . it is not impossible that these unfortunate people may have arrived before this Dispatch reaches you."[123] Portland was correct: some 560 Maroons soon arrived in Halifax. The Maroons proved to be an asset, rather than a liability. They were Jamaica's problem, and the Jamaican Legislature was expected to pay for them. Initially, Wentworth was delighted with the "very considerable Sum of Money to be applied toward the settlement and maintenance of the Maroons." Even better, the Maroons were not the savage rebels Wentworth expected, but rather a people "who have behaved orderly, peacefully and quietly since their arrival." Wentworth noted, "It cannot but afford pleasure to every serious and human mind, to be informed, that means of instructions are liberally provided for the children . . . as are also the most provident means for instructing all of them in the Christian Religion."[124] The Maroons were a double blessing to Wentworth: a source of cash and an opportunity for a civilizing mission.

Wentworth settled some of the Maroons in the villages of Boydville and Preston. The Preston group went on strike, "still deluded with false schemes of returning to Jamaica." So Wentworth stopped their rations. The Maroons threatened to get their own provisions through cattle raiding, and Wentworth sent in two officers and thirty soldiers to keep order. "Their present refusal to work," he wrote, "is an artifice to procure subsistence without labour . . . I am fully persuaded, that these People are situated in the only part of the World, where they can do no mischief, and by a firm and temperate perseverance be reclaimed to civilization."[125] Wentworth understood that Balcarres' decision to send the Maroons into exile without getting approval from London had pinioned the Jamaican Legislature. He sent a copy of his expenses to London, with this smug aside: "I trust that Government [i.e., of Jamaica] will provide reimbursements, as it is certainly incurred by their own Act—for their own safety, service and even preservation."[126] Wentworth charged bills of exchange amounting to at least £10,379 toward the expenses of maintaining the Maroons during their time in the province, expecting Jamaica to pay up.[127]

Portland, the Secretary of State for War, into whose portfolio the management of the Maroons fell, had little interest in their civilization, but he had a strong interest in keeping Jamaica secure, and in keeping imperial finances as disciplined as possible. When the Jamaican Legislature refused to pay Wentworth's expenses, Portland was embarrassed and angry. As early as

February 1799, he was considering Sierra Leone as a new home for the Maroons. In a private letter, one of his confidential advisors suggested that "the whole expense of their transportation to Africa & the purchase of a settlement for them there should cost from 10 to 12,000£. It is a sum that will soon be expended on their account in Nova Scotia."[128] Portland complained to Wentworth about a set of Treasury bills for £2,944, for which Wentworth had not bothered to send receipts, and warned him that, until the receipts appeared, "you will stand personally charged with and accountable."[129] Portland put out feelers for a new, more responsible host for the Maroons. On 18 June 1799, Portland wrote to Wentworth that the government intended to resettle the Maroons in Sierra Leone.[130]

To Portland, the Maroons were imperial pawns. He wrote, "The terms on upon which the Maroons will be received at Sierra Leone . . . [are] granted [to them] altogether as a matter of grace . . . I do not think it necessary or expedient that their inclinations should be consulted."[131] The Secretary of State treated the Maroons as objects to be moved back and forth across the Atlantic, but they were objects which he believed belonged to Britain, and whose (limited) care it was Britain's burden to discharge. The "care" of the Maroons was the Sierra Leone Company's first significant government contract, and was parlayed into the Company's first official contact with the British armed forces.

In March 1799, Henry Thornton wrote to John King, Portland's confidential secretary, in a "private & extra-official" capacity about the possibility of taking on the Maroons as emigrants "as chiefly preparatory to some more regular communication from our Court." He estimated that each Maroon would cost the Government £20 per year for provisions, and that the Maroon families' houses would cost £3 or £4 to construct, plus the costs of surveying, purchasing new land, and constructing new houses for their European minders. To make it simpler he urged Portland to consider the Sierra Leone Company as their agents. Thornton suggested that Parliament ought to consider annual grants to the Company, "partly on the ground of our being burthened with the charge of these Maroons & partly on that of our having so long voluntarily charged ourselves & of our still purposing to do so with the Burthen of supporting a Civil Establishment at Sierra Leone." The colony, he explained disingenuously, had been founded "much more to benefit Africa thru the Civilisation which it promotes & ultimately to benefit Great Britain than to benefit our own Proprietors."[132] Soon after this "extra-official" letter was sent out, the Company announced that they were willing to absorb the

Maroons into the colonial population of Sierra Leone, so long as the Company were not expected to pay "the expenses necessary for their establishment and maintenance." Moreover, the Company expected that they would retain the right to appoint or to dismiss "the persons placed over" the Maroons.[133] Portland was happy to send the Maroons to Sierra Leone, since the Company's "well-known character" reassured him that the Treasury would not be taken advantage of in the deal, and that it would be completed "in the most oeconomical manner."[134]

The Maroons, in theory, were valuable as settlers in the same ways as the Nova Scotians. They were expected to pay quit-rent on the land they were granted, and further grants were made contingent on putting at least three-quarters of the first grant under cultivation.[135] But quit-rents and produce in the market were incidental to the real value of the Maroons to the Company. The Maroons were a bargaining chip even before they left Nova Scotia. The Company's staff in Freetown tried to get as much as they could from Wentworth in Nova Scotia along with the Maroons, demanding at least two 12-pound, four 6-pound, and four 3-pound cannons, as well as four months' worth of basic provisions, 25 or 30 tons of rice, pine boards, barrels, brick, flour, butter, and other supplies. Wentworth refused, dryly noting that "you will receive everything that may be considered necessary, in the *Asia*," the lead transport ship carrying the Maroons.[136]

London was more willing to deal. The Company used their offer to take in the Maroons as leverage to secure Royal Navy protection for their ships, both in the coastal trade and for longer-haul voyages. The Company planned to settle the Maroons on the Banana Islands. In March 1799, Henry Thornton requested a Royal Navy cutter to secure the island before their arrival, claiming that French privateers threatened the Company's lightly armed ships.[137] In November, Zachary Macaulay, back in London, stressed to the Office of the Secretary of State for War that rumours of the Maroons' arrival had inflamed local chiefs and slave traders. He hoped that "on account of the urgency of the occasion Government may be disposed to yield them the requisite support by stationing a vessel of force for a few months at Sierra Leone."[138] But a Royal Navy vessel would do more than secure the Banana Islands. It would also protect Company vessels, and perhaps overawe the Company's enemies. Shortly after the Royal Navy sent a ship to Freetown, in 1800, the Royal African Corps garrison arrived. Now that both the Royal Navy and the British Army had advance parties in Sierra Leone, the Company pressed for more and better troops and ships, again on the pretense of controlling the Maroons. In 1802, Zachary Macaulay requested that a West India Regiment be sent to the colony, due to "the Sickness and mortality which have prevailed among the white Troops at Sierra Leone," as well as "the difficulties of executing the British Laws among the Maroons in all cases in the want of their not being controlled by some superior force."[139]

Granville Sharp, the moving spirit of the original British settlement at Sierra Leone, was a committed democrat and political innovator, and built new institutions of representative government into the constitution of his 1787 "Province of Freedom." Some of these institutions, including the elected offices of "Hundredor" and "Tythingman" (terms Sharp borrowed from Anglo-Saxon history), carried forward into Company rule.[140] By 1800, the Hundredors and Tythingmen of Freetown represented the interests of the settlers in opposition to the Company. In February 1800, a dispute between a Liverpool slave-ship captain and the Company's landlord, King Tom, expanded into conflict between the Company and a group of Nova Scotian settlers, led by Nathaniel Wansey and James Robertson. The settlers demanded that the captain pay anchorage duties to King Tom; the Governor had promised him free passage. The dispute brought the grievances of the settlers to a head, and in September the Hundredors and Tythingmen published their own code of laws, demanding that the Company give up their right to manage anything but their own affairs. A group of about fifty settlers took up arms and left Freetown.

In October, the *Asia* arrived. The Maroons agreed to track the rebels through the bush outside the colony, capture them, and return them to Freetown. Some of the rebel leaders were exiled for life, two others were hanged.[141] The emigrant Maroons had already benefited the Company by intimidating the Nova Scotians. They also proved to be a financial windfall. Their arrival brought the Sierra Leone Company into the same orbit around the Treasury as the slave-trading British forts in West Africa, many of which were supported by Parliamentary grants. From 1800 to 1805, the Company received £67,000 in grants, beginning with £7,000 in February 1800 to pay for fortifications, followed soon after by £4,000 "for the Service of the Year."[142] In 1800, hard on the heels of the Parliamentary grants, the colony was granted a Charter of Justice, allowing its Governor to appoint magistrates to enforce the British common law.[143] In 1801, the directors began a campaign to convince Parliament formally to take over Sierra Leone as a Crown Colony.

In a memo to the War Office, Zachary Macaulay and Henry Thornton made four arguments for the takeover. First, the British government was bound to the Nova Scotians and Maroons, "by every consideration of Justice and good faith," and it would be much cheaper to keep the settlers in Sierra Leone. Second, Macaulay and Thornton slyly suggested that "this character of permanency, including the expectation of effectual support, will certainly attach to it when it shall be known to be in the possession of Government." Third, the Company had eaten through so much of its capital that "in the want of any extraordinary and unforeseen emergency the Directors feel that should be unable to proceed . . . even to the personal safety of the Colonists." Fourth, and perhaps most important, the directors stressed that Sierra Leone might be a valuable station for Royal Navy ships: "The Harbour is safe and commodious . . . Wood and Water of the best quality are procured with facility . . . The position of the Settlement renders communication easy with the whole line of Coast from Gambia to Cape Palmas."[144] The Maroons and Nova Scotians bound the government in London to Sierra Leone, making the transfer a moral imperative, the costs of which could be written off against the strategic value of the colony. Thornton put it plainly in the House of Commons: "Sierra Leone, indeed, now assumed nearly the same character as various other African forts to which parliament had been used to grant from 20,000£ to 30,000£ per annum."[145] The analogy between Sierra Leone and Britain's other forts was made possible by the arrival of the Maroons.

Macaulay, the Garrison, and the New Crown Colony

In the 1820s, the long-serving colonial official Daniel Molloy Hamilton declared, "I have no reason to believe that the . . . original possessors of the Peninsula of Sierra Leone have either derived benefit or sustained injury by the occupation by the British."[146] By the 1820s the British armed forces had subdued, dispossessed, or expelled any local people on the Peninsula unwilling to accept the permanent presence of the colony. And, as the next chapters of this book will show, the Royal African Corps' importance in the colony, and the antislavery prestige of its officers, grew enormously, particularly after the end of the slave trade. But those first years of the nineteenth century were violent and uncertain for the small garrison sent to guard Sierra Leone. The local Temne were well armed, often with British-made firearms. But unlike European soldiers who fought in ranks, Temne warriors avoided open spaces in favour of firing from behind trees or other cover. They also didn't look like European soldiers: they covered their bodies in chalk, hung amulets around their necks and wrists, painted their knees and elbows red, and used vegetable oils to make the dark skin of their faces even darker.[147] The garrison was on perpetual alert. One of their officers recorded in his diary for 5 July 1803, "An attack on this colony being suppos'd to be at present planning by the natives on the Bullom Shore . . . all the men (not sick) are to be under arms in their Block Houses every morning at 4 o'clock until further orders and have everything clear for action."[148] In 1804, the half-pay Royal Navy officer William Day was appointed Governor by the Sierra Leone Company. Day's priority (when his gouty foot permitted), was to augment the colony's defenses.[149]

On 11 March 1805, Day organized a procession to lay the foundation for a Martello tower to overlook and protect the settlement. That morning, a procession of Nova Scotian and Maroon militiamen, along with "all the curious and African fashionables," marched up a hill just outside the settlement. A missionary living in Freetown noted that, in order, "first was carried by Volunteers the Union Flag, guarded by Soldiers of the African Chor; then followed the Governor, Mr. Ludlam, and myself between them, carrying the Tower of the world; the refuge of the miserable; the Word that endures when heaven & earth pass away; then followed a train of white and black Ladies; then the Company's Flag, guarded by Soldiers."[150] This march up what is now Tower Hill in Freetown (although the tower is long gone), with the Company's flag guarded by soldiers, was a symbol of the increasingly robust connection between the British armed forces and the colony. A visitor to the colony in April 1805 remarked that when he met Day, "he was then occupied in forming plans of defence in the colony; and had he lived . . . it would in a short period have opposed to an enemy a formidable resistance."[151] However, Day died three months later, and Thomas Ludlam was appointed Governor of Sierra Leone.

The Company's moribund trade briefly revived, thanks to the burgeoning relationship between the colony and the military. Zachary Macaulay kept up a lively correspondence with the Navy Board, the War Office and the Transport Office, appealing for grants to feed and house the Maroons, and bidding on contracts to transport goods and dispatches via Sierra Leone to other West African forts like Gorée.[152] Macaulay, already familiar with the routines of slave traders in Africa, soon learned the routines of bureaucrats in London. His new connections in the Treasury and the War Office raised his profile. He became a valued advisor to the government on British affairs in West Africa. In August 1802, Macaulay urged Lord Hobart to consider Sierra Leone as a base for British explorers looking for the source of the Niger, and for any traders hoping to establish long-distance trade with the interior of Africa. He boasted (incorrectly) that Port Loko, a town up the Sierra Leone River from Freetown, was less than four hundred miles from the putative source of the Niger. "Sierra Leone," he wrote, to encourage Hobart to adopt the plan, "is also recommended by other considerations, such as the Establishment of a British colony, and the erection of a British Fort at the entrance of the River."[153]

In 1807, the Sierra Leone Act passed, and on 1 January 1808, Sierra Leone became a Crown Colony. In a lucky coincidence for the Company, the official transfer of the colony to the Crown happened soon after the abolition of the slave trade. The directors of the Company, no longer encumbered by their greatest liability—the cost of governing the colony—were free to benefit from government contracts from the War Office. But the end of Company rule did not mean the end of Company influence. Shortly after the transfer, Henry Thornton wrote to Lord Castlereagh to call "your Lordship['s] early attention to the several measures which may be rendered necessary both by this Bill & by the Bill for the abolition of the slave trade . . . the Directors are of opinion that it is extremely material that a ship of war, perhaps that two ships of war, should be sent immediately to the coast."[154] Castlereagh agreed to send H.M.S. *Derwent* to West Africa.

The end of the Company's role in the formal government of Sierra Leone allowed the former directors, particularly Zachary Macaulay, to fantasize about the growth of Sierra Leone from a small colony to the heart of a new empire in West Africa. In May 1807, Macaulay laid out for Castlereagh a plan for reorganizing the colony and West Africa more broadly around a network of coastal bases from which to conduct the campaign against the slave trade. Macaulay began with confidence: "I take the liberty of addressing your Lordship on the general subject of African Affairs. I am encouraged to do this by the desire which your Lordship has expressed of obtaining information respecting that country." Macaulay stressed the concentration of power and influence in Sierra Leone, complaining that the various forts and settlements in West Africa "form at present a very loose and disjointed whole subjected to great diversity of management and pursuing ends which widely differ from each other." He suggested instead that West Africa be organized as a "presidency," like the Indian presidencies, with Sierra Leone as its capital, although he provided no explanation of how a West African presidency might be organized.[155] He urged the government to dispatch more vessels to the West African coast, to Gorée and the Gold Coast as well as to Sierra Leone, "with a view both of giving effect to the provisions of the Act for abolishing the Slave Trade and for other purposes of considerable moment." The prestige of Royal Navy captains, he suggested, would give them considerable influence among the local rulers. They would relay information about trade, agriculture and social conditions in Africa back to England. By virtue of their commissions, they would have the power to make treaties to further the goal of the abolition of the slave trade. The captains would be able "to encourage and patronize every rational scheme for improving the condition of Africa." They would also have the firepower to bully British merchants out of the slave trade, and into legitimate trade, and the influence to show local chiefs "the various Channels into which the Industry of their people may be advantageously directed."[156]

Under Macaulay's scheme, a Royal Navy officer (like the former Governor, Captain Day) would relay information about the coast to the Government, and would put into force the abolitionists' schemes for "improvement." The captains would bully British slave traders and protect and promote "legitimate" commerce. They would make treaties and add to British territory. Antislavery commerce would acquire a military and an imperial character. In a letter to Thomas Ludlam, Macaulay gloated, "I have *no doubt* that Government will be disposed to adopt almost any plan which we may propose to them with respect to Africa provided we will but save them the trouble of thinking."[157] Macaulay, ambitious and intensely pious, was no braggart. His candid remark to Ludlam about his ability to dictate terms to Government was true: after abolition passed into law, West African affairs all but passed into the hands of the Clapham Sect. On 7 December 1808 Wilberforce described his inner circle as "a little conclave on Sierra Leone, indeed generally speaking African affairs."[158]

Between Macaulay's return to England in 1799 and the transfer of the colony in 1808, Sierra Leone was transformed. Private merchants took over trade from the Company, and the colony acquired a garrison and a permanent Royal Navy presence. The Company, before it dissolved, fulfilled government contracts and sold supplies to the armed forces. The original Company experiment had faltered. The Nova Scotians did not meet the directors' expectations as plantation workers. They were, Wilberforce wrote to Henry Dundas, "as thorough Jacobins as if they had been trained and educated in Paris."[159] The Company's trade was not enough either, burdened as it was by the expense of governing the colony. Wilberforce blamed the slave trade, but declared that despite its commercial failure the colony "had taken deep root, and would be the means of civilizing a considerable portion of Africa."[160]

From 1800 to 1807, the roots of the colony not only sank deeper into the soil of Africa. They also grew out, tapping into the resources of the British government, like mistletoe on an English oak. As the Company's experiment wound down, the principles of British antislavery as defined by the movement's public face and private centre of gravity, the men of the Clapham Sect, began to shift from passive economic transformation toward active imperial rule. The Nova Scotians were disciplined for refusing Company orders. The Maroons were treated as tokens to be traded for favours in London and Halifax. Local kings were alienated from their land, and enslaved people in Africa worked harder to grow the things that Freetown needed. British military officers were conscripted into the cause. British antislavery had been planted in African soil.

2. Let That Heart Be English

A Royal Navy officer described Freetown in 1805 as a quiet town "built on a gentle declivity, with the streets very broad and arranged at right angles." Most of the houses had small gardens growing pineapples, bananas, and other produce. This was the Freetown of the roughly 1,500 Nova Scotian and Maroon settlers and European traders. Grass grew at the edges of the grid of unpaved streets, flattened by wheels, feet, and hooves. The richer townspeople lived in clapboard homes, some with shingled roofs, built on top of stone cellars. The poor lived in huts built from salvaged canvas and wood. On the western outskirts of the town several hundred itinerant Kru longshoremen lived in a dense village of wattle-and-daub huts. At sunset, the town came alive with outdoor cooking fires and shrieking children. At the end of the dry season, settlers saw columns of smoke rising from the Bullom villages across the river, as farmers set fire to patches of eight-foot-high grass, preparing swiddens for planting. Fort Thornton overlooked the town. The wide front wall of the fort faced the harbor, bracketed by two taller bastions armed with rusting cannons. The shorter back wall faced the mountains. The walls protected the termite-infested Government House, the Company store, and the squalid barracks of the Royal African Corps (fig. 5). The son of a mathematician, Governor Thomas Ludlam was 32 years old. He was tall but thin from bouts of malaria and dysentery. He preferred to dress in the style of Royal Navy officers at ease, in white trousers and an open blue jacket.[1]

In late 1806, Ludlam received a letter from Zachary Macaulay, his patron in London. Macaulay wrote that the Sierra Leone Company was close to a deal to surrender Sierra Leone to the Crown. Macaulay instructed Ludlam to hold

Figure 5. Freetown as seen from the harbour, ca. 1800. Fort Thornton is at far right, flying the Union Jack; the waterfront structures are warehouses. (From Thomas Masterman Winterbottom, *An Account of the Native Africans in the Neighbourhood of Sierra Leone*, vol. 1, [London, 1803]; copy in the British Library)

on to the Company's valuable warehouses, wharves, and other assets, and to liquidate its other property.[2] Macaulay also enclosed a copy of an Act of Parliament, preliminary to the complete abolition of the British slave trade, banning the sale of slaves in foreign ports by British subjects, or in British ships.[3] Ludlam was charged with preparing Sierra Leone for a transformation from a trading post with an antislavery mission into a Crown Colony that would shelter former slaves and act as staging area for the end of the slave trade in all of West Africa.

In 1808, the first people freed from the Middle Passage by British ships arrived in Freetown. Between 1792 and 1808, European traders in the colony (including Zachary Macaulay's trading partnership, Macaulay & Babington) had come to rely on the infrastructure of the slave trade to buy and sell commodities like gold, ivory, rice, and coffee. Concomitantly, colonial officials had made it clear that "freedom" for former slaves in Sierra Leone would be carefully managed and attenuated. In Britain, 1807 was a bright line between slavery and antislavery; in Sierra Leone, the line faded into the backdrop of colonial practice and local traditions of slave trading. After the colony passed to the Crown, no one was sure "how [it] would work, who would govern it, how it would be defended, who would pay for it."[4] In consequence, Ludlam improvised, adding his intuitions about the meaning of the Slave Trade Act to older practices of Company government, factory commerce, and escalating military activity.

In March 1808, H.M.S. *Derwent* entered Freetown's harbour with two captured slave ships under convoy, and 167 enslaved people onboard. Ludlam decided that the abolition of the slave trade as legislated in Britain required him to free the slaves from the captured ships, and to reward Captain Frederick Parker of the *Derwent* with an $800 bounty for his effort.[5] Ludlam bound the former slaves as apprentices to European merchants and to Nova Scotian and Maroon settlers. He charged each new master $20 (the pound sterling had not yet been adopted as the colonial currency, and money in the colony was still reckoned in either Spanish or Company dollars) as a premium, in order to raise the money for Captain Parker's prize.[6] Ludlam was replaced in July 1808 by Thomas Perronet Thompson, a former Army officer and the son of a friend of William Wilberforce. Thompson had been groomed for office by the Clapham Sect and urged to follow Ludlam's example. He rebelled. When he learned what happened to the slaves freed by the *Derwent,* Thompson was furious: he did not see a distinction between slavery and "apprenticeship" as it was practiced in the colony. Thompson came to see the colony as a grotesque parody of antislavery, and to believe that the Sierra Leone Company had bamboozled the British public into supporting an "abolitionist" project that was actually a slave colony.

Thomas Ludlam fit former slaves into a familiar model of apprenticed labour in Freetown. Thompson imagined them as soldiers and pioneers, cutting swathes into the backcountry of the Peninsula and beyond. He fantasized that the end of the slave trade in West Africa would transform the coast into a second India. After sending a series of prolix, paranoid dispatches to England, Thompson was hastily recalled. But his frenzied innovations survived him. Before Thompson, the Sierra Leone Company's officials assumed that former slaves were uncivilized, and that European-style commerce would begin the civilizing process. In this model, the civilizing mission was passive, an emergent property of exposure to British economic folkways. Thompson claimed the right to enlist former slaves in schemes for imperial expansion and systematically to impose the practices of civilization.

The Slave Trade Act in Freetown

In the first volume of his history of the end of the British slave trade, Thomas Clarkson included a remarkable map, depicting the watershed accomplishment of the 1807 Slave Trade Act as a literal watershed (fig. 6). Clarkson

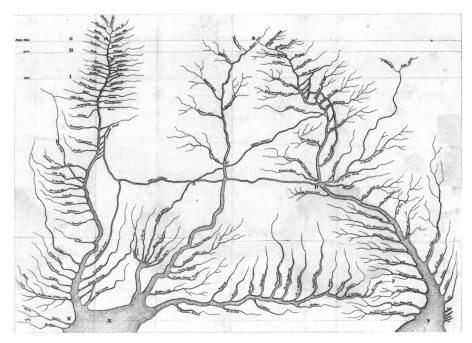

Figure 6. Representation of the intellectual lineage of British antislavery as a system of rivers gathering momentum before emptying into an ocean. (From Thomas Clarkson, *The History of the Rise, Progress, and Accomplishment of the Abolition of the African Slave-Trade by the British Parliament*, vol. 1, [London, 1808]; courtesy of Houghton Library, Harvard University)

imagined antislavery as "so many springs and rivulets, which assisted in making and swelling the torrent which swept away the Slave-trade."[7] Clarkson's map showed how British antislavery drew strength and resilience from its many sources. It was a tide that would never be turned back, Clarkson concluded, "For let us consider how many, both of the living and the dead, could be made to animate us."[8] In London, the end of the slave trade had a clear pedigree as the product of generations of work by enlightened Europeans. The Slave Trade Act itself was a formidable, irreversible, and self-evident achievement. In Sierra Leone, the legislative terminus of the campaign to end the British slave trade was a piece of paper. It was up to colonial officials to figure out what British antislavery would be in practice.

The Slave Trade Act was clarified and put into force by an executive Order-in-Council, published on 16 March 1808. Two days later, and months before the order reached the colony, Thomas Ludlam learned about the *Derwent*'s prizes. Ludlam explained abolition to the colony's local allies. He wrote to Amrah, the "Mandingo" Alimami based near Forekaria, a town on the Rio Pongas, in the hinterland of Freeport, the Company's old trading factory, "This place now belongs to the King of England who has made [me] Governor for him." The King, he explained, "has ordered the English to buy no more slaves, because he thinks the people of Africa will be happier in their own country, than they can be in another; and because the Headmen of this country may become very rich if they make the people work for them here & employ them trading to the back country."[9] But what abolition meant to the colony itself was vague. Ludlam had clearly been warned by Macaulay that abolition was likely, and that the Royal Navy would be responsible for enforcing the law. He offered no advice on how to turn people of the Middle Passage from slaves into free people. Manumission was routine in the West Indies, but it was a mechanism for individual, not mass, emancipation. The abolition of the slave trade had created a new category of people who had once been capital and who were at a stroke transformed into something else.

In the gradual-emancipation schemes of the northern United States, former slaves often "earned" the value of their freedom, either in cash or in "good conduct." In Africa, slavery and freedom were part of a wide spectrum of kinship and labour relations. Neither slave owners nor abolitionists assumed either that the end of one's status as a slave meant breaking ties between masters and former slaves, or that emancipated people would be allowed to set the terms of their own lives. But notwithstanding the complexity of the transition from slavery to freedom, Ludlam had little sense of what had actually happened when the slave ships had been captured. Had the *Derwent* made the captives free just by catching the ships? Were they free when they landed? And what was "freedom" to people who were, by any British measure, untutored in the obligations, values, and conduct of "civilized" society?

Ludlam may or may not have had much to say about the meaning of emancipation in the abstract. But in 1808 he had a pressing practical problem to solve: Freetown desperately needed labour. European merchants, colonial officials, and many Maroon and Nova Scotian settlers wanted servants for their homes, and longshoremen, watchmen, and porters for their warehouses and docks. Unsurprisingly, the emancipation Thomas Ludlam imagined in 1808 was a path from slavery to domestic service and manual work in the shipping industry. Ludlam ordered that the enslaved people—or free people, or people somewhere in between—be taken off the ship and marched together up Tower Hill to the back gate of Fort Thornton. On the way up the hill, an officer in the Royal African Corps, Frederick Forbes, tried to take three children from the group to work in his household. Alexander Smith, the Mayor of Freetown and an old Company servant, insisted that Forbes could not take the children immediately, and that all the merchants and settlers ought to get a fair chance at a servant or two.[10]

The "slaves" were brought into the fort, and the jailer, Jack Reed, a Nova Scotian, proclaimed to the settlers and European traders, "'O Yes,' 'O Yes,' 'O Yes' this is to give notice that no person is to take away any of the slaves without paying the sum of twenty Dollars."[11] The relatively low price of the "slaves" nearly caused a riot: "The cry of everybody was, 'I've got twenty Dollars.'" Ludlam intervened. He ordered everyone out of the fort, and told the crowd that the captives "would come one by one," to be given to "respectable people . . . who would maintain them."[12] John Prime, an officer of the Royal African Corps, saw many of the slaves "removed to a cattle-pen at the back of Fort Thornton . . . by the name of the Slave-Yard."[13] For all intents and purposes, the people freed from slavery by the *Derwent* were sold at auction two days after Parliament put into force the law against the slave trade.

Although the Slave Trade Act was focused on West Africa, Thomas Ludlam complained, "I have been placed in a situation of some embarrassment. I had to act at once for Government and for the Company . . . I had no assistance; and scarcely one particle of information."[14] He believed he had arranged an auction to sell the right to bind former captives as indentured servants. He applied the $20 surcharge for two reasons. First, he wanted to make sure that only colonists of means could benefit from the labour of an apprentice. Second, Ludlam wanted to raise enough money to convince Captain Parker and the crew of the *Derwent* that their pursuit of the slave ships had been worth it, and would be worth doing again.[15] Zachary Macaulay had written to Ludlam in November 1807 that although Parker "probably [wanted] in general information and talents," he would prove suggestible, and was "much pleased with the service on which he is sent."[16] Taking a ship away from an enemy, condemning it as prize, and turning both the value of the ship and the ship itself over to a British owner was a long-established practice in the Royal Navy. However, if a ship "liberated" from the Portuguese became British property, the slaves aboard a Portuguese slave ship, when liberated, were nobody's property. And yet, being property was not the same as being "free." The Order-in-Council of 16 March 1808 affirmed that slave trading was illegal, but stipulated that slaves were to be condemned like any other "contraband," and either enlisted in the Army or Royal Navy, or bound as apprentices.[17] Former slaves were not free to do as they chose. By binding former slaves to the British empire, the architects of the Slave Trade Act hoped to avoid a revolution like Haiti's, or—perhaps worse—the recruiting of former slaves by the French.

In 1808, the vast majority of Britons would have agreed with the idea that the male head of a household had the right to control the labour of the women and children under his protection; even industrial labour depended on family hierarchies to discipline workers.[18] Antislavery activists relied heavily on the conceit of representing enslaved and recently emancipated people as the children or younger siblings of Britons in order to assert their right to continue to hold authority over legally "free" people.[19] In Britain, apprenticeship formalized a householder's paternal rights in a contract; an apprentice became a subordinate member of a household in exchange for room, board, protection, and—if the owner of the indenture was a tradesman—training in skilled work. In Sierra Leone, indentures were far more rudimentary contracts, if they were signed at all.

In the 1820s, Joseph Reffell, a long-serving colonial official, quoted from the "standard" colonial indenture in use in Freetown. The obligations of the apprentice were left undefined; they served at their master's pleasure. Masters, for their part, were expected "to teach and instruct, or cause to be taught and instructed the said apprentice in the English language, the principles of the Christian Religion and also to treat the said apprentice humanely, finding and providing unto him or her good sufficient meat, drink, wearing apparel, washing and lodging and all other necessaries." The contracts also usually required would-be masters to teach women "useful personal domestic service" and men a trade or occupation, if the indenture called for it. "I know of no other regulations," Reffell concluded, "prescribed to the Master or Mistress towards the apprentice."[20] Even in the 1820s, only one copy of each contract was made for the master's records, and many former slaves, especially children, were apprenticed without a contract. It is easy to imagine just how crude the instrument for apprenticeship was twenty years earlier. In Britain, apprenticeship was vulnerable to abuse, but apprentices had (in theory) recourse to legal protection from bad masters. However, the laws of "apprenticeship" in the post-slavery labour regimes of the British empire were very different from their metropolitan ancestors.[21] The apprenticeship scheme developed for the British West Indies after 1833 drew on a long tradition of unofficial regimes of time-limited forced labour for freedpeople after emancipation.

In Freetown, indentures were usually signed only by masters, not apprentices. Only by serving as apprentices could former slaves reach the level of civilization necessary to understand the contract they had "agreed" to. When, in 1827, the leading merchant Kenneth Macaulay commented that the main struggle for colonial officials was "to avoid giving [apprentices] to improper persons," he was pointing to the central problem of apprenticeship in a colony devoted to the abolition of slavery.[22] Apprenticeship reproduced the paternal power of the adult male householder, who was, ideally, also white and pious. Giving out apprenticeships to Nova Scotian or Maroon settlers meant acknowledging in a written contract the "superiority" of the black settlers in the colony over the newly arrived former slaves. Ludlam's informal sale of indentures in 1808 thus used the Slave Trade Act as the charter to formalize an informal colonial hierarchy, with Europeans at the top, settlers below, and former slaves at the bottom.

Ludlam tried to limit the right to receive indentured apprentices to only the most successful settlers, but apprenticeship of former slaves was well known in the settler community. In 1792, John Clarkson allowed at least one "captain" of the Nova Scotians to have an apprentice, purchased as a slave from a local African village and manumitted into apprenticeship. Clarkson offered to pay for the apprentice's room and board provided his new master paid "attention to the boy" and did not mistreat him. Clarkson wrote that he was willing to offer apprentices "to any other people to a certain number as an inducement to industry."[23] Before 1808, there were effectively two kinds of informal apprenticeship in Freetown. One was for a small minority of the sons of settlers who were apprenticed to other settlers to learn skilled work, in an arrangement much like apprenticeship in Britain. For example, George Bath was apprenticed to Peter Francis, a joiner.[24] The majority of "apprentices" were domestic servants, "redeemed" from slavery in nearby villages and unofficially bound to serve for an indeterminate period. In the records, these apprentices are identified as 'living with' their purchaser. Manumitted slaves were expected to earn the cost of their manumission. Some settlers saw this kind of apprenticeship as a religious duty. In 1805, a missionary met a Nova Scotian preacher who "recommended redeeming slaves . . . in this way he thought they might be led by degrees unto God."[25] The settlers Thomas Wilson, Mary Perth, and Ann Smith had "Native" boys and girls living with them.[26] Demand among the settlers for domestic servants was buoyant. In 1811, a visiting merchant noticed how "fond" the settlers were "of haveing a Number of Servents about them."[27]

The Company also "redeemed" apprentices to work as its employees' servants in the colony. Records from the early 1800s identify at least two boys, Samuel Garvin and Thomas Gray, as "Native boy[s] apprenticed to the company."[28] The Company employee Michael Macmillan is listed along with "Isaac Watt, a Native Boy [who] lives with him."[29] Like nearly all people given near-absolute power over others, the new masters could develop a taste for sadistic violence toward their apprentices. One European, who burned an eight-year-old girl with a hot iron for "insolence," excused himself by saying that he "paid money for the girl & therefore she is [mine] . . . I did not buy her, I redeemed her."[30] In 1809, a settler named Susannah Caulker was prosecuted for torturing her apprentice, "Nancy." Caulker accused "Nancy" of having sex with a male apprentice. She stripped Nancy naked, invited the local boys to look at her, beat her with a switch, and then rubbed hot peppers into her vulva. A young African boy, called "Buonaparte" by the Europeans, testified that he was "sent by the defendant to fetch pepper and salt, fetched some green and red pepper, & mashed it in his hand" and gave the paste to Caulker to apply.[31]

Fifty-eight men, fifty-one boys, fourteen women, forty-one girls, and three infants were brought from the ships captured by the *Derwent*.[32] Ludlam reserved some of the apprenticeships for the Company, "to be employed in the first instance as labourers in the fort on public works," and later to "be formed . . . into a Military Corps."[33] In the end, the Governor claimed thirty former slaves for the "Military Corps," which he renamed the "Corps of Labourers." The rest were apprenticed to Europeans and settlers who could pay the fee.[34] The Corps of Labourers were put on rations. Four days a week they were served three pints of rice with a pint of palm oil. On the other three days they received two pints of rice and a half-pound of fresh meat, washed down with a weekly gill of rum. They lived in wattle huts inside the walls of Fort Thornton. A European was paid £100 per year to manage their rations and lodgings.[35] When the Corps did farmwork, three Nova Scotian settlers carrying switches acted as overseers.[36] The Royal African Corps officer Frederick Forbes was promised £500 per annum to serve as their Superintendent.

Five hundred pounds a year would have been an outrageously rich salary to be paid for managing fewer than forty people, so it is likely that Ludlam hoped to expand the Corps as more former slaves arrived.[37]

At least eleven of the Corps deserted, fleeing inland to Robiss, a Temne village on the Sierra Leone River. Of the other apprentices, some twenty escaped from their new masters. The eleven apprentices from the Corps of Labourers and a handful of other runaways were captured and put in irons in the Freetown jail.[38] According to the jailer, George Stephen Caulker, the jail was a small hut, locked from the outside. Caulker remembered there being roughly twenty former slaves packed into the room, some nineteen men and one woman. All but "three or four" of the men were in irons. The woman was chained to a "a piece of log, a piece of wood . . . made round and long . . . for she could take it up with one hand and . . . work with the other."[39] For Europeans and settlers, apprenticeship and slavery were different in both theory and practice. An apprenticeship had a theoretical time limit, established in the terms of the indenture. It imposed obligations on masters as well as on servants. It was made by signing a written indenture and not a deed of sale. However, from the perspective of the people apprenticed in Sierra Leone in 1808, the differences would have been difficult to detect.

Training Governor Thompson

On New Year's Day 1808, in front of the Freetown church (which was used for most public meetings, and which also served as a courtroom) Captain Parker of the *Derwent* took the Sierra Leone Company's charter from Thomas Ludlam. The colonial Volunteers, mostly Nova Scotian settlers, laid down their arms. Parker hauled down the Company flag and raised the Union Jack. The Royal African Corps fired three volleys. Then Parker indicated to Ludlam that he could resume the government, the Volunteers picked up their guns, and, in an instant, Sierra Leone became a Crown Colony.[40] The Sierra Leone Company surrendered its charter, but not its influence. Ludlam wrote to Stephen Caulker, chief of the Banana Islands, "The long expected transfer of this colony from the Sierra Leone Company to His Majesty has at length taken place. No changes will be made however in the principles on which we proceed."[41] That continuity was mirrored in London. Eight of the fourteen directors of the Sierra Leone Company in 1807–8 joined the steering committee of the new "African Institution." The

Institution, a lobby group whose subscribers included the Duke of Glouces-ter and dozens of high-minded merchants and pious bankers, was founded expressly to influence British policy in West Africa. As one historian puts it, the Institution was "almost a de-facto slave-trade department of the Foreign Office."[42] Eli Akin, a settler, remembered that the Company "told us all pub-lickly the very day that they was giving Sierra Leone up to Government that although they ceased governing that they would seek for our welfare."[43]

Thomas Perronet Thompson, the first Governor of Sierra Leone ap-pointed by the Crown, was expected to protect the continuity between Com-pany and Crown rule. Crown Colonies were adaptable, and their Governors enjoyed substantial executive power.[44] In Sierra Leone, Crown Colony status was meant to preserve, not replace, the oversight which the Company had en-joyed. Thompson was vetted and appointed by the same Clapham worthies who had appointed Ludlam. He was ordered to report to Freetown and spend some time as (fittingly) Ludlam's apprentice, to learn how to exercise the power accorded to him by the Crown in accordance with the wishes of the an-tislavery lobby. When Thompson arrived in Freetown, he was distressed and disoriented, submerged in a nightmare of imprisoned apprentices and wink-ing, salacious Company servants. He soon determined that Thomas Ludlam had not "applied the general direction of the Abolition Act at all . . . he ap-plied everything which it was the direction of the Abolition *should not be*."[45]

By 1809 Thompson had been recalled, but he continued to govern until Edward Columbine arrived in 1810 to replace him. Thompson is a footnote in the historiography of Sierra Leone. Christopher Fyfe casts Thompson as grandiloquent and foolish, "the flail of republican Freetown." Another histo-rian characterizes him as an "energetic and idealistic 'friend of Africa' . . . just the kind of governor needed by Sierra Leone."[46] Thompson deserves both less contempt and (much) less praise. He was macho and callow, insecure and eager to be liked, especially by men he perceived as soldierly. Ludlam fol-lowed orders from London and responded to immediate needs in the colony when drawing up plans for the lives of former slaves after emancipation. The transfer of the colony from the Company to the Crown was supposed to be a change in ownership, not in policy. Thompson was more grandiose. He im-agined former slaves as soldiers and pioneers, expanding Sierra Leone far be-yond the Freetown Peninsula. Thompson proposed to remake the colony with former slaves as "a race of active cultivators attached to the soil . . . a free and hardy peasantry."[47]

Thompson was born in Hull in 1783. His father was a wealthy merchant banker and a Wesleyan preacher, and represented Midhurst in the Commons from 1807 to 1818. His mother, Philothea Perronet Thompson, belonged to a prominent Methodist family. T. P. Thompson took a degree at Queen's College, Cambridge, in 1802, and was elected to a fellowship in 1804. He served unhappily in the Royal Navy from 1804 until 1806, and then transferred to the Army, where he participated in a disastrous attack on Buenos Aires in July 1807.[48] Wilberforce wrote that Thompson's father wanted "to make him a banker."[49] Thompson commented in 1811, "my early inclination had been for the Army, but finding this displeasing to my friends I had applied to the study of mathematics from the persuasion that the naval service from its connections with those sciences might appear to them to be less objectionable."[50] For Thompson, pushed along by his family's connections, Sierra Leone was both a field for adventure and an attainable prize. Situations in the colony were in the gift of his family's friends. He claimed to admire the colony from "principles of hostility to the slave trade . . . heightened by personal and hereditary respect for many of its principal supporters."[51] However, it was Wilberforce who planted the idea of going to Sierra Leone in his mind. After meeting Wilberforce at the abolitionist's home, Thompson wrote that he laid awake "combining arrangements ashore and afloat for opening and improving the communications with the interior of Africa." Wilberforce was impressed by Thompson's brio, and resolved to try and secure him a place in the government.[52] Thompson was young but he was keen, and Wilberforce trusted his father.[53]

On 19 January 1808, Wilberforce, in his looping, scribbly hand, wrote to Lord Castlereagh to recommend Thompson as Governor of Sierra Leone. As he wrote to Castlereagh, "Our experience in respect to Sierra Leone has strongly enforc'd on us, the necessity of having, for this, in many particulars, peculiar kind of service, men well qualified, & well-disposed also, to their work." Thompson, Wilberforce wrote, was "A gentleman . . . to whom after his having been for a few weeks under Mr. Ludlam's instructions, we conceived the Gov't of Sierra Leone might be safely intrusted." Wilberforce mentioned Thompson's Cambridge degree and connections and concluded, "After he should have received an apprenticeship at Sierra Leone and have got acquainted with the African character . . . I should hope he might move in a line which would require more energy & genius." In Wilberforce's reckoning, Sierra Leone could be Thompson's first step into the Clapham elite, just as it had been for Macaulay.[54] Affable, funny, and suave, William Wilberforce hoped for the radical transformation of the British empire at a slow, deeply conservative pace. He was repelled by slavery but also by social disorder, and was a gradualist by temperament and conviction. To make sure that the former slaves in Sierra Leone did not become restive or "idle," Wilberforce wanted his friends to remain as much in control of the colony as possible. Thornton explained to Thomas Ludlam that the end of the slave trade was "a new era in respect to African affairs . . . I feel therefore a strong desire . . . to place in the hands of zealous and proper persons the general direction of the British concerns in Africa."[55] Defining the terms of freedom was delicate and discreet work, and it required management from London.

Before sailing, Thompson tried to learn about Sierra Leone. The papers he received from Zachary Macaulay, he wrote, "were filled with . . . histories in which nothing was treated of," full of anodyne praise for the Sierra Leone Company.[56] When he asked for further information he was told, cryptically, "that some further projects were in agitation for advancing our intercourse with Africa." He reflected that he sailed without any information about his new post or the plans of his new Clapham patrons, "except what might be collected from works already before the public."[57] Thompson was frustrated. "I never saw such a set of men," he wrote. "they are all heart and no head."[58] He bucked against the embrace of the Clapham Sect. He wrote to his fiancée, Nancy Barker, "I am already blasted with good names; grave, steady, hopeful, promising, and the other titles which being interpreted mean fool. I have been *well disposed* a long time," he continued, mocking the prissy euphemisms of the Clapham Sect, "at present there are *great hopes of me,* and I should not wonder at waking up some morning an *established character* on Clapham Common."[59] Thompson was being told only what his patrons felt he needed to know. Macaulay was particularly and acutely aware of the difference between the rhetoric of freedom and slavery in antislavery publicity and the compromises that he and his fellow colonial officials had made with slave traders in West Africa. In order to protect Sierra Leone, those compromises needed to be concealed from a public that might not understand or accept them. Macaulay must have thought it simpler to train a new Governor on the ground, to show rather than tell the ways abolition in practice differed from abolitionism in theory.

Thompson's patrons might have guessed that their new hire wouldn't work out. Before he sailed for Africa, Thompson argued with Zachary

Macaulay about the well-established practice of buying, or "redeeming," slaves from African villages as farm labourers and servants. Thompson asked Macaulay "what the West Indians did, but *redeem* negroes & employ them in cultivation"?[60] The difference between Sierra Leone and the West Indies, in Macaulay's mind, was that masters in Sierra Leone were expected eventually to free their apprentices and to make an effort to educate and to civilize them, ideally beginning with conversion to Christianity. Thompson did not accept the distinction. He wrote, "Macaulay . . . said it was ransoming, and I said it was buying and as is usual in such cases we both ended where we began."[61] Thompson complained that whenever he suggested that he might do away with "redemption," Macaulay would reply, "But we hope you will not."[62]

On 11 April 1808, Lord Castlereagh sent Thompson his final instructions. He was ordered to shadow Ludlam until the beginning of the next rainy season, in December, in order to "obtain such information . . . as will enable you to assume the Government of the colony with advantage."[63] On 5 June 1808, Thompson sailed. He wrote to Nancy, from onboard the *Mutine,* that "I am beginning my course of study for a governor, consisting for the time being of Adam Smith on the Wealth of Nations, as fitting a subject I guess for Sierra Leone as can be devised."[64] Smith's views on slavery were straightforward; slavery was both inhumane and inefficient: masters, for one thing, needed to maintain their slaves, rather than the slaves maintaining themselves. Smith also stressed a division of labour between nations. Families divided their labour according to the special roles of each family member, and, Smith argued, "What is prudence in the conduct of every private family can scarce be folly in that of a great kingdom."[65] Smith's economics impressed Thompson. First, and most obviously, he imbibed Smith's critique of slavery. Second, and more subtly, Smith gave shape to Thompson's sense of the relationship between trade and national virtue.

William Dawes, who had served as interim Governor several times during Macaulay's tenure, accompanied Thompson on his voyage out. Dawes also wouldn't tell Thompson much about what he could expect in Freetown. Thompson reflected, "There was a mystery about his communication on subjects connected with the government and political economy of the colony." For example, when Dawes explained that chickens were expensive in Freetown, and Thompson inquired why the settlers didn't raise their own, Dawes replied, cryptically, "That *they had something else to do than rear fowls.*"[66] The table thus set with Thompson's burgeoning suspicion of the

Company, his arguments with Zachary Macaulay, and his awkward relationship with William Dawes, the new Governor's first days in the colony could
not have been worse.

Soon after he arrived in Freetown, a European merchant approached
Thompson with "300 *apprentices* in the Col[ony] to *work out*."[67] Thompson was
probably correct to assume that the man was a slave trader who had learned
about Ludlam's new plan for turning people freed from slave ships into apprentices, and was hoping to sell off as many people as possible before moving
his operations away from the colony or cashing out. The next day, Thompson
confronted Dawes. "Mr. D. answered with vehemence," Thompson wrote, "I
always thought slavery necessary in the colony; I think so still." Thompson
asked for proof, and Dawes mentioned "the men who had run from their native masters in the time of Gov. Mac[aulay] & for whom for the sake of peace
& to avoid giving them up as slaves he made satisfaction to their masters."
Dawes was referring to slavery among Freetown's Mende, Temne, and Bullom
neighbours—in order to "redeem" locally enslaved people and to preserve the
peace, Macaulay needed to acknowledge the existence of slavery within the
Company's territory. But he didn't explain that to Thompson, perhaps because
the Company was committed to concealing the real limits of their control over
the Freetown Peninsula. As far as the public was concerned, the Company
commanded all the land it had purchased for its colony. But Thompson couldn't
be *told* that; he needed to learn it for himself, as part of his training. Thompson
was mortified. He shot back that Dawes's views were "a horrible perversion."[68]
According to Thompson, Dawes perseverated, arguing that "Slavery had existed among the Greeks & Romans & that the improvement of society had
abolished it."[69] Dawes later swore that this conversation with Thompson had
never happened.[70] He might have been lying, or Thompson might have invented or embroidered the conversation. Still, it was Company policy to
tolerate slavery in local politics, and the Company had come to the consensus
that people redeemed from slavery required many years of "civilization" to
value and to exercise their freedom. As Ludlam explained to Thompson, "Our
colonists are seldom correct reasoners; they enter not into nice distinctions."[71]
Regardless of what Dawes said or meant, what Thompson *heard* was that the
Company was made up of incorrigible hypocrites.

On 27 July, to his surprise, Thompson was handed the government
of the colony by Ludlam, who would "attend exclusively to settling the
affairs of the Sierra Leone Company."[72] Ludlam may have assumed that

anyone selected by Macaulay, Wilberforce, and Thornton would be a known quantity. Thompson, reflecting on his time as Governor, claimed that when he assumed the government he was "without instructions, without information on the designs of government . . . I had only to form my own conjectures on the path to be pursued."[73] On 31 July 1808, Thompson was invited to a dinner with the prominent citizens of the town. At the dinner, Thompson was alarmed to see a military officer drunk and swearing loudly. Because he was a former officer in both the Army and the Navy, it is impossible that Thompson had never seen a similar piss-up. However, perhaps because it was a civic dinner, or because he associated Sierra Leone with the fussy manners and teetotalling of the Clapham Sect, Thompson was scandalized. When he got up to leave, Ludlam stopped him, telling him that he would need to "get used to such things as this."[74] "Getting used to such things" was, in the minds of the Clapham Sect, crucial to the long-term survival of the colony and the progress of antislavery in the British empire. The compromises made by Macaulay (explored in Chapter One) with European and African slave traders and with British military officers had taken years to refine. Just as Dawes expected Thompson to understand that Sierra Leone had to tolerate slavery among its neighbours, Ludlam expected Thompson to understand that cooperating with military officers in West Africa meant accepting a bit of debauchery. Ludlam, however, failed to persuade his successor.

Thompson soon discovered the imprisoned runaways from the Corps of Labourers. When he visited the one-room prison, he was shocked. He reported in his diary that the most affecting sight was the lone woman chained to the log, "a load for an ass." Thompson brought the prisoners into the courtyard of Fort Thornton. A crowd appeared to watch; maybe they hoped for another auction. Thompson felt they were "ready to pull [him] in pieces." He recruited interpreters from nearby villages, and asked the prisoners why they had fled. They replied that it was because they feared they would be sent across the sea. Thompson asked whether they would work in the colony if they were released. He asked them if they would follow him to war as free men. According to Thompson, when the interpreters repeated his words, they were "roaring out their assent at the end of every sentence." One of the Maroons objected that he had paid $20 for his apprentice. Thompson piously told him, "if the old governor sold slaves, the new one did not."[75] He redistributed the former slaves as apprentices, and wrote in the *Sierra Leone Gazette*, "The Governor congratulates the inhabitants of H.M. colony on the great eagerness shown to obtain free labourers, as proof of their increasing industry and prosperity."[76]

Thompson had very positive first impressions of the Maroons. Two Maroon war-leaders, Captain Shaw and General Montague, recognized that Thompson was easily flattered. In turn, the Governor paid them a compliment by wearing his sword slung on a belt across his shoulders, "Maroon fashion," rather than at his waist. He took care to solicit their opinion on how to defend the colony.[77] Thompson believed that Dawes had deliberately set him up to snub the Maroons by inventing a pretext to take him away from meeting the Maroon leaders. "We went to the back of the fort," Thompson wrote, "among heaps bricks & rubbish. . . . The secret was out, & the reservedness of the Maroons was easily to be accounted for."[78] More evidence accumulated in Thompson's mind of the duplicity of the Sierra Leone Company.

Thompson also had a high opinion of the dignity of the Crown, and refused to honour the agreements made between the Company and its local African partners. On 2 August 1808, the Company's landlord, King Firama, came to the colony to collect duties which the Sierra Leone Company paid him for the use of the harbour. Thompson refused to pay, arguing that now that the colony belonged to the Crown, George III had no responsibility to pay the debts of a private corporation. He sent Firama away. In his diary, Thompson wrote that Firama was "a stupid drunken beast, dressed up in mockery in an embroidered coat by some slave trader." Thompson fumed that after meeting with Firama, he went to the Company store, where he met "the ill-omened visage . . . who burns his *redeemed* with hot irons made its appearance." Thompson went berserk, and "broke forth furiously against this despicable system of government."[79] To Thompson, Freetown was nearly a hallucination, a carnival parody of the abolition of slavery. The young man who was supposed to be an "established character" became the scourge of the Sierra Leone Company.

The Abortion: Thompson against Freetown

The world of the Freetown settlers was dense with subtle distinctions of class, origin, and status. For example, the language of the settlers, which began as an English patois and, in time, evolved into Krio, one of the official languages of present-day Sierra Leone, was a minefield for outsiders. One visitor to the colony was upbraided by a Nova Scotian woman for asking,

"What *matter* for you no done bring him?" instead of "What *fashion* for you
no done bring him?"—"matter" was a Maroon word, and "fashion" a Nova
Scotian one, and each signified subtle distinctions in colonial societies and
culture.[80] The signs and symbols of everyday life in Freetown were not the
same as in Britain and required immersion to understand; Thompson misread
them all. The young Governor sent many angry letters and dispatches to
England. His letters raised an alarm, but not in the way he had anticipated.
The "friends of Africa," fearing embarrassment, arranged for Thompson's
recall. In Freetown, his bile and suspicion pushed him to the social margins
of the colony, where he began to develop a theory connecting the Sierra
Leone Company to slavery, sexual exploitation, and rebellion.

In July 1808, Ludlam told Thompson some local gossip about Anne
Edmonds, the daughter of David Edmonds, a wealthy Nova Scotian merchant and shipwright, and an ally of the Company. He whispered that Anne
had been tried and acquitted for the murder of a bastard child and that "another unmarried daughter of the same family had been proved with child,
but the child had been suppressed . . . and this same daughter was known at
that very time to be a second time with Child." The rumour in the colony,
Ludlam continued, was that Mrs. David Edmonds was well aware "that a European was . . . having indecent connexion with her daughter in the next
room" and procuring abortion or infanticide as needed.[81] Ludlam, according
to Thompson, explained that on the day of the birth "a number of children
were collected by the relations & made to dance for the purpose of drowning
any cries . . . the woman was insensible for some time after the delivery & on
asking for the child was answered *That it was taken care of & if she was not
quiet she would be taken care of too.*"[82] Ludlam may have been starved for company or for opportunities to gossip, or perhaps he assumed that as white men
he and Thompson could speak frankly. Maybe Ludlam was hinting that
Thompson should feel free to seek out "indecent connexions" of his own (although Ludlam, on his deathbed, denied having a mistress in the colony).[83]
Intent notwithstanding, Ludlam's gossip gave Thompson material to build a
conspiracy theory, connecting the alleged infanticide to slave trading, and
slave trading to the Sierra Leone Company.

Perhaps because of his military background and Tory principles,
Thompson despised the United States. He projected this hostility onto the
settlers in the colony. Ludlam's sleazy hints that they pimped out their daughters to the Sierra Leone Company in exchange for preferment confirmed his

bias. Thompson's disgust began to transform into political critique. "The greater part of the inhabitants of this colony," Thompson wrote, "are in the greatest degree disaffected to His Majesty's Government . . . being composed of the runaway slaves of American masters; & full of every species of ignorant enthusiasm and republican frenzy."[84] In another letter, Thompson expressed his shock at the European pretensions of the settler who must have "English broad cloth" for himself and finer fabrics for his wife. Thompson also complained that "one of the most respectable of our colonists . . . came to beg of me a coffin for his mother."[85] How, he wondered, could the colonists maintain apprentices if they could not even afford to bury their parents?

Thompson concluded that since the Maroons were not "American" they must be both political allies and moral exemplars. "The first object," Thompson wrote, "of a young Maroon is to save money for a house, and to marry. The Nova-Scotian discourages his children from marrying, that the sons may not be encumbered with families and that the daughters may have the chance of being supported by some European."[86] The Maroons, Thompson argued, had been neglected by Ludlam and the other previous Governors. Ludlam preferred to gallivant around the town "in his slop jacket & trowsers to talk politics with the lying-in negresses of the Nova-Scotians." The Maroons, in contrast, were loyal to the King, untainted by "American" mores.[87] Shaw, the captain of the Maroons, impressed Thompson when he told him, "I heard a few of the ten commandments, & by them I have tried to rule my life. . . . The Maroons," Thompson swooned, "seem to have maintained a sort of ferocious morality of their own."[88] Thompson wrote to his sweetheart that the Nova Scotians "are *le diable*, & God has certainly given them up to follow their own hearts' inventions."[89] He felt that the Maroons would form a fine light infantry, provided they were not "contaminated" by marrying "cast-off mistresses and other Nova-Scotian women."[90] Illicit sexuality, republicanism, rebellion, and hypocrisy were a potent brew.

The linguistic sleight between "slave" and "apprentice" obsessed Thompson. He wrote to Ludlam, "You will say that people were *apprenticed*, or *disposed of*, according to the provisions of the order in Council. If so, where are the Indentures? You know well that the people of this Country," he inveighed, "never spoke of the natives brought by the Derwent but as their 'slaves,' 'my *slave boy*,' 'my *slave girl*,' 'the people I bought from the Governor.'"[91] Thompson rejected the equivocations of Company government. In contrast, he boasted that *he* governed "with the plainness of soldiers."

"Surely," he continued, "this contemptible system needs only to be exposed to cease to exist."[92] Thompson believed that by collecting instances of misconduct by the Nova Scotians and the Sierra Leone Company, and faithfully transmitting them to Lord Castlereagh, he would invite the wrath of the Secretary of State for War and the Colonies, and the public at large, and reform Sierra Leone. And yet, in late 1808, Thompson still maintained a distance between the colony and its backers in London: "It is but justice to say that I have never found anything which did not do credit to my friend Macaulay," he wrote, "though we must still quarrel in England on the subject of redemptions & apprenticeships."[93]

On 1 November 1808, Thompson passed a busy day in Council. He wrote up a new treaty with the empire of Futa Djallon (it is not at all clear that the Alimami was aware of the change) and voided the colony's treaty with King Firama. He abolished the volunteer militia, and ordered the whole male population of the colony over 12 under arms.[94] A group of leading Nova Scotian settlers met and declared that they would not comply with this "Militia Act." Thompson promptly ordered the Maroons and the remainder of the Nova Scotian settlers to assemble. He arrested the protestors and threatened to hold them hostage.[95] Enraged, Thompson changed the name of Freetown to Georgetown; "Freetown," he wrote, "has been found to have been perverted to the purposes of insubordination and rebellion." He also changed the currency of the colony, creating a "Sierra Leone Pound" to replace American and Spanish dollars, exchangeable at the rate of one dollar for four shillings and sixpence (fig. 7).[96]

In December 1808, Thompson used the colonial newspaper, the *Sierra Leone Gazette* (which he would soon rename *The African Herald*), to tell his version of the first months of his governorship, praising the Maroons and condemning the Nova Scotians. The Maroons were few but virtuous, he wrote, while the Nova Scotian majority were contaminated "with every maxim of inflammatory politics which half-comprehended notions of American independence . . . joined to a high degree of the ferocity of the savage." Overall, he reflected, his time in Government House had given him "lamentable proof of the effects of a weak government" on people not raised in what he took to be British martial virtue and self-discipline. But that was the old Sierra Leone, Thompson concluded. He would make something new. He imagined a near future when, under his command, Sierra Leone would be raised by martial values and vigorous commerce to the forefront of the Brit-

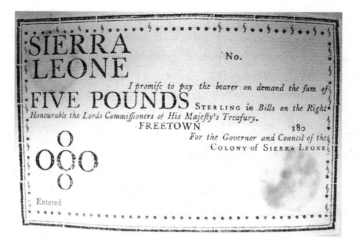

Figure 7. A £5 note issued by Thomas Perronet Thompson for circulation in Sierra Leone. This note was one of several short-lived, disruptive reforms launched by Thompson to rid Freetown of "American" influence. (Records of the Colonial Office, The National Archives, Kew 267/25)

ish empire. Thompson insisted that it would not be the Company, or the Nova Scotians, or even the Maroons who raised Sierra Leone to imperial prominence. Rather, "The Natives of Africa introduced into this colony by the operations of the Act for the Abolition of the Slave-trade" would be the "foundation for the most rational expectation of its future prosperity." He would, he promised, "make a heart to this people oppressed and peeled, and . . . let that heart be English."[97] This promise was made as part of a grandiose and paranoid diatribe against the Company, but it was crucial. Thompson, in his frenzy, had stumbled on what would, within a decade, become the centre-piece of colonial policy, a civilizing mission aimed at people released from the slave trade.

But in 1808, Thompson's reforms were paper tigers, and made him an outcast. The new Sierra Leone "pound" made commerce more difficult, and nobody except Thompson seems to have accepted that he or she lived in "Georgetown" rather than Freetown. The leading settlers closed ranks with the old guard of the Company. On Thursday, 16 February 1809, the friends and family of John Leedam Morgan, a Maroon clerk in government service, and Anne Edmonds (the woman exonerated from charges of killing her child) were married.[98] Thomas Ludlam sat at the head of the table at the wedding feast. Thompson was not invited. On the walls of Fort Thornton, within sight of the town, Thompson had his servants build a gallows. He scribbled out an inscription and tacked it to the scaffolding: "To the memory of a Mulatto male child found murdered in the colony, August 10, 1807, to remain until the execution of the guilty."[99] The next Sunday, Thompson burst into the colonial chapel and demanded that the chaplain, Reinhold Nyländer, read a letter about the gallows. Ludlam and the Edmonds family walked out. "The murder of a European's bastard," Thompson wrote, "is not one of those worldly concerns which may be attended to upon the Sabbath."[100] He resolved to try Anne Morgan again, claiming that his status as Governor entitled him to convene a special sitting of the new colonial Vice-Admiralty Court, and to sit as judge—a right that he seems to have invented on the spot.

In March 1809, Morgan was tried not for the murder of her child, since she could not be tried again for a crime for which she had been acquitted, but rather for concealing the birth. The transcripts of the trial were printed in the *African Herald* and sent back to London in official correspondence. At the trial, midwives called upon to testify agreed that she had borne a child. A young girl, Linda Bennett, recounted the moment when she found a child's corpse under a lime tree. "The side of the jaw was stabbed," the girl testified. "If it had lived it would have been a fair mulatto."[101] Morgan was convicted and sentenced to death. She was locked in a shed used to store barrels of gunpowder. She was marched to the gallows and mocked by the executioner as he put the rope around her neck. At the last second, she was pardoned. Thompson's nerve had failed him. Two days later, he received a letter from London. He had been sacked. He burst into tears.[102]

Redefining Antislavery by Accident

By July 1809, Thompson knew that he would return to England as soon as his replacement arrived.[103] Confident that posterity would exonerate him, Thompson made plans to overhaul the colony. His paranoia and half-cocked ideas about political economy became new—and ultimately enduring—imperial policies. Although neither Thompson nor Zachary Macaulay would have seen the justice of the comparison, the two men had something in common as they approached the implementation of antislavery legislation. Each took stock of the resources available in Sierra Leone and weighed them against his own understanding of the principles of British antislavery. To Macaulay, that was a rigid, hierarchical social order and a commitment to legitimate trade, even with slave dealers. To Thompson, it meant a military empire in West Africa driven on by pioneer-soldiers recruited from slave ships. Thompson argued for a new way to manage the abolition of the slave trade. "This colony," he wrote, "has certainly exhibited a fearful warning of the effects of emancipation upon slaves when managed by religionists and weak disaffected fanatics."[104] He agreed that emancipation required careful management, but rejected the Company's views on how to treat former slaves. "If the black people," he wrote, "were not as steadfast as saints, the European devils would lead them into all manner of evil-doing."[105] Thompson would not accept, "stripped of sophistry and verbal distinctions," that the emancipation of people from the Middle Passage assumed that "that the persons proposed to be *civilized* should for a greater or a smaller period be the slaves of the *civilizers*."[106]

On 4 September 1809, he opened the colonial Court of Vice-Admiralty for another special session, a sequel to the trial of Anne Morgan. This time, Thompson used the Court as a bully pulpit. He had discovered, among the papers of the Sierra Leone Company, two letters from Zachary Macaulay, one about the practice of apprenticeship, and the other about his influence in the Colonial Office.[107] "I have fallen on such a *bonne bouche*," he told Nancy, "I have the original of this & a thousand other curiosities. I believe *ferax monstrorum Africa*, which being interpreted is Africa abounding with monsters, never produced such a monster in his way as Zachary Macaulay."[108] Both letters were from Macaulay to Ludlam, and, for Thompson, they connected the fallen state of the colony to the hypocrisy of the elite abolitionists in London. On 1 May 1807 Macaulay wrote, "While the slave trade lasted I certainly felt very opposed to the giving [of] any direct encouragement to the purchase of slaves with a view to the benefit of their labour for a certain given period." In short, Macaulay was reluctant to endorse the "redemption" of enslaved people in West Africa. "But," he continued, "I always looked forward to the event of the abolition as removing many objections to that system."[109]

Macaulay was arguing for the continuation and expansion of a system of purchase and indenture that was already common in Freetown. Thompson was right: Macaulay was proposing that the Company or its successor purchase enslaved people, manumit them, and then apprentice them to colonists. Thompson still could not wrap his mind around the distinction between slavery and apprenticeship. He soon found a second letter, which pushed him into even greater fury. On 4 November 1807 Macaulay wrote to Ludlam, "A word in private respecting the African Institution—I cannot help regarding it as an important engine." He explained that many powerful people supported antislavery, but urged Ludlam to be discreet. Not every powerful Briton supported antislavery, Macaulay warned Ludlam, and so he ought to censor the seedier aspects of colonial life in correspondence, to blunt "the *effect* of what you say on lukewarm friends." In the end, as we saw in Chapter One, Macaulay was confident that "Government will be disposed to adopt almost any plan which we may propose to them with respect to Africa provided we will but save them the trouble of thinking."[110]

This second letter confirmed to Thompson that the Sierra Leone Company was deliberately lying. He began to see the entire colony as an elaborate conspiracy concocted in London, instead of being a cancer in situ on the African coast. The Company officials in London were no longer well-meaning but uninformed patsies of their colonial employees. Now they were a "canting, lying sect . . . extending their arms to East & the West & to the uttermost parts of the earth, grasping at all power."[111] He imagined the former Company directors on the board of the African Institution had tentacles in every sphere of British life. "They step into their carriages," he wrote, "and straightaway they are the Sierra Leone Company; and again, and they are the Society for Missions to Africa and the East; another transformation makes them the Society for the Suppression of Vice; a fifth carries them to the India House; and sixth lands them at the House of Commons."[112]

In a sense, Thompson was exactly right. Among the former directors of the Sierra Leone Company were men who *did* dominate the board of the African Institution, *did* serve on the board of the Society for Missions, *did* lead the Society for the Suppression of Vice, and *were* welcome at India House and in the House of Commons. Thompson was being removed by inches from his sanity, but he had grasped three ideas that were essentially true. The end of the slave trade in Sierra Leone *was* built on compromise with slave traders, and assumed that people released from slavery would be subject to coerced labour of one kind or another, in "preparation" for freedom. Moreover, the end of the slave trade *had* increased the influence and ambition of the Clapham Sect. Finally, the end of the slave trade had opened up a path for the Clapham Sect to more and more diverse schemes for moral reform, both in Britain and abroad.

Thompson developed his own eccentric vision of African political economy after the slave trade. He was gratified by the changes in the price of labour he managed to effect in the colony; before his arrival, he reported, manual labour cost three times what it would have been worth in England. However, by the lucky "competition of the labour of the inhabitants, the prices of labour and of the necessaries of life have been reduced more than one half in the colony."[113] He believed, based on his own (abstruse, indecipherable) calculations, that "The expense of work done by slaves, is to the expense of the same quantity of work done by Kroomen, as 33/2 to 25/3, as 2 to 1 nearly."[114] And indeed some of the slaves freed under Thompson were not indentured; like the Kru, they were wage labourers, a condition Thompson associated indelibly with freedom. They were, he wrote, "more loyal, orderly and respectable; receive the lowest wages in the colony, nine pence a day & rice. No other expence."[115] Africans, he insisted to Lord Castlereagh, in a distant echo of Adam Smith, were cultivators by nature. England was a place for making finished goods and for trade; if Sierra Leone did not produce agricultural products it would be "utterly ruinous."[116] He explained, in defiance of the global continuum of free and unfree labour, that "there is no medium between absolute slavery & absolute freedom of labour which does not destroy the advantages which are derived from either."[117]

Now that he knew that Company representatives in Freetown and their superiors in London spoke with one voice, Thompson looked frantically for allies. Ironically, Thompson fell in with local slave traders who told him they had given up the trade, and with military officers eager to expand their influence in the colony. Compounding the irony, these were often also the same people with whom Zachary Macaulay had worked out his most delicate compromises in the 1790s. The officers and traders took advantage of Thompson's mania and isolation to try to claw back lost privileges. One of Thompson's friends, Daniel Botefeur, had worked as supercargo of the Spanish slaver *Casualidad* in 1804 and by 1810 had returned to slave trading aboard his ship, the *Fourth of July*.[118] Thompson also became friendly with a trader named Davies, and assisted him and other agents at Bance Island, in putting down a revolt of the island's domestic slaves in 1810.[119] Davies warned Thompson, "Whatever you may conclude upon doing [to stop the revolt], should be done speedily & *secretly*, if the *Citizens* get wind of your intention of paying this place a visit they will all be off immediately."[120] Davies knew that calling the settlers "Citizens," echoing the American and

French Revolutions, would resonate with Thompson. Thompson rewarded Davies with a plantation of more than 200 acres between Fourah Bay and Susan's Bay.[121]

When Edward Columbine arrived, Thompson moved from Government House to Davies' house, where he told Columbine that he felt himself "exactly in the predicament of a man seizing a felon, & being immediately seized in turn himself, & charged with felony."[122] Davies later purchased a condemned slave ship, the *Cuba*, and renamed it the *Governor Thompson*.[123] Columbine had a shrewd view of Thompson's relationship with the traders, who had "found an easy and certain road" to Thompson's friendship "by calumniating the officers of the Company."[124] African rulers also took advantage of Thompson's paranoia. Sierra Leone's trade partnership with Futa Djallon had ebbed when the Company abandoned Freeport factory in the Rio Pongas. Perhaps tipped off by European and Euro-African slave traders, and hoping to reopen trade, the Alimami wrote to flatter Thompson. Of Macaulay, the Alimami wrote, "If a man looks at [his] writing he will not see the truth, so much as a single word."[125]

Thompson was just as easily seduced by military officers. In London, Wilberforce had told him that the colony could resist "six frigates." Thompson suspected the colony was much worse off than that. On his voyage to Sierra Leone, the dour William Dawes had hinted to him that the Martello Tower built in the colony was never manned by the soldiers of the Royal African Corps, because the tower overlooked the fort and the Governor's residence. Thompson was stunned: what kind of colonial garrison was not trustworthy enough to be within a gunshot's range of the Governor?[126] This gave Thompson an idea. Instead of the white convict soldiers of the Royal African Corps and the "republican" Nova Scotian settlers, former slaves might become "the Colonist & soldier . . . combined." Sierra Leone, he reasoned, with its "naturally fortified position" and an "infantry trained to the country" would be "invincible."[127] Under Ludlam, people released from the slave trade were apprenticed to meet the immediate needs of the colony. Thompson imagined them as soldiers, colonists, and pioneers. And yet, Thompson, like Ludlam and like the Clapham Sect, never conceived of a post-emancipation society where former slaves were not put to British use in one way or another.

It isn't clear exactly how many people freed from slavery arrived in the colony while Thompson served as Governor. The records were indifferently kept.[128] However, as former slaves arrived in the colony, Thompson sent many into the bush to build new villages, including a village at the "Hogbrook" (warthogs wallowed in the stream), which he renamed Kingston-in-Africa after his hometown, Kingston-upon-Hull.[129] According to Thompson, they "cut their way into the woods . . . we advance into the country like a conflagration."[130] After Thompson's proclamations, Kingston-in-Africa virtually disappears from the archive (although there are roads in present-day Hull called Freetown Road and in present-day Freetown called Kingston-upon-Hull Way). Five years later, Hogbrook was renamed Regent and (as Chapter Five shows) became the object of intense missionary and colonial scrutiny. In the interim, settlers sometimes complained that villagers from the mountains raided their farms, stealing crops and livestock.[131] Otherwise, they were virtually invisible until colonial officials found it necessary to find, count, concentrate, and "civilize" them again.

Thompson had a distinct preference for the apparently more warlike of the former slaves. In his mind, the "Joloffs" and "Bambarrans" had the "dress & figure of an ancient Roman."[132] Among European soldiers, Thompson had a cozy relationship with the Royal African Corps. Major Maxwell, the Commandant of Gorée and eventual Governor of Sierra Leone (an important figure in the second half of this book) helped Thompson to import racehorses to Sierra Leone. Thompson seized on the friendly gesture to inquire about the possibility of uniting Sierra Leone and Gorée, another prescient idea arrived at through paranoia, as later Governors would attempt to unify British possessions in West Africa under Sierra Leone.[133] He also made Frederick Forbes, the ranking Royal African Corps officer in Sierra Leone, First-in-Council, giving Forbes the responsibility of governing the colony in case of Thompson's death or absence. Forbes was a dissolute descendent of a noble family, who styled himself the "Honourable Frederick Forbes."[134] The African Institution panicked. James Stephen worried that Thompson would die, leaving Sierra Leone in the hands of a man "of very bad character, in desperate circumstances" instead of "those old & tried servants of the Company whom he has such an outrageous and insane dislike to."[135]

Thompson contrasted Muslim with animist Africans. He imagined that a few guns, positioned near Government House, could intimidate local non-Muslim chiefs, "a few beggarly Caffres" to Thompson at negligible cost. "I say *Caffres*," he continued, "because the Mahometan Chiefs were men perfectly capable of comprehending the effects of the position of guns."[136] He warned the Secretary of State about "the subtle cool Mahometan . . . duly transmitting into the interior his contempt."[137] Thompson insisted that the Company had ignored the "polished, sensible, & acute" Muslim Africans in favour of "savage" animists.[138] During his hearings at the Vice-Admiralty Court, Thompson called Dalu Mohammed, a "Mandingo" chief from the Bullom Shore, to the stand. Dalu Mohammed said just what Thompson wanted to hear: "From what I have seen of English Law . . . English law is nothing but power, when you have power there is law for you."[139]

Thompson saw a different kind of power in West Africa. He proposed that Sierra Leone be the base for wars of conquest based on antislavery. Expeditionary forces would crush restive tribes, and then offer the defeated parties membership in a political union, organized from Freetown, "our Presidency at Sierra Leone."[140] He made the hopeful prediction that, if the Bank of England printed official African pounds to supplement the "pounds" he had had printed, they would become the common currency of West Africa.[141] Thompson failed in all of these ambitions. But Thompson's failures were a conceptual revolution. In his crazed letters home, the leading lights of the African Institution saw their plans reflected back at them through a lens of ever more grandiose ambition. If they set aside Thompson's animus and paranoia, they could see new possibilities for African empire.

The Antislavery Omertà

In 1808, as a ship entered the harbour, William Dawes told Thompson it was rumoured to be the *Derwent*. "I shall be very glad indeed if it is," he said. Thompson wrote in his journal, "Does the insulting old man mean to say . . . that he means to write home against me?" He wrote that he had snapped at Dawes that a ship belonging to his ally Davies would sail well before Parker could even drop anchor.[142] Thompson assumed that if he sent enough letters, he could alert the public to the misdeeds of the Company. He was wrong. Thompson was recruited because he was well connected, but his connections were conditional. When Thompson rebelled, the Clapham Sect closed ranks in London, and even skeptical administrators kept silent to avoid embarrassment.

The leaders of the African Institution did not exaggerate their superior access to the levers of government in African affairs. All of Thompson's "confidential" dispatches to Lord Castlereagh had been copied for William

Wilberforce by Castlereagh's secretary. Wilberforce quickly organized a meeting with the "friends of Africa."[143] At the meeting, the "friends" resolved to remove Thompson, and James Stephen quickly worked out the legal details.[144] Wilberforce, who agreed with Thornton and Macaulay in removing Thompson, was ashamed that his former protégé had been such a disastrous Governor. "I durst not," he wrote privately to Thompson, "take on myself the responsibility of endeavouring to counteract the judgement & wish of so many men of superior understanding, experience, [and] integrity."[145] Henry Thornton had answers for all of Thompson's critiques. The sale of apprentices was written off as a "material error." Ludlam deserved "the most indulgent consideration."[146] After all, the banker argued, Thompson had done worse when he voided the indentures made to the colonists, but did not refund their $20 fees.[147]

Thompson tried to marshal a defense. He asked his brother in a letter for a copy of the *Christian Observer*, the magazine edited by Zachary Macaulay, to keep an eye on what was happening in England.[148] He was suspicious that members of the Clapham Sect were intercepting his letters: "Nancy, there is foul play somewhere," he wrote to his fiancée.[149] He wrote a rambling letter, more than 20 pages long, to a ship captain whose boat he had had searched, in the hopes that the trader would communicate the plight of the colony in Britain.[150] When Columbine arrived to assume the government, Thompson claimed to be too sick to attend the hand-over ceremony, and refused to accept Columbine's right to govern, calling him "the Officer appointed by His Majesty . . . *ad interim*."[151] He tried to steal documents from the Council Room, and threw a bag of Columbine's letters into the sea from the deck of the ship that took him home to England.[152]

Columbine set about undoing the disaster. His primary goal was to cut costs; Thompson's grandiosity had cost the British government far more than it imagined its new Crown Colony to be worth. Columbine also pardoned Anne Morgan unconditionally.[153] He concluded that the father of the child had been the Company surgeon, Mr. Robson. Columbine heard, but could not prove, the rumours that Robson had procured an abortion.[154] He dissolved the colonial militia, and set to work figuring out how to take Thompson's new "Sierra Leone Pound" out of circulation.[155] When Columbine looked through the Council books, he found the proceedings of the hearing Thompson held on the Company, which Columbine considered to be "the most scurrilous public document that ever I read."[156] He was also definitive about Thompson's gallows. "Anne Edmonds," he wrote, "was married, & as is customary, a great supper was given; to which Mr. Ludlam, Dawes & Smith were invited; but Thompson was omitted. This mark of respect to others . . . he seems never to have forgiven."[157]

When he returned to England, Thompson continued to demand an investigation. He imagined that Lord Liverpool "would not think [him] unreasonable in requesting that either a full and public investigation might take place" and demanded a government job, as a platform from which "to silence those whom in the discharge of my duty I have made the enemy of my character."[158] However, the Clapham Sect erased him. In the third annual report of the African Institution, usually full of specific praise for colonial officials, Thompson was referred to only as "the Governor of Sierra Leone."[159] And Wilberforce warned him, "The manner of your coming home will be such I trust, as will prevent public discredit."[160] Thompson, isolated and unemployed, took the hint. Wilberforce relaxed. "Mr. Thompson," he wrote, "begins to cool."[161] Thompson found a post in the Persian Gulf, where he learned Arabic and spent most of the 1810s and 1820s.[162] When he returned to England, he eventually became a leading polemicist for the Anti-Corn-Law League. In the 1840s an admirer wrote, "The governor, too liberal for Sierra Leone, was sent home—ALIVE . . . His experience in Sierra Leone had shaken his faith in Toryism, and his views rapidly assumed a more liberal cast," but Thompson, even in his very public late career, rarely mentioned Sierra Leone.[163]

Still, the cat had been let out of the bag. Thompson had not maintained the discretion demanded of him by Wilberforce and Macaulay. Thompson had histrionically publicized the difficult compromises and ambiguities of antislavery in practice. He had unwittingly put grist into the West Indian pro-slavery mill. After 1807, the patriotic good feelings associated with the end of the slave trade meant that it was very rare for British supporters of the slave colonies of the West Indies to offer any public defence of slavery as such. Instead, pro-slavery advocates generally took one of two positions, arguing not for slavery, but against abolition. Some argued that slavery needed to continue until enslaved people were "ready" for freedom, an argument that appropriated claims for gradual emancipation made by the abolitionists themselves. The second common position was that the advocates of antislavery were hypocrites who hoped to destroy the West Indian planter class in order take their place. In the decade after his dismissal, Thompson's letters became key evidence for pamphleteers making this second argument. Robert

Thorpe, a colonial jurist (see Chapters Three and Four) who wrote a series of pamphlets attacking Zachary Macaulay and defending the West Indian planters, wrote that Thompson was "a true, zealous, and practical abolitionist" who had been unfairly recalled by a hypocritical Clapham Sect. "Truth and honour were his disqualifications," Thorpe declared.[164] In another pamphlet, Thorpe wrote of the Sierra Leone Company's sale of indentures, "Governor Thompson made it sufficiently notorious."[165] Thorpe quoted Thompson's papers at length in his pamphlets, using them to discredit the African Institution and, by extension, antislavery. Zachary Macaulay replied with a pamphlet of his own, which included full versions of several letters, including the two letters which led Thompson to place Macaulay at the centre of the Company's conspiracy.[166] But Thompson himself said nothing.

In March 1809, Thomas Perronet Thompson slept in Government House, in Fort Thornton. It was hot and humid, and the young Governor dreamed of England. He later recalled his dreams in a letter to Nancy, his fiancée. "I came to your house in Fishergate," he wrote, "wrapped in a great coat as hath generally, I think, been my look." After waiting for some time, he continued, "you came & looked 'well-liking' like one of Pharaoh's kine . . . with that sort of respectable & goodly look which characterizes people who begin to grow 'elderly.'" In the dream, Nancy, her eyes vacant, said, "'O Thompson, how bad you look." Suddenly, Nancy's father came out of the house, and mocked the young governor, asking "whether the river of Sierra Leone was much improved or not." Upon reflection, Thompson remarked, "If some dreams are foolish & others super-naturally wise, this I appreciated is what might be called an orderly common-sense sort of dream."[167]

The vast archive of the British empire is not particularly rich in fever dreams, but Thompson's fractured vision is more than a curiosity. His description and interpretation of the dream shows his pride, his misogyny, his sense of irony, and an occult comment on his place in the history of British antislavery. Thompson said a lot of things we might agree with: that the Sierra Leone Company made astonishing compromises with slave traders in order to try to turn a profit; that Zachary Macaulay was a stern, sinister figure; that the Clapham Sect had global ambitions and considerable influence; that life in Freetown was veined with violence and sexual exploitation; that distinctions between "apprenticeship" and "slavery," particularly immediately after the abolition of the slave trade, were largely semantic. Thompson was expected to take up the same nuanced view of the actual practice of abolition as that of Macaulay and the Company, and accept that the abolition of slavery would be incremental, and that redemption and apprenticeship would be the basic instruments of the civilizing mission. The public didn't need to understand the subtleties. Thompson was supposed to be initiated into this privileged understanding of West African affairs, and into the Clapham elite, but he refused. His wild criticisms of the Sierra Leone Company offer a vivid window into the first days of abolition, in a place where the end of the slave trade meant a profound reversal of centuries of economic, political, and culture routine.

And yet, Thompson's belief in the potential of people rescued from slave ships to be colonists, pioneers, and soldiers was prescient, and his cockamamie schemes cast improbably long shadows over the history of the post-emancipation societies of the British empire. Thompson *agreed* with Macaulay that former slaves would need "civilization" after emancipation; but he was committed to a more martial, expansionist version of that mission. Under the Company Governors, people "redeemed" from slavery were expected to serve the people who had paid for their manumission. Thompson proposed that since people freed from slave ships had been rescued by Britain, they ought to serve Britain. Antislavery would be not a commercial concern but an imperial project. Still, for all of Thompson's praise of the former slaves as soldiers and pioneers, he did little beyond the founding of a few villages, which he promptly ignored. Future Governors far more simpatico with the African Institution took up some of Thompson's plans: the use of former slaves as soldiers, the creation of mountain settlements, the expansion of the colony by force. Thompson licensed future colonial Governors to act as though a slave freed from the Middle Passage was effectively nothing, a blank slate—and could therefore be anything.

3. The Vice-Admiralty Court

The air in the barracks was thick. Heavy rain made the wooden structure swell, and cockroaches crawled out from between the boards to avoid being crushed. A boy walked into the yard outside. He was around fourteen years old and about five feet tall. He had noticeable scars on his right elbow, his back, his chest, and his left calf. Months earlier he had been sold at Calabar, in the Bight of Biafra, with 244 other people and imprisoned aboard the Spanish-owned brigantine *Intrepida*. Before it could begin the Middle Passage, *Intrepida* was captured by H.M.S. *Comus* and brought to Freetown. When the captured ship arrived in port, the colonial Superintendent of Captured Negroes was instructed to "receive, protect and provide for" the boy until he could be "disposed of according to the true meaning" of the 1807 Act of Parliament that had abolished the British slave trade.[1] If the boy's "African name" was not "sufficiently easy, clear and distinctive," the Superintendent was entitled to give the former slave any name he chose. He could not resist a sour little joke. The boy was renamed "Tattoe": many of his shipmates wore ink, but he wore scars.[2]

In the Court of Vice-Admiralty of Sierra Leone on 8 August 1815, the *Intrepida* was condemned as a prize. Kenneth Macaulay (Zachary Macaulay's cousin and employee), who from 1810 until 1814 had served as the first Superintendent of Captured Negroes, was present in the court as both Proctor and as the prize agent for the captain and crew of the *Comus*.[3] Macaulay recently had sat on the bench as acting Judge, but, on that day, Thomas Wilford presided.[4] Wilford had no formal legal training. He was a merchant, appointed, in the words of Governor Charles MacCarthy, because "the colony has been placed under the greatest embarrassment for want of a person qualified."[5] The Marshal of the Court, George Macaulay (another relation) copied and notarized the lists of people, alongside lists of cargo and rough appraisals of the value of the ship itself.[6] Wilford was too anxious about his lack of legal training to serve in criminal cases.[7] However, he had enough confidence in his legal skills to claim that the jurisdiction of the Slave Trade Act extended beyond Britain and its empire to any port with a British merchant community. The Act as written applied to Britons, and to merchants using British ports, and made it illegal to buy and sell slaves or any of the equipment associated with slave trading—the shackles, iron collars, specialized netting, and reinforced doors required to imprison hundreds of people at sea. Wilford ruled that since the *Intrepida* had bought its gear in a territory belonging to a British ally, and from a British subject, it was a legal prize. The Court awarded the auction value of the *Intrepida* "with her Cargo, Boats, Guns, Tackle, Apparel and Furniture" as prize to the *Comus*, and the 245 slaves "with the apparatus for feeding and coercing . . . as forfeiture to his Majesty."[8] Although Tattoe didn't know it, this pageant of money, bureaucracy, and nepotism had been organized on his behalf. He was no longer a slave; he was a "captured Negro."

The Court of Vice-Admiralty was perhaps the most important institution in Freetown from 1808 until the end of the Napoleonic wars. It was also the first court in the British empire with a mandate not only to manumit individual enslaved people, but to emancipate shiploads of captives. And yet, the Court wasn't particularly interested in what happened to the people it released. Instead, it inventoried, condemned, auctioned, and redistributed the cash value of any property, which in the Court's view included people, captured at sea. Because they could not legally be resold, "captured Negroes" were less valuable than trade goods. One visitor to Freetown noticed that captured ships with just a few captives aboard caused the most excitement. The presence of a few slaves made the ship eligible for capture, but "her cargo not being completed rendered her still more valuable, as she had a considerable quantity of cloth and spirits on board."[9] The officials of the Court didn't systematically keep track of "captured Negroes" until after 1815, publishing "incomplete and contradictory" statistics.[10] In wartime, former slaves were most carefully scrutinized at moments when they impinged upon a commercial transaction. The people who had been imprisoned aboard the *Intrepida* were present only as a list of names.[11]

The transatlantic slave trade was a finely tuned machine for turning people into commodities, into "bodies animated by others' calculated investment in their physical capacities."[12] Just as antislavery trade in Sierra Leone relied on local institutions of slave labour, and on the physical plant of the transatlantic slave trade, the Court applied to people the same legal processes that it applied to the capture of contraband cargo. The Court "condemned" former slaves, making them the property of the Crown. The Crown then refused to exercise its putative right to "own" slaves. This made former slaves "property" without an owner, and so "free" in a sense. However, this kind of freedom is best understood as a freedom from direct legal ownership, and not a positive right. "Captured Negroes" could be apprenticed, enlisted in the military, or compelled to work for the colonial government.

Some legal scholars rush to declare the slave-trade Courts of Sierra Leone the "first courts of human rights."[13] However, as Lauren Benton and Lisa Ford point out, much of the jurisprudence of British anti-slave-trade courts at the imperial level rested on making a legal analogy between slave trading and piracy.[14] Moreover, as Benton puts it, insofar as the courts defined rights in any capacity, they defined "the property rights and legal prerogative of slave traders and slave owners within the imperial order."[15] On the ground in Freetown's "captured Negro yard" or bustling auction-houses, any putative connections that might be drawn between the origins of "human rights law" and the doings of the Vice-Admiralty Court are even more specious, tenuous, and unlikely. Tattoe and his shipmates were released from slavery like bolts of cloth or casks of salt pork "liberated" from the hold of a French merchant vessel. The concept that a slave freed or self-emancipated in war had a legal status analogous to contraband goods was common in the slave-holding societies of the Atlantic world until at least the American Civil War. Escaped enslaved people were "contraband"; "property" that had, absurdly, "stolen itself."[16] As Rebecca Scott writes, "Slave status had come to be naturalized, regularly reinforced, and made to appear inviolate" in the eighteenth-century Atlantic world, to the point where even freedom from slavery was defined according to the terms of slave-holding societies.[17]

Tattoe was one of at least 14,500 people released from the Middle Passage between 1808 and 1823 and repatriated in Sierra Leone.[18] Ultimately, the history of the Court is important because of what happened to these people. The archive, however, is almost exclusively about what happened to money. After the passage of the Slave Trade Act, the elite abolitionists of the

Clapham Sect oversaw the design of the prohibition on slave trading. Their solution, out of convenience and principle, was to rely on the power of the market. The Court in Sierra Leone provided commercial and military incentives to encourage the capture of slave ships. In his *Commentaries,* William Blackstone described early modern courts of "piepoudre," "the court of such petty chapmen as resort to fairs or markets . . . of which the steward of him, who owns or has the toll of the market, is the judge."[19] The Vice-Admiralty Court was a piepoudre court with an antislavery mandate. Its judges were merchants, devoted above all to prolonging and expanding the flow of captured property moving from the Court to the market. The first colonial instrument of mass emancipation in the British empire was designed to create freedom as an emergent property of vigorous commerce.

A second crucial feature of the Court was its deep connection to the practices of eighteenth-century naval warfare. In 1806 the Whig politician Charles James Fox had two dying wishes: peace in Europe and the end of the slave trade, but in a pinch, he declared, he would choose abolition over peace. Britons, he said, "could much better protect ourselves against our own external enemies, than this helpless people against their oppressors."[20] Had he lived, Fox would not have had the choice; the abolition of the slave trade was designed for wartime. The Slave Trade Act made slave ships into lawful "prizes," eligible for capture by British ships and regiments. The Court of Vice-Admiralty made it quick and easy for military officers to benefit from the Act: an officer could bring a captured slave ship into port and then quickly receive a portion of the auction value of the ship and all its cargo as "prize money." Former slaves released from the Middle Passage were sent by colonial officials to meet whatever immediate need for labour presented itself. In wartime, the two biggest consumers of labour in Sierra Leone were the military and the industries that sprang up to support the military: food, drink, supplies, and other services. In line with its wartime mission and design, the Court pushed many "captured Negroes" toward the military, recruiting prized black soldiers without the hassle of purchase.

This chapter sprawls from London to Freetown, from the markets to the barracks, following the ragged network of London activists, Freetown merchants, and British military officers built by the Court of Vice-Admiralty. The military and commercial functions of the Court overlapped and reinforced one another. More goods were an incentive to hunt for slave ships; more soldiers recruited from those ships meant greater military capacity for future missions. The Court was informal, even corrupt, by design. In 1827, an inquest into Sierra Leone's place in the British empire concluded that in the Court, as in the wider colony, "plans were chiefly adopted as the exigencies suggested them . . . without any established rules for their guidance."[21] The antislavery lobby reasoned that if it were easy and profitable to prosecute slave ships, it would encourage the British armed forces to be aggressive. The informality of the Court also made it easier to control. Like a market steward of a piepoudre court, Zachary Macaulay was steward of the Freetown slave-trade Court. His employees served as officers of the Court and dominated "prize agency" in the colony. His firm, Macaulay & Babington, distributed contracts to preferred vendors and traders in Freetown. This power abetted Macaulay & Babington's trade in Africa with both African and European merchants. As Macaulay wrote at the peak of his influence, "It is my policy . . . to discourage everything which tends to draw us beyond Sierra Leone. That is our place."[22] Macaulay connected the Court, a colonial institution operating at the margins of the "law of nations," to the ambitions and moral prestige of London antislavery. In turn, the Court churned up money and goods for the military, reinforcing antislavery policy and cementing Macaulay's position at the centre of the market.

Designing a Slave-Trade Court

In 1807, after a series of stunning victories over the French, the Royal Navy was perhaps Britain's most popular national institution. In a global war, British officers could justify searching ships belonging to virtually any other nation, by making a vague distinction between the "right to search," which applied only in limited circumstances, and a "right to visit," which applied to virtually every ship afloat.[23] The incentives weighed in favour of capture: prize money was a significant portion of naval pay, and in wartime the "law of nations," already weak, became effectively unenforceable. Even ships belonging to the United States, the most powerful neutral party in the Napoleonic wars, were fair game. Until the War of 1812, British policies on the press-ganging of naturalized American sailors implied that naturalized Americans from Britain were excused from British service only while physically within the United States.[24] Public support, loose regulations, huge incentives, and little chance of reprisal made the Royal Navy accustomed to impunity in search and seizure.

Vice-Admiralty Courts reflected the loose rules governing the capture of foreign ships. The Courts sprouted across the empire in order to make it easier for Royal Navy officers to collect prizes far from London and, to a lesser extent, to adjudicate on crimes committed at sea. The competition between European empires and a high volume of local shipping made the Courts in the British West Indies especially important. For example, in the Leeward Islands, home to six independent Courts of Vice-Admiralty, planters made regular use of the Courts, and often appointed judges without legal training to the bench, in order to speed up and smooth over the seizure and sale of enemy shipping.[25] The share of every prize paid to the Royal Navy brass as "droit of Admiralty" guaranteed that the Courts were valued by admirals as well as by planters and post-captains. James Stephen learned the culture of prize money as a young lawyer in Barbados, defending American traders whose ships had been seized under the mercantilist Navigation Acts.[26] Stephen planned and wrote most of both the 1806 Act that banned British participation in the foreign slave trade, and its successor, the 1807 Slave Trade Act. He must have had his time in the West Indies in mind, as both of the antislavery laws he wrote were structured to add slave ships to the list of lawful prizes. Stephen must also have relished the opportunity to turn a popular institution among slave-holding planters to antislavery purposes.

However, Stephen and the Clapham Sect were anxious about turning over the administration of the slave-trade laws to the existing regime of Vice-Admiralty Courts, and particularly to the Courts of the West Indies. If, for example, Jamaica became the headquarters of antislavery, any people freed from the Middle Passage there both would have endured the trauma of the voyage, and would pass from the Court into the hands of a slave-holding colonial government. Stephen also believed that the Caribbean held a greater risk for former slaves to be captured and enlisted by the French, or to be inspired to violent rebellion by the example of the Haitian Republic. To make sure cash and people passed through the right hands, Zachary Macaulay and William Wilberforce urged Lord Castlereagh to establish a new slave-trade Court in West Africa.[27] By November 1807, Macaulay was confident that "If a prize court is established at Sierra Leone, and that this will be the case I have no doubt, all difficulty will be at an end."[28] The War Office followed Macaulay's suggestion, and drew up a warrant for a Court of Vice-Admiralty for Sierra Leone.[29]

Vice-Admiralty Courts turned captured property into money quickly, with little attention to procedure. As Benton comments, the Courts were convenient mechanisms for regulating trade and did not constitute "a regime of well-ordered practices."[30] The High Court of Admiralty, to which the

Vice-Admiralty Courts were subordinate, was reformed during the early nineteenth century by an able Chief Justice, William Scott. But reform at the top did not percolate down, and the Vice-Admiralty Courts remained informal and difficult to regulate.[31] Even the reforming Justice Scott admitted to an appreciation for the "tenderness . . . usually shewn to mere informalities in the practice of Vice-Admiralty Courts."[32] The unregulated structure of the Courts was a function of their purpose. In a British prize court's jurisdiction, Royal Navy sailors could expect their prize money relatively quickly, as the Court quickly surveyed, appraised, and auctioned off the ships they had captured. During the Napoleonic wars, British prize courts handled £30 million of business in captured ships, and £10 million more for military posts ashore—or roughly £2.5 billion in 2015 currency.[33]

Douglas Hay and Paul Craven comment that in most jurisdictions of the nineteenth-century British empire, justice was "speedy, cheap, shorn of doctrinal formality and procedural complexity."[34] Even in an empire of laissez-faire legal practice, the Vice-Admiralty Courts were famously corrupt. The Courts were notorious for having personnel who held multiple offices. Lord Cochrane, in a popular memoir of his career at sea, described the Court of Vice-Admiralty at Malta, where a clerk named Jackson was both Marshal and Proctor. "Very profitably," Cochrane wrote, "did Mr. Proctor Jackson perform the duty of attending and consulting himself as Mr. Marshal Jackson!"[35] And yet, the corruption of the Courts was "honest graft" to the abolitionists, who hoped that the incentives the Courts offered would encourage the interdiction of slave ships. In 1810, Zachary Macaulay defended the captors of a slave ship whose prize decision had been appealed because of poor paperwork. He explained that "irregularity in the Information is . . . to be attributed to the ignorance of the Parties prosecuting . . . who had no opportunity at Sierra Leone of obtaining the aid of professional men there being none such in that colony." Macaulay admitted his clients had not obeyed the law. But, he continued, they should not be punished for being zealous in the pursuit of slave ships. If they lost their prize, other officers would be scared off, and the overall effect would be to "damp the zeal and relax the activity of the individuals whose duty it is to enforce the due execution of the said acts."[36] Did the appellate court, he asked, really want to be responsible for the continuation of the slave trade?

The body nominally responsible for overseeing the government of Sierra Leone after 1808 was the Office of the Secretary of State for War and the

Colonies. The office was uninterested in Sierra Leone and unequipped to manage it. Responsibility for Britain's colonies had been passed from department to department after the American War of Independence, and eventually was folded into the portfolio of the Secretary of State for War. Sierra Leone was a low priority, compared with the West Indies, India, or the growing settler colonies. The Treasury, also tasked with oversight of colonial matters, likewise remained largely unreformed until the 1820s.[37] Confidential information about Sierra Leone was routinely leaked to the "friends of Africa." James Stephen was reprimanded for turning over files on Jamaica to the African Institution, but not for materials on West Africa.[38] Unstructured, unregulated, and unsupervised, the new slave-trade Court in Sierra Leone could be easily influenced by anyone with the means and the inclination. Macaulay & Babington soon became the principal broker of the Court, and the hub of its connections with the military.

The Monopoly

Prize agency was Zachary Macaulay's way into the Court. In Vice-Admiralty cases, when a British officer captured a vessel and brought it to port, he often hired a prize agent to act on his behalf. The agent would instruct counsel, arrange for the sale of condemned property, and pay out the officer and his crew in exchange for a commission. Prize agency was not a career in itself. It was an additional service provided by merchants, flag secretaries in the Royal Navy, bankers, and small-time moneylenders. Most prize agents charged 5 percent commission on the value of prizes they managed, and were essential but overlooked middlemen in the British maritime world. Prize agents were brokers, but also unofficial financial and legal advisors to overworked officers far from their home ports. Zachary Macaulay was well suited to the precision and vigilance in arbitrage, money-changing, and brokerage required by prize agency.[39] And Macaulay & Babington benefited from the information Macaulay and his employees gathered in their communication with officers applying for prize money.

When the Court opened in 1808, Macaulay & Babington was the only firm in Freetown with an office and a reserve of capital back in London. Macaulay's influence in West African policy infuriated his enemies, who complained that, despite the dissolution of the Sierra Leone Company, nearly all trade in the colony "was secured to their managing secretary."[40]

The firm was well placed to do business in the Court of Vice-Admiralty. In London, in his role as Secretary of the African Institution, Macaulay managed a clearinghouse of information about West Africa.[41] The Institution's annual reports included lengthy appendices of excerpted legislation and regular mentions of the "pecuniary advantages which would accrue . . . from a rigorous enforcement of the Abolition Laws."[42] The reports were effective. An officer serving in West Africa wrote that some "information from Mr. Macaulay" had convinced him to seize a number of ships which he suspected were fitted out for slave trading.[43] In London Macaulay could tempt individual officers. In Freetown his firm could fulfill promises made in London and benefit from the commissions on captured slave ships. As the firm's client base grew, Macaulay & Babington came to enjoy a near monopoly over prize agency.

Monopoly in prize courts was neither rare nor frowned upon. One Jamaican firm, Willis & Waterhouse, managed more than 90 percent of business in Kingston from 1793 until 1801.[44] Macaulay & Babington dominated Sierra Leone just as completely. Between November of 1808 and March 1817, at least 179 cases were prosecuted in the Vice-Admiralty Court in Freetown. The fewest (3) were heard in 1808, and the most in 1815 (33). In that time, the Court reported that it freed 10,022 enslaved people in total. The extant archives of the Court, arranged by individual captured vessel, specify that these 10,022 people included at least 4,799 men, 1,874 women, 2,214 boys, and 814 girls; records of the age and sex of the remaining 301 people either were never kept or have been lost.[45] Of those extant cases, all but 18 have a listed prize agent. Either Zachary Macaulay in London or one of his employees in Freetown (first Michael Macmillan, and later Kenneth Macaulay) was sole or joint prize agent in 105 cases, or 59 percent. Zachary Macaulay himself was named as either sole or joint agent on 58 captures (or 55 percent of his firm's business and 32 percent of the total). Of the remaining cases, D. M. Hamilton, a former employee of the Sierra Leone Company and a close associate of Kenneth Macaulay's, was named as either the sole or joint agent 19 times. Consequently, across nine years of Court business, prize agents with no connection to Macaulay & Babington managed only 37 cases, or 21 percent.[46]

Before Macaulay & Babington entered the market, other well-established trading firms, like the West Indian partnership of Ommaney & Druce and the London-based firm of Bouverie & Antrobus, managed prize cases in Freetown.[47] In October 1811, Zachary Macaulay and D. M. Hamilton jointly

managed the capture of the slave ship *Calypso* on behalf of H.M.S. *Thais.*[48]
The same month, Macaulay hired Michael Macmillan as a subcontractor. Macmillan agreed to pay half of his prize commissions to Macaulay, and to trade
privately only up to £400 per year.[49] The firm's share of the market expanded
quickly. In 1811, of 19 cases prosecuted, Macaulay or his agents took on 6
(32 percent). In 1812, the proportion rose to 57 percent. In 1813, it was 64 percent. In 1814, Zachary Macaulay or his agents in Freetown were sole agent or
joint agent in all 17 recorded cases. In 1815, Macaulay or his agents managed
30 of 33 cases, or 91 percent. In 1816, the firm controlled 89 percent of the
market, and 90 percent in 1817.[50]

Macaulay was admired by his peers for his administrative talent and astonishing memory. George Stephen, in his memoir of the antislavery campaigns, remembered Macaulay as a superhuman bureaucrat who "could reduce
to ten or twenty pages all that was worth extracting from five hundred."[51]
Macaulay had privileged access to prize agency and information because of his
political and financial connections, and those connections were reinforced by
his prize agencies and the information they generated. He soon became, as one
biographer puts it, "effectively the chief executive of the enterprise."[52] The
Court kept few reliable written records. As early as 1827, British officials complained the Court's paperwork was "very defective, owing to the absence of
some records, and the imperfect manner in which others have been made."[53]
Macaulay turned the threadbare records to his advantage: anyone who wanted
to know about the Court needed to consult him personally. By 1811, even
James Stephen, who had designed the Slave Trade Act, forwarded requests for
information about the Court to Macaulay, "my own oracle . . . respecting the
slave court."[54]

There is no record of how much Macaulay & Babington earned on
commissions from prize agency, but command of the market must have been
lucrative. The Order-in-Council, which put the Slave Trade Act into force,
also provided for cash bounties to be added to the prize money for slave
ships, based on the number of people imprisoned aboard. These bounties
were more difficult to claim than prize money since they were paid from London, not Freetown. However, because bounty claims required applications to
London, they are slightly better documented than prize agencies. Total bounties are a poor proxy for the total value of prize ships and goods in Sierra
Leone, and the extant data is patchy, imprecise, and no doubt much inflated
compared to the amount paid out, but out of necessity the bounties have to

stand in for richer, more precise data. Christopher Fyfe estimates that from 1807 to 1815, £191,100 was on the books.[55] Christopher Lloyd claims that the total was £318,380 from 1807 to 1822.[56] I found records indicating that, between 1808 and 1815, some £126,490 was listed as paid out by the Navy Board in bounties, of which at least £58,110 went unclaimed. Some sailors to whom bounties were owed died, some did not know they were eligible, and some were unable to make it to the offices of Macaulay & Babington in Water Street, Freetown, in time to collect.[57] However weak the data, it is clear that prize money could be a spectacular windfall, and was worth pursuing.

Control of prize agency helped Macaulay & Babington command Freetown's economic life. Macaulay protested that although he was "grateful indeed for this proof of confidence . . . by me it was neither expected nor solicited." His firm, he explained, simply offered goods "on better terms than they could be procured from any other merchant."[58] A rare bundle of extant receipts in the archives of the Vice-Admiralty Court hint at the way the firm did business. When H.M.S. *Comus* captured a slave ship, it was managed as a prize by the firm, which renovated it with new rigging and canvas, paint, and cannon, "Bot of Messrs. Z. Macaulay Babington," and then arranged for the vessel's sale at auction.[59] Prize agency allowed Macaulay & Babington to integrate their businesses in Freetown vertically from the Court outward and to take a cut from nearly every transaction. It managed legal work, sold the goods necessary to refit, restock, and refuel warships, and recommended surveyors and shipwrights to repair prize vessels, auctioneers to sell them, and assortments of trade goods to carry in them.

Macaulay protested that his firm made its monopoly by outworking any rivals. However, sharp practice was easy in Freetown. In 1814, John Caton, a merchant from Liverpool, complained that his ship, the *Margaret*, had been shaken down by the colonial customs officers. The ship, captained by Richard Baker, brought a cargo of gin, anchovies, ham, and puddings to Sierra Leone, along with iron goods, cloth, beads, and tobacco to sell in the African trade. In Madeira, Baker picked up seven more cases of "India goods" and wine to import on behalf of Michael Macmillan, Macaulay & Babington's agent in Freetown. When the *Margaret* arrived in Freetown, George Macaulay, acting as Collector of Customs, seized the gin and anchovies, allegedly for violating the Navigation Acts. The goods were condemned in an "Instance Court" presided over by Robert Purdie, colonial surgeon and acting Chief Justice of the Vice-Admiralty Court, and then sold at auction.[60]

Baker was angry, but not surprised. "Not a vessel comes here," he complained, "but gets into some dilemma or other." He claimed that Sierra Leone's customs routinely demanded a 2-percent fee on the total value of all imports as a kickback. Reluctant captains would have their papers examined, and the "least flaw" would result in the loss of the entire cargo.[61] Macaulay & Babington did not endorse this practice, although Zachary Macaulay must have known about it. However, regardless of intent, the firm, as the largest and best connected in Freetown, benefited from the insecure conditions under which less-well-connected merchants had to operate. Its agents could buy cheap trade goods seized by customs, and could offer merchants more secure commercial arrangements at an appropriate price.

Prize agency also gave Macaulay & Babington the power to distribute contracts and piecework within Freetown. The firm held many powers of attorney, many of which survive in the archives.[62] But the bulk of the business generated by prize agency involved renovating and restoring captured slave ships for sale at auction. The records of the High Court of Admiralty include a bundle of receipts, signed by Kenneth Macaulay, for accounts paid to various contractors in Sierra Leone for the management of seven prize cases from 1815.[63] These receipts show just how many people might benefit from a captured slave ship. Settler foremen and Kru mariners were hired to keep the ships in good condition. Benjamin York, a Nova Scotian merchant, sold supplies and food to feed the former captives, and William Grant, another Nova Scotian with a trading factory in the Rio Pongas, was hired to refit the ship with new ironwork. Macaulay & Babington itself also sold other supplies needed for renovation under the supervision of David Edmonds, the Nova Scotian shipwright and merchant to whom Governor Thompson took a passionate dislike.[64] In this admittedly limited sample, the average prize brought to Sierra Leone generated about £132 pounds in contracts and fees. Assuming that sum represents something close to the actual average cost, the contracts and fees associated with prize management in the Vice-Admiralty Court—not including the value of captured ships, the value of apprenticed workers, or the sale of goods and cargo—generated roughly £23,628 across all 179 cases heard by the Court between 1808 and 1817 (*very* roughly £8,531 per prize case). Compared to the amount of money generated by bounties or by the sale of prize ships, this was negligible, but it shows the place of the Court at the hub of a wider system of commerce.

Many settlers hoped for a portion of trade in the colony. Some asked visiting merchants to take on their children as apprentices.[65] Other settlers rented out parts of their homes and shops as warehouse space. By 1826, more than 52,292 cubic feet of storage space was under lease in Freetown, mostly to the Royal Navy.[66] As a naval and military station, the colony was enormously thirsty for liquor. The Nova Scotian settlers, who, according to one visitor, were famously "fond of Spiritual Liquors," dominated alcohol sales in Freetown.[67] The poor might visit moonshine stands, like the basement premises of Anthony Davis in Howe Street, and get drunk safe in the knowledge that Davis was "willing to accommodate any person who might get intoxicated in the House." "The better sort of company," could order from the "very decent Tap" in Richard Waistcoat's public house in Wilberforce Street.[68] Anyone interested in trade with African kings and chiefs could buy rum in wholesale quantities. In an audit of his family's business, Zachary Macaulay's nephew commented, "The only persons whom we could expect to deal with us for whole packages are the grog-shop keepers."[69] There is a social history of drunkenness in the colony swaying and muttering beyond the edge of the archive, but what we can know about the brisk sale of booze in Freetown shows another way the Vice-Admiralty Court catalysed economic life in the capital. Liquor seized on captured ships was added to the stock of imported liquor and resold to merchants, who either distributed it to smaller retailers or sold it in bulk to coastal traders.

The Vice-Admiralty Court was made for commerce. It did not produce a coherent body of antislavery law. Robert Thorpe, who served as Chief Justice in Sierra Leone in 1811, complained that he could not fathom how he could be legally permitted to condemn captured Portuguese ships. The tenth article of an 1810 treaty between Britain and Portugal had restricted the Portuguese slave trade to Portuguese territory, but Thorpe had no idea what part of the coast " 'belonged" to Portugal. He noted that the legality of seizing French and Spanish slave trades was just as vague, and that the Sierra Leone Vice-Admiralty Court lacked any "Registrar, Advocate, Proctor, Marshal, or Interpreter, that understood his duty."[70] In another letter, to Chief Justice William Scott, Thorpe asked questions about the jurisdiction and rules of search and seizure that seemed so fundamental that an appalled Scott refused to answer.[71] Even the Commissioners appointed in 1813 to reform the Court excused themselves for their relative ignorance, and remarked that what information they did have they had "obtained from Mr. McAulay . . . as well as from bills of Costs, in possession of an Agent for a King's Ship which had brought the greatest number of Prizes to adjudication in the Court."[72] The Court was the source of Macaulay's private fortune. Christopher Fyfe estimates that he made more than £100,000 in profits in Sierra Leone, and assumes that "so vast a profit can only have come from public sources."[73] However, Macaulay did not make his money by skimming off grants to the colony. Instead, monopoly allowed him to control the direction and velocity of both public monies and private enterprise in Freetown; rather than stealing from the Court, his business *was* the Court.

Debt, Slavery, and Trade in West Africa

Most of the money circulating in Freetown in the heyday of the Vice-Admiralty Court was not specie. It was debt. In his work on economic life in Baltimore in the early 1800s, Seth Rockman reconstructs a world where most people were paid "on the books." Instead of paying in scarce cash, most poor people in Baltimore paid their bills with the debts owed to them, written in ledgers or on promissory notes. Employers could easily exploit employees paid in unstable, easily counterfeited or highly conditional paper debt. For example, if a debt could be redeemed only in one place, like a company store, it could be easily devalued at a profit to the issuer.[74] This phenomenon was epidemic in the cities of the early nineteenth-century Atlantic world, including Freetown. What specie there was in the colony was a mixture of British, Spanish, Portuguese, and French coins, but most former slaves and other low-wage labourers were paid in unofficial promissory notes redeemable for goods, rather than in cash.[75] This made the poor vulnerable to losing the money held on the books whenever debts were called in, which was often. In the late 1810s, the back pages of the Freetown newspaper were full of notices that one merchant or another had died or returned to England, and expected cash for the debt on his books. This system made a feedback loop, rendering the economic lives of the poor even more unstable, draining more cash from Freetown and increasing the amount of debt circulating as money.

Macaulay & Babington was a prominent broker of debt. In coastal trade, the firm would barter only in goods for reliably expensive luxury commodities like gold and ivory. For other transactions, Zachary Macaulay's nephew Henry wrote, "We get all our African Produce from our debtors," mostly cattle, rice, and palm oil. The firm, having bought goods in exchange for debt, resold the goods for cash or for more debt to merchants in the colony and to coastal traders.[76] The limited amount of currency circulating, and the high risk of commerce in a climate where Europeans died at a brisk rate, gave even more weight to owning debt and being able to extend credit. Macaulay & Babington, because of its size and London offices, was more resilient than any other Freetown merchant or banker; the death of one of the firm's employees would not threaten the entire partnership. Ready credit made it easy quickly to buy and sell ships and goods condemned by the Court. The firm also loaned money, on three- to six-month terms, without interest.[77] Instead, Macaulay & Babington would seize defaulters' property. For example, the firm gave George Stephen Caulker, the long-standing owner of the Banana Islands, a mortgage on which Caulker defaulted in 1828. Caulker forfeited the island to Sierra Leone.[78] And in a colony where a creditor was as likely to die of malaria as to default, the firm managed the estates of many prominent Europeans.[79] In Jamaica, executors of wills filled an important social function for whites as symbolic protectors of social continuity. Macaulay & Babington may have filled this role for Sierra Leone's merchants, and they may have charged the standard Jamaican fee: between 5 and 10 percent of the net value of the estate.[80]

Merchants in the Atlantic world were brokers in knowledge as well as in goods.[81] It was no different for Macaulay & Babington. The firm sold valuable goods, but it also held valuable paperwork: ledgers of debt and folios of powers-of-attorneys, wills, and testaments. These documents were valuable in themselves, since they could be liquidated. But taken together they comprised a detailed picture of who owned and who owed, who was improvident and who was wealthy. Since the Court's records were so poorly and intermittently kept, the firm had a more detailed and accurate picture of the market than anyone else, including the Colonial Office. The firm could assist local merchants in purchasing condemned vessels, but its ready credit also made it easy for Macaulay & Babington to buy the ships, refit them, and sell them. For example, Kenneth Macaulay advertised the former slave ship *Esperanza* as "new sheathed: well found, and excellently adapted for the timber or rice trade."[82] Would-be timber or rice traders found that Macaulay & Babington played a prominent role in those industries as well. The firm sold imported European goods wholesale to Freetown retailers.[83] In turn, European retailers accepted African cash crops and commodities like rice and camwood as payment from African traders, as well as goods and cash from Europeans, and promissory notes from freed slaves and migrant workers. Retailers in the colony then sold the goods and promissory notes to Macaulay & Babington for more retail goods. When retail goods began to decay in the unremitting heat and humidity, the firm would auction them off, despite relatively heavy auction fees. "In Sierra Leone," one employee wrote, "such a security should be well paid for."[84]

Shopkeepers in Sierra Leone could not afford to be specialists. Most shopkeepers sold their goods from large rooms on the ground floor of their houses, offering both wholesale and retail services. Shops sold "every article, from tons of ivory and teak, gold-dust and camwood, to a single needle or a wafer, a nail of tape or a yard of thread," often simply arranged in piles on tables and shelves.[85] Shopkeepers catered to Europeans, settlers, locals, and "captured Negroes" and needed to offer their goods for cash, credit, or barter. For example, the retailer Daniel Sutherland sold his goods for specie or on credit, but also accepted rice, camwood, or palm oil as payment.[86] In turn, most of Sutherland's inventory was either consigned by Macaulay & Babington or purchased with credit extended by the firm.[87]

As Chapter One shows, the African goods bought and sold in Freetown were not usually cultivated in Sierra Leone. By the time the Court was in full swing, a significant proportion of the colony's rice and palm oil was grown in the delta of the Rio Pongas, a region with which Macaulay & Babington had long-standing ties. Zachary Macaulay had contacts there since the failed experiment of Freeport Factory in the 1790s, which he nurtured through patronage of several British missionary societies. In 1800, because of his resolute support for missionary work in Africa, Macaulay was appointed Visitor to the General Committee of the Society for Missions, "as he is . . . peculiarly capable of giving the Committee very important and useful information."[88] Macaulay urged the Society to choose the rice-growing areas of the Rio Pongas and Rio Nuñez as "the most eligible sphere for their labours."[89] In Sierra Leone, the missionaries met William Fantomani, the son of a chief whom Macaulay had taken with him to England in the 1790s to a school in Clapham, the "African Academy," at his father's request. William told the visitors, "Mr. Macaulay told me I must trade with the colony and build a house for the Missionaries and treat them well."[90] The missionaries themselves tried their hand at trade. One missionary bought European goods in Freetown, and forwarded them to his colleagues in the Rio Pongas, to "purchase as much rice as possible, and to sell it again to Mr. Macmillan, Zachary Macaulay's agent." He turned a profit of £500.[91]

The growing population and surging economy of Freetown in wartime exerted ever greater pressure on nearby rice-producing regions, most

of which relied on slave labour for agriculture. Some of those goods would
have been consumed locally, but a significant portion of the crop was exported from the river's trade factories, south along the coast to Freetown.
Other major trade goods and commodities were also slave-produced. The
amount of palm oil exported from the Bight of Biafra grew from an annual
export of 40 tons in the mid-1780s to some 450 tons in the mid 1800s, to 3,000
tons in 1819. A significant quantity of palm oil found its way to Freetown
markets. The trade in Sierra Leone timber began in 1816, when an Irish
trader named John McCormack opened a sawpit on an island in the Sierra
Leone River. Macaulay & Babington followed suit in 1820 with their own
sawpit on Tasso Island. This timber was sold to the Admiralty, after an initial
contract in 1817. Much of the wood came from stands of forest on the banks
of the Sierra Leone River, and from the Sherbro' Peninsula south of Freetown. Virtually none of the timber came from the colony. Consequently,
African subcontractors were free to use slave labour.[92]

The records of the Vice-Admiralty Court, and of colonial trade in
wartime, are remarkable and absorbing, evoking a nearly tangible everyday
world of exchange and credit in hot, dusty shops full of goods from Africa,
North America, and Europe. It is easy to forget that all of this commerce
centred on a Court with a mandate to make enslaved people free, because
emancipation had so little to do with the business of antislavery. Former
slaves were incidental to the market in its day-to-day operation but essential
to the market's existence. For all of the granular specificity of the archive of
trade in Sierra Leone in wartime, there are very few records that give any insight into the lives of former slaves. It isn't even clear what became of many
of the people released from the slave trade before the end of the Napoleonic
wars—they were counted and registered upon disembarking from slave
ships, but then they disappear from the records. As in Ludlam and Thompson's time, some "captured Negroes" were apprenticed to settlers or merchants. But demand was at low ebb. One visitor to Freetown noticed that
nearly every family had at least one apprentice, and some had as many as
twenty.[93] Remember, however, that the Slave Trade Act was designed with a
compact between commerce and military service in mind; remember also
that the Vice-Admiralty Court relied on wartime practices of search and seizure to function. Consequently, for many "captured Negroes" military service was the most significant way that the economy of antislavery intruded
upon their lives.

The Court and the Military

The partnership between the Clapham Sect, military officers, and Freetown merchants that made antislavery possible was built in the Vice-Admiralty Court and directed by Zachary Macaulay. Among many other officers, Macaulay personally acted as prize agent for Charles MacCarthy in at least nine cases in 1814 and 1815.[94] The future Governor and Macaulay became close enough that when MacCarthy took a leave of absence from Sierra Leone in 1821, he asked Macaulay to help him find a wife "to fill the throne at Sierra Leone," as Macaulay put it.[95] However, no officer left behind a larger personal archive than James Chisholm, a Scottish officer in the Royal African Corps. Chisholm's papers show how the prize system attracted officers and kept them on task in their pursuit of slave ships, and how the exchange of money and information came to form a sturdy and long-lasting connection between the Clapham Sect and the Royal African Corps. In the process, prize money extended beyond the boundaries of the market and into the lives of former slaves.

The scars on Lieutenant-Colonel James Chisholm's body were a map of the British empire. He had served for 17 years in the 50th Regiment, including a stint, from 1780 to 1782, in the British garrison under siege at Gibraltar. He was present at the captures of Martinique, Guadeloupe, and St. Lucia in 1794 and 1795. In 1796, with money advanced by his relatives, he purchased a commission as Ensign in the 88th Regiment, and, in 1798, a Lieutenancy. He fought in Gujarat, Bombay, Calcutta, and Ceylon. On 13 November 1804, at the battle of Deej during the Second Anglo-Maratha War, he was stabbed with a spear. The weapon plunged through his right hip and the right side of his groin. Although the wound closed, it often split open, weeping pus, with "pieces of Cloth & Shirt coming away."[96] In 1805, at the Siege of Bhurpore, an exploding shell burned the skin off his chest. During the ill-fated British assault on Buenos Aires (in which Thompson also served) in July 1807 Chisholm was shot twice in the left leg. The next year, Chisholm was promoted to Major in the Royal African Corps. He served as Commandant of Gorée and was eventually promoted to Lieutenant-Colonel.[97] In West Africa, his wounds often reopened, oozing reminders of British wars for the Bombay Presidency and for influence in Latin America.

Chisholm continued to climb the ranks, physically battered but professionally thriving. After his death in 1822, Chisholm was remembered in *The Gentleman's Magazine* as brave, gallant, and lucky. Early in his career, Chisholm enjoyed the patronage of Wellington and General Lord Lake, but while in the Royal African Corps, his patrons were abolitionists. The obituary noted that Chisholm was regularly praised by the African Institution for "his cordial exertions in favour of the unhappy natives of Africa," exertions for which was rewarded "by all his fellow-labourers in human emancipation."[98] And yet the Royal African Corps had an awful reputation. As Chisholm complained privately to a friend, his regiment was "the most villainous set of Rascals."[99] The Corps was an unlikely instrument for antislavery, and an unlikely client for the Clapham Sect. Its rank and file were convicts from other regiments, local African volunteers, and, after 1808, former slaves enlisted for life. But, like James Chisholm, the Corps was widely praised in the *Reports* of the African Institution. The Evangelical leaders of Parliamentary antislavery needed the cooperation and enthusiasm of the British armed forces in order to enforce the Slave Trade Act. The Vice-Admiralty Court was a forum for the abolitionists to encounter an unlikely group of officers, and to "convert" them to the cause.

While in India, James Chisholm relied on Allan Maclean & Company of Calcutta to manage his money.[100] When he arrived in Gorée in 1809, he needed a new agent, one with West African expertise. Chisholm also needed a reliable source of information about the legal and financial details of antislavery in an outpost that was often among the last to receive official information about changes in British law and policy. When the Abolition Act passed, for example, the then-Commandant of Gorée, Charles Maxwell, complained, "I am left entirely in the dark as to the wishes of Government in carrying into execution the slave laws; I am not furnished with any instructions, or power to act." His garrison learned the contents of the Act from a visiting merchant captain who happened to have a brought a copy with him.[101] Soon, Macaulay reached out to Maxwell with information that proved valuable in the capture of several slave ships, in which Chisholm took part.[102] Chisholm thanked Macaulay for the advice, and for "having done me the honor of enrolling me as a member of the African Institution," and solicited him to act his prize agent.[103]

James Chisholm is listed in the records of the Vice-Admiralty Court of Sierra Leone as the sole or joint captor in four captures of slave ships, and as the sole or joint captor in four cases where a total of 71 enslaved people were released from the Middle Passage. Either Zachary Macaulay or Kenneth Macaulay represented him in all but one of those cases.[104] One surviving receipt from Chisholm's papers suggests the sort of payouts he expected. For his share of the bounty on 14 slaves, including 11 men, 3 women and 1 child who were "condemned to the King at his suit" in February 1811, Chisholm was awarded £176. Macaulay deducted £35, 5s, 4d in fees, including £7, 8s "to Commission on nett proceeds £148, 2s, 6d @ 5%," and paid out £140, 14s, 6d to Chisholm.[105] Chisholm's files also include a handwritten copy of an advertisement from the Freetown *Royal Gazette* reporting that the offices of Macaulay & Babington were ready to disburse prize money for two ships, *Empecinado* and *Dos Hermanos*. Chisholm, perhaps hoping to make a case that he had been instrumental in the capture of the vessels, copied down that a first-class share of the *Empecinado* was worth £675, 10s, and that second- and third-class captors received £86, 7s and £69, 1s.[106] Chisholm also lobbied his agents for shares of prizes he may or may not have been entitled to claim. For example, Kenneth Macaulay paid out £410, 10s, 9d to Charles MacCarthy for his role in the capture of the *Tentativa*, *Desemperados*, and *Empecinado* in 1816. Chisholm seems to have tried to claim a share of these prizes as well, although the records suggest he was only involved in the capture of *Empecinado*.[107] In 1818, Chisholm received a memorandum that reckoned his share of prize money at £407, 10s, 9d, although the document does not specify what ships or groups of slaves were condemned to generate the prize.[108] In addition to prize money, which could be handled in Freetown, Macaulay also managed Chisholm's share of bounties for freeing individual slaves, filing claims with the Navy Board and Treasury in London. After his death, Chisholm's executors continued to apply for the bounties he had earned for the *San Jose*, captured in 1815.[109] When the bounty was finally paid to his estate in 1825, the executors were urged to "see Mr. Macaulay on the subject."[110]

The abolitionist and the officer traded favours. Macaulay stumped for Chisholm's appointment as Governor of Senegal when Charles Maxwell was promoted to Governor of Sierra Leone after Columbine's death.[111] In turn, Chisholm was especially solicitous toward missionaries, and enthusiastically supported Evangelical causes in West Africa. On 27 February 1813, Leopold Butscher reported from Gorée that Chisholm gave missionaries "every possible kindness & attention."[112] In 1818, Chisholm placed an African boy, christened "Allan," with his friend Ninian Bruce, a surgeon at Sandhurst.[113] James Chisholm's enthusiasm for missionaries and the education of African children were the cause and the consequence of increased attention from missionaries to West Africa at the beginning of the 1810s. Chisholm's professional prospects came to depend on collaboration with the Anglican-Evangelical "friends of Africa."

In one extant receipt in Chisholm's archive, Macaulay made a mere £7, 8s out of a bounty of £176.[114] But these small increments could add up. One of Zachary Macaulay's most bitter critics, the pamphleteer James McQueen, argued that Macaulay's commission amounted to "£13,000 per annum, during the last seventeen years, clear gain . . . the very *cheese parings and candle ends*' of which are annually worth more than the salary of the Prime Minister of Great Britain!"[115] McQueen's histrionics notwithstanding, Macaulay did profit from prize agency. However, commissions on prizes were only a base on which a more profitable business was built. James Chisholm and other officers sent letters thick with information back to London, and talked at length with agents in Freetown. That information was more valuable than a five percent cut.

Some letters were sources of anecdotes of missionary and Evangelical successes in West Africa. For example, Chisholm helped to repatriate a former slave captured in the West Indies and apprenticed in Antigua, where his unusual skills as a linguist, and particularly his mastery of Arabic, came to the attention of the Governor. The man, Mohammed, was baptized with the new name "Job."[116] Chisholm helped Mohammed find a passage inland after he returned to Senegal. Chisholm reported that "Job" kneeled and kissed the beach when he came ashore, and thanked Providence, and "those who had been the means of sending him to his native Shore." In the same letter Chisholm commented on the possibility of establishing a missionary school in Senegal, the progress made by two missionaries from Sierra Leone who had been seconded to Gorée, the rumours of slave ships sighted near the shore, and the progress of various cases in the Court of Vice-Admiralty.[117] Sometimes Chisholm was able to provide Macaulay with fine-grained details on the structure of the slave trade, and the practices used by slave ships to avoid capture. An American prisoner told Chisholm about three American-owned slave ships that planned to sail under Portuguese colors in Africa, and to swap for Spanish flags off Tenerife.[118]

By 1813, Macaulay & Babington were the dominant prize agency in West Africa, and by 1815 they managed virtually every prize adjudicated in the Court of Vice-Admiralty in Freetown. In that year Chisholm could not have found another prize agent even if he had wanted to. He badly needed money, particularly to buy military commissions for younger relatives.[119] The Royal African Corps offered few of the usual perquisites commissioned officers relied on to top up their pay. For example, many regiments allowed officers to sell uniforms and gear to private soldiers, who were expected to

buy their own equipment. In the Royal African Corps, when the convict recruits arrived at their recruiting depot in Guernsey "entirely destitute of necessaries," in an "uncomfortable and naked state," the officers of the Corps
had to advance their own money to the soldiers to buy kit.[120]

The relationship between Chisholm and Macaulay & Babington was
sufficiently important and public that Chisolm's professional enemies wrote to
the Clapham Sect as well as to the Horse Guards to try to disrupt his career.
Thus, Major Edward Lloyd, who had clashed with Chisholm over their respective rights to African servants while in West Africa, wrote to Macaulay to
accuse Chisholm of permitting the slave trade in Gorée, and of calling for a
brutal punishment of 500 lashes on a free black man accused of stealing a mus-
ket. Lloyd described the man's back as being in "a putrid state" after being
whipped by "two stout black men" with a whip made of "the skin of a fish,"
perhaps sharkskin, with its hard, jagged scales. "Instead of our commandant
being civilizing," Lloyd concluded, "he is quite the opposite."[121] In response,
Wilberforce wrote frantically to the Secretary of State for War and the Colonies, demanding an investigation.[122] Chisholm was ultimately exonerated of
the charge of permitting the slave trade, and his enthusiasm for flogging was
written off as an unfortunate excess of zeal.[123] Chisholm retired on good terms
with the African Institution, and Wilberforce helped him to secure a pension
when he was finally invalided.[124] For the officers of the Royal African Corps,
pursuing slave ships had become a path to money, patronage, and promotion.

Volunteer Soldiers for Life: Former Slaves in the Corps

The benefits of prize agency were not only monetary. The 1807 Slave Trade
Act allowed British officials to enlist people released from the slave trade into
the armed forces. Before the abolition of the slave trade, the Royal African
Corps relied on white convicts to fill out its ranks. The Corps' officers established a routine of drill and drink, in the hope of preventing mutiny with violence and alcoholic torpor. In comparison with white convicts, former slaves
were a very attractive alternative. The Royal African Corps had a bad reputation, and the patronage of the abolitionists, through the Vice-Admiralty
Court, helped to rehabilitate its officers.

In 1811 the *Royal Military Chronicle,* a semiofficial publication founded
by the Duke of York and in wide circulation among British officers, published a letter purporting to be from a private in the Royal African Corps:

MY OLD FRIEND—I take the earliest opportunity of stating to you, that all the detachment came safe, and in good health, to this place, excepting Quail, who was drowned in endeavoring to swim on shore at Madeira. I request you will inform me if my wife came to Castle Cornet, and be pleased to desire her to come when the next transport goes out to Africa. This is the best place for a soldier on the coast of Africa; there is abundance of meat and everything else for the men, so that they are not served with salt ration. The ration to each man is one pound of fresh beef per day, one pint of wine, one pound of bread, and one half pint of peas, besides rice, coffee, sugar, and pumpkins, and all for six-pence a day. We are masters of our own time till five o'clock in the evening, and then we are never more than ten minutes on parade. I believe we have the best officers in the service, and particularly Major Chisholm, who, it was said, used the men so ill at Guernsey. He takes all the care he can of us. The days are 13 hours long. This is the cold season. The inhabitants say it is the best time of year for soldiers to come from England ... I hear that the detachment at Sierra Leone expect to have their old commanding officer with them, and they are greatly rejoiced to hear, that he is honorably acquitted of the charges which were sent against him. Wishing you all happiness, I remain, yours sincerely, J. Rennicks, private in the royal African Corps.[125]

The piece was a joke at the expense of the Corps. Its European privates were usually sick, often starving, and were issued poor-quality equipment, if they received any at all. Most regiments were not allowed to bring their wives with them to their barracks; a convict regiment would never be allowed the privilege. Instead of ten minutes' marching a day, the Corps was perpetually on parade. The slightly colder rainy season, the "best time of year," was particularly lethal, as it was the peak of the mosquito breeding period. The "old commanding officer" of the Sierra Leone detachment of the Regiment to which the letter refers was Frederick Forbes, who, rather than being acquitted, was cashiered out of the service. Finally, "the best officer in the service," the same James Chisholm whose archive gives so much insight into the relationship between London activists and officers in Africa, had a reputation as a violent disciplinarian, with no scruples about ordering thousands of lashes at courts-martial.[126] The fluent, jaunty prose of the letter is itself tongue in cheek. Among the privates there were very, very few soldiers who could even write their own names.[127]

Before the abolition of the slave trade, the Corps' predecessor, the Gorée Corps, was legendarily atrocious. Joseph Wall, an infamous colonial administrator in the short-lived British colony of Senegambia, punished a mutinous soldier in the Gorée Corps by hanging him, then strapping his still-warm corpse across the mouth of a cannon and blowing it apart in a spray of gore.[128] J. J. Crooks, an official in the colonial government of Sierra Leone in the latter part of the nineteenth century, is the Corps' only dedicated historian. It has no regimental archive. Its history exists in scraps scattered across continents. One historian claims that the Corps was formed in 1792, but I have found no evidence to support this.[129] According to Crooks it was first raised, as "Fraser's Corps of Infantry" (after its commander, Colonel Fraser) in August 1800, shortly after the French Garrison at Gorée fell to the British.[130]

Despite its reputation, the regiment was officially styled the "Royal" African Corps by 1804, perhaps because one of its most senior officers, whose high-ranking commission in the Corps was a sinecure, not a military duty, was Sir James Willoughby Gordon, a close friend of the Duke of York.[131] The new establishment of the regiment included two companies, each with one captain, two lieutenants, one ensign, four sergeants, two drummers, and one hundred private soldiers. These companies were formed up at Hilsea, outside of Portsmouth. Initially, the soldiers were recruited from garrison regiments in England and from men enlisting for the Gorée Corps. When the companies were increased after this initial mustering of officers and men, the new soldiers were recruited from among "deserters and persons confined on board the Hulks," the rotting decommissioned ships used to relieve the pressure on Britain's overcrowded prisons.[132] In November 1800, a detachment of 50 soldiers from the Corps arrived. The reputation of West African service was a powerful deterrent to volunteers, even among soldiers who would be spared hundreds of lashes if they signed up, and the Corps was always eager for recruits. Colonel Fraser was given permission by Lord Castlereagh to recruit local Africans as soldiers, and to offer a limited term of service as an inducement.[133] Initially, black soldiers served on better terms than did white soldiers and the soldiers recruited at Gorée were free men. Beginning in 1795, Britain had begun to purchase enslaved men to serve as soldiers in the West Indies, but free Africans were believed to be even better value since they did not need to be rewarded for their service with emancipation. As Henry Dundas warned a subordinate, "I cannot help intimating to you the absolute necessity of avoiding forming any eventual engagements with Persons who have not previously acquired their liberty, which might lead them to any expectation of future Emancipation, as a reward."[134]

One commanding officer of the Corps called its white rank and file "the sweepings of every parade in England . . . They were not a bad set of fellows when there was anything to be done, but with nothing to do, they were devils incarnate."[135] So the white soldiers of the Royal African Corps always had plenty to "do," their lives defined by a routine of roll call, parade, rum, and punishment. John Kingsley, an Irish officer, commanded the detachment at Sierra Leone at the turn of the nineteenth century. He took command on 25 May 1800. Two days later, he handed down his first whipping: 75 lashes to a private named Connor. This failed to correct Connor's behaviour. On 1 June, Kingsley noted, "Tolerably dry. Stopped Connor's liquor for 6 Days, for being basely drunk & absent at roll call at 10 o'clock in the morning also confined him to the Fort. Parade as usual."[136] Desperate alcoholism and violence were common. On 13 March 1801, Private Alexander Ross was dismissed as hospital orderly for bad conduct. He was flogged the next day, badly enough that he was admitted to hospital for 10 days to recover. As Ross was leaving the hospital, the surgeon on duty discovered that Ross had swilled twelve bottles of wine without permission. He fled but was caught in the jungle outside of Freetown by a Maroon tracker. When the Maroon caught him, Ross moaned that he "was going to cut his throat as he was ashamed of his comrades & everyone he met."[137] On Saturday, 11 December 1800, Lieutenant Kingsley gave another soldier, confined for drunkenness, permission to leave Fort Thornton to go to the river to bathe. He didn't return. A party of soldiers found him a few days later. He had hanged himself at a sawpit outside of Freetown.[138]

The white soldiers of the Corps, like many in British regiments, were often only nominally "British." When the Corps assembled in Guernsey in 1807, the rank and file included 142 Englishmen, 3 Scots, 12 Irish, and 108 "Foreigners."[139] The soldiers lived in privation and squalor. In 1808, Lieutenant Colonel Lloyd reported on serious food shortages in Gorée, where the troops had been living for three months only on the "rice of the country," without any other provisions.[140] At Sierra Leone, the men lived within the walls of Fort Thornton in decrepit barracks. Thomas Perronet Thompson was shocked to find that one of the ground-floor rooms where the men slept was windowless, and they could be barred from outside as punishment, leaving them trapped and sweating in near-absolute darkness.[141]

Drill was another horror of army life. British soldiers were trained in the "nineteen manoeuvres," a series of rote marching patterns. The manoeuvres were meant to break complex military strategy down into simple moves. "There will not be seen," a correspondent of William Cobbett wrote, "in any assembly room in England, nineteen country dances whose figures are not more complicated . . . than the evolutions of those nineteen manoeuvres."[142] Drill structured the lives of the soldiers in the Corps, but it didn't teach sophisticated military skills. For example, no one in an entire battery unit sent to the Cape Colony in 1847 had ever learned to harness a horse.[143] But drill could make British soldiers into formidable combatants. James Belich argues that rigid training was so coercive and unpleasant that "the sudden release from discipline, in the form of an order to charge, unleashed an almost berserk ferocity."[144] But those moments of violent ecstasy were rare interruptions in a tedious and miserably uncomfortable life.

For white soldiers in the Corps, the counterpoint to drill was drink. As in the rest of the armed forces, alcoholism was rampant—the rum ration was distributed every day before breakfast, and teetotalers were generally ostracized, and sometimes savagely beaten.[145] But it was disease that claimed the most lives. Philip Curtin, adapting and refining a military census commissioned by Parliament in the mid-nineteenth century, estimated that from 1810 to 1816 the annual death rate from disease among British troops in Sierra Leone was 483 out of every 1,000.[146] Other records show that in Gorée for the year 1810, 63 out of 243 noncommissioned officers and rank-and-file soldiers died. In Senegal, 66 died out of 308, and in Sierra Leone 11 out of 98. In 1812, 174 out of 347 soldiers in Senegal died in service, 116 out of 260 at Gorée, and 40 out of 304 at Sierra Leone.[147]

Crime was common, especially theft.[148] Courts-martial prosecuted most crimes. The records of the courts-martial of major regiments are relatively easy to recover, but those of the Royal African Corps are few and far between. Thomas Maxey, a private in the Corps, was confined on 30 October 1810. Onboard a transport, the *Royal Yeoman*, Maxey regularly refused his officers' orders and threatened to strike anyone who continued to bother him. According to a sergeant, Maxey threatened the captain on the quarterdeck, saying, "He would as soon knock down an Officer as a Soldier." The court-martial, assembled at Gorée, gave Maxey a sentence of 950 lashes. In the margin of the decision, James Chisholm, who served on the court that handed down the sentence, noted that the prisoner received 700 of the lashes.[149] Another soldier, named Michael Gallagher, was arrested for theft and died while imprisoned in a "place of confinement . . . so small and close" that he suffocated.[150]

For the officers of the Corps, keeping privates under discipline was one practical problem, and keeping them from dying of disease was another. The Corps' convict identity and terrible reputation also made its leaders nervous about missed promotions. The Vice-Admiralty Court offered a convenient solution to all three problems. "Captured Negroes" were presumed to be more tractable than white deserters, and more resistant to tropical fevers. Moreover, enlisting former slaves as soldiers pleased the abolitionists, and abetted the Vice-Admiralty Court. These perks were enticing enough, and black soldiers were at a premium in the British empire by the 1790s.

From 1795 to 1797, the West Indies service claimed to be in deficit by 50,000 troops.[151] Tens of thousands of soldiers had died of disease in the Caribbean, above all in the disastrous attempt to invade Saint-Domingue to stop the Haitian Revolution. Some white soldiers would mutiny rather than serve in the sugar islands. In September 1795, the 105th and 113th Regiments rioted in Cork when they were ordered to the Caribbean.[152] In nascent Haiti, black soldiers fought effectively on many different sides of the conflict, and seemed to be less susceptible to diseases like yellow fever. So, on 22 December 1794, Sir John Vaughan proposed to the Duke of Portland to create a thousand-man corps of "Blacks and Mulattoes" raised by grants and gifts from the West Indian colonies, and completed by enlisting free blacks with a bounty. In 1795, a unit from the Revolutionary War, the Black Carolina Corps, was merged with Malcolm's Rangers, recruited from Martinique into a new regiment which was soon renamed the 1st West India. Many of the soldiers in the 1st were freedmen, but the desire to recruit black troops, who were believed to be virtually essential for tropical warfare, soon outstripped the supply of free recruits.[153] Planters in the West Indies feared the influence of the enslaved soldiers on "their" people. In the late 1790s, for example, a council of planters on Saint Kitts demanded the withdrawal of the 4th West India Regiment after one enslaved soldier's drunken boasts triggered a wave of panic at the prospect of a mass conspiracy to surprise and massacre the planters.[154] However, the imperial Parliament was more concerned with protecting the West Indies from foreign conquest than with reassuring resident white planters and overseers, and what began as an expedient came to be seen as a necessity. Between 1795 and 1807, at least 19,000 slaves were purchased by the British government for military service, roughly 1 out of every 10 slaves purchased in the West Indies from 1795 to 1808.[155] In the historian Brian Dyde's reckoning, the British army bought more slaves than did any other single person or institution in the islands, and was willing to spend £70 or more for a single enslaved man—or more than £900,000 in total—even though a white recruit could be trained and outfitted for a fifth of the cost.[156] By 1798, 6,000 black soldiers had already been recruited and were on active duty in the Caribbean.[157]

The abolition of the slave trade threatened these practices. In 1806, the Horse Guards secretly ordered "2 to 4,000 slaves of the tribes from the Gold Coast . . . before the Act takes effect."[158] An officer in one of the West India Regiments reminded officials in Dominica in 1806 that "the Abolition of the Slave Trade will preclude the possibility of procuring suitable Negroes in this Country."[159] The Duke of York, Commander in Chief of the British Army, was especially anxious. "Since the abolition of the Slave Trade the West India Regiments have had no means of Recruiting their numbers," he wrote, "the longer the consideration of this important question is posted, the greater will be the danger." White soldiers were needed to fight the war in Europe, and, without a steady supply of soldiers of African descent, European troops "would in a great degree be frittered away in the supply of West India Garrisons."[160] Soon after the Slave Trade Act was passed, William Wilberforce proposed filling "our Black Reg'ts & perhaps raising new ones, in Africa."[161] In an another letter, to Castlereagh, he made a similar plea promising black soldiers from Sierra Leone "in almost any Number you can desire."[162]

The possibility of recruiting African soldiers directly from West Africa, rather than purchasing slaves in the West Indies, circulated even as the campaign to abolish the slave trade gained traction in Britain. Officers mooted plans to replace some of the slaves in the West India Regiments with African volunteers. Colonel Fraser wrote in 1800, "The Africans near Gorée, are in general stout, well-made men, accustomed to arms, and prefer a military life to labour of any kind. Recruits raised according to this plan, clothed and drilled in Africa and accustomed to the English language, would arrive in the West Indies as soldiers."[163] In 1808 James Willoughby Gordon, who had been instrumental in buying thousands of slaves to fill the ranks of the West India Regiment, was promoted to Colonel of the Royal African Corps by the Duke of York, thereby enabling him to benefit from abolition in much the same way he had benefited from the slave trade.[164] Being Colonel of a British regiment was a sweet sinecure. A Colonel had the right to sell uniforms to his soldiers, to take a cut out of victualing and other contracts, and to style himself as a military bravo. Edward Columbine guessed that with Gordon in charge, the ranks of the regiment would grow and grow, allowing Gordon to fill his pockets. "The sole object of all these enlistments," he wrote, "so injurious to the public service, is to raise a regiment for Col. Gordon" despite the Corps' reputation as "a set of villains who are ready to cut our throats at any favourable opportunity."[165] As Columbine predicted, the Royal African Corps soon increased to eight companies, of 100 rank and file each.[166]

After 1807, "captured Negroes" released from slavery by the Court were required to join the Corps if they happened to catch the eye of a recruiter. A. B. Ellis, historian of the 1st West India Regiment, described the scene in Freetown, as any fit-seeming captive man was sized up by noncommissioned officers, "given high-sounding names, such as Mark Antony, Scipio Africanus, etc. their own barbaric appellations being too unpronounceable, and then marched down in a body to the Cathedral to be baptized."[167] White soldiers remained highly vulnerable to the disease environment, and the supply of deserters and felons was insecure. Moreover, although a high rate of desertion guaranteed a regular stream of privates for the Royal African Corps, it didn't augur well for the British armed forces as a whole. African soldiers were considered to be more robust, less likely to rebel, and much easier to recruit—even if they arrived in the Corps without a word of English. The end of the slave trade increased the demand for black soldiers and changed their terms of service from voluntary enlistment to permanent service.[168] Linda Colley writes, "In some respects, white soldiers overseas shared levels of unfreedom with black slaves."[169] In the Royal African Corps, before abolition, white soldiers served for their natural lives alongside free blacks on limited service. After the end of the slave trade, former slaves recruited into the Corps served for life. By February 1810, among all 624 rank-and-file black and white soldiers in the Royal African Corps mustered that month, only 78 were enlisted for limited service.[170]

Despite their alleged imperviousness to disease, the black recruits were often ill. James Higgins described seeing more than 100 formerly enslaved soldiers suffering from skin ulcers when he arrived in the colony in 1810. The men had been penned in the former barracks that served as the forcing-house of the colonial Captured Negro Department, and "had been neglected with respect to medical treatment, and their habitation [was] extremely offensive.[171] Another surgeon remarked on "the great number of inveterate ulcers and chronic diseases which abound among the Captured Negroes, rendering the Colonial Hospital a Lazar House."[172] Another colonial medical man, Samuel Curry, estimated that 60 to 80 black soldiers were in hospital at any given time from 27 November 1810 to 9 May 1811.[173]

In addition to their vaunted "immunity" to disease, former slaves were valued as soldiers because they were imagined to be blank slates, and easy to train. The West India Regiments made a ritual of renaming each enslaved soldier, symbolically erasing his past. Army recruiters, in this sense, had a lot in common with colonial officials responsible for managing the lives of former slaves. For a "captured Negro," this might mean a second new name in a short time on shore. One officer remembered hanging brass tags around new soldiers' necks listing their new names, and hearing in roll call "men answer to the names of Gibraltar 1st, Gibraltar 2nd, London 1st, London 2nd, etc."[174] By July 1814, some 5,925 former slaves had been received in Sierra Leone, of whom 1,861—or more than 3 in 10—had been enlisted.[175]

The lives of the black soldiers in the Royal African Corps are even more obscure than the lives of white soldiers. Most of what we know about the regiment's white soldiers appears in disciplinary records. Analogous records for black soldiers, if they were ever kept, have disappeared, and black soldiers were punished without the formality of a court-martial. However, former slaves had a good reputation with their officers, especially in comparison with white convicts. That reputation might have been grounded in reality. Serving in the Corps was significantly more comfortable than the Middle Passage. Soldiers received pay and rations. They had a higher status than former slaves compelled to farm or work as domestic servants, and, at least among the local Temne, Mende, and Bullom people, farmwork was considered work for women and slaves. Free men palavered and fought in wars. Serving in the Corps was not the same as being a village warrior, but it was closer than farming. Moreover, black soldiers were permitted to build their huts in a prime location, on the high ground near the fort, providing some relief from the heat and the mosquitoes. The huts were also far more comfortable than the stuffy, stinking hell of the barracks, where white soldiers were quartered.[176] In the end, though, it is impossible to reconstruct how the "captured Negro" soldiers heard, understood, obeyed, or disobeyed their orders. E. P. Thompson made a plea for "more studies of the social attitudes of criminals, of soldiers and sailors," with an eye for "the tenacity of self-preservation."[177] At the very least, we can be sure that the soldiers, black and white, tried to survive in exceptionally difficult circumstances.

In Sierra Leone, thanks to the connections between the Clapham Sect and the Royal African Corps, crates of Bibles and devotional tracts were sent over from London to the soldiers, a common practice in other parts of the empire.[178] It is likely that these Good Books were put to good use. In Britain and the empire, paper from cheap books was used to stiffen boxes and trunks, to wrap up food, or for other purposes. For example, 3,000 copies of Saw's 1776 German Bible were used to wrap up cartridges. Paper was used for lighting fires in twists, or in "necessary houses."[179] Soldiers' books were especially disposable. Of the hundreds of thousands of copies of the *Soldier's Companion* (first published in 1803) known to have been printed, only a very few copies survive, mostly from the 35th and 65th editions.[180] For the convicts and former slaves of the godly Royal African Corps, perhaps the only benefit of the Corps' antislavery bona fides was a good supply of kindling and toilet paper.

The Court in Decline

When the Napoleonic wars ended, the Vice-Admiralty Court became less useful. In wartime, enemy ships could be seized and taken with little legal justification. When peace was restored in Europe, the seizure of slave ships became a provocation.[181] Anti-slave-trade laws needed a new legal footing. Moreover, Parliament began to scrutinize the money that had been made fighting the slave trade, and to rein in the corrupt, but productive, practices of prize courts across the empire. In July 1814, the House of Commons ordered up reports on the Sierra Leone Court's docket from 1 May 1807 until as far as returns were made, as well as a report on the number of "captured Negroes," and copies of all of the certificates claiming slave bounties.[182] Despite its promises to better regulate anti-slave-trade activity in Sierra Leone, the Royal Navy continued to seize ships, and the Court continued to award prizes. The lawyer Stephen Lushington complained, "There exists . . . at Sierra Leone a great misapprehension as to the state of the existing law upon the subject, and a lamentable ignorance of the principles that govern the rights of nations in amity with each other."[183] By 1821, Parliament had passed an Act that set up a slush fund for paying out the claims of slave-ship owners whose ships were taken after the end of the war, or who might have other claims on the Court.[184] The Vice-Admiralty Court continued to sit occasionally, mostly as a criminal court for offences committed at sea, but its jurisdiction over captured slave ships was effectively abolished.

In 1818, the first of several bilateral Courts of Mixed Commission was founded in Freetown to try to secure the cooperation of the other slave trading powers. In London, in part because of the wealth he had earned during the war, Zachary Macaulay's philanthropic causes were proliferating. He described his more and more wide-ranging interests in a letter to his son, the famous historian and jurist Thomas Babington Macaulay. "No sooner was Africa disposed of," Macaulay the elder wrote, "than Asia called for our exertions."[185] The interests of the antislavery lobby had grown far beyond West Africa, and Zachary Macaulay was keen to promote missionary work to India. Indeed, by the early 1820s, Macaulay & Babington had moved a great deal of its business on to India, although evidence of its work there is scarce.[186] In 1823, Macaulay retired from business to become a full-time philanthropist. He turned over day-to-day business to his junior partner, T. G. Babington, who took only three years to run the business into the ground, forcing Macaulay to return to work and sort out the firm's affairs.[187] In 1829, the partnership was dissolved, although, Macaulay admitted, "with a fair prospect of gradually recovering from abroad the means of satisfying [our] more indulgent creditors."[188] In Sierra Leone, the firm gave up its retail store, leaving a ruined foundation and an empty lot full of rusting ironmongery.[189] For a long time after 1827, no English firms with London offices opened branches in Freetown, preferring to offer goods on credit to European traders on their way to Africa, in exchange for a commission on sales.[190]

During the Napoleonic wars, the campaign to end the British slave trade relied on the union of commerce and military force built on a foundation laid down during the last years of Company rule in Sierra Leone. The Vice-Admiralty Court was the centre of the antislavery economy in Freetown, and provided a set of tools for turning captives into "captured Negroes," and "captured Negroes" into soldiers or labourers. The Court was especially useful as a tool for filling the ranks of the growing Royal African Corps. The

Court was also a nexus in which the "friends of Africa" in London, through Zachary Macaulay, built up relationships with military officers. The Court made it possible for the African Institution to influence the governance of Sierra Leone after the transfer of the colony to Crown government, and to experiment with the possibilities offered by the Slave Trade Act for the "civilization" of West Africa. They resolved "to adopt such measures as are best calculated to promote their civilization and happiness." These measures would be coercive. "Indolence," the Institution insisted, "is a disease which it is the business of civilization to cure."[191]

4. The Absolute Disposal of the Crown

When the well-fed and well-disciplined black soldiers and sergeants and white officers of the West India Regiments appeared in the streets of Freetown and in the yard of the Captured Negro Department, they wore matching scarlet and blue uniforms, and spoke mostly in English (fig. 8). The recruiting party carried new firearms and polished sabres. They brought musical instruments: cymbals, clarinets, oboes, tambourines, drums, trumpets, French horns, bugles, and triangles. They performed unfamiliar martial songs and gave out food and liquor.[1] The sergeants flourished yards of cloth to be made into new uniforms for anyone who joined, and displayed crates of new white and checked shirts and huge rolls of canvas for trousers. Volunteers were given an £8 bounty, along with new kit: a tin dish, a mirror, a pocketknife, a mug, beads, coral, and a snuffbox, "with a painted portrait of a Black Soldier under arms."[2] The comfortable army life put on display by the recruiting party was an illusion, a far cry from the real material conditions of service in the West India Regiments. But no one had ever before tried to offer "captured Negroes" the *choice* to join the armed forces. Compared with the malarial, paranoid martinets, poorly equipped former captives, and despondent white drunks of the Royal African Corps, the West India Regiments must have been immediately appealing.

As the previous chapter showed, a mechanism to enlist former slaves as soldiers was built into the operation of the Vice-Admiralty Court, and the Royal African Corps depended on the Court for nearly all of its recruiting after 1808. The West India Regiments, however, had a much more distinguished history than the Corps. The Regiments had first been raised to fight in the

Figure 8. Shoulder belt plate, 1st West India Regiment, ca. 1800. The West India Regiments were considered essential to the security of the British Caribbean. Until 1807, rank-and-file soldiers in the Regiments were enslaved, and were recruited by purchase. (Courtesy of the Council of the National Army Museum, London)

sugar islands. They fought the French, the rebel armies of Saint-Domingue, and the restive plantation slaves hoping to hack open, crush, bleed, and boil their masters like sugarcane. Private soldiers in the Regiments were slaves, but they enjoyed far more autonomy than those enslaved on plantations. The Regiments had recruited by the mass purchase of slaves before 1808, but their officers were pragmatic. They wanted the best soldiers, regardless of how they were enlisted. In the age of the slave trade, officers could select likely warriors; in the age of abolition, the officers hoped that likely warriors would choose to join up. When the West India Regiments' recruiting sergeants arrived in Sierra Leone, they hoped to attract volunteers from among the "captured Negroes," the apprentices in Freetown, and local villagers living outside the colony. If "captured Negroes" weren't enslaved, the officers reasoned, they ought to be able to choose to serve. New recruits for the West India Regiments would be free in the same way white recruits were free: free to enlist, but not free to be discharged. However, when the recruiting party arrived, Charles Maxwell, Lieutenant-Colonel of the Royal African Corps and Governor of Sierra Leone, was furious. In his view the Slave Trade Act meant that former slaves were not free to choose whether to enlist, not free to imagine themselves as the picturesque soldier on a new snuffbox. They belonged to him.

The judicial mechanisms put in place in Sierra Leone to manage the abolition of the slave trade gave the Governors of Sierra Leone control over the "disposal" of former slaves. Thomas Ludlam, in 1808, opted for apprentice-ship. T. P. Thompson imagined an army of loyal pioneer-soldiers, although he lacked the resources or the wherewithal to do much more than imagine. After Thompson, Columbine looked for expedients, and aimed to shove former slaves out of sight and off government rations by whatever means. Charles Maxwell, a career soldier, imagined former slaves in uniform or, if not in uniform, then under military discipline. The Vice-Admiralty Court was indifferent to the people released from the slave trade by its decisions. The Court united the commercial and military aspects of the antislavery program, and gave London activists a platform to build and strengthen ties with both the colonial government and the armed forces. Consequently, Charles Maxwell was free to imagine ways that he might turn not only prize money but also "captured Negroes" to his advantage. In the eighteenth and nineteenth centuries, many British-controlled regiments and armies re-cruited from among local, "native" people relied on elaborate, trumped-up "ethnic" categories.[3] Maxwell had little interest in finding the martial races among the "captured Negroes." In his view, he could use antislavery laws to make the "captured Negroes" into a martial race—or anything else he chose.

The action in this chapter pivots on a series of squabbles between mili-tary officers, and tracks Charles Maxwell's growing ambition as he discovered and explored the limits of the power he had inherited from his mandate to en-force the Slave Trade Act. Maxwell is at the centre of the archive, and so the records of his time in office place him and his preoccupations and prejudices in the foreground. But remember: Maxwell's experiments and adventures oc-curred against a backdrop of oppression and violence. The most important records of Charles Maxwell's campaign against the slave trade were written on the bodies of the people on whose behalf he claimed to fight, the "captured Negroes" released from the slave trade by the Court of Vice-Admiralty in Freetown. The soldiers who fought or fled under Maxwell's command died and decomposed, leaving few traces in the paper archives of Government House, beyond head counts and occasional muster lists. We can, however, be confident that life in Sierra Leone in the late days of Britain's long war with Napoleonic France had a distinctly martial flavour. Above all, Charles Maxwell put antislavery on a war footing. He did not declare war against slav-ery; rather, he used the tools provided to him by antislavery laws to go to war. He competed with Edward Columbine and the Royal Navy for control of the West African coast, and in the process made the Royal African Corps even

more important to the day-to-day life of Sierra Leone. He aggressively recruited "captured Negroes" for the Corps, and used his expanded regiment to
suppress the independence of the settlers. He undermined, arrested, and de-
ported the commanding officer of the West India Regiment recruiting party,
took over the recruiting drive himself, and used the regiments to rid Sierra
Leone of "captured Negroes" he felt might be a burden to the colony, sending them across the Atlantic to lifetime service in the Caribbean. He deployed
the Royal African Corps in an extended military campaign against local kings,
making a bid for Sierra Leone's supremacy on the Upper Guinea Coast. The
vague logic and military incentives written into the 1807 Slave Trade Act and
embodied in the Vice-Admiralty Court became, in Maxwell's hands, the charter for an aggressive, expansionist British empire in Africa.

In 1807 Zachary Macaulay had dreamed of military "consuls" in charge
of "every fort and station, from the Gambia to Angola."[4] At the time,
Macaulay thought the "consuls" would be Royal Navy officers. Charles Maxwell proved that the Royal African Corps, despite its bad reputation, could be
a reliable source of officials. Maxwell showed the abolitionists how the Corps
might connect Britain's coastal outposts in a thin but durable network of
goods, ideas, and personnel. In a process familiar to students of British imperial history, military adventuring called the tune for official territorial expansion.[5] Linda Colley comments, "Imperial Britain was always overstretched.
The thin red line was more accurately anorexic."[6] Anorexia may not be the
right metaphor. Anorexia is the clinical loss or absence of appetite, but the
military officers at the edges of the British empire were insatiably hungry.
The thin red line was gluttonous but emaciated, always eating but never satisfied. In Sierra Leone, turning over the day-to-day work of abolition to military officers expanded Britain's footprint in West Africa.

Edward Columbine, Company Man

In December 1808, Captain Edward Columbine, a distinguished officer and
hydrographer, a subscriber to the African Institution and a friend of William
Wilberforce, was appointed to replace Thomas Perronet Thompson as
Governor of Sierra Leone. Columbine was given command of the 32-gun
H.M.S. *Solebay* and ordered to lead a convoy to West Africa. Columbine
accepted the new post on the condition that he retain command of the *Solebay*
while serving as Governor.[7] Columbine hoped to profit from his position by

cruising the West African coast in his new ship. He understood what Thompson could not or would not: that serving a term in Sierra Leone meant winning favour with a powerful and wealthy clique of antislavery businessmen and politicians. As he reminded himself in his memo-book, "although the Sierra Leone Company had been divested by Law, of the right to direct the colony," the British government was "very liberally disposed to attend to the requests & suggestions of the leading members of that company in all such matters as relate to the welfare of Africa."[8]

On 21 June 1809, the *Solebay* anchored off the coast of Senegal, at Gorée. Columbine stopped for fuel, water, and victuals, and met the Commandant of the island, Major (soon to be Lieutenant-Colonel) Charles Maxwell. Columbine and Maxwell discussed the weakness of the French force on the mainland, at Fort-Louis, Senegal: their lack of provisions, the ill-trained troops of the garrison, and the incompetence of their leaders. Columbine wrote that "A very general desire prevailed here to take Senegal."[9] H.M.S. *Derwent* joined them from Sierra Leone, and on Friday, 8 July, 120 Royal Navy sailors, 160 soldiers of the Royal African Corps, and 50 Royal Marines attacked.[10] The element of surprise was on the British side, and on 20 July 1809 Columbine reported to the Admiralty that he and Maxwell had successfully claimed Senegal for Britain, although the *Solebay* ran a reef and sank in the course of the battle. "I determined," Columbine wrote, "not to let slip the possible chance of expelling the French from Africa, and of annexing another of their Colonies to the British Empire."[11]

After this triumph, Columbine returned to England to face the formality of a court-martial for losing his ship. He was quickly acquitted and returned to Sierra Leone in February 1810 as captain of a second ship, H.M.S. *Crocodile*. Columbine had been ordered to enforce financial austerity in the colony. Thompson had spent £59,000 since his arrival, far more than the British government would tolerate.[12] At his swearing-in, held in the colonial chapel on 12 February 1810, Columbine warned the colonists that "a very considerable reduction of the contingencies & of the number of people employed on public works [would] be the principal object" of his government.[13] Thompson had spent nearly £60,000 in less than two years. Columbine had been granted £17,360 for the colony's annual expenses, a sum inflated by a one-time grant of £5,000 to pay for a survey of the coast, and another single grant of £1,200 to pay the legal fees incurred in writing up a new colonial charter.[14] Columbine wrote glumly to a friend that his orders "brought upon me a tolerable share of odium and opposition."[15] However, he wagered that the anger of Freetonians would be balanced out by the good opinion of the Clapham Sect. He wrote privately to Zachary Macaulay that "all the money which Thompson spent here, has not bettered the condition of the inhabitants, who are, and I think always will be, miserably poor, owing to their unconquerable indolence, and improvident dispositions."[16] In conversation with Paul Cuffe, he complained about the slave trade and the settlers.[17] However, unlike Thompson, Columbine kept his opinions on the progress of the colony out of print. He would keep quiet, undo as many of Thompson's manic reforms as he could, and capture as many slave ships as possible to fill his pockets with prize money.

As Columbine prepared his campaign against the slave trade, the rules governing prize money were changing and expanding to include Army officers. Looting conquered camps and settlements was as essential to the pay of British soldiers as the (slightly) more regulated system of prize money was to British sailors.[18] Consequently, regiments needed to be perpetually on the march to be profitable. In 1809, the Duke of York introduced new rules requiring that the Army and Royal Navy share equally in the proceeds of amphibious assaults, and that the Army's portion of prizes be "divided among the army alone," carefully divided out from the Royal Navy's share.[19] In the African Institution's fifth annual report, published in 1811, Army officers were invited to join the Royal Navy in taking a share of the "pecuniary advantages" of abolition.[20]

For his part, Columbine was eager to govern Sierra Leone from the quarterdeck of the *Crocodile*. He feared that coastal traders were destroying his correspondence. He lay awake in his cockroach- and termite-infested room, "so wretchedly small that when we shut the windows to keep out the rain we are stewed alive," fantasizing about the open ocean.[21] Thomas Ludlam, the former Governor, died from a fever in 1810 while surveying the coast north of the colony. Columbine saw an opportunity. Since he had been appointed to the same surveying commission as Ludlam, he declared that he would fill Ludlam's post, and cruise as far south as the Gold Coast, "to complete what has been left defective."[22] Before he could set out to sea, Columbine fell ill. He was feverish, and seized by vomiting and diarrhea so uncontrollable that only ether-induced unconsciousness gave him any relief.[23] Columbine, unlike most colonial officials, had brought his wife, Anne, and his young daughter, Charlotte, with him to Freetown. When he was finally well enough to stand, Columbine learned that Anne and Charlotte had died. He mourned "the wreck of my family" as he put the *Crocodile* to sea.[24] Despite Columbine's hollowing by illness and grief, the *Crocodile* captured at least 12 slave ships in 1810 and 1811.[25]

Charles Maxwell, Columbine's partner in the taking of Senegal for Britain, perhaps urged on by the enthusiasm of the abolitionists and encouraged by the success of the Vice-Admiralty Court, began to eye taking a share of the slave ships sailing near Senegal and Gorée for himself. Like Columbine in Sierra Leone, Maxwell was eager to extract what he could from his new post as Governor of Senegal. One of his first acts after receiving the appointment had been to formulate ad hoc commercial policies for Senegal, promptly rejected by the Board of Trade, including opening the port of Saint-Louis to non-British ships, and eliminating duties on foreign imports and all exports.[26] For an entrepreneurial colonial official, prize money was a more secure source of income. In August 1810, Maxwell fitted and sent out a schooner on Senegal's behalf to search for slave ships.[27] The colonial schooner was lucky. By 15 December 1810, on Maxwell's account, eight vessels had been captured and condemned in the Vice-Admiralty Court at Sierra Leone.[28] Columbine and Maxwell were bound to come to loggerheads. Columbine believed he had been promised exclusive access to slave ships off Sierra Leone, and Maxwell refused to give up on his own claims.

During the wars with France, prime sailors were in high demand everywhere; by 1807, the Royal Navy needed 12,000 new sailors every year to maintain its strength.[29] When he left Senegal in 1809, Columbine left behind some of the crew of the *Solebay*. When he returned, Columbine ordered them to report to his new ship.[30] Maxwell countermanded the order and assigned the sailors, along with a group of soldiers from the Royal African Corps, to act as the crew of the new Senegal Colonial Schooner, *George*. He put the ship under the command of Lieutenant Charles Moore. Columbine was livid. Moore, he wrote, "was never at sea, except taking the passage to Africa."[31] Moore and the *George* may have had beginner's luck on their side. On its very first cruise, the *George* surprised five slave ships at anchor near a fort on the Gambia River. Much to Columbine's fury, Moore put small crews onboard each of the ships and sent them to Freetown to be adjudicated and condemned.[32] Soon the *George* began regularly to sweep the mouth of the river, which, from Columbine's perspective, was a particularly desirable slice of the coast.

The tension between Maxwell and Columbine did not lead to ever-bolder adventures in pursuit of slave ships, but rather to backbiting over a small but convenient portion of the coast. The authors of the Slave Trade Act counted on a simple market heuristic to put their new law into action: the more prize money, the fewer slave ships at sea. However, the law did not account for the tendency of military officers looking for easy money to take the path of least resistance. There were strong incentives to compete for the relatively small number of slave ships near Sierra Leone, rather than cruise further afield. By 1810, most slave ships sailed far from the colony, near the equatorial bights of Benin and Biafra. The voyage south was easy, but sailing back was long and technically challenging, was pitched against prevailing winds, and could be nearly as gruelling for captives as the Middle Passage.[33] Consequently, the cruising ground nearest Sierra Leone became a prized "fishery," with a finite number of prizes. The right to cruise the Gambia River was especially desired. The river, relatively close to Freetown, was also nominally British territory, ceded to Britain under the terms of the 1783 Peace of Paris. Columbine complained to Moore that cruising rights there belonged exclusively to Sierra Leone. He wrote that having Moore's ship in Sierra Leone's "neighbourhood" "would derange my plans . . . it could not be consistent that the Government schooner of a distant settlement should fix upon this place as her cruising ground."[34]

Soon after the *George* returned from its first cruise, Columbine received a letter from some of the sailors from the *Derwent*, pleading to return to their old ship, "for we don't wish to stay on board of the Schooner George any longer."[35] In response, Columbine challenged Moore on his legal right to cruise out of Sierra Leone, and on the legality of his commission to command a British vessel. "You act upon the coast near my Government," he wrote, "as if the whole range of it were under the control of Senegal—and that the naval authority on the Coast was in the hands of your Commanding Officer, and not in mine."[36] Moore replied that the sailors were "employed on a particular and very important service" under the orders of "Lieut. Col. Maxwell—Lt. Gov. of Senegal, Gorée, &c.—and Commander of His Majesty's Troops on the Western Coast of Africa."[37] On 9 August 1810, Moore made a cheeky offer to carry letters to Gorée for Columbine. Columbine retaliated by attempting to press all of the sailors out of the *George* and keep her in port, and on 10 August Moore agreed to leave Freetown and to release the Royal Navy sailors from his crew.[38]

The Corps struck back against Columbine in their own "home waters." The *Dart*, a cutter with a privateering license (sometimes called a "letter of marque"), signed by Columbine, which entitled it independently to pursue slave ships, was seized by the Corps off Gorée. Columbine complained, "They also set up a pretension that the *Dart* should not board any vessel in the road, nor even off the island! Their pretensions are the most unjustifiable that can be imagined."[39] In addition to cutting off Sierra Leone ships from capturing prizes off Senegal, the Corps tried to interrupt communication between Columbine and his correspondents in Britain. Captain Frederick Forbes of the Corps boarded a packet boat carrying letters from England that stopped at Senegal on its way to Sierra Leone, and opened dispatches addressed to Columbine. "It contained nothing but the articles of war—but this is nothing to the purpose," Columbine wrote, "It is plain that my chance of hearing from England, except by a man of war, is most precarious."[40] Columbine was also threatened in Freetown itself: the garrison were housed in barracks only yards from Government House. Forbes insisted to Columbine that Maxwell commanded the Sierra Leone Garrison, and not Columbine. "This," Columbine replied, "*I* will never concede."[41]

The competition between the two officers increased the overall number of slave ships captured in Sierra Leone, which also increased the number of "captured Negroes" processed by the Vice-Admiralty Court. Governor Thompson had grand plans for former slaves, but Governor Columbine wasn't sure what to do with them. In 1810–11, Sierra Leone absorbed 594 captives, all of whom needed to be "disposed of," in the nasty euphemism of the Slave Trade Act.[42] Columbine sent some formerly enslaved people inland to found new villages, particularly near the new school on Leicester Mountain, above Freetown, founded by the Church Missionary Society. In 1811, when Paul Cuffe was in the colony to plan for the emigration of a group of African American families to Freetown, he became friendly with Columbine, and noted that the census taken by the Governor did not even include soldiers or any of the former slaves sent outside Freetown to "the Subburbs Without the pale."[43] Indeed, Columbine's census took careful count of the 1,917 Freetonians, but not of the nearly 1,000 people who had already been emancipated under the 1807 Act but who lived outside the capital.[44] Cuffe, curious, rode into the mountains early in 1812 with two settlers and was surprised to find that one of the country lots originally deeded to the Nova Scotians was now a small village occupied by the "the Jolon Native Captivs about 12 or 15."[45]

For the most part, people freed from the slave trade in Columbine's time were simply given rations and perhaps some tools or seeds, and then were left to organize themselves.[46] In Freetown, Columbine commandeered one of the few structures large enough to serve as a temporary shelter for "captured Negroes" in transit, the lower storeroom of a warehouse at Falconbridge Point used by the Royal African Corps, and ordered the Corps to provide guards.[47] Forbes asserted that Columbine had no right to command his troops, or to use military buildings for civilian purposes. Columbine reminded him "that it is an old wooden building in very bad repair belonging to the *civil* government—my *right* to use it is therefore unquestionable."[48]

The Royal African Corps, as the previous chapter showed, was always keen to absorb able-bodied new recruits from among the "captured Negroes." In fact, Forbes had been one of the first officers in the Royal African Corps to propose recruiting among former slaves to Thomas Ludlam.[49] Maxwell, as Governor of Senegal in 1810, supported forming new companies of the Corps composed exclusively of "negroes adjudged to His Majesty by the Vice-Admiralty Court at Sierra Leone.[50] But the Corps was not required to enlist "captured Negroes."[51] And so, when Forbes refused the offer to recruit the former slaves into the Corps, they remained in Sierra Leone, a burden on an overstretched Governor Columbine. Columbine complained that although 40 men had been enlisted, the *George* would only take 6 on board, and Forbes refused to take any, leaving 34 captives with nowhere to go.[52] Of another group of recently freed people, Forbes took only 38 out of 128.[53] When Forbes was ordered back to Senegal, and replaced by Captain Maling in May 1810, Maling arrived with orders from Maxwell to continue to refuse to enlist former slaves as soldiers.[54] If the "captured Negroes" remained in the warehouse at Falconbridge Point, they would continue to distract Columbine.

To further harass Columbine, Maxwell moved mutinous white soldiers from Senegal to Freetown. In September 1810 a group of white recruits arrived at Senegal, fresh from convictions for desertion in other regiments. The soldiers plotted to kill their officers, commandeer a ship, and escape to America. A snitch in the regiment turned in the ringleaders, who were tried and shot.[55] In November, the mutiny spread to Gorée, and two more soldiers were executed.[56] James Chisholm (who became the Commandant of Gorée after Maxwell was promoted) wrote to his boss, "If it is possible to get rid of them without taking any more . . . it would be in my humble opinion more desirable."[57] Maxwell tried to turn the mutiny to his advantage by sending some of the mutineers to Freetown. Sierra Leone, he explained, was the only place that could absorb the convicts, "as that colony is strictly British, and has a considerable body of Militia, as the soldiers already there are regular, steady, and well-behaved; and as there were three Ships of War upon that part of the Coast."[58] At the same time, sending the mutineers to Sierra Leone would threaten Columbine and force him to remain in the colony in case of a riot or disturbance, and prevent him personally from going to sea.

Soon the mutineers clanked onto a transport in irons, under a 12-man guard. The ship stopped in at Gorée on its way to Sierra Leone to pick up, according to Columbine, "the very fellow who . . . was to have murdered Chisholm."[59] Columbine was bedridden at the time, prostrated by the fever that would soon kill his wife and daughter. Lieutenant Christie of the Royal African Corps told Columbine's secretary that the soldiers on the transport were "fine strong healthy young men . . . Their being handcuffed," Columbine seethed, "was not mentioned!"[60] The next day, the assistant surgeon of the garrison in Sierra Leone ("as stupid a blockhead as you could see," according to Columbine) wrote to inform the Governor that 10 of the soldiers aboard (presumably the mutineers) were ill, and needed to be brought ashore. In exchange, the surgeon proposed that 10 men from the Sierra Leone garrison be sent to Gorée. Columbine detected the ruse, and ordered the transport back to sea on 8 October.[61] Columbine, livid, informed Maxwell and Chisholm that if the Corps' detachment were withdrawn, he would not allow it to be replaced.[62]

In Sierra Leone, a European with a stout constitution was as likely as not to bury an enemy or two every rainy season. Columbine left Sierra Leone on the *Crocodile* in May 1811, worried for his health. He died a few weeks later at sea. Maxwell became Governor of Sierra Leone. Maxwell's appointment brought the Royal African Corps fully into its own, connecting it to London and to the Vice-Admiralty Court. Soldiers, not sailors, would govern Sierra Leone for decades to come. It was an unlikely marriage between upright Londoners and the officers of regiment whose European rank and file were described as "the men with whose presence . . . Sierra Leone has been afflicted."[63] But, from the perspective of the elite antislavery lobby, the Corps was valuable. Its officers were hungry for prizes, even to the point of foul play, which might hasten abolition. At the same time, the transfer of troops between the various stations of the Royal African Corps created a rough coastal integration of officers, men, and materiel. The officers of the Corps were arrayed in a comprehensible command structure, with a clear leader and regular communications. The Royal Navy could provide that as well, but its connections in West Africa were diffuse, whereas the Royal African Corps manned a dense cluster of outposts. When Columbine wanted to protect his letters from perlustration, he had to hope they would be carried in a warship. The Royal Navy was expert at long-range logistics, but the Royal African Corps was more nimble and more rooted in West Africa.

More importantly, there was an established place for former slaves in the Royal African Corps, unlike the Royal Navy. The Royal Navy had a strong preference for skilled workers; press-gangs roamed ports looking for sailors to capture, not landsmen.[64] There were many black seamen in the Royal Navy, but there was little demand for "captured Negroes" without nautical skills. The Royal African Corps always needed recruits, and seemed to offer a clearer pathway to the "civilization" of former slaves. In August 1811, Zachary Macaulay noted that with an estimated 80,000 people making the Middle Passage each year, "a very large number of slave ships might very soon be brought in for adjudication" in Freetown.[65] He proposed that the West India Regiments (once composed of enslaved soldiers) become the British imperial army in West Africa, and an engine for the civilizing mission. The Royal African Corps beat the West India Regiments to the mark as the means of marshalling the labour of former slaves, forming them into an imperial military force, zealous to enforce the abolition of the slave trade.

Charles Maxwell's Abolition

Maxwell arrived in Sierra Leone on board H.M.S. *Thais* on 29 June 1811, and was sworn in as Governor on 1 July. He wrote that Columbine had departed in May without leaving any instructions, and that none of the settlers or European staff knew much about the government of the colony, since so few residents "possessed [Columbine's] confidence."[66] Columbine also took most of his papers with him. Maxwell took advantage of the vacuum, filling colonial posts with loyalists from Senegal. Maxwell had a vision of a more permanent Freetown. He proposed to replace "perishable damp wooden huts" in Freetown with sturdy stone buildings. Temporary huts, he insisted, had "impressed the Inhabitants with doubts as to the intention of Government to return possession of the Settlement."[67] To ensure security in the colony, he proposed to embody another Company of the Royal African

Corps composed exclusively of "captured Negroes," to "afford the means of saving the European Soldier, and curtailing the expense of the police."[68]

Where Columbine had his eyes on the sea, Maxwell used his regiment to enforce his will in the colony. First, he bent communications on the coast toward himself. He demanded that the British packet boat the *Tweed*, and all men-of-war, touch at Sierra Leone no matter their errand on the coast.[69] Second, he vied with Robert Thorpe, the Chief Justice of the colony and Judge of the Vice-Admiralty Court, for control over judicial appointments. Before he left Sierra Leone on medical leave, Thorpe conceded to Maxwell, and wrote out a blank commission, allowing Maxwell to appoint anyone he liked as deputy judge in the Vice-Admiralty Court.[70] Under Columbine, the Royal Navy and the Royal African Corps had been in conflict. Once a soldier was in Government House, however, the advantages of sailing without the responsibilities of government became clearer to naval officers. The African Institution praised the new solidarity and coordinated action among the two branches of the service, a "perfect union of sentiment" between Maxwell, Thorpe, and the leading Royal Navy officers on the coast.[71]

Maxwell also imagined other, more sophisticated ways to "dispose" of former slaves. By the 1810s demand in Freetown for apprentices was low.[72] There were too many new people arriving in Sierra Leone to be apprenticed, and too few "respectable" settlers to hold new indentures. Maxwell argued that instead of being assigned to individual settlers, the " 'captured Negroes" belonged to the colony. He believed that the stability of Sierra Leone depended on the creation of "a regular body of Labourers belonging to the colony who have no other country."[73] Many were sent to pioneer villages outside of Freetown. Maxwell divided these groups roughly by their native language, but not with any particular diligence—the important thing was that former slaves went where they were told to go. Most worked building roads and buildings for the colonial government, both in Freetown and in their own villages.[74]

Maxwell also tried his hand at running a plantation on the site of Zachary Macaulay's old farm. The land near his plantation, he argued, had already been cleared, and so it "afforded, it was judged, the best spot" for a new village.[75] Maxwell paid adults from the village wages to work on his plantation. However, "a number of boys [also] resided in the farms," who were not paid, but rather "were attended by one of the Native Soldiers of the Royal African Corps, for the purpose of keeping them together till a proper establishment could be provided for them."[76] Maxwell did not use freed slaves exclusively as military labour, and he did not compel adult former slaves to work without wages. However, Maxwell's control over where former slaves were assigned to live, and his use of Royal African Corps soldiers to police the colony and the labour of boys and girls on his farm, suggest that although the labour of former slaves was not exclusively military, it was significantly militarized. Farmworkers were deployed to strategic locations; children were placed under officers.

Maxwell also asserted his claim over former slaves by pursuing and capturing runaways. When several "'captured Negroes" fled Freetown to Bompetuk, a village near the Plantain Islands south of the colony, Kenneth Macaulay, acting on Maxwell's orders, demanded that George Stephen Caulker, chief of the Islands, return them to Freetown immediately. "Should you not choose to make these proper concessions (but which he has no doubt you will readily do)," Macaulay wrote, "[the Governor] will be under the unpleasant necessity of appealing to force, and you will be answerable for whatever consequences may happen."[77] Caulker was stunned. He promised to comply, but was dismayed by Maxwell's attitude. "We have never made a contrary motion," he wrote, and "we do not deserve such a threatening letter for so trivial a cause."[78] A Quaker missionary who visited the colony commented that former slaves "at times watch favourable opportunities and run away," and approved of the Corps' efforts to recapture them.[79] Maxwell, unlike Columbine, intended to control the labour of former slaves.

The growing Royal African Corps allowed Maxwell to intimidate and marginalize the Nova Scotians and Maroons. Accustomed to military discipline, Maxwell demanded that the settlers place themselves at his orders. In 1812, he issued a new Militia Act, which required an oath of allegiance and, if called upon, military service from every man in the colony which, unprecedentedly for the militia, might include service outside the colony. The Nova Scotians resented being conscripted. The settler Eli Akin remembered that Maxwell issued "a Proclamation in such like bounding terms that we all conceived ourselves to be entering into a state of bondage. We was," Akin continued, "British subjects eighteen or twenty years before we came here." The settlers refused to comply with Maxwell's orders, just as they had Thompson's Militia Act. Maxwell simply used his soldiers to seize the farms of anyone who disobeyed him.[80] The Maroons objected for a different reason. Their leaders wrote that they were willing to fight for the colony, but only under their own traditions of discipline. They also feared being conscripted as marines onboard colonial ships. "We cannot be learnt how to fight by Sea," their leaders protested, "nor be disciplined no other way to fight by land."[81] Maxwell would not bend to what he took to be "the most unqualified sentiments of insubordination," guided by faith in "those barbarous customs, and usages, which they practiced in the fastnesses of Jamaica." Maxwell boasted that he already commanded "a sufficient force of the captured Negroes, completely organized, to overawe, and repress them."[82] Maxwell cursed the institutions of settler self-government that survived in Freetown, as the remains of the "ill-judged efforts of Mr. Granville Sharpe, in his attempts to establish Saxon institutions among men incapable of appreciating their worth." The Maroons who objected to the Militia Act were sent into exile on the Bullom Shore, across the wide mouth of the Sierra Leone River from Freetown.[83]

In 1814, while Maxwell was in England on leave, Major Maling of the Royal African Corps served as interim Governor. In Freetown, raising the alarm of "native" attack had long been a form of political protest. Under Thompson, for example, the Nova Scotians had raised rumours of Temne attack to disrupt his government. When Maling assumed the governorship, another rumour of attack began to circulate. Maxwell understood that, generally speaking, a rumour of "native" attack was likely to be a ruse. "If I had attended to each report," he wrote to reassure Bathurst, "which the European and Native inhabitants of the colony brought to me, of attacks and poisonings . . . the colony would have been in a constant state of alarm."[84] In 1814, the settlers' usual warnings of invasions were compounded with a claim "that the Captured Negroes and native Soldiers would join in the attack on the colony." Maxwell was dismissive. "The truth is," he wrote, "the Captured Negroes are becoming the most useful and creditable part of the population; of their respectability and prosperity the old vile scum are viciously jealous."[85]

On 17 December 1814 many of the "old vile scum" attended a town meeting, and signed a petition demanding that the Nova Scotians, Maroons, and "English European Settlers" be immediately armed against the natives of the Rokele River and the Sherbro' who, the petition claimed, planned to overrun the colony on Christmas Day. The petitioners demanded that the "captured Negro" troops be disarmed at nightfall and locked in their barracks overnight.[86] The protestors led a procession through Freetown, firing muskets and beating drums. Maxwell was pleased to learn how Maling responded. Maling had a notice put up around Freetown, proclaiming that the petition was an illegal gathering, and that the procession after the meeting was "was nothing less than what is defined Riot, by the Law of England."[87] The old settlers, faced with the reality that they were now outnumbered by people released by the slave-trade Court, backed down.

The West India Regiments

The end of the British slave trade did not end the demand for African soldiers to fight in the West Indies. The West India Regiments remained desperate for recruits, with a strong preference for "saltwater" soldiers who had never worked on a sugar plantation. A regimental folklore about the martial capacities of different West African ethnic groups—invented, more or less, by the officers themselves—had settled into place. The officers wanted to exercise without interference what they took to be their superior discernment of the relative strengths and weaknesses of "Eebo" or "Coromantee" soldiers (who may not have been Igbo or Akan at all). "Saltwater slaves" were also judged to be more loyal than enslaved people from the plantations. Third, and perhaps most important, West Indian planters were anxious and resentful at the idea of *any* enslaved people carrying arms. Most planters were willing to accept that the West India Regiments were a necessary evil, but they were not willing to see any of the black people they claimed they owned dressed in red coats, with bayonets leveled at their well-fed white bodies.[88]

The antislavery interest in London was well aware of both the desire of the regiments for soldiers and the distrust of the planters toward the regiments. As early as 1807, Wilberforce had invited the West India Regiments to establish a recruiting depot in or near Sierra Leone, in order to recruit from among the "captured Negroes." However, Thomas Perronet Thompson refused to allow the plan to move forward while he was in office.[89] After Thompson was recalled, the idea gained new impetus. For the officers and abolitionists in London, a Sierra Leone recruiting station seemed mutually beneficial—a source of recruits and a way to reinforce the relationship between antislavery and the military. In Sierra Leone, Charles Maxwell had a different idea. Maxwell agreed with the general principles of the antislavery laws, but he intended to use them to serve his own interests first. Maxwell seems to have conceived of the Royal African Corps as his personal colonial army, which served him as Governor. Although he was theoretically duty-bound to obey superior Army officers, he began to defy orders sent from

Horse Guards, the Palladian pile in London that served as the British Army's headquarters. Maxwell planned to reserve the best recruits for his Corps, and to use the West India Regiments as a reservoir for more "raw" former slaves. Africans, he reasoned, never saw anyone return from the Middle Passage, except for the sick, exhausted, and disoriented captives released in Freetown. If "captured Negro" soldiers from the West India Regiments eventually came back to Sierra Leone, they would "remove those unfavourable impressions, too justly made on the minds of the natives, during the slave trade."[90] As well as fighting France in the West Indies, Maxwell insisted, black soldiers could expand the British empire in Africa.

Maxwell's plans were not communicated to London while the recruiting depot was being planned. In September 1811 William Wilberforce met with Major R. J. Wingfield, who had been appointed to lead the recruiters, and introduced him to Lord Liverpool.[91] Initially, Wingfield imagined that the recruiting station would be based at Gorée, independent of other military authorities, rather than at Sierra Leone. The system of prize money in Sierra Leone had made it easy for officers to support the settlement. But when it came to recruiting soldiers for the valuable, undermanned West India Regiments, Horse Guards was less willing to follow the antislavery line set in Clapham. Its priority was to get as many potential soldiers from Africa to the West Indies as soon as possible. Army officers worried about the quality of recruits released from the slave trade, in contrast with those who were selected and purchased. One officer worried that "appropriating the Cargoes of Negroes Captured under the Slave Abolition Act to the Corps in the West Indies" would compromise training and discipline. Still, the officer admitted any recruiting "could not admit of rejection under the present want of Men."[92]

From Zachary Macaulay's time in Freetown, the "friends of Africa" were anxious to preserve their authority and their own best practices in West Africa. Horse Guards, concerned that the Vice-Admiralty Court would not provide high-quality recruits, pushed for a system of voluntary recruiting from among former slaves and local villagers rather than recruiting directly from the Court of Vice-Admiralty in Freetown, and even mooted the idea of establishing the recruiting station at another British possession on the coast, like Gorée. The leaders of Parliamentary antislavery applied pressure on behalf of Sierra Leone. "Almost every African Man fit for a Planter's purpose," James Stephen wrote, "must be fit also for a soldier." He worried that recruiters located somewhere other than Sierra Leone would be unable to convince former slaves of the differences "between military service & slavery." Stephen also hoped that the presence of black noncommissioned officers would help to ensure that recruits did not confuse lifetime service in the British armed forces with lifetime labour on British plantations.[93] He reminded military officers that "Many hundreds of slaves have been condemned & enfranchised by the Court of Vice Admiralty in S. Leone," and that "many more may be expected every season & among these many more eligible recruits might be found."[94] Zachary Macaulay reminded the Secretary of State for War and the Colonies that "voluntary enlistment of Africans for West Indian service has hitherto been found impracticable."[95] Eventually, Robert Peel weighed in on behalf of the abolitionists, insisting that Sierra Leone would be the site of the recruiting station, that the drilling of the recruits would take place in West Africa, and "that no presents should be permitted to be given to the Native Chiefs, except such as are of so trifling a value as to preclude the possibility of their operating as any temptation to bring down men as Recruits."[96] The "friends of Africa" believed that they had won the argument, and that recruiting in West Africa for the West India Regiments would be exclusively from among the "captured Negroes" released from the Vice-Admiralty Court. Maxwell had won their favour with his single-mindedness and newfound spirit of co-operation with the Royal Navy.

However, the influence of men like Macaulay and Wilberforce, although significant, was not unlimited. The British armed forces were happy to collaborate with the Clapham Sect, but when their interests clashed with the interests of the Saints, the soldiers did not yield. For example, even after Wilberforce's direct intervention, the Admiralty refused to release sailors pressed from the African American merchant Paul Cuffe's vessel, *Traveller*, a ship engaged in "legitimate trade" and heartily endorsed by the African Institution.[97] The Duke of York, a great believer in the West India Regiments, was annoyed that his preference for voluntary enlistment on the coast was opposed by the Clapham Sect and its allies, and had only reluctantly agreed to recruiting from among the former slaves. Consequently, Wingfield's orders were a compromise between activists and officers in London. He was instructed to recruit from among "such eligible Negroes as may be found amongst the Cargoes Captured under the Slave Abolition Act." At the same time, in line with the expectations of the Duke of York, and in order "to bring the military service into repute," Wingfield was entitled to offer volunteers—including local villagers, as well as former captives—eight guineas as a bounty.[98] The *Royal*

Military Chronicle cheerfully papered over the issue. "Major Wingfield," the *Chronicle* reported, "has now the satisfaction to find himself strenuously supported by . . . all the advocates for the abolition of the Slave Trade."[99]

The tension between Maxwell's plans and Wingfield's orders was shaped by the network of influence built up around the Vice-Admiralty Court. The Court gave Macaulay and his friends direct access to the Royal African Corps, and gave the Corps' officers access to antislavery patronage. But the Corps served two masters. It was still an Army regiment, in theory commanded from London. However, before the West India Regiments arrived in Africa, bringing the attention of the brass with them, the leaders of the British Army took very little interest in West African affairs. After all, the Royal African Corps was a convict regiment, and West Africa was not a particularly important theatre in the war with France. The apathy of the Horse Guards may have given the Clapham Sect the impression that they were in command of the Corps, and may also have given the Corps' officers the impression that they could act independently. This intimation of independence was compounded by the close association between the Corps and the business of colonial governance. It wasn't clear who had the last word on the military implementation of antislavery laws.

For his part, Charles Maxwell loathed the idea of voluntary service among both former slaves and local African villagers. He was jealous in protecting the control he enjoyed over "captured Negroes." He was able to recruit as many troops as he needed from the Vice-Admiralty Court for the Royal African Corps. But not every former captive could be recruited, nor was every former captive fit to serve—and although demand for former slaves as labourers in the colony was rising, too many captives were arriving to assimilate smoothly into the colony. The West India Regiment recruiting depot offered Maxwell an opportunity to send out "surplus" captives to the West Indies, and eventually to receive "civilized" veterans in exchange. He proposed to Lord Liverpool that Sierra Leone and the West Indies ought to exchange new recruits from slave ships for discharged soldiers. The old soldiers, he wrote, would be living proof of British integrity and generosity. The soldiers would "set on foot a spirit of inquiry" in their communities, and their ties to the British Army would provide a ready supply of loyal African subjects to extend Britain's influence far into the interior.[100] The recruiting station would be a money-laundering operation for Maxwell's surplus human capital.

Maxwell and the London antislavery lobby were united in their opposition to recruiting in the villages near Freetown, but for different reasons. The Clapham elite did not want to encourage African chiefs and kings to sell recruits; Maxwell did not want the West India Regiments to bypass the pool of potential recruits that he controlled. And so, when a lieutenant and 23 noncommissioned officers from the West India Regiments arrived in Sierra Leone from Barbados aboard the transport ship *Scorpion* in April 1812—without Major Wingfield, who arrived soon after, on another ship bound from London—Maxwell acted quickly. He immediately loaded the *Scorpion* up with 50 recruits and sent it back to the West Indies.[101] Back in Barbados, General Beckwith complained that the new recruits were of an "indifferent description, and such as would not have been purchased by him for military service."[102] Maxwell, however, had no intention of improving the West India Regiments in the short term. He hoped to improve Sierra Leone in the long term by controlling the number of people who needed support from the colonial government, and perhaps by receiving English-speaking retired soldiers in return.

Maxwell chose Bance Island, the old slave-trading fort in the Sierra Leone River, as a site for the recruiting depot. The qualities that made Bance Island a valuable fort also made it an ideal recruiting station. The island was close enough to local settlements and farms to make provisioning convenient, but rocky and isolated enough to make escape difficult. Even more convenient for Maxwell's purposes, almost all of its old buildings still stood.[103] Wingfield arrived in September 1812. Maxwell remained adamant that no local Africans would enlist in the West India Regiments. He wrote in a dispatch, "Though [Wingfield] has made many enlistments, they are, with a solitary exception or two, entirely from the captured negroes who were reserved for him; or from apprentices, who . . . have preferred being soldiers, to agricultural or mechanical labour." He noted that not one Temne, Mende, or Bullom man had enlisted, and explained that none ever would, "till a revolution takes place in the sentiments of the African." It would be difficult to erase the legacy of the slave trade, and even more difficult to overcome the fondness of "the African" for "his country, and the veneration he has for its customs."[104]

With few local recruits choosing to volunteer, the regiments began to make overtures to the "captured Negroes," offering the eight-guinea bounty to them in exchange for voluntary enlistment. Maxwell was angry. The regiments had misunderstood just what kind of people the "captured Negroes" were, and who was entitled to speak for their interests. Wingfield and his officers were, Maxwell wrote to the Earl Bathurst, "under the impression that captured Negroes, and government apprentices, are free agents." But they were mistaken. It was admirable, Maxwell wrote, that the West India Regiments were observing all of the usual formalities in their recruiting efforts. However, he insisted, giving bounties "to persons regularly condemned as lawful prize to HM, in the court of VA, is not only an unnecessary waste of Public money, but a disingenuous attempt to pass off, as recruits voluntarily enlisted, men who are at the absolute disposal of the Crown."[105] Maxwell took very seriously the provisions of the Slave Trade Act that placed former captives under the command of colonial officials, and took at face value the logic of the Vice-Admiralty Court. Men freed from slave ships could not voluntarily enlist, because their labour was not theirs to sell. They had been recaptured, *not* emancipated.

In November 1812, when Wingfield sent the *Herald* troopship from Bance Island, with 312 recruits aboard. without stopping at Freetown to be cleared by colonial officials, Maxwell had had enough. He ordered that the eight-guinea bounty given "to captured Negroes, as if they were voluntary recruits" be replaced immediately with "no greater amount than was absolutely necessary, to clothe persons of this description."[106] Maxwell then seized on the provisions of the Slave Trade Act to take control of the recruiting depot. Maxwell demanded that Wingfield show him the manifest of goods the West India Regiments had brought with them to the colony. Maxwell confronted Wingfield with reports from the chiefs near Bance Island that Wingfield had been engaged in what the chiefs had called the "small man slave trade."[107] He had Wingfield arrested. Kenneth Macaulay searched the regimental storerooms at Bance Island. Among Wingfield's stores Macaulay found embroidered jackets, gold-laced hats, flashy canes, and silver-inlaid pistols and fowling pieces, which suggested that the Regiments planned to trade with African kings, presumably offering goods in exchange for slaves.[108]

Maxwell then sent Kenneth Macaulay up to villages near Bance Island to investigate. A Temne headman told him that the "Major sent for him & he went down to see him. The Major gave him an umbrella & a bar of tobacco & told him he would give him twenty more if he would find him some soldiers." In another village the chief, Pa Yara, told Macaulay that he had sent some of his people to Bance Island "because the Major said the King was in want of Men & they would have allowed these men's wives to have gone had they had any—They said—people had told lies upon the Major, they had not sold the people—they were their own and they gave them fairly." Later that night, though, the chief changed his story. Pa Yara told Macaulay that Wingfield had greeted him and his brother warmly, and told them that "the King had sent him to Africa to get soldiers to fight the French." The Major then offered the chief and his brother a "handsome Sabre" and a "fine cane" as well as "a great many strings of Coral & Amber also a quantity of cloths & taffetas." Wingfield promised the chiefs "plenty more when they sent him five men each." Pa Yara sent a few of his people to the recruiting depot. He gave up the men, he said, "because the King sent them such a handsome message, & such fine presents, & because they wish to see Bance Island prosper again."[109] Based on this report, Chief Justice Robert Thorpe concluded that Wingfield was buying slaves. "It is evident," he wrote, "that by presents the Major has induced the Chiefs of this River, and in the vicinity of the colony to seize on Negroes, throw them into Irons, & by force send them to his Depot to be Recruits."[110] In November 1812 Maxwell imprisoned Wingfield, took control of the recruiting station, and sent off 608 recruits for the West India Regiments aboard H.M.S. *Kangaroo,* the *Herald* transport, and a former slave ship, the *Anderinha,* which he bought at auction from the Vice-Admiralty Court for the purpose.[111] Until the depot was finally closed in 1815, many men released from the Middle Passage into the hands of the Captured Negro Department were sent to Bance Island, where they were sent on a new Middle Passage, to serve for life as British soldiers in the West Indies.

As Chapter Three showed, the lives of the thousands of former captives who arrived in Sierra Leone during the Napoleonic wars are obscure at best. Even the most basic data are threadbare. The Department kept a Register of Captured Negroes, but it is patchy and incomplete, especially in the war years. This obscurity was partly accidental. Record-keeping was difficult; hot, humid weather and pests ate through ledgers; petulant officials threw whole boxes full of records into the Atlantic (like Thompson) or smuggled them out of the colony (like Columbine). But it was also partly a design feature of a court built to turn slave ships into money quickly, with few procedures and little official jurisprudence or paperwork. The West India recruiting depot on Bance Island is even more obscure. There are scant records even of the numbers of soldiers enlisted, to say nothing of what conditions were like for former slaves sent to live in the confines of the old slave fort.

A few dark reports discrediting antislavery advocates percolated out into the parts of the London press loyal to the planters of the West Indies. The

Monthly Magazine called the recruiting depot "a most cruel expedient . . . equivalent to the slave trade itself," duping each recruit into taking an oath and becoming a "volunteer-soldier for life."[112] And within the archives of the Church Missionary Society, a few reports from the recruiting station have survived. Peter Wenzell was reassigned from the Church Missionary Society's station in the Rio Pongas mission to Freetown, where he and another missionary, Reinhold Nyländer, baptized 400 recruits at Bance Island, and married 32 couples. Wenzell reflected, "It was indeed an interesting scene, though we could not speak with them, except by interpreters." Despite the linguistic challenges he faced, Wenzell was confident that baptism removed "the wild slavish fear . . . from their countenances, and willing and loving submission was to be seen in their appearances."[113] The "wild slavish fear" of the recruits was probably not a function of their unsaved souls. Many may have recognized the distinctive buildings and fortifications of a European slave fort; some might even have already spent time imprisoned on Bance Island.

The "marriages" officiated by the missionaries were an early attempt to impose European family organization and sexual morality on a colony with an overwhelmingly male population, and a predominantly military character. Even as late as 1818, there were only 68 women to every 100 men in the colony. Polygamy was routine among local peoples, but monogamous marriage was a priority for the colonial government.[114] The parties to these military marriages, according to the African Institution, were "carefully informed, that though they were free to act as they pleased, and could not be forced to do anything contrary to their inclinations, yet that, if they were once united as man and wife, they would not be allowed afterwards to separate."[115] And yet, many of the "wives" sent to the recruiting depot are listed in the records as being as young as nine or ten.[116] Perhaps the evidence most suggestive of the grim treatment of recruits of Bance Island is the acknowledgment of the suffering of the recruits by the African Institution, whose publications were usually unrelentingly positive. One Association report admitted, "The Directors have learnt, with great regret" that some of the recruits at Bance Island "suffered, at one time, great hardships," but promised that "the captured Negroes have lately enjoyed all the advantages compatible with their situation."[117]

Wingfield was sent back to England in December 1812. Maxwell hoped he would stand trial as a slave trader, but was content to have him gone in any case. Wingfield fell ill on the voyage, spent eight months bedridden, and died on 8 August 1813.[118] It isn't clear from the archives whether Wingfield was planning to buy slaves for the West India Regiments in violation of the Slave Trade Act, and even less clear if he had been ordered to do so by his superiors. That kind of order would have been a scandal if it were public knowledge, so if it was given it likely would not have been recorded. It is possible that the West India Regiment recruiting station was a last gasp from the British Army at buying enslaved soldiers, or that Wingfield took the initiative himself. However, what seems most likely is that Wingfield's orders were intended to take advantage of the ambiguous legal status of both "captured Negroes" and domestic slaves in West Africa; if he had secret orders, they were likely to be orders that violated the spirit, and not the letter, of the Slave Trade Act.

Regardless, Wingfield's corpse was a useful scapegoat for what had proved to be an embarrassing miscommunication between the military and the abolitionists, although his wife, Jane, insisted that he followed his orders with "*zeal and attention to his instructions.*"[119] In spring 1813, the Horse Guards announced that the recruiting station would be closed as soon as possible, although the Duke of York hoped that there might be a chance to keep the project going, perhaps by sending a second recruiting party to Freetown.[120] James Stephen defended Maxwell in the House of Commons. The people confined to Bance Islands, Stephen explained, "had all the allowances of British soldiers, and might one day return with the rudiments of civilization to their native land." Stephen declared that recruitment based in Sierra Leone and exclusively from the slave-trade Court had always been the plan. Wingfield, he concluded, had "exceeded the line marked out for him."[121] Despite the order to close down the depot, there were still more than 275 recruits on Bance Island in July 1814, and more arrived with every captured slave ship.[122] Governor Charles MacCarthy, who succeeded Maxwell, finally closed the station a year later, striking a deal with Captain Harvey of H.M.S. *Porcupine* to remove in several transport ships the 805 men and boys, 62 women, and 15 children who were living in temporary huts on Bance Island.[123] The 882 people set off on a passage from West Africa to the West Indies in a convoy of refitted slave ships.

Charlie Maxwell's War

Charles Maxwell understood that the Slave Trade Act had empowered military officers, giving them a source of recruits and a chance to line their pockets. Maxwell used the Act and the Vice-Admiralty Court to overawe Edward Columbine, expand the Royal African Corps, dominate the Freetown settlers, and transform the West India Regiments' recruiting station into an instrument for sending away surplus or otherwise undesirable "captured Negroes." But his most dramatic campaign was a series of raids on slave forts along the coast north and south of the Freetown Peninsula. The 1811 Slave Trade Felony Act, designed to build on the Slave Trade Act, made slave trading by British subjects a crime punishable with transportation. Maxwell interpreted the Felony Act as a charter not only to pursue ships at sea, but also to hunt down and capture slave traders on shore, and to claim their forts as British territory. Maxwell believed that this would retroactively make even non-British slave traders subject to the Felony Act, making illegal raids into legal raids ex post facto. Maxwell's raids show the wartime military and financial logic of the Slave Trade Act legislation at its most aggressive. They also represent a critical but overlooked moment in British imperial history, a moment when the campaign against the slave trade tipped from being a campaign of national self-purification conducted at sea, and became a justification for expansionist imperial war on land.

In 1810 Henry Brougham, eventually Lord Chancellor, was a young Scottish barrister and a client of the Clapham Sect. In Parliament he argued forcefully for the need for more coercive measures to enforce the abolition of the slave trade. "I must protest loudly against the abuse of language," he proclaimed, "which allows [slave traders] to call themselves traders or merchants." He rhapsodized that he would not allow trade to be "prostituted" by slave dealers when instead it should "humanize and pacify the world."[124] Under the 1807 Act, the penalties for slave trading were economic: a captured slave trader lost his ship and his goods, and was fined. In 1811, Brougham pushed a law through Parliament that made it a felony for "any British subject, or any person residing in the United Kingdom, or any island, colony, dominion, fort, settlement, factory, belonging thereto or being in his Majesty's occupation thereto" to sell slaves.[125]

Under the Felony Act, slave trading would be punished with transportation for 14 years. The Felony Act also gave colonial officials the right to buy captured slave ships at auction, fit them with new gear and weapons, and commission them for the purpose of prosecuting the abolition of the slave trade.[126] When Charles Maxwell governed Senegal, he had commissioned the *George* in exactly the same way for exactly the same purpose. Now the Felony Act seemed to Maxwell to have enshrined his improvisations in statute. Like the Slave Trade Act itself, the Felony Act provided a legal framework for antislavery that was not always clearly understood, and often very flexibly interpreted by colonial jurists and officials. Henry Brougham argued that even considering slave dealing "trade" at all was an abuse of language. The terms of his Act were just as prone to slips in meaning.

The African Institution egged on British officers like Maxwell by re-printing and distributing a long abstract of the Felony Act, followed by a re-port on the case of the *Amedie*. The *Amedie* belonged to a merchant named Groves from Charleston, South Carolina. In 1807, en route to Cuba from Bonny, in the north of the Bight of Biafra, it was captured with slaves aboard by the Royal Navy. The ship was condemned in the Vice-Admiralty Court of Tortola, and Groves appealed to the High Court of Admiralty. The Court denied the appeal. In the decision the judge explained that, after the abolition of the slave trade by Britain, the slave trade "cannot, abstractedly speaking, be said to have a legitimate existence." Although Britain could not "compel the subjects of other nations to observe any other than the first and generally received principles of universal law," the judge continued, "we are now en-titled to act, according to our law . . . where there is no right established to carry on this trade, no claim to restitution of this property can be admit-ted."[127] Under this precedent, it seemed that virtually any ship suspected of slave trading was susceptible to capture.[128] This collection of legal materials told the officers who read it three things: the slave trade was illegal, a law was in place that gave captors wide rights of seizure, and if British officers en-forced the law, the High Court of Admiralty would protect them.

In 1811, Maxwell launched a raid on Samuel Samo's slave factory. The factory was located just past the mud bar at the mouth of the Rio Pongas. The transport ships carrying the troops dropped anchor before they ran aground. The soldiers climbed overboard into canoes. Thick mangroves lined either side of the bank. They arrived at "Charleston," Samo's factory. A few years later the missionary Edward Bickersteth described Charleston as "a small vil-lage . . . of six or eight houses, belonging to Mr. Samo. Here was once a slave factory." Bickersteth was moved: "The view was very beautiful," he wrote. "I could almost fancy myself on some parts of the Thames."[129] In 1811 Char-leston was still a slave fort, a group of huts, warehouses, and paddocks for hu-man cargo. Samo must have been very surprised to see British troops (and doubly surprised to see so many black troops) appear on the river. He surren-dered, and was taken prisoner. The people imprisoned at his fort were piled into a transport ship to Freetown, to be processed by the Captured Negro De-partment and the Vice-Admiralty Court.

The trial of Samuel Samo was the first time the Felony Act had been used to prosecute a slave trader in the British empire. In the trial Chief Justice Thorpe used the Abolition Act and the Slave Trade Felony Act to insist that people outside the borders of Sierra Leone were nonetheless subject to British laws. Mary Louise Pratt, in *Imperial Eyes*, identifies a phenomenon she calls " 'anti-conquest": "the strategies of representation whereby European bourgeois subjects seek to secure their innocence in the same moment as they assert European hegemony."[130] For Charles Maxwell, armed assaults on slave factories were both conquest, since he used the raids to intimidate and overrun territories that did not belong to the colony, and "anti-conquest," since they disrupted the slave trade.

The Slave Trade Act drew impetus from the Napoleonic wars. The Felony Act was also shaped by the struggle between Britain and the United States over naval and military manpower and citizenship during the War of 1812. One of the causes for hostilities in this war was the pressing of naturalized American sailors into the Royal Navy. In the view of the British government, emigrants from Britain were not excused from the duties of British subjects. As Alan Taylor comments, emigration, "seeking citizenship and forsaking the status of a monarch's subject" seemed like a reenactment of the American Revolution to many elite Britons, especially in the military.[131] Maxwell may have thought of West Africa as another front in the war, and not without some justification. Most of the slave traders residing in the Rio Pongas either had been born in the American colonies when they belonged to Britain, or were closely connected with slave dealers in the United States.[132] Maxwell's raids were valuable in and of themselves, but they also had the additional value of intimidating American traders.[133]

An account of Samuel Samo's trial was soon published in London, bankrolled by the African Institution. The short pamphlet made the case for Maxwell's military operations against slave forts, framing the trial as part of a military and legal assault on slave trading by both Europeans and Africans. Samo's lawyer argued that he was not a British subject, and the Rio Pongas was not British territory, and so he could not be subject to the Slave Trade Felony Act. According to a statement read aloud in court, Samo had been born in Amsterdam in 1770, had worked from 1788 to 1795 as a bookkeeper on a sugar plantation in Suriname, and then emigrated to the United States. He had moved to West Africa to run his factory in 1797. "I do not only declare that I am innocent of the charge laid against me," Samo's statement read, "but that I have, for a considerable time, been doing all in my power toward the grand object, the total abolition of the slave trade." He claimed he had been arrested just before he could move from the Rio Pongas to the Iles-de-Los, where he swore he had "the promise of a good piece of land, and (if it please the Almighty) I will convince the inhabitants and natives of Africa what can be done in respect to agriculture."[134] Despite this plea, Samo was convicted. However, several white European merchants (and former Company employees), including George Nichol, Alexander Smith, and Michael Macmillan, all testified that he "was a very quiet man, one of the best of the factors" and "a good man," and ought to be released.[135]

The report on the trial in London announced that three petitions, written in Arabic, from three chiefs from the Rio Pongas region, including "Mandingo," Baga, and Susu leaders, arrived in the colony soon after Samo's conviction. Each king vowed that his people would abandon slave trading. Maxwell pardoned Samo, on condition that Samo also agreed to abandon the slave trade. "To have the 'father of the trade,'" the pamphlet proclaimed, "converted into its avowed enemy . . . was a great point gained, and infinitely preferable to sacrificing an individual slave trader to the rigour of the law."[136] The pardon was as effective as punishment, as far as Maxwell was concerned. It had justified both the first raid and any further attacks. Earl Bathurst was pleased with the outcome. "I see every reason to approve of the ground upon which you have thought fit to extend the Royal Mercy to Samuel Samo," he wrote, "and have every hope that the expectations which you have formed of thus securing the influence of the neighbouring chiefs in putting a complete stop to the slave trade will be speedily realized."[137] The threat of punishment would turn Samo into an agent of antislavery, both as Samo worked to convince his African clients to stop trading in slaves and as Maxwell used Samo's case to justify more attacks on slave forts.

Samuel Samo's capture was a physical threat to the slave traders of the Rio Pongas, but not a formal conquest. However, the pamphlet which praised Samo's decision to give up the slave trade in exchange for freedom proclaimed that the river now belonged to Sierra Leone and thus to Britain. Since it was virtually impossible to prove that Samo was actually a British subject, the authors of the pamphlet argued instead that the African chiefs residing in the Rio Pongas had already accepted British jurisdiction. Since Samo was their "'stranger," he was also a British subject, even if he didn't know it. Thorpe proclaimed that "the chiefs of that country consider the white men as British subjects, and they also consider themselves British subjects; they have claimed, in cases of distress, British protection . . . they purchase, reside, and trade as British subjects, not as Africans."[138] Maxwell believed that European slave traders held local people in corrupting thrall. Thorpe gave Maxwell's conviction another legal justification by arguing that participation in the transatlantic slave trade with British traders had made the rulers of African polities subject to British law.

In consequence, each witness was sworn according to custom. A Temne man named Banta "swore by his mother, and wished she might die if he did not speak the truth, and he hoped that God might strike him dead as the earth (on which he rubbed his two forefingers and applied the dust to his tongue) if he did not relate the whole truth." Dalu Mohammed, the Muslim "Mandingo" sub-chief (who had been Thomas Perronet Thompson's closest African ally) "spoke English well; he was sworn on the Koran, with great solemnity." Another witness, Duboo, was "sworn on the Old Testament; he believed in a state of future rewards and punishments"; Yangyarra was sworn "by praying that God would cause the earth to open and receive him, if he told not the whole truth"; "Monday was sworn on the New Testament and on the earth . . . Quiepa knelt down and kissed the earth, and was thus sworn to tell the truth."[139] By accepting a wide spectrum of African swearing practices in his courtroom, Thorpe seems to have imagined he had absorbed the witnesses into the British empire. Having sworn an oath, the witnesses had affirmed and formalised the informal dominion Britain claimed over them. Thorpe relied on this same strategy in the case of another slave trader, Joseph Peters, who was arrested with Samo. Peters, a former Royal Navy surgeon's mate who served for six years as factor at Bance Island, was arrested there. The *Edinburgh Review* commented, "It is not stated from what country he came . . . at any rate, he committed the acts of slave trading within the limits of British settlement."[140]

Thorpe returned to England on sick leave in 1813. Maxwell chose the colonial surgeon, Robert Purdie, who had no legal training, to replace him. The two men proceeded to launch ever bolder attacks on slave forts. Maxwell argued that a robust force in Sierra Leone was "indispensably necessary for the protection of its numerous new population, and for the maintenance of the respectability of the colony in the eyes of the surrounding nations, especially the Mandingoes."[141] In August 1813, Maxwell dispatched the *Thais*, under the command of Captain Scobell, south to Cape Mesurado, where the ship shelled and destroyed a factory, and claimed 230 slaves to be condemned as property in Sierra Leone, and sentenced the two slave traders who ran the factory, Bostock and McQueen, to 14 years' transportation in Australia.[142] In February 1814, the *Princess Charlotte* and the *Doris* sailed with orders to attack and burn every American factory in the Rio Pongas. The ships captured Samuel Gale's factory on the Bangalan branch of the river (sometimes called the "Congo" by local traders) on 15 February, and John Ormond's factory at Bangalan on 20 February, before sailing on to capture Samuel Perry's factory near Canoffe, one of the villages in which Church Missionary Society missionaries had taken up residence. In March 1814, Maxwell deployed the Royal African Corps to capture three more slave traders named Brodie, Cooke, and Dunbar. Cooke's factory, "South Carolina," later valued at more than $30,000, burned to the ground in the assault.[143]

Captured slave traders were pressured into signing affidavits by the officers of the Royal African Corps. One of the affidavits signed by an African trader in slaves and other goods gives a sense of the combination of threat and incentive offered to slave traders by British officers. The trader promised to "undertake that in consequence of the inhumanity, pointed out to us by the Thais, which exists in the Slave Trade and also wishing to be friends with King George of England, we will not henceforward enslave any of our fellow creatures." The *Thais*'s cannons and the promise of British trade made a compelling case. The trader vowed not to allow people "to be shipped away from our territories as heretofore done to America, principally by the concern of Charles Mason and Robert Bostick who are the Owners of the Slaves and small craft, accustomed to carry them and this day captured by the Thais."[144] The slaves and the small craft, it is worth noting, may actually have belonged to the trader—the slaves might not have been sold yet, and the craft might have been loaned by African traders to their European clients. But in order for the property and the slaves to be eligible to be seized under the Slave Trade Act of 1807, they needed to belong to British subjects, not African factors. The affidavit made the European slave traders liable to prosecution, and made all their gear and all their slaves open to seizure.

In another affidavit, traders living near Cape Mesurado confessed that they had sold slaves to Mason and Bostock, "the former we believe being an American now there and receiving the return of Cargoes in that Country and the latter being an Englishman living in this neighbourhood." The traders "received payment for the said slaves in Tobacco, Rum &c. consequently the small craft, names unknown and the said slaves captured by the Thais are the property of Mason and Bostick." They made the usual genuflection to anti-slavery principles and British policy: "We further declare and depose to Captain Scobell and Lieutenant Wilkins of His Majesty's Ship Thais that (made sensible of the inhumanity and unlawfulness of bartering the liberty and persons of our fellow creatures) we will never henceforward be conducive in any way to the enslaving of African Negroes."[145] In this affidavit as well, the officers of the Royal Navy made sure that the ownership of the slaves had already passed to the European traders, and that at least Bostock was declared to be a British subject. Local slave traders were intimidated. Malcolm Brodie, a trader who was prosecuted under the Slave Trade Felony Act, complained that although he had the documents to defend himself, "These kind of documents taken in Africa are of no use here . . . I see no prospect of recovering for anything else, but for false imprisonment and personal sufferings."[146]

These raids made bold territorial and legal claims on regions to which Britain had made no prior claim. In order to prosecute Samo and the other slave traders, Maxwell sent the colonial Attorney General to the Rio Pongas to find witnesses for the Crown.[147] Melchior Renner, a missionary in the region, refused to testify. "We are watched by the Natives with a jealous eye," he explained, "considering us always as 'Sierra Leone people' and they cannot help of telling that by our means the Susoo country will gradually become King George's."[148] The Rio Pongas, already politically fractured, became even more unstable. The intensification of slave-trade interdiction brought European traders into a more equal partnership with their landlords. Beginning in 1811, white traders began to take part in the council of the Susu king, Kadi, participating for the first time in palavers about disputes with Sierra Leone.[149] Renner's caution was warranted. In 1814 the slave trader George Ormond had threatened to burn the Church Missionary Society's mission station at Bashia to the ground, and King Kadi had Renner briefly imprisoned.[150]

In 1814 a caravan from Moria, a Muslim kingdom in the Rio Pongas, arrived in Freetown. A group of slaves fled the caravan, claiming Maxwell's protection. Soon Daniel Gospel, a merchant resident in Forekaria, a town under Moria's control, died under mysterious circumstances. Many colonial officials and local traders assumed that he had been murdered.[151] In March 1814, Maxwell received a letter from Amara Touré, Alimami of Moria, and his subordinate chief, Solyman. The kings demurred about the killing: "About Daniel Gospel I know no more than you do Sir; but I will bring the transgressor to trial—& whatever my book says, that I will put into execution." But the kings were less equivocal about Maxwell's campaigns against the slave trade. They warned Maxwell not to attack any more slave ships in their rivers, or any more forts in their territory. "If you do," they threatened, "take care of yourself—don't think you will get any black man's thing in all this Country either to buy or to eat." The Alimami remembered when "white people come to this country for trade palaver . . . but today white people come to take the country away from us & to make slaves of us in return." They explained that the Quran entitled them to keep slaves, and that their traditions required them to treat European traders as "strangers" entitled to protection. Maxwell's campaigns had forced them to endure the humiliation of breaking that trust. "We beg you Governor," they concluded "let this war be over . . . you know this country belongs unto us the natives of it—you are a stranger here, we are the proprietors." If Europeans no longer wanted to buy slaves, then they should not visit Moria or the northern rivers. And, Amara concluded, if "any white man buys slaves, & you trouble him for that palaver, you trouble me."[152]

Amara and Solyman called Maxwell's raids a "war," and that was exactly what Maxwell intended them to be. As John Thornton notes, "African wars [before European conquest] that aimed at acquiring slaves were in fact the exact equivalent of Eurasian wars aimed at acquiring land."[153] Maxwell wanted to "make Sierra Leone very large" at the expense of local rulers, by capturing enslaved people and conscripting them into colonial service. The abolition of the slave trade gave him both a reason to go to war, and the troops to make it happen. Maxwell believed that the letter had been written for the chiefs (who were certainly literate in Arabic, if not English) by Peter Hartwig, a disgraced German missionary who had abandoned the church to work in the slave trade.[154] Maxwell saw Hartwig as a sinister puppeteer. Maxwell believed that the letter was not a true account of African opinion on the conduct of the anti-slave-trade campaign, but rather proof that Europeans "have poisoned the minds of the natives."[155] Hartwig may have transcribed and translated the letter, but he certainly didn't write it—he worked for the king, not vice versa. Maxwell was already angry with Amara Touré, who had threatened to cut by half the supply of rice his people sold to Freetown, in order to raise the price. Maxwell believed that this plan was also a white invention forced on a guileless African by white viziers, this time by American traders rather than defrocked Germans.[156]

In retaliation, Maxwell deployed 150 soldiers of the Royal African Corps in a transport to the Rio Pongas and ordered the brig *Princess Charlotte* to support the troops with cannon fire from the river. "The steady conduct, and orderly behavior of the troops," Maxwell wrote, "has effected a complete change of opinion in the chiefs of the different rivers." Intimidated, the Alimami was compelled to arrest the alleged murderers of Daniel Gospel. Maxwell was invited to the palaver that would decide their punishment. He refused. "I wish to do away [with] the absurd custom," he wrote, "which in former time prevailed here, of sending a representative to attend, at their endless palavers."[157] The point of the attack had not really been to achieve justice for Daniel Gospel's slaying, but to apply British laws to Moria by force in retaliation for the polity's defiance. The attack was also profitable: Maxwell captured three ships and 240 slaves, and arrested four European slave traders.[158] One of the slave traders captured in the raid was pardoned on condition that he teach the Susu about "agricultural pursuits; with which, I hear, he is well acquainted." His 60 "domestic slaves" were liberated and turned over to colonial officials.[159] The raid was an unqualified success. It took more slaves to be made into "captured Negroes" and so raised Maxwell's prestige and power; it removed Europeans from the rivers, and it overawed local chiefs. If "captured Negroes" in Freetown were a new kind of resource for the use of British officials, the raids were intended to extend the claim to the nearby rivers, to flatten out complex interdependence into simple dependence.

Maxwell used the 1811 Felony Act to justify his raids, but he may never actually have read the Act. According to Robert Thorpe, Maxwell got his information from the African Institution's published abstract.[160] Thorpe, who has the dubious distinction of being the focus of an entire fat file of Court transcripts and character assassinations among the Colonial Office records, became famous as Maxwell's enemy. He left the colony in 1813 for health reasons, and a grievance over unpaid salary pushed him to excoriate his former patron and friend in the press.[161] While in the colony, Thorpe acted as Maxwell's right hand, devising legal justifications for the slave raids. When he first left the colony, Thorpe wrote to Maxwell, "Permit me to express the first wish of my heart, which is, that the happy terms in which we have lived for two years might be as well known in England as it is here." He asked Maxwell for a good reference with the Secretary of State. He hoped Maxwell would write to Bathurst, and "relate, as I feel you think, that I have done my duty strictly, that what little aid I could give to your administration I have performed cheerfully, that I have made some exertions in support of the Abolition, and that in private I have not poisoned the convivial banquet."[162] Back in London, though, a disappointed Thorpe was unrelenting. Thorpe called the raids a "repeated breach of public faith . . . the most unpardonable insult ever offered to the honour and feelings of Great Britain."[163] Maxwell's conduct, he raved, "will scarcely find a parallel in the history of any civilized nation on earth."[164] In his own defense Maxwell claimed that even if the slave traders he had prosecuted were not British subjects, they were Americans. Since most of the raids took place during the War of 1812, American slave traders were enemies of Britain, and, as slave traders, enemies of Sierra Leone.[165]

When Maxwell was promoted from Senegal to Sierra Leone after Edward Columbine's death, Zachary Macaulay, as usual, received a copy of his instructions. Macaulay—rather presciently—complained to his contacts in the Secretary of State for the Colonies' office that Maxwell seemed too eager to go on the offensive, and that he might benefit from "the cultivation of an amicable intercourse with the different native powers" to help cement the colony's place in the local political economy.[166] Still, from the perspective of abolitionists in London, every charred slave fort was at the very least a step toward total abolition, and one less competitor in the coastal trade. Governor Maxwell "has continued to make every possible exertion for the further suppression of the Slave Trade in the neighbourhood of his government," the African Institution reported with approval in 1813, and praised Maxwell's initiative in enforcing the Felony Act.[167]

The African Institution also blamed Thorpe, not Maxwell, for establishing the pattern of condemning slave traders from outside of the jurisdiction of the Court—a betrayal which may have accounted for Thorpe's fury at the Clapham Sect. Remember that Robert Purdie, who had no legal training, replaced Thorpe in Freetown. The Institution insisted, though, that Thorpe had established the precedent for convicting slave traders when he was in the colony, and that Purdie, "*following the precedents of his learned predecessor Mr. Thorpe himself*, had tried and convicted those men without any lawful jurisdiction."[168] In 1817, Cooke (owner of the burned "South Carolina" factory) sued Maxwell. The report of the case noted that Cooke's indictment in Sierra Leone "is imperfect as a record . . . since it does not appear to have been found by any persons who were competent to find an indictment . . . the mere statement that a fact amounts to a felony will not render it a felony."[169] Cooke also made quite a performance in court. He claimed to be an American citizen, and his barrister, Mr. Scarlett, announced that he had been "from Affluence to beggary." He claimed Maxwell had gone to the "Congo" river, "150 miles from the seat of his authority, and much beyond its limits." Major Appleton of the Royal African Corps arrived at the mouth of the river, and sailed for 60 miles up it, with three ships. Appleton set up camp in the town of King Kadi, and took Cooke captive. Meanwhile, according to Cooke's lawyer, the soldiers of the Royal African Corps looted ivory and other goods from the factory, and then burned it to the ground.[170] Cooke was tried in Sierra Leone, and then sent back to Portsmouth, where he was imprisoned. He was then sent to the *Laurel*, a hulk floating off Spithead, where Mr. Scarlett inveighed, he was imprisoned for six months without access to counsel. "Redress," Scarlett told the Court, "could not be hoped in the colony where the governor was almost absolute."[171]

Had the appeal been heard in 1812, the appellate Court might not have been convinced by Cooke's claim of American citizenship. In 1812, the naturalized American citizen Jenkin Ratford was hanged from the yardarm of his old vessel, H.M.S. *Halifax*, after being pressed from U.S.S. *Chesapeake*, to make a point about the futility of attempting to escape by emigration the obligations of a British subject.[172] Moreover, Maxwell's raids had been looked on with favour partly because there were so many Americans trading in the Rio Pongas. But by 1817 the terrain of Anglo-American relations had changed; American citizenship had achieved greater recognition in British law—and the Court awarded Cooke £20,000 in damages. The legal question was settled. The case cast a chill over plans to enforce the abolition of the slave trade by attacking slave forts.[173] Malcolm Brodie, another slave trader prosecuted with Cooke, was delighted. He wrote to a business partner that if came to England to file suit, he might "easily recover" any money he had lost, "now the ice is broken."[174]

Maxwell, who did indeed feel that his power in Sierra Leone was "almost absolute," and who used the mechanisms of antislavery laws to secure his power, had become the first official both to prosecute anyone under the Felony Act, and to encounter its limitations. "No doubt," Cooke's lawyer declared in court, "the excuse of the defendant would be his zeal for the abolition of the slave trade." But, he reminded the jury, Maxwell had made a lot of money as well. Perhaps "his zeal had not been a little inflamed by his love of money as well as humanity."[175] And yet, Charles Maxwell was no hypocrite.

Under the 1807 Slave Trade Act, "love of money" and "humanity" aligned ideologically and practically, and military power was designed as the backbone of antislavery policy. Elite abolitionists like Wilberforce and Zachary Macaulay believed that making money in a fair market was evidence of God's favour. The 1807 Act's provisions echoed this spirit, and expressed it in the idiom of naval warfare. The principles and legal framework of the abolition of the slave trade synthesized humanitarianism with capitalist accumulation, and drove it forward by military force. Slave-fort raiding generated prize money and expanded the labour force at the disposal of the government of Sierra Leone, while chipping away at competition on the coast and benefitting traders in London and Freetown who hoped for a greater share of the West African market.

Charles Maxwell is largely forgotten. He is not included in the *Dictionary of National Biography*, and is peripheral to most histories of Sierra Leone. Only Maxwell's Duiker, a tubby little antelope native to West Africa, carries his name, since he brought a specimen back with him when he was recalled to England in 1814.[176] However, he had an outsize impact on the early history of the practices of antislavery in the British empire. In 1849, when Lieutenant-General Sir Charles William Maxwell, Companion of the Order of the Bath, died in Broadstairs, Kent, at 73, he could look back with pleasure at a successful career in imperial government. Maxwell enjoyed a long career after his time in Sierra Leone, acting as Governor, at one time or another, of Dominica, Saint Kitts, Nevis, Tortola, and the Virgin Islands. He claimed to have been born a gentleman, the eldest son of Charles Maxwell of Terraughty, Dumfriesshire.[177] However, a genealogist in the later nineteenth century concluded that "nothing is known of any Charles Maxwell of Terraughty, and no one of that name ever owned Terraughty or resided there . . . Sir Charles Maxwell's father may have been the Charles Maxwell in London, son of Charles the upholsterer."[178] The upholsterer's son, it seems, began his long trajectory from a purchased officer's commission to the Order of the Bath with a stroke of insight into the relationship between war, money, and antislavery embodied in the Slave Trade Act and promoted by the elite antislavery lobby in London.

Maxwell's guiding policy in Sierra Leone was the use of former slaves as soldiers to tighten his control over the Freetown settlers and the colony's neighbours. With Maxwell's approval, his officers suppressed the settlers.

Since Macaulay's time, the colony had been enmeshed in a complicated network of political and economic ties with local polities, and with the coastal trade in slaves and legitimate goods. Maxwell tried to use raids on slave forts to slash at those ties, and replace them with top-down control of the coast by the Governor of Sierra Leone. When the West India Regiments came to recruit near the colony, Maxwell refused to allow recruitment among villagers outside his control. In all of these projects, Maxwell treated the "captured Negroes" as blank slates. He imagined them as police in Freetown, as soldiers in the West Indies, as warriors against the slave trade in Africa. Charles Maxwell could not succeed in removing the previous lives and identities from the "captured Negroes." However, he acted as though it were possible, and used the Slave Trade Act to give him the leverage, the means, and the authority to try it out.

5. The Liberated African Department

On 22 April 1821, five men argued on the outskirts of Campelar, a village on Sherbro' Island, 50 miles south of Freetown. A few months earlier, 88 African American settlers had arrived in the village, the staging area for a new colony on the mainland banks of the Sherbro' River. However, the local chiefs refused to give up any land, stranding the settlers in a tumbledown village built around a long, rectangular church with a thatched roof. Soon, nearly two dozen were dead of fever, along with two white agents of the American Colonization Society (ACS).[1] Their graves had been dug in a makeshift cemetery near the tide-line, where the ground was saturated with water. Nothing stayed buried for long, and the smell was nauseating. Two of the men present, Ephraim Bacon and Joseph Andrus, had come from America to settle accounts. Two other men, William Tamba and William Davis, Liberated Africans from Sierra Leone, accompanied the Americans as interpreters. Their services were unnecessary that day, because the fifth man, John Kizell, spoke English. Kizell, headman of Campelar and one of the first Nova Scotian settlers in Sierra Leone, had been hired by the ACS as a fixer. He had promised more than he could deliver. Still, Kizell expected to be paid. He had sent a bill for $800 to the ACS for services rendered to the colonists, but "his avaricious attitude," Bacon wrote, "was not satisfied."[2]

William Tamba had been born on the coast of what is now Liberia. He was kidnapped as a child and raised in a slave factory. In addition to his native tongue, Sherbro', he had learned English and at least six other African languages while working on the canoes that brought goods and enslaved people to and from the shore. It isn't clear whether Tamba was rescued from a slave ship or released in a raid on a slave fort, or whether he moved to Sierra Leone by choice, but by the 1810s he lived in Freetown, where he served as the colonial jailer. He later moved to Regent, a village in the mountains above the capital, and converted to Christianity.[3] He had dreamed of children burning their hands, and remembered hearing W. A. B. Johnson, the missionary superintendent of Regent, preach that "Sinners when they die must go to hell for the fire." Tamba was moved. "I knew," he remembered, "it was like my dream, and I thank God that he kept me from it."[4] William Davis was from the Grand Bassa region, also in present-day Liberia. "My father die, my mother die," he remembered, "& I had no one to take care of me. Then they sell me, but it pleased God to bring me" to Regent. He too had converted, inspired by Johnson and set on fire by prophetic dreams.[5] In Regent, Tamba and Davis were Johnson's lieutenants. As early as 1817, Davis had begun to walk down from Regent to Cockle Bay, just outside Freetown, to preach in the Bassa language.[6] By 1820, both men taught in the missionary school in Regent, led evening prayers in nearby mission stations, and made preaching circuits of nearby "native" villages.[7] In 1821, they were recruited to accompany the agents of the American Colonization Society as translators.

The argument on Sherbro' Island and the lives of Tamba and Davis hint at a profound transformation in British antislavery after the end of the wars with Napoleonic France. During the wars, the prize system drove the colonial economy. If "captured Negroes" could not be recruited as soldiers for service in West Africa or the West Indies, or apprenticed as labourers in Freetown, they were sent outside of the capital to live in informal settlements and all but ignored. After Waterloo, Royal Navy cruisers kept capturing slave ships, but the distribution of seized money and goods was more closely regulated, and demand for African soldiers fell sharply. While the torrent of prize money slowed to a trickle, formerly enslaved people kept arriving in Freetown. After 1815, the business of governing the colony reoriented around managing the people, who, by the early 1820s, began to appear in the colonial records as "Liberated Africans" rather than "captured Negroes."[8] "'Civilization" replaced prize money at the heart of the colonial economy. Just as the Vice-Admiralty Court and its long trail of money and military campaigning expressed in practice the abstractions of the Slave Trade Act, an abstract idea of "civilization" became a program to teach former slaves European folkways: wage work, scheduled and timed labour, dress, consumption, and church attendance. The idea that the end of the slave trade would "civilize" West Africa had, in theory, been important to the British antislavery program from its inception. But until the end of the war in Europe, there were few incentives for colonial officials to put plans for the "civilization" of people liberated from the slave trade into action. However, by 1827 two Commissioners of Inquiry sent to survey the colony commented that the Liberated Africans' "manner of life . . . is altogether artificial; and a certain control is requisite to prevent their return to their former habits."[9]

The institution responsible for the "civilization" of former slaves was the Liberated African Department, and its basic administrative unit was the Liberated African Village. The villages, established from 1816 to 1823, included Regent, Kissy, Gloucester, Waterloo, Wilberforce, Leopold, Charlotte, Bathurst, Wellington, York, Hastings, a village on the Banana Islands (off the southern coast of the Freetown Peninsula), and a more far-flung village on the Isles-de-Los (fig. 9). Each village was managed by a missionary, paid partly by the Church Missionary Society and partly by the colonial government, who had free rein to preach in exchange for acting as local administrator for the Department. The missionaries collected vital statistics, and distributed rations and other goods to former slaves, making the villages into centres for the circulation of information and the distribution of labour. By 1822 nearly 8,000 people lived in the villages, compared with 5,600 in the capital.[10] Concurrently with the increasing capacity and sophistication of the Department and the village system, MacCarthy built a network of colonial outposts subordinate to Sierra Leone, including Bathurst, at the mouth of the Gambia River, and the Isles-de-Los, off the coast of present-day Guinea. He imagined himself as "Captain-General and Governor-in-Chief," with the power to colonize new territories, "make, enact, and ordain laws, statutes, ordinances for the peace, welfare &c. &c. &c."[11] Sierra Leone continued to represent in practice the ambitions of British antislavery for Africa. The massive expansion of British sea power in the Napoleonic wars, and the comprehensive defeat of France and its allies left Britain to rule the waves after 1815. In consequence, the horizons of right-minded Britons quickly expanded: missionary societies bloomed and antislavery projects flourished from Cape Coast to Mauritius.[12] Sierra Leone had once been a pilot plant for "legitimate trade"; it became a pilot plant for a kind of British colonialism and territorial expansion previously unknown in West Africa. The civilizing mission and expanding colonial footprint helped to persuade the Colonial Office and the Treasury to send money and supplies, while the missionary press published reams of approving articles and pamphlets.

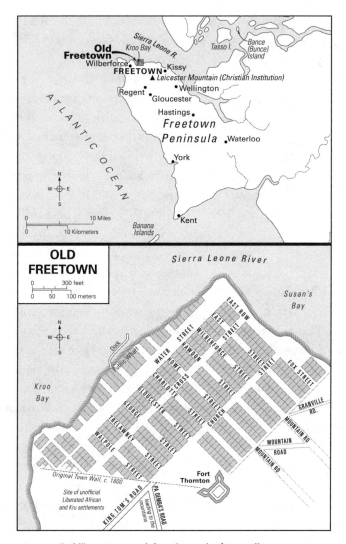

Figure 9. "Old" Freetown and the Liberated African villages.

The ideology of British antislavery, in the hands of a few officials looking for a new way to make money from the practices of stopping the slave trade, was transformed into a colonialism that proposed to transform former slaves into Christians, wage workers, and consumers.

The reorientation of the practices of antislavery away from an overwhelming emphasis on interdiction and toward a civilizing mission coincided with the growth of interest among white Americans in the founding of an African colony for freedpeople from the United States. In 1822 the American colony that would become Liberia was founded at Cape Mesurado, some 250 miles southeast of the Freetown Peninsula. Liberia and Sierra Leone seem as though they ought to be easy to place in the same frame of reference. And yet, although traders and missionaries in the two colonies competed for goods and access to markets, their histories have only rarely been compared, much less combined.[13] Partly, this is an accident of geography. On twenty-first-century maps, Liberia and Sierra Leone share a land border. In 1822, "Sierra Leone" was the Freetown Peninsula and "Liberia" was a hamlet on Cape Mesurado. The colonies were separated by a wide hinterland, and contrary winds and currents made the voyage north from Liberia to Sierra Leone tricky for inexperienced sailors. More important, British and American abolitionists had wildly different expectations of the African colonies founded in their respective images. From Charles MacCarthy's perspective, the village system would maintain colonial prosperity. From the ACS' perspective, the villages offered proof-of-concept that a group of former slaves might, "under the political government of a few white men," be subdued enough as to found a colony.[14] However, the "political government of a few white men" in Sierra Leone was not quite what the Americans thought it was.

Americans had been present in Sierra Leone from the colony's founding. The Nova Scotian settlers had been enslaved on American plantations; Zachary Macaulay bought rice from Rhode Island merchants calling at Freetown and worried about the "American" intransigence of the settlers; Maxwell went to war with American slave traders and their allies in the Rio Pongas. Moreover, the British and American versions of abolitionism had a common history in Quaker activism, transatlantic religious revival, a common cult of sentimentality, and a shared sense that slavery would wither away before "efficient" wage work.[15] However, the three decades since 1792 had driven a wedge between British and American abolitionists. In the United States the cotton gin exploded the idea that antislavery might be a natural consequence of economic development; suddenly, slavery was more profitable than it had ever been. The internal slave trade surged in size and value. American abolitionism turned inward toward frontier states and territories, where every new bid for statehood prompted furious arguments over the expansion of slavery. Slave owners in the United States dreamed of new territories and new colonies; slavery was expansionist.[16] In Britain, ending the

slave trade (and, after 1833, ending slavery itself) became more and more en-
twined with Britain's imperial projects: with commerce, with missionary
work, and with the British armed forces. While American slavery and antislavery wrestled for the frontier, British antislavery pushed the borders of the
empire outward.

The policies and ideology of white supremacy were different on either
side of the Atlantic. The Liberated African Villages expressed British ideas
about the cultural superiority of Britons over Africans that diverged in theory and practice from white American fears of African American freedom
and citizenship. Still, the idea that emancipation ought to be gradual, and that
a coercive "civilizing process" ought to be prerequisite to the end of slavery,
persisted in both Britain and the United States. But even this apparent common ground was shifting. To MacCarthy, Liberated Africans were a flexible
labour force at his disposal for colonial projects, and an advertisement for his
administrative acumen to his superiors in London. In the United States, "civilizing" the emancipated, especially in West Africa, was intended to defuse
the tension between white abolitionists' desire for an end to American slavery, and their fear of the possibility of social unrest caused by mass emancipation. In practice, as the Americans on the beach on 22 April 1821 discovered,
all it took was a high tide or two to show where the bodies had been buried.

The Origins of the Village System: Postwar Crisis

MacCarthy, like officials across the British empire and in Britain itself, experienced the end of the war with France as a shock. As Linda Colley puts it,
"Waterloo finally slew the dragon; and the immediate reaction among many
Britons was less complacency than disorientation."[17] For the Clapham Sect in
London, peace meant the narrowing of some horizons of activism, and the
opening of dizzying new vistas in others. First, it became clear that the abolition of the entire European slave trade would be postponed, perhaps indef-
initely. In 1815, at the Congress of Vienna, with the spectre of Napoleon
exorcised, the other European powers demurred at ending the slave trade.
The Treaty of Paris included vague affirmations of antislavery principles,
but did not include any formal commitment to abolition. Castlereagh claimed
in Parliament that "a great moral triumph was achieved," but activists in
London were furious, and petitions poured in demanding action.[18] However,
there was little British negotiators could do, and the Treaty was ratified.

Without a ban in place, and absent the weak regulatory climate of wartime, the Royal Navy would need to be more circumspect in attacking slave ships.

In 1816 the staff of the High Court of Admiralty advised naval officials that even detaining a foreign slave ship in peacetime might expose British officers to lawsuits and other legal penalties.[19] The Court of Vice-Admiralty in Freetown did not immediately stop prosecuting foreign slave ships in 1815. In fact, 37 cases were prosecuted by the Vice-Admiralty Court at Sierra Leone in 1816 and 1817, and 2,645 slaves were freed from the Middle Passage and settled in the colony. But the Court's proceedings were subject to more scrutiny. When the case of the *Louis,* a French slave ship captured in 1816, came up for appeal at the High Court of Admiralty, Chief Justice Sir William Scott praised jurists in Freetown for their "proper zeal for the purposes of the establishment of *Sierra Leone.*" But he worried that colonial jurists were failing to pay attention "not only to the common forms of law, but to the rational principles on which they are founded."[20] In another appeal, Lord Stowell refused to blame Royal Navy officers for illegal captures, since their "zeal frequently outruns their prudence and knowledge." Instead, Stowell blamed "persons at *Sierra Leone,* who give advice much beyond their authority."[21] Britain would not stop the hunt for slave ships, but it would need to carry it on within a new, multilateral regulatory framework, in order to reduce the likelihood of successful lawsuits by foreign slave-ship owners.

Although the commitment of many European powers to the end of the slave trade was weak at best, Britain's negotiating position was strong enough to make sure that countries like Spain and Portugal could not simply resume an unrestricted slave trade. The slave-trading powers were willing to accept British interdiction north of the equator, provided they were compensated for their wartime losses and given a cut of future revenues from slave-trade interdiction, and could continue to ship slaves across the South Atlantic. For this raw deal, Britain paid hundreds of thousands of pounds to Spain and Portugal in "restitution."[22] To normalize the operation of slave-trade Courts, Britain signed several bilateral treaties in 1818 and 1819 to establish Courts of Mixed Commission to prosecute slave-trade cases. Where the Vice-Admiralty Court had a single jurist, each Mixed Commission had four: Britain and the other party to each treaty appointed a Commissary Judge and an Arbitrator. To encourage cooperation the Mixed Commission treaties also established slave-trade Courts in Havana, Rio de Janeiro, and Suriname (although from 1819 to 1845 only 50 cases were heard in Havana, 44 in Rio, and 1 in Suriname, compared with 433 in Sierra Leone).[23] Cases that the Judges could not agree on were sent to the Arbitrators. The Mixed Commission turned over half of all prize monies directly to the representatives of the foreign government at the Court.[24] After the establishment of the Mixed Commissions, regular sittings of the Freetown Court of Vice-Admiralty were suspended, and the Court convened only to judge serious crimes committed at sea.[25]

The new legal regime for abolition threatened the economic survival of Sierra Leone. The colonial schooner *Prince Regent* was taken out of commission, "from principles of extreme economy," after its right to capture slave ships was voided by the Courts of Mixed Commission.[26] MacCarthy lost control over patronage appointments; appointments to the Mixed Commissions were made directly by the Foreign Office.[27] The new Courts were diplomatic as well as judicial instruments, balancing the interests of foreign judges against the interests of British officers. The Judges and Arbitrators discussed cases in a private office on the lower floor of a rented house in Freetown, "furnished with one table, four chairs, & two desks and decorated with a few of the maps officially sent out."[28] The number of chairs is a telling detail: Charles MacCarthy literally did not have a seat at the table.

The Mixed Commissions continued to process captured slave ships, and to generate prize money. For example, by August 1820 six captured Spanish ships had been sold, with a total value of £3,603, 1s, 6d, as well as two Dutch ships, valued at £353, 16s, 9½d.[29] Crucially, the prize money generated by the new Courts did not immediately begin to circulate in the colony. "A practice of pilfering," the British Commissioners complained to the Foreign Office, "is always carried on in prize vessels condemned."[30] "Pilfered" goods and money no longer seeped into colonial markets, and officers in Freetown had less cash to spend. The British "moiety" of prize funds was paid into a military account, and the foreign commissioners received the other half.[31] As one nineteenth-century historian commented, although the Courts had full dockets, their proceedings were "tedious and annoying," full of miscommunications and miscues.[32] The foreign judges in the Mixed Commissions were entitled to protect their home countries' interests, to the frustration of both the British judges and high-ranking British officers.[33] The British Commissioners, Edward Gregory and Edward Fitzgerald, had to ask the permission of the Foreign Office to use funds earmarked for England to pay the salaries of Court officers.[34] The new slave-trade Courts' rules and regulations also irritated military officers accustomed to the Vice-Admiralty Court. After the Mixed Commissions published a decision he disagreed with, Sir George Collier, the highest-ranking Royal Navy officer in the colony, began to disparage the British Commissioners at parties around Freetown, and to threaten legal action against them.[35] The compact between the slave-trade Court and British officers was dissolving.

From a military perspective, the advantages of Sierra Leone as a headquarters for slave-trade interdiction had been more economic than geographic. The treaties permitting the trade to continue south of the equator confirmed a long-term trend in the geography of slave trading. The trade north of the equator had been in decline for decades, in favour of the specialized slave-trading ports of the Bights of Benin and Biafra. From 1819 to 1826, among the 69 ships tried at Freetown, only 4 were captured north of Sierra Leone. The average distance from the point of capture to Freetown was 790 miles, and at least one slave ship was brought back to Freetown from more than 1,200 miles away.[36] Getting to Freetown was often inconvenient, but the port had good facilities for prize agency and trade. With prize money more difficult to obtain, some officers lobbied for more geographically convenient headquarters. In a widely published letter, Sir James Lucas Yeo insisted Sierra Leone was "not so well calculated for forming a settlement for emancipated or captured Negroes, as the Gold Coast."[37]

Along with the Gold Coast, the island of Fernando Po (now called Bioko, a part of Equatorial Guinea) was mooted in the press as a possible headquarters. "Fernando Po," read one comment, "certainly offers a favourable position for landing the slaves captured in the two Bights, while the passage to Sierra Leone from thence, averages at least six weeks."[38] In the House of Commons, Frederick Marryat, a novelist and pamphleteer with deep ties to the West Indies, remarked, "In the crowded state of slave ships, the mortality on board them must of course be dreadful; and would be almost wholly avoided, by their being sent to Cape Coast Castle."[39] Marryat and other representatives of the West India planters did not dare hope to reverse the abolition of the slave trade; given popular support for abolition, that would have been politically suicidal.[40] Instead, propagandists agitated to move the headquarters of military antislavery in order to diminish the power of the London antislavery elite—if the Royal Navy were based at Cape Coast Castle, for example, the Clapham Sect would have fewer eyes and ears on the ground, and no long-standing relationships with local merchants and administrators. This campaign was supplemented with publications claiming to reveal the "corruption" of the London abolitionists and their clients in Sierra Leone.[41]

In 1818, in the face of this campaign, William Wilberforce protested on the floor of the House that he "had no particular partiality to Sierra Leone."[42] In 1808 or even 1815, Wilberforce's demurral would have been unthinkable. Three years after Waterloo, it was a sign of the times.

Building the Liberated African Department

After 1815, as prize money became scarcer, thousands of people continued to arrive in the colony from slave ships. "Unless some more enlarged plans are adopted as to the mode of rendering the case of Captured Negroes . . . useful to themselves and the Colony," wrote Charles MacCarthy, "the increase we daily receive of these individuals will rather retard than promote our advance toward Civilization."[43] Former slaves were arriving in Freetown in too great a volume to be managed in the ad hoc style adopted by previous Governors. Demand for apprentices had been mostly satisfied, and the end of the wars had also dried up demand for black soldiers for service in West Africa and the West Indies. The steady supply of cheap labour pushed the children of the old settlers out of many skilled and unskilled jobs, and into work as sailors and carpenters onboard foreign and British merchant vessels.[44] Settlers expected higher wages than those of the Liberated Africans or migrant Kru. One colonial editorialist wrote that a migrant or former slave would receive 20 or 30 pence per day, and could "live well on five shilling per month," while a settler was too inclined to "sport finer clothes than any gentleman of the colony, [to] have his mutton for dinner, his fish for supper—his spirits, his wine, his porter for daily drink." Moreover, the writer continued, although Liberated Africans usually lacked the maritime skills of Kru workers, they were more numerous, and had the virtue of being "attached" to the colony, "in preference to men who are continually passing to and fro."[45] MacCarthy faced a complicated labour problem, of shortage in some sectors and surplus in others. More former slaves in the colony meant cheaper labour, but falling wages were pushing English-speaking tradesmen and apprentices out of Freetown. He worried that former slaves not apprenticed or enlisted were not growing rice, cassava, or other staples, but relying on "occasional employment at King's Works, and bringing on their backs to the market a small quantity of wood or lime."[46] He needed a system to command and distribute labour where and when he felt it was needed.

MacCarthy had been born in France, and christened Charles Guèroult. He was the descendant of Irish Catholic Jacobites, who had gone into exile

with King James II after the Glorious Revolution. He took the surname
"MacCarthy" from his uncle.[47] After serving in the Irish Brigade under the
French monarchy, MacCarthy fled the Revolution to fight under British com-
mand.[48] After several years in British North America, largely as a coordinator
of recruiting rather than in combat, he joined the Royal African Corps in 1811
as Lieutenant-Colonel. In 1812, he was appointed Governor of Senegal. After
Maxwell was recalled in 1814, MacCarthy became Governor of Sierra Leone.
His talents notwithstanding, MacCarthy was a Frenchman and a Catholic.
"My serving in North America or the West Coast of Africa," he complained,
"was not a matter of choice."[49] MacCarthy was nominally Catholic, but he
was not observant or pious. He imagined Christianity more as a baseline
guarantor of social order and valued the Church of England as a symbol of
British values, not as a guardian of revealed truths. Christian practice, he assumed, was simply part and parcel of "civilized" behaviour. His colony
needed teachers, clerks, and bookkeepers to organize and pay former slaves
for their labour. Missionaries, MacCarthy reasoned, could be both managers
and teachers. He proposed to "divide the Peninsula in Parishes, settling a
Clergyman in each." The parishes would be sources of unskilled labour; as
Liberated Africans arrived, they would be distributed to villages as needed.
To shore up the supply of skilled workers, the most promising young men
would be taken on by the colonial government as apprentices to learn trades.[50]

Freetown had many Christian communities, including an official Church
of England congregation, three Methodist meetings, a Baptist meeting, and
various nondenominational evangelical groups.[51] However, MacCarthy noted
that Freetown's churches often excluded Liberated Africans. In the Anglican
chapel, colonists and white merchants filled the pews, while former slaves
stood in "a kind of ante-chamber," near prisoners from the jail. In the Methodist chapel favoured by prosperous Maroons and Nova Scotians, Liberated
Africans attended only as apprentices and servants.[52] Without a place for Liberated Africans in these communities, how could conversion to Christianity
occur? Historians have struggled to understand conversion: was it fundamentally coercive? Could converts "use" conversion to their own advantage?[53] To
MacCarthy, conversion was a bureaucratic act which occurred when a baptism
was recorded in a parish register, and which confirmed that the convert was on
the road to British civilization.

MacCarthy also hoped that conversion would keep former slaves from
leaving the colony to return to "native" life. If too many Liberated Africans

fled to the Mende, Temne, and Bullom villages scattered throughout the Peninsula, it might tip the balance of power from the British colony to the "native" chiefs. Indeed, the recorded population of "natives" in Freetown, living in ethnic enclaves like "Foolah Town," was growing alongside the population of Liberated Africans, from 997 in 1818 to 2,174 in 1826.[54] Other "runaway" Liberated Africans settled in a village known as Bambara Town, a half-mile east of Freetown, "an African hamlet in the centre of a British colony."[55] The discharged black soldiers of the 4th West India Regiment lived in another informal settlement, Soldier Town, close to Bambara Town, unofficially called "the Camp," and well known as a market for stolen goods.[56] To MacCarthy, fixing Liberated Africans in villages in the colonial hinterland would help to prevent their "escape" from the colony.

With all this in mind, MacCarthy reached out to the Church Missionary Society (CMS) in 1815 through a subordinate, Major Appleton of the Royal African Corps. Appleton dropped in on a meeting of the central corresponding committee of the Church Missionary Society (known at the time as the Society for Missions to Africa and the East) in London. He complained to the committee about the settlers and the Maroons, "a bad race . . . slothful and fond of liquors." Among the black residents of Sierra Leone, Appleton declared, "the recaptured ones [were] the best." Appleton reminded the members of the corresponding committee that "the Governor, by his oath, must encourage the Church—cannot commit the schools, except from mere necessity, to any one not of the Church."[57] The implication was simple: if the CMS would provide teachers, MacCarthy would be both delighted and required to accept them. For his part, MacCarthy sent solicitous letters to Josiah Pratt, the Secretary of the CMS. The "captured Negroes" were, he explained, "extremely zealous to be taught the Christian religion, and if a clergyman were settled with them . . . material progress would be made in their civilization."[58]

The Church Missionary Society had established a foothold in West Africa in 1804. Between 1804 and 1816, although the CMS supplied chaplains to Sierra Leone, and operated a school on Leicester Mountain above Freetown, its main West African mission was based in the villages and forts of the Rio Pongas. By 1816, partly due to backlash against Charles Maxwell's campaigns in the region, the Rio Pongas missions had many enemies and few converts.[59] The committee in London sent one of its members, Edward Bickersteth, to survey the missions and make recommendations for their reform. When he reached Freetown, Bickersteth was easily convinced to relocate to

Sierra Leone. "In the absence of supernatural inspiration," he wrote, "such circumstances may be considered as the call, 'Come over and help us.' "[60] Bickersteth arrived with a list, and renamed children at the Leicester school according to the wishes of British donors who had committed to donate at least £5 per year for six years.[61] Bickersteth spoke to a few of the children being renamed, "telling them the character of those whose names they bore. Could we but give them the souls of these good men," he exclaimed, "what a blessing these children would be to Africa!" The "black faces" of the children, he remarked, "seemed gratified with the labels we put round their necks."[62] This was exactly what MacCarthy had hoped for: missionaries would rename and educate Liberated Africans, and transform them into subjects with British names, British manners, and British attitudes toward work and social order. The Governor, delighted, promised to double the salary of any missionary who joined the village system, from £125 to £250 a year. In celebration of the deal, he gave the oldest of the informal villages in the colony, Hog Brook (Kingston-in-Africa in Thompson's time) a patriotic new name: Regent's Town.[63]

Liberated Africans at Work

The village system was designed to keep Liberated Africans from dispersing throughout the colony in order to better manage their work. Missionaries in the villages were expected to convert villagers to Christianity, but conversion (from MacCarthy's perspective) was mostly a catalyst to convince former slaves to take wages and work when and where they were told. The Captured Negro Department was renamed the Liberated African Department, and soon replaced the fading Vice-Admiralty Court at the centre of the colonial political economy. The Court was concentrated in Freetown; the Department was responsible for many thousands of Liberated Africans throughout the colony. The Court managed ships and goods; the Department managed people. But both institutions were centres for organizing economic life, hubs at the centre of networks of contracts and supply chains. Both permitted the colonial government to distribute the labour of former slaves. Both were informal, with few written rules, affording considerable latitude to colonial officials. Both were sources of patronage. Above all, both relied on a steady supply of slave ships arriving in Freetown to function and to thrive. However, there was at least one very important difference between the Department and

the Court. The Court was shambolic but it ultimately added value to the colonial economy; more money came out of the Court than was invested in it.
The Court's productivity was cut off by the end of the war, but in wartime it
was self-sustaining, and benefited several Governors of Sierra Leone. The
Liberated African Department operated at a loss. MacCarthy pumped money
from Britain through the Department, using it as a kind of device for economic stimulus. He also used the Department to concentrate and conceal data
about colonial finances. "Civilization" attracted money to stimulate a sagging
economy, and the village system came effectively to "belong" to MacCarthy
himself.

One of the most important documents produced by the Department,
the Register of Liberated Africans, is a collection of names, physical descriptions, and, occasionally, notes about the nationality of more than 10,000
former slaves. Historians have used the Register to write innovative cultural
and demographic histories of diasporic communities in Sierra Leone.[64] The
records, however, were not intended to be ethnographic. The Register was
an actuarial document: by recording the name, physical appearance, and ethnicity of former slaves, the colonial government hoped to maintain closer
watch over them. Moreover, for a time the British government paid out a
base fee of 2d per day for each adult Liberated African, and 1½ d for each
child, for the first six months after landing. The Register served as a kind of
invoice for support from Britain.[65] The Liberated African Department also
produced a second ledger, the "Liberated African Department Statement of
Disposals," of which the volume for 1821–33 has also survived in the Sierra
Leone Public Archives in Freetown. The Statement is a more precise instrument, a record of the total number of individuals in each slave ship, broken
down by where they were "disposed" of.[66] The Liberated African Department recorded which people were assigned to clear forests, learn trades, row
boats, repair buildings, or farm crops; the Statement was a spreadsheet, balancing demand for colonial labour against the supply of former slaves.

MacCarthy maintained tight control over the Department. While Governor, he would personally deliver his instructions to his second-in-command,
the Chief Superintendent, and occasionally to individual missionary superintendents.[67] The Chief Superintendent was the official liaison between individual villages and other colonial staff. He was expected to ride a regular circuit,
"to inquire into all complaints, and to observe that the system is acted up to."
He revised lists of Liberated Africans in collaboration with the missionary

superintendents.[68] When a ship arrived with freed slaves aboard, he and the Governor would assign people to villages as needed. When goods from England arrived, the Chief Superintendent organized their distribution. In general, Freetonians who needed apprentices for domestic service or to work in their warehouses and docks had first choice, after which likely looking young men were assigned to the public works in Freetown as "Government" apprentices. The remainder were distributed to the villages. In MacCarthy's time, there was no particular order as to which people from what slave ship went to what village; the Department had an unofficial policy of keeping "friends" together, but not people from the same region.[69]

MacCarthy, like many of his predecessors and many of his patrons in London, hoped to improve commercial agriculture in Sierra Leone. However, expansion and extensive farming were checked by geography: much of the Freetown Peninsula was jungle, growing out of thin, rocky soil. MacCarthy and the Department established villages in strategic locations, to compel villagers to clear land as part of the process of building homes and gardens. From 1816 to 1819, most of the villages were founded in the mountains, with the expectation that villagers would, as the long-serving Chief Superintendent Joseph Reffell put it, "clear the Forest in the rear."[70] One writer in the colonial newspaper reminded readers, "The importation of redeemed negroes had enabled the governor of Sierra Leone to clear some parts of the woods."[71] After 1819, people released from the Middle Passage were joined by large numbers of discharged soldiers from the Royal African Corps and West India Regiments. The next wave of villages, settled mostly by these former soldiers, was built in the swampy coastal lowlands, after the new fields cleared in the mountains proved less productive than expected.[72]

MacCarthy and the Department established villages in particular places so that villagers would clear jungles and drain swamps for agriculture. The villages were also placed such that they would cement the claim of the colonial government over the whole Freetown Peninsula, pushing out local kings and chiefs. In July 1819, MacCarthy purchased a tract of land from the Temne up to the bank of the Ribi River, south of Freetown, for 50 bars' worth of goods (as described in Chapter One, the "bar" was the local barter currency, used in the coastal trade and based on the nominal value of an iron bar). MacCarthy boasted that he did not *need* to make the treaty. In the hands of local chiefs, he reckoned, the land was "a useless forest and waste." Still, when the land claimed under the treaty was added to the land claimed by the new villages, MacCarthy could boast that his colony had grown into its "natural" geographic borders: the Sierra Leone River to the north, the mountains to the east, the Atlantic to the west, and the Ribi to the south.[73]

The villages helped MacCarthy claim greater control over the labour force and geography of the colony, giving him more control over the colonial economy. Much of the financial business of the Department was confined to the colony itself, concealed (whether by happenstance or by design) from auditors in London. The CMS archives, for example, do not preserve early financial records. According to one Department official, it was the Chief Superintendent's job to make out returns of the cash spent in each village, and the amount of provisions brought in and issued. These reports were apparently kept in a Freetown office, and although nearly all are lost, some of the data were copied in 1827.[74] All of the day-to-day expenses of the Department, including the cost of settling former slaves, building and repairing government-owned buildings, and paying out salaries, were recorded in the Cash Account. As early as 1827, Cash Account records for 1814 and 1815 were missing. By the second decade of the twenty-first century, none seem to have survived; I was unable to locate them in London, Freetown, or elsewhere. However, other sources indicate that funding flowed straight from the Governor's accounts, with all payments made with bills drawn on the Treasury by the Governor in his role as public accountant.[75]

The money passing through the Cash Account was not small change. There is slightly more data on money sent from London to Freetown. The village system, supported by the Clapham Sect and praised in the thriving missionary press, drew much-needed money to the colony. The Liberated African Department attracted grants from Parliament that the colonial government of Sierra Leone could not: £29,000 in 1815, £41,000 in 1816, and £39,000 in 1823. However, the expenses of the Liberated African Department also rose from £10,849 in 1815 to £59,629 in 1822.[76] The basic grant to the colony for the support of colonial officials barely changed, and grants to the Liberated African Department inflated the colonial budget.[77] From these numbers—and bearing in mind that the data are probably inaccurate and certainly incomplete—it appears the Department ran a significant deficit. But it was not in and of itself a business. It was a hub of contracts, labour, services, and other sources of economic activity. By pushing money through the Liberated African Department, it could be redirected as needed.

Because so few records remain, it is hard fully to understand how money passed from the colonial government through the Department into the colony at large. There are hints: one of MacCarthy's successors complained about the salaries of two French Catholic nuns whom MacCarthy seemed to have employed as nurses. "Why the whole of this sum was paid by the Liberated African Department," he wrote, "I can form no idea."[78] MacCarthy probably used the Department's funds to pay contingent expenses as they came up, although that is also a guess, as MacCarthy preferred to carry many colonial records with him when he travelled, and they are now lost.[79] In the archives, I found Colonial Office files that show that on at least 55 different occasions between 1817 and 1820, MacCarthy drew bills directly on the British Treasury without an itemized advice slip, "'on account of the expenses of Captured Negroes," for amounts ranging from £100 to £1,000. In response to these bills, the Treasury sent memoranda to the Colonial Office, inquiring whether it ought to pay. Each time, the Secretary of State for the Colonies signed off on MacCarthy's claims. The Secretary, the Earl Bathurst, was friendly to antislavery, but signing the bills was also easier than trying to claw back the money. Since MacCarthy was likely to have already spent whatever he had claimed before the bill even arrived in London, it was easier to sign and return to the thousand other matters calling for the attention of his small office. In this way, former slaves were a steady source of ready cash.

When MacCarthy went on furlough to England in 1820, acting Governor Charles Grant made at least another 16 charges on the account of the Liberated African Department. These (at least) 71 extant bills charged on the account of the Department amounted to £32,379, 16s 14d. Adjusted for inflation, these charges amount to roughly £2,560,000—not astronomical, by Treasury standards, but still a significant sum to be granted with virtually no oversight.[80] Moreover, a huge swath of the budget provided for Liberated Africans was devoted to the costs of building and maintaining Department buildings. From 1818 to 1825, the colony spent a reported £242,419, 6s, 11½d in total on Liberated Africans, of which roughly £110,092, 2s, 4½d was spent on feeding the colony and paying colonial officials, leaving more than £132,327 to be spent on buildings and repairs, or roughly £9.5 million in 2015 pounds sterling.[81] Given the relatively small size of the colony and the ready availability of timber, thatch, and other building materials, the construction budget seems to have been inflated beyond the immediate needs of the Department and the colony. It is easy to imagine that the remainder of the money earmarked for construction and repairs served as a convenient, all-purpose slush fund.

In addition to grants and per-head subsidies, the Liberated African Department received enormous loads of clothing, tools, and heavy machinery that could not be produced in Sierra Leone, sometimes at the expense of the British Treasury, sometimes at their wholesale cost. London was willing to ship over slate, lead, bells, clocks, and even weather vanes, provided that the hardware was going toward building churches. School supplies like slates, notebooks, and ink were also shipped over by the ton.[82] In one typical order, placed in 1818, Joseph Reffell requested thousands of shirts, pairs of pants, bars of soap, and blankets, as well as 26 tons of iron in different shapes and lengths, 10 bundles of iron rods, an expensive industrial lathe, and a screw chuck.[83] In another order, placed in 1822, he requested almost 19 miles of cloth.[84] These goods meant fees for transportation, inventory, warehousing, and distribution. Moreover, they were valuable trade goods. Before 1819, most cloth was sent to the colony as finished garments. After 1819, Mac-Carthy specifically requested whole cloth be sent. Whole cloth, he explained, would create work for apprentice tailors and seamstresses (and was, coincidentally, preferred by caravan traders).[85] In general, men and boys received "a frock made of duck cloth, a check shirt, a pair of duck cloth pants, and a pair of braces," while women and girls were usually given "a frock of printed calico, check, blue baft cloth and a white cotton chemise."[86] The Department also distributed doors, window shutters, nails, hinges, locks, and other hardware to the men to add to their houses, which village superintendents were expected to guarantee encompassed at least 70 square feet of internal space.[87]

The village system allowed MacCarthy to claim territory, and to gather and distribute money and goods. He also hoped it could help move the colony toward agricultural self-sufficiency. From the perspective of the colonial government, rice was by far the most valuable crop that could be grown in the villages. Tubers like cassava were difficult to preserve; rice was much easier to dry and store, and could be sold for export. In the best years, the mountain villages might yield two harvests of rice. In the lowland villages, farmers planted rice in between patches of cassava and coconut. However, the villages never produced anywhere near enough rice to satisfy demand, even within the colony.[88] The demand for rice, and for palm oil, the most common condiment served with the staple, had a number of consequences. First, growing demand presumably intensified slave labour in rice- and palm-growing regions. The Liberated African Department offered tenders to local merchants, including European merchants like Kenneth Macaulay and old Nova Scotian settlers like Stephen Gabbidon and the colonial printer James Wise, to supply rice to the villages. The amount of rice imported to Sierra Leone rose from 422 tons in 1818 to 1,091 tons in 1823, and the amount of palm oil imported from 13,788 gallons in 1820 to 31,546 gallons in 1823.[89] The bills may have been paid with funds funneled through the Liberated African Department.

The demand for rice also inspired the Department to invent a calculus for "converting" the crops that were grown in the villages, including cassava and coconut, into an equivalent value in rice in order to demonstrate increasing productivity (coconuts are usually referred to as "cocoa" or in the records of the colony, but to avoid confusion with the cocoa bean, used to make chocolate, I use "coconut" instead).[90] Through the village superintendents, the Liberated African Department purchased coconuts and cassava grown by villagers. In the early 1820s the price of a bushel of coconuts in the market in Freetown was 1s, 6d, and cassava 1s. The distance of the villages from Freetown, and the power of the village superintendents to distribute valuable goods and hardware, made it easy to convince farmers in the villages to sell their crop to the Department for a below-market rate of 1s per bushel of coconuts and 9d per bushel of cassava.[91] From 1819 to 1824, the Department purchased 175,130 bushels of cassava and 27,918 bushels of coconuts in this way, operating as a kind of agricultural cooperative. Assuming that all of these crops were purchased at the same rate, the Liberated African Department turned a profit of £697, 19s on the coconuts it bought, and £2,189, 2s, 6d on the cassava, or £2,887, 1s, 6d in total. However, in the same period, the Department spent at least £33,356, 5s, 1d on rice purchased from local merchants. In an attempt to balance the books, the Department reckoned that the total production of coconuts and cassava had been equivalent to the production of 53,964 bushels of rice.[92]

But production did not meet demand, and accountancy could not turn cassava into rice. Consequently, the village superintendents were expected to get as many Liberated Africans into the rice fields as they could. And where, in Freetown, employees of the Department were expected to implement "one uniform model of treatment" when it came to "feeding, clothing and working" the Liberated Africans, village superintendents could do as they saw fit.[93] Many chose "from amongst the negroes the most intelligent to act as overseers," and punished the "idle" either by withholding wages or by locking them up in sheds, warehouses, and other makeshift prisons overnight.[94] As usual, "idleness" was defined as the unwillingness among former slaves to grow the crops they were commanded to grow, rather than unwillingness to farm. Even as the villages "failed" to meet rice quotas, they grew a wide variety of other fruits and vegetables for their own consumption, and for village markets, including ginger, arrowroot, bananas, okra, yams, and papaya.[95]

Liberated Africans who did not work as farmers were often assigned to the public works in Freetown, or in the villages. While in " 'the King's service," former captives worked alongside settlers and Kru migrant workers, and lived in temporary huts built out of mud, or in makeshift sheds at the Colonial Forge Yard and Forge House.[96] The Department loaned out groups of workers to various colonial departments. When loaned to the Ordnance Department, Liberated Africans were not paid wages.[97] In 1825, the Department of Public Works employed 440 workers for wages, and 300 more without wages, although apparently they were "employed in carrying Bricks and lime, being a lighter work and one more easily apportioned to the strength of the individual."[98] There are very few sources that give much insight into the working lives of the Liberated Africans in the age of the village system. In 1827, the Commission of Inquiry sent to survey Sierra Leone interviewed a few dozen prominent Liberated Africans, primarily prosperous farmers who sold the bulk of their surplus crop to the Liberated African Department. Some, like George Sawyer, recruited farm labour exclusively from among their "country people" arriving from the Middle Passage. Disbanded soldiers from the West India Regiments were folded into the mass of the Liberated Africans, but tended to have slightly more diverse business interests. A demobilized soldier called Sergeant Maitland settled in Kent, where he opened a shop selling liquor, tobacco, and trade beads; he hired up to six Liberated Africans to work his farm and employed crews of sailors from the Sherbro' to bring his goods around the tip of the Peninsula into Freetown.[99]

Despite their productive work, which seemed to be evidence of their acceptance of British civilization, the Liberated Africans puzzled European observers. The most prosperous, like the farmer Peter Renner, enthusiastically employed newer arrivals in the colony, bought European clothes, and sold their crops, keeping careful records of the profits. But even Renner could "give no satisfactory account of the time or labour bestowed" on his farms.[100] "In an enlightened country like England," the Commissioners of Inquiry explained, it would be unthinkable that someone would be as innocent of time kept by clocks or as heedless of land ownership as defined by fences and deeds as some of the Liberated Africans appeared to be. "One will scarcely conceive," they wrote, "the difficulty experienced in ascertaining from . . . even the most intelligent liberated African, his age, the length of time he has resided in the colony or the village, the quantity of land he has cultivated, of seed which he sows, of produce which he reaps, or the number of months or weeks which he is employed in its cultivation." Even market-gardeners didn't appear to know how much they had grown: "His produce he never measures but that which he sells and this by a measure which is seldom regulated by any fixed stand."[101] The Liberated African Department intended for agriculture to be civilizing; but if farmers didn't come to market on time, or didn't fence their fields or measure their crop yield, then perhaps they had not absorbed the lessons agriculture was supposed to teach. The Liberated African farmer, the Commissioners concluded in dismay, "has eaten one part of his produce, planted another part, and sold the remainder" but had little sense of the "proportions either in gross or in detail."[102]

The Liberated African Department struggled mightily to convince villagers to observe European folkways of time and quantity. By the mid-eighteenth century, keeping time with clocks was considered to be a particular mark of civilized life, and essential to organizing labour; convincing people who had never worked by the clock to adopt its particular way of imposing discipline on the passage of time remained a preoccupation for European colonial powers throughout the nineteenth and twentieth centuries.[103] In Mac-Carthy's time, attempts to govern time with clocks were more symbolic gestures than practical reforms. Sometime in the 1820s, colonial officials ordered the works from Britain for a clock tower with four faces to be built in Freetown, in the hope that "that dwellers in each point of the compass [would] meditate upon the flight of time." The clock was never properly installed. Most watch repairs in Freetown were done by Fula whitesmiths, who could not install the larger, more complicated works that drove the four clock faces. No one else in the colony had any experience with building or repairing timepieces, and by the 1830s only one of the four dial plates had hands at all, much less kept time.[104] The one-faced clock, assembled by men with more expertise repairing tinware and pocket watches, missing many of its parts and barely correct twice a day, was in the centre of a prominent, much-trafficked public space, and must have been a reminder to colonial officials of the limits of the Liberated African Department and the civilizing mission. In Freetown,

workers were expected to work from six to nine in the morning, then from
ten to four, but Liberated Africans required constant supervision to remain at
work during these "business hours"—in part because colonial officials were
also often unsure of the time.[105]

In the early days of the colony, the Nova Scotian settlers were frequent
litigants in the colonial courts on questions of land tenure. Many colonial officials resented the Nova Scotians for their stridency, but they understood
why the settlers would want to go to law. The desire to own land seemed self-
evident. In MacCarthy's era, Liberated African Department officials were
puzzled that Liberated Africans did not immediately claim farms for themselves. Joseph Reffell commented, "Every individual has made his own
choice; and so long as he did not interfere with the ground cleared by others,
no objection has been made to his occupying any part of land he chose, no
fixed portion being allotted."[106] According to Reffell, like the people of the
Bullom Shore, the Liberated Africans practised swidden agriculture, moving
from field to field throughout the growing seasons, burning brush and plough-
ing the stubble. Most cultivated more land in their second year of farming. By
the third year, some simply abandoned the land or went back to previously
cleared land that had returned to bush. "When a man abandons the ground he
has cleared and cultivated, leaving nothing on it, and it grows up into bush,"
Reffell concluded with astonishment, "I rather think he considers his interest
lost in it."[107] Moreover, many former slaves abandoned their villages when
their time on rations ended. Since farmland in the villages "frequently lay at a
considerable distance from any settlement," a colonial official admitted, Liberated Africans could easily leave for the fields and never return.[108] A similar
effect occurred when wages fell. One of the village superintendents noted
that a sag in wages had "much thinned the population."[109]

Reffell and his colleagues were unable completely to solve this problem. By the 1830s, Liberated Africans were more willing to assert claims to
land, but many had abandoned farming in favour of trade. Despite the insist-
ence of the Department that civilization was built on small holdings and
peasant agriculture, many Liberated Africans cleaved to their own under-
standings of the meaning of farmwork, and rejected it. Liberated Africans
came from across West Africa and beyond, but nearly all had either been
born enslaved, or forced into slavery in war or in a judicial proceeding. Many
came from societies where slaves did most of the farming. For example,
among the Mende, Temne, and Bullom living around the colony, the work of

freemen included clearing land for rice, building and repairing houses and other buildings, hunting and fishing, and participating in palaver.[110] Maintaining and harvesting fields was work for women and slaves. If they were no longer slaves, Liberated African men might have thought, why would they do the work of slaves? Liberated Africans confronted the civilizing mission with their own complicated set of expectations and cultural norms—a set of beliefs and practices that are invisible in the archives of the MacCarthy era. The gender politics and division of labour in the villages, for example, are effectively inaccessible. Like the broken clock keeping indifferent time in Freetown, the demands placed on Liberated African farmers—rations, land tenure rules, cooperative sale of cassava and coconuts, missionary management—were intrusive and demanding, but uneven. But if the civilizing mission couldn't be imposed, it could at least be displayed.

Regent: Converting Labour

MacCarthy was proud of the villages and visited them as many as three times a week, often bringing guests with him.[111] To European visitors, the villages were like living dioramas-cum-experimental-farms. The colonial newspaper often featured accounts of official visits taken to observe the former slaves at work or at prayer, and occasionally to take an "elegant dinner in *humble Style*."[112] In the view from Freetown, the villages were a source of workers and contracts that could be rendered in registers of names and charts of imports, exports, and bushels of rice. Up close, the most successful villages prospered because white missionaries "lost control," sharing power by choice or by necessity with African converts.

The records of the religious life of the village system are deceptively rich. In the later nineteenth century, Freetown became a hub of Christian evangelism in Africa, and the home of the Church of England's first black bishop.[113] But in the 1820s, the lives of Liberated Africans lay just beyond the edge of the archive: most people freed from the Middle Passage were illiterate, and even those who learned English left behind few records. Although missions produced enormous archives, their records preponderate toward "those segments of the global chains that connect donors with practitioners."[114] Missionaries wrote down some of the sayings and prayers of former slaves in the pages of the journals they were required to keep and send to London and which were published for the consumption of potential donors. "Send

us particular narratives of what takes place," the CMS implored one missionary, "that you think will interest our friends."[115] Some top-ranking African
converts kept journals themselves. These letters and journals are shaped by
the generic conventions of Bible stories and narratives of perdition, redemption, and conversion.[116] The journals offer a detailed view of life in the villages, but one focused almost exclusively on converts to Christianity—a
minority of villagers even in the most famous village, Regent. Regent's superintendent, W. A. B. Johnson, produced some of the most complete documen-
tation on the everyday work of the village system, but his letters and journals
overwhelmingly privilege his closest allies, a group of polyglot African converts who did much of the administrative work in the village. In this sense,
Regent is an especially good case study of the quotidian life of the village system, and of the key role African converts came to play in it, just beyond the
ken of officials in Freetown. It is also a crucial case study because it shows the
optical illusion of missionary archives in sharp detail: the records make it seem
possible to know a lot about the Liberated Africans who lived in Regent in
MacCarthy's era—but we may not know anything at all.

Johnson was a working-class immigrant to London from Hanover,
zealous but with little theological training.[117] Despite his limited education,
Johnson was pious and charismatic. As an administrator, he saw eye to eye
with MacCarthy. As a cleric, he was less tractable. Many of the missionaries
working in Sierra Leone realised that Charles MacCarthy was interested less
in Christianity as such and more in what he thought it could do for the colony. "He has two faces towards us," the colonial chaplain William Garnon
wrote. "While your servants do his dirty work, i.e. build houses & plant
vineyards—all is well, but if they talk about their people's souls . . . it is then
nothing."[118] When Johnson was in Freetown preaching to an audience including MacCarthy and a clique of military officers, the officers laughed and
talked throughout the service. After services, the missionary hiked five miles
up from the town to the mountains. "I felt," he wrote, "as if I had come into
another world."[119]

When Johnson arrived in Regent, it had been settled by former slaves
since at least 1809. Because the archives of early colonial Sierra Leone are
mostly European, and because few Europeans visited the village until Johnson, we have only his journal as a source. He wrote that the village was "a
complete wilderness. But God says, 'that in the wilderness shall waters break
out, and streams in the desert.' "[120] Johnson's biblicism occludes. To evangel-

ical eyes, a tidy village could be a "wilderness," and a lush jungle a desert, because the expectations of missionary writers demanded that their arrival cause "waters to break out." Because the village was visited so rarely, Johnson found the registers of the former slaves who had been assigned to live in the village to be "in the greatest confusion . . . some have received rations, & some have not for some time & are actually in a state of starvation."[121]

As Johnson began to distribute regular rations and supplies, and because many were eager to learn English, the language of trade in Freetown, the village grew quickly. The villagers regularly attended church services, but Johnson was distressed that, when he finished his sermons, "they would come & ask me for clothing &c. which gave me reason to think that they only came for that purpose."[122] Later, when William Tamba visited a local village to preach, the headman told him that he and his people "did not want Sunday, but clothes."[123] However, some villagers were moved, and in October 1816 a shingle maker named Joe Thomson became Johnson's first convert. By January 1817, 41 of the villagers had been baptised and invited to become full communicant members of the church.[124]

From a historian's perspective, conversion is confounding, both ephemeral and profoundly material. For converts, it was an ecstatic spiritual experience that by definition cannot survive in an archive, but it was also an invitation to join a political and economic community of believers that kept dense records of village life and work. Salvation was free in Regent, but getting saved was valuable. MacCarthy wrote to the village superintendents that he hoped the villages would "keep the uncivilized in due order & reward the industry of the well behaved."[125] After services, when people lined up for clothing or food, Johnson told them he would inspect their farms, "and give . . . according to their industry."[126] Villagers whose farms passed muster received surplus clothing from the Napoleonic wars; Johnson referred to his favourite schoolboys as "my little Red Jackets."[127] But the material advantages of conversion were distributed not only by Johnson. The communicants established a mutual aid society for themselves, for the support of the sick and the unfortunate.[128] Communicants could be disciplined by the revocation of their privileges. A man who fought with his wife in public was warned, "Another misdemeanor might deprive him of the privileges which God's people enjoyed."[129] The relentlessly positive tone of missionary journals presents the village as nearly conflict-free, but a few hints of the hostility other villagers directed toward the communicants and missionaries speaks to their power.

Some schoolgirls complained to Johnson, "Them other girls make too much noise, and some of them would do us bad, but they fear you."[130] In another instance, a group of boys being trained as carpenters threw stones at the missionaries after one of their cohort was arrested for making a bed out of wood stolen from a colonial building site.[131] A Maroon rum seller declared he would murder Johnson, although Johnson declined to have him prosecuted.[132]

Johnson was convinced that "the Christian negroes shew a strong attachment to the simplest views of religion."[133] In a village where beating rice was part of the rhythm of everyday life, Johnson explained the doctrine of election in familiar terms. As villagers beat rice stalks, the grains remained as the husks blew away, like wheat separating from chaff; communicants, Johnson explained, were the grains, chosen for eternal life.[134] "The simplest views of religion" may have given communicants the space to understand Christianity on their own terms. In the accounts of their lives preserved in Johnson's letters and diaries, the communicants remembered the "miracle" of their rescue from the Middle Passage, and were especially fearful of eternal damnation. "I thank God he bring me to this country," one man testified to his fellow converts.[135] Another communicant experienced terror at the idea that he only had learned how to imitate a Christian, and had not been authentically converted.[136] Ironically, Johnson was sometimes annoyed by the communicants' preoccupation with their sins. He wrote, "They seem to have all the old usual disorders, complaining & mourning over the depravity of their [hearts]."[137]

Conversion could spread as new villagers found groups of people who spoke their language. Others converted and joined new communities of believers. One communicant, named George Paul, who was freed from the Middle Passage in 1815 and who lived with a settler in Freetown until 1817, was sent to Regent and apprenticed to a tailor. Paul, who "had very little connection with his country people," and no other home to go to, lived in Johnson's house, and found companionship in his church.[138] In 1818, at the age of roughly 14, he founded a nightly prayer meeting under the supervision of William Tamba.[139] At the meetings, the boys and girls of the church would meet to sing and pray. By lamplight a 10-year-old boy implored, "O Lord . . . Take us away from Hell fire. We want you to do it now! This night! Our sins too much!," while Johnson eavesdropped outside under a window, weeping.[140]

MacCarthy, who prized church attendance, was duly impressed by the communicants. Some attended divine worship as many as six times on

Sundays.[141] When communicants married one another, they wore European clothes, "The brides . . . dressed in white gowns, black beaver hats, ribbons . . . the men in blue coats, light waistcoats, frilled shirts, white neck-handkerchiefs, light trowsers, white stockings, shoes, and fine hats."[142] On a visit to the village in 1821, the newly knighted Sir Charles MacCarthy was overwhelmed with emotion when he saw the communicant villagers lined up along the road into town, dressed in European clothing, led by 12 girls in white.[143] MacCarthy was also pleased because Regent was especially productive. Henry Düring, a missionary in another village, complained that the Liberated Africans under his supervision were suspicious even of subsistence farming. When he demanded they set to sowing and plowing, they would answer, "What for we work? King take all we make," probably a reference to the Department's habit of buying up surplus crops at a below-market rate.[144] But in Regent, schoolboys cleared land for farms growing subsistence crops like cassava, coconut, yams, plantains, and bananas and cash crops like coffee. Regent produced more surplus coconuts and cassava than did any other village.[145] In 1818 and 1819, villagers from Regent cut a new road down to Freetown.[146] Later, more than 300 villagers built a road from Regent to York, a fishing village south of the capital. "The poor people have worked almost beyond their strength," Johnson wrote. "The rocks are immense."[147]

And yet, there weren't enough communicants to satisfy MacCarthy. In 1823, out of a population of roughly 2,000, there were only 410 communicants in Regent.[148] MacCarthy saw religion as social cohesion and baptism as paperwork. He expected Johnson to baptize every former slave in Regent, and to treat church services as patriotic rituals. Johnson refused. He claimed the ability to distinguish true from false conversions, and insisted that since only a fraction of humanity had been elected to salvation, only a minority of the villagers could be full members of the Christian community. MacCarthy paraphrased the Archbishop of Calcutta, arguing for more baptisms because "Christianity and Religion may be expected . . . to follow the success of a Christian state."[149] Johnson disagreed. On 13 May 1818, he wrote in his diary that the Governor "wished I would baptize more people. I told him that I could not, unless God first baptized their hearts." MacCarthy was furious, and threatened to censure Johnson. He promised to send the entire population of unbaptized people in Regent to the Methodist chapel in Freetown, since "as far as he thought, [Methodist] Baptism [was] as good as ours." "I told him," Johnson wrote, "that God only could make Christians."[150]

MacCarthy did not have much leverage; if he sent Liberated Africans to be baptized by the Baptists or the Methodists, it might make more Liberated Africans mobile and itinerant, weakening the village system. Moreover, Johnson was obviously successful, while most other missionaries in the colony were unimpressive, and some were violent and brutal: for example, William Randle, superintendent of Kent, beat his servant to death in front of a group of horrified Liberated African villagers.[151] Still, MacCarthy complained, "A good moral conduct, a Christian appearance, and an assurance of an anxious wish to become Christians is all that can be expected" of candidates for baptism.[152] He praised three more senior missionaries, Leopold Butscher, Charles Wenzel, and Melchior Renner, who were willing to baptize "their" villagers.[153] "What can I do?" Renner asked in a letter. "Our good Governor is always present, and is sponsor for all, old and young."[154]

As church membership became more desirable, Johnson became nervous that "the Devil is about to sow tares amongst the wheat," encouraging false conversions.[155] Johnson's desire to limit membership in his church was practical, but it was also theological: if 50 applied for baptism and only 16 were received, it insured that village resources remained highly valued, but also that salvation was scarce.[156] Consequently, there were high barriers to entry into the communion, policed by Johnson and the communicants. Church membership was managed through a system of evaluation and public scrutiny. As early as 1818, Johnson met with a council of six to evaluate candidates for baptism.[157] By 1820, the council included Johnson, two local tradesmen, and seven Africans, including William Tamba and William Davis. Candidates were invited to "relate the dealings of the Lord" to the committee. They were then questioned, and "such were allowed who had manifested a change in their conduct, convinced of sin & had a view of the Saviour to save them."[158]

In one of his journals, Johnson transcribed one of these interviews. The young woman seeking baptism was first asked why she wanted the sacrament. She replied that it was because of something Johnson said in a sermon that terrified her, that a person "not born again by the spirit of God, they cannot go to God." Johnson asked the woman if she "had been bad before, you do not anything bad now; you are very good this time, are you not?" She replied that her heart was full of sin. Johnson asked, "I suppose then, when you are baptized, you think you shall be better?" The woman replied, "No . . . that no make me good, the Lord Jesus Christ . . . can save me." Johnson asked whether baptismal water washed body and soul, to which the woman replied, "The Holy Ghost must baptize the soul."[159] Johnson wanted to confirm that the prospective communicant understood the Calvinist doctrines of election and total depravity, that baptism would not wash away their sins, and that their fate in the afterlife was already sealed, and no individual choice they made would affect their salvation or damnation. Every week, after these theological quizzes, Johnson would announce the names and "places of abode" of candidates to the communicants, who would watch them, "and if they should observe any improper conduct . . . inform me of the same." This week of surveillance was repeated after three months of candidacy, and again just before baptism.[160]

In Regent, baptism was not what MacCarthy wanted it to be, because it was indexed to access to resources, community, and social power and because it was controlled and limited by a committee composed mostly of Liberated Africans. It was also not exactly what the CMS expected it to be. The CMS had a scheme in place to make baptism a fund-raising tool. Donors could give Liberated Africans new names as they chose, and in return receive brief accounts of their "character" and "nation." For example, "John Essex Bull," age 20 in 1821, was reckoned to be Susu, and was judged "quiet, diligent, attentive," while "Cradock Galscott," age 13, was described as "very idle . . . runs away continually."[161] Johnson was censured by the CMS central committee for allowing communicants to be "baptised with names of their own choice." Edward Bickersteth reminded Johnson that women who changed their name at marriage from a donor-selected name ought to be encouraged to keep their donor's name, "which is of importance to their English Friends . . . it would be well if the Surname given by Benefactors were considered and used as the principal *Christian* name; as this would more distinctly show their relation to their Benefactors."[162] Part of the success of Regent inhered in Johnson's belief in the capacity of the villagers to be "genuinely" converted, and his willingness to share power with an inner circle of African church leaders.

Johnson's inner circle of communicants had a few traits in common: all were men, all were polyglot, and all were skilled labourers.[163] Other missionaries sometimes believed that their converts were feigning conversion to bamboozle them. One wrote, for example, that the "first thing the [African] mother inculcates into her child is deceit."[164] Johnson, in contrast, delegated so much authority to his communicants that the European missionaries became jealous. When Johnson was on leave in England, William Davis was accused of drinking wine and burning wax candles, forbidden as sinful and wasteful, respectively, under missionary regulations. David Noah had his modest salary of £80 a year stripped from him. "David Noah," Johnson fumed on his return, "is more useful than some Schoolmasters and Missionaries who enjoy a Salary of £200 & £250."[165] Noah, Johnson wrote, taught school, issued rations, kept the inventory of provisions and the registers of villagers, acted as village surveyor by measuring out and distributing house lots, entered marriages and baptisms into parish records, and more. "In short," Johnson wrote, "he is everything at Regent's Town!"[166]

Regent, then, hints at a concealed history of the village system, a counterpoint to MacCarthy's statistics and to the frictionless just-so conversion stories of the missionary press. Regent prospered less because of Johnson's particular skill as a missionary, and more because he allowed a group of elite Liberated Africans access to considerable power, particularly over the distribution of rations and other goods. And because Johnson trusted that converts in Regent were not feigning conversion, he allowed the villagers to invent new devotional practices, like the nightly prayer meetings. Regent seemed so successful precisely because Johnson ceded some control of the colonial "civilizing mission" to the Liberated Africans.

Greater Sierra Leone

The colonial civilizing mission emerged in Sierra Leone as Charles MacCarthy looked to reorient the colonial economy around the Liberated Africans as the prize-money economy cooled. The territorial expansion of Sierra Leone's "empire" in West Africa was also a consequence of straitened postwar circumstances, as Britain began to revise the loose rules of wartime commerce in ways that disquieted MacCarthy. From 1812 until 1814, MacCarthy had served as Governor of Senegal. While Senegal was occupied by Britain, many British subjects moved there, and built factories and trading posts. Many of these traders dealt in gum arabic, the sap harvested from acacia trees, valuable in the manufacture of many industrial chemicals. When Senegal was restored to France, MacCarthy hoped that the British subjects remaining in French territory would bring their goods to Sierra Leone. When MacCarthy mooted the idea in a dispatch, the issue was referred by the Colonial Office to the senior politicians and jurists of the Privy Council, invested by the Crown with substantial power to review and amend domestic and colonial legislation. The Council ruled that, under the Navigation Acts, trade between French and

British colonies was illegal, even if all the traders involved were British sub-jects.[167] MacCarthy was disappointed by the ruling. In response, he did what he could to encourage local trade on a smaller scale by quietly amending the weights and measures used in the colony and dropping many duties on goods, in order to encourage a greater volume of caravan trade.[168] Without imports from other parts of the coast, Freetown merchants would have nothing to sell to African traders. The only way for Sierra Leone to trade legally with other British settlements in tropical West Africa was for the colony to absorb or annex them. And so, just as the Liberated African villages consolidated British rule in the Freetown Peninsula, MacCarthy enlisted Liberated Africans as set-tlers and pioneers in new trading posts.

After Britain agreed to turn Senegal back over to France, MacCarthy received permission to establish a trading post on the Gambia River. The river was nominally a British possession, and MacCarthy's orders were to dispatch a small military force to fly the British flag and hold the territory in case French traders sought to expand south from Senegal. Few French mer-chants seemed particularly interested, but rumours circulated that American merchants hoped to stake a claim.[169] MacCarthy sent Captain Grant of the Royal African Corps to renew treaties with local rulers and build a makeshift fort on the site of the old trading post of Saint James, some 60 miles inland from the mouth of the river. However, as MacCarthy reported to Earl Bathurst in April 1816, Grant was more impressed with Banjul, a swampy is-land at the mouth of the river, which "appeared to him perfectly well adapted for a military and commercial establishment."[170] Grant explained that Banjul would be an upgrade, "a facility of preventing Vessels for Slaves from enter-ing the River," that "would at the same time be . . . advantageous as a Com-mercial Establishment." Grant explained that local natives would be happy to cross the shallow river between the island and the mainland to trade hides, beeswax, and ivory. He reported that many British traders at Saint James had already applied for grants of land on the new settlement at the river's mouth. In a time of retrenchment in Britain, a new colony was unwelcome, but pos-session was nine-tenths of permission, and the new town of Bathurst, on the renamed Saint Mary's Island, was added to the new "greater Sierra Leone."[171] The claim that Britain would eventually make on the colony of the Gambia originated in part from MacCarthy's short-term scheme to recapture a slice of the gum trade from French and American merchants. MacCarthy also mooted the idea of claiming Arguin, an island off the coast of present-day

Mauritania, far north of Sierra Leone.[172] Nothing came of this second plan, but the proposal shows how eager MacCarthy was to claim territory in order to secure colonial trade.

After claiming Saint Mary's Island as a dependency, MacCarthy set sights on the Isles-de-Los. The islands had been important both to the slave trade and to "legitimate" trade for centuries, and had long been occupied by a mix of British, French, Euro-African, and American traders. The islands were also well known in Freetown as a safe haven for debtors and suspected slave traders.[173] MacCarthy explained to Bathurst that British traders were losing business as American goods were smuggled through the islands into the colony to "the prejudice of the fair trader, and the African trade carried on by foreigners."[174] Two British traders had factories on the islands. They purchased most of their goods from Americans whose forts were based in the nearby rivers, and then traded directly with Sierra Leone.[175] MacCarthy was furious that Americans could benefit from what he felt ought to be British trade. It would be easy, MacCarthy reasoned, to send a small military force to occupy the islands to dissuade smugglers, and cut off American smugglers' access to trade in Freetown. MacCarthy also formally annexed Bance Island and the Banana Islands to Sierra Leone, to make trade easier, and to exclude American and French merchants.[176]

In the rainy season of 1818, the three most prominent European traders at the Isles-de-Los left the islands. W. H. Leigh and Charles Hickson died. Samuel Samo, the slave trader tried by Maxwell, decided to return to England. Leigh, according to Charles MacCarthy, left behind £20,000 of trade goods in his warehouse, and on his deathbed apparently asked MacCarthy to protect his property. That solemn (maybe fictional; certainly convenient) vow, coupled with "the thorough conviction of their proving of great importance to British Commerce," gave MacCarthy impetus to claim the islands for Britain.[177] He heard rumours in Freetown that Leigh and Hickson had been planning to sell their property to their American clients, "falsely pretending that they could dispose of Islands not their property." MacCarthy received word from the "Mandingo" Alimami Dalu Mohammed that he and the local Baga chiefs would support MacCarthy's claim to the islands. On 2 July MacCarthy attended a palaver on one of the islands and signed a new treaty that turned over possession of the islands to Britain. MacCarthy landed thirty soldiers from the Royal African Corps to occupy the forts. He renamed the islands: Crawford became Bathurst; Tammara became Liverpool; Whiteman's Island was renamed Wilberforce, and Allen Coral became Clarkson.[178] Symbolically and officially, the Isles-de-Los belonged to Sierra Leone.

The Wages of Gradual Emancipation

The success of the village system and the growth of Sierra Leone's footprint did not go unnoticed, as the American Colonization Society began to plan a colony of its own in West Africa. The intellectual and cultural history of the American Colonization Society is a history of white appropriation of African American initiative, and a crucial point of connection between the histories of American slavery and emancipation and the history of American empire. The ACS is best known for promoting what historian Nicholas Guyatt has called "an idea of double emancipation," that "blacks would be freed from slavery, then whites would be freed from blacks."[179] The ACS coalesced in the wake of the War of 1812, as slaveholders in the upper South reckoned with the thousands of enslaved African Americans who had taken advantage of the fog of war to escape to freedom behind British lines, following in the footsteps of the many thousands of people who had emancipated themselves during the American Revolution. In turn, antislavery advocates in the North focused on colonization as a means of convincing Southern slaveholders of the wisdom of gradual emancipation. Christian clergy and proponents of missionary work on both sides of the sectional divide saw in colonization the possibility of spreading Christianity to West Africa. This odd union of white leaders in the slaveholding South and gradualist North soon collapsed, but in the 1810s and early 1820s, the ACS was able to paper over the conflict over slavery in the United States by appealing to the common cause of removing African Americans to West Africa.[180] However, long before colonization captured the white imagination, the idea of founding a colony had flourished in free black communities in the mid-Atlantic states. Sierra Leone was an early model for these communities. After all, Thomas Peters, the Nova Scotian leader, had lobbied for the emigration of his community by visiting London to lobby the Sierra Leone Company. In 1787, the Free African Union Society published a letter announcing they were "waiting and longing to hear what has been the issue and the success of the attempt to make a settlement of Blacks in Africa, hopeing this will open the way for us."[181] In the same way, a delegation of African Americans belonging to Samuel Hopkins's congregation in Newport, Rhode Island, visited Freetown in 1795, to inquire about emigration. Zachary Macaulay offered the same terms of settlement as the Company had offered to the Maroons.[182] However, white slave owners also saw the appeal of "ridding" America of former slaves. As early as 1802, Thomas Jefferson had proposed sending free blacks from Virginia to the colony.[183]

Colonization had dissonant meanings in the United States. To some free black Americans, it represented a chance to escape oppression and the threat of reenslavement. To many white Americans, both abolitionists and slave owners, it represented a chance to hive off free black Americans to Africa to work around the problem of managing mass emancipation. A similar tension was built into the Sierra Leone Company's plans: the Nova Scotian settlers wanted good land and genuine freedom, and the Company wanted a suggestible workforce. But the Company was based in Britain, not one of Britain's slave colonies. The problem of freedom was much more immediate to the Americans. The ideological tensions within the ACS worked out in practice as a disaster for the first colonists to arrive in West Africa. The ACS contacted Nova Scotian settlers in Sierra Leone through the agency of Paul Cuffe, an African American merchant and proponent of colonization.[184] Cuffe planned to create a transatlantic trading network between African Americans in America and Africa. Consequently, Cuffe's allies in Freetown were primarily traders who were from the first generation of Company settlers and who hoped for a greater share of colonial trade.

Cuffe died in 1817. The white agents of the ACS co-opted his plans without appreciating their context, nuances, or radical aims. In one of its first official reports, the ACS praised Sierra Leone for controlling "the fugitive slaves of the southern states . . . a useless and pernicious, if not a dangerous" population. That was precisely *not* Cuffe's reason for admiring Sierra Leone; he proposed to establish a kind of transatlantic chamber of commerce with the "useless and pernicious" Nova Scotians.[185] And so the ACS arrived in Sierra Leone in a motley of white supremacist fantasy, stitched from the scraps of a plan for black liberation. At the same time, the ACS agents were deeply impressed by the village system and the expanding footprint of Sierra Leone. However, the agents of the ACS projected their own, distinctly American anxieties about emancipation, black freedom, and the purpose of an "anti-slavery" colony in West Africa onto Sierra Leone. The American agents were oblivious to MacCarthy's resentment of American trade in and around Sierra Leone. The agents did not recognize that the villages were not designed by the Liberated African Department as a mechanism for either creating a racially integrated society or removing free people of African descent from the white-dominated territories of the British empire. The villages were part of MacCarthy's strategy for harnessing the labour of former slaves for the benefit of his own ambitions as an imperial administrator.

On 6 January 1796, Theodore Foster, United States Senator from Pennsylvania, addressed a convention of American abolitionists in Philadelphia. The audience included both black and white delegates, but Foster directed his remarks to the free people of African descent in the audience. He declared that he wished "to see you act worthily of the rank you have acquired as freemen . . . to justify the friends and advocates of your colour in the eyes of the world." He proceeded to outline nine recommendations for the freedpeople in the audience, so that they might show that they had "earned" freedom, recommendations that would probably have been immediately familiar to antislavery supporters in Britain. Foster urged them to worship in public, and to teach their children to read, write, and do arithmetic. Their children should learn "useful trades," he continued, "or to labour with their hands in cultivating the earth." They should be "faithful in all the relations" that they might enter into, and be "simple in . . . dress and furniture." They should never drink alcohol, a vice "not necessary to lessen the fatigue of labour, nor to obviate the extremes of heat or cold," and always "avoid frolicking." Their marriages, Foster reminded his black listeners, should be legally performed, and they should arrange birth certificates and death certificates for their relatives. They should save money, so that they might be able to pass down property to their children. Finally, he expected that emancipated people would know to "behave . . . to all persons in a civil and respectful manner, by which you may prevent contention." It was only through constant self-discipline and respectful obedience that African Americans might "refute the objections which have been against you as rational and moral creatures."[186]

Cuffe, a pious and wealthy African American Quaker who traded out of Westport, Massachusetts, hoped to connect with a community of similarly upright black merchants in Freetown. Foster's speech was bundled with a short and admiring account of Cuffe's plans to trade with settlers in Sierra Leone, evidence of the strained and ambiguous relationship between white and black Americans' hopes for an African colony. Historians have attributed to Cuffe all sorts of anachronistic ideologies. Although Cuffe felt instinctive solidarity with Africans and people of African descent, he was not a "pan-Africanist"; although he was an enthusiastic proponent of voting and property rights for black residents of Massachusetts, he was not a proponent of modern "civil rights discourse."[187] Cuffe was an abolitionist Quaker, and, as Sarah Levine-Gronningsater argues, "while antislavery Quakers were radical in their position on slavery, their emancipation schemes hewed to contemporary norms about work, family, and the right of local leaders to supervise households in their midst."[188] Cuffe's property, prominence, and fame were radical, but his understanding of emancipation, and his expectations of emancipated people, were very conservative. Cuffe was also a businessman who hoped to create a network of Quaker merchants in England, Africa, and the United States "from Africa to England, and thence to America."[189]

When Cuffe visited Sierra Leone in 1811–12, with the support of William Allen and other leading British Quakers, he was dismayed to find many settlers' homes "Without Bibeles and other who had bibles Without the Living Substance of the Spirit."[190] In his private log, he excoriated the Nova Scotians for their participation in the rum trade in the colony, for being "Very fond of haveing a Number of Servents about them" and for allowing "the industery on their farmes" to be "too much neglected."[191] But Cuffe was warmly welcomed by the settlers and Governor Columbine, and invited to dinners, parties, and public events, including a sitting of the Vice-Admiralty Court. Leading Nova Scotians brought him to visit King George of the Bullom and King Tom of the Temne, to whom Cuffe presented copies of the Bible and of writings by Elizabeth Webb, a famous Pennsylvania Quaker. Cuffe had little contact with Liberated Africans—or rather, neither his logs and letters nor the published accounts of his visit make much of a mention of the "captured Negroes." When Cuffe needed to hire short-term labourers, he did not hire "captured Negroes." Instead, he recruited from among the migrant Kru workers residing in the colony, at a rate of $3 per month, plus meals.[192]

Cuffe dreamed of bringing black settlers from the United States to Sierra Leone, and the Nova Scotians seemed to be of similar mind. While Cuffe was in Freetown, a group of settlers petitioned Columbine to request of Parliament first to encourage "all our Brethren who may Come from the British Colonies or from America and Become farmers in order to help us Cultivate the Land," second to encourage anyone with a vessel to "Establish Commerce" and third to encourage "all those who may Establish whalefishery" in Sierra Leone.[193] Cuffe read these resolutions and imagined they aligned perfectly with his dreams for Sierra Leone, that it might become "a Nation to be Numbered among the historians nations of the World."[194] The Nova Scotian merchants had much more pressing reasons to hope for more English-speaking African American settlers in the colony. An influx of farmers would protect their claims on the farmland granted by the Sierra Leone Company against the growing population of Liberated Africans. More shipowners and merchants would pry a larger share of the colonial trade from European firms. Whalers would establish a new source of economic activity outside of the prize Courts, and connect the settlers to a lucrative global trading network. The increasing importance of the Liberated Africans made many settlers anxious. By the 1830s, the surviving Nova Scotians and their descendants were openly resentful of the Liberated Africans, whom they referred to as the "Captives." "We are becoming poorer and more despised every day," one young daughter of a Nova Scotian merchant complained, "and those Captives are the great people now."[195] Paul Cuffe's scheme seemed like an opportunity to begin to balance out the growing Liberated African population with more voluntary settlers.

In March 1815, Cuffe wrote to an African American preacher in Baltimore, Daniel Coker, to invite member of his congregation, "the ancestors of africans who have to do or may feel their minds Zealously inguaged for the good of their fellow creators in africa and have a mind to Visit or remove to that Countery," to sign up as colonists.[196] In April he wrote to Nathan Lord and Samuel Mills, young scholars at the Andover Theological Seminary, urging them to assist in the recruitment of free black settlers. Cuffe worried that "if the colony that was settled at Sierra Leone was not aided by further addition there was a danger of loosing what labour was already bestowed."[197] Groups in Philadelphia and Baltimore recruited from the free black people of the cities, "whose characters are guaranteed by some of the most respectable individuals in society."[198] In December 1815 Cuffe sailed back to Sierra Leone, and arrived in February 1816 with just under 40 settlers aboard. The settlers were welcomed, but Cuffe was not allowed to land many of his trade goods, including tobacco, soap, candles, and naval stores. "The few articles I am permitted to land," he wrote, "pay Such a duty that the expenses of the Voyage will fawl Very heavy on me."[199]

By 1818, a year after Cuffe's death, both Daniel Coker and Samuel Mills were in Sierra Leone as representatives of the American Colonization Society, on a mission to find a site for a new American colony to be settled by freeborn black people and former slaves from the United States. The Society's first report mourned Cuffe, since, in their estimation, his "character alone ought to be sufficient to rescue the people to which belonged from the unmerited aspersions which have been cast on them."[200] Cuffe's commercial ambitions and racial politics died with him. In the ACS's first published report he was recast as a "credit to the race," and his plans for a trading network supported by prosperous black volunteer emigrants was reconfigured in the image of white desires. A different legacy survived in African American congregations. In one published eulogy from an African American church, Cuffe's eulogist reminded the congregation that Cuffe had "wished to see that part of our nation, which are dispersed and kept in a state of bondage and degradation in christian countries, returning to the land of their ancestors."[201]

John Kizell had been born in the Sherbro' and sold into slavery, arriving from the Middle Passage in Charleston, South Carolina, a few years before the city fell during the Revolutionary War. Kizell joined the British ranks, was moved to Nova Scotia, and returned to Africa in 1792 as a settler.[202] From 1802 he worked as a trader and commercial agent for the Sierra Leone Company in Freetown and in the Sherbro' River. By 1809 he owed the directors of the now-defunct Company at least $1,450, and perhaps as much as $1,995. In 1810, he settled the debt by turning over his town and country properties to his creditors.[203] Edward Columbine encouraged him to move back to the Sherbro', establish a trading post, and act as an unofficial colonial envoy to the local kings and chiefs.[204] While visiting Freetown in 1811–12, Kizell met Paul Cuffe and joined the "Friendly Society," which Cuffe had helped to found to encourage trade between African Americans on both sides of the Atlantic. Cuffe bought camwood and other tropical lumber from Kizell.[205] At the Friendly Society, Kizell must have convinced Cuffe to make him his liaison in West Africa. Cuffe recommended to Samuel Mills that the American colony be situated on "a river about 50 leagues south of Cape Sierra Leone, called the Sherborough" where "a citizen of Sierra Leone . . . has ever been desirous that a settlement should be established at that place."[206] When he arrived in Sierra Leone, Mills met with the Friendly Society, of which Kizell now served as president.[207] He was delighted with Kizell, "A second Paul Cuffe."[208]

Kizell understood how to speak to both white and black colonizationists. There are no surviving minutes of the Friendly Society, but it is clear that Cuffe found common ground with Kizell. Kizell, a Baptist, was pious, respectable, and entrepreneurial—the three qualities which Cuffe prized in trading partners and potential colonists. To the white agents Kizell promised

that the Society's new colony would "Prevent insurrection among the slaves
. . . bring into this country some good men . . . give an opportunity to masters who are disposed to release their slaves, and thus promote a gradual
emancipation."[209] Kizell also wrote to Bushrod Washington, the son of
George Washington, a Supreme Court Justice and leading figure in the ACS,
"God bids you, 'colonize.' "[210] Kizell had his own agenda, set with Cuffe,
which he hardly concealed, but which the ACS did not seem to register. After
all, how could a former slave have commercial and political ambition independent of white leadership?

"Mr. K[izell]," Samuel Mills wrote, "thinks the greater part of the
people of colour, who are now in America, will yet return to Africa."[211] In the
winter of 1817, Ebenezer Burgess and Samuel Mills went to London, where
they met with William Dillwyn, a leading Quaker who had fled Pennsylvania
during the American Revolution, and Dr. Thomas Hodgkin, William Allen's
private secretary. In February 1818, they sailed for Sierra Leone.[212] When
Mills saw the Liberated African Villages, he was rapt. "The altars on these
mountains," he wrote, "which the natives had dedicated to devils, are falling
before the temples of the living God, like the image of Dagon before the ark
. . . Ethiopia will stretch forth her hands unto God, and worship."[213] Mills described the villagers of Regent as "a spectacle of grateful admiration."[214] He
was convinced that he and the Americans were welcome on the coast. "The
minds of the leading men here," he noted, "were found favourable to the establishment of an American colony; but some difference of opinion existed,
as to the expediency of locating it in the vicinity of Sierra Leone."[215]

The physician of the ACS transport ship, *Elizabeth*, Samuel Crozer, explained
to Charles MacCarthy that the ACS planned to settle at the Sherbro', and that
"having appointed agents to provide an establishment for liberated Africans,
the Society conceive it will be mutually advantageous, to fix upon the same
local position."[216] The language of "Liberated Africans" had seeped into the
ACS's vocabulary.[217] On an individual level, MacCarthy welcomed African
American settlers and their valuable skills.[218] The question was the extent to
which any settlement of free American blacks in West Africa would be an
American colony. Would it undercut Sierra Leone by importing finished goods?
Worse, would conflict between the two colonies renew the hostilities of the
War of 1812? "As *war* had already existed between Great Britain and the United
States," one colonial writer exclaimed, "that calamity may be expected to

recur." Perhaps worse, competition between the two settlements might "scandalize the cause of Christianity and social improvement." Even the "good of Africa" was not worth another war between the United States and Britain.[219]

Abolitionists in London corresponded regularly with their counterparts in the United States. But in Sierra Leone colonial trade and sovereignty took precedence. MacCarthy had not been in Sierra Leone when Paul Cuffe first arrived. MacCarthy averred, "I believe they have some idea of proposing to their friends in America, on their return to that Country, the forming of an establishment on the Sherbro', and that they look also upon the Isles de Los, as a desirable Station." MacCarthy resented the American interest in a West African colony. "However philanthropic & benevolent the views of the society may be," MacCarthy continued, "it becomes my duty to employ every honourable means to secure to British Merchants the advantage of a trade to which England by immense sacrifice in the cause of oppressed Africa has obtained the fairest claim."[220] To MacCarthy's horror, the ACS sent the *Elizabeth*, with a group of settlers aboard, to found a settlement there, in 1820.

At the Sherbro', where Kizell had promised they could build a colony, the passengers of the *Elizabeth* discovered that they had made a bad bargain. The ACS explained to its subscribers that the settlement at Campelar on Sherbro' was "only taken as a temporary shelter, till they could get the land on the Bagroo, which is high and healthy, and abounds in good water, and where the settlement was intended to be located."[221] In the end, they reflected, "they have been deceived and imposed upon by the natives, among whom John Kizzell, an influential man among them."[222] Soon, Ephraim Bacon and James Andrus arrived to evacuate the settlers from Campelar. Before returning to Sherbro' to settle scores with Kizell, the agents visited Regent. Andrus told Johnson "he never had seen a Church in America filled with more attentive hearers." Johnson, who knew that William Tamba and William Davis were keen to preach outside the colony, suggested that they accompany the Americans as interpreters and negotiators, in exchange for free passage on their ship to a new mission field.[223]

Tamba and Davis accompanied the ACS missionaries on one of their reconnaissance trips to the Grand Bassa. Davis, a native of the region, was on fire for the conversion of the world to Christianity. He hoped to guide the Americans there in order to found a mission of his own, a project Johnson supported with enthusiasm. The headmen of Grand Bassa were "suspicious that we had some unfriendly object in view," but Davis tried to convince them otherwise.[224] Davis also negotiated with the king of Grand Bassa on behalf of the ACS.[225] The bargain struck between the ACS and the king of Grand Bassa included a provision for the education of the king's son, at Regent. The ACS agents, with the same hateful whimsy that led to generations of slaves being named "Scipio Africanus," renamed the Bassa prince "Bushrod Washington." They chortled when the king ordered the American flag hung near his village, "which the people consider a white man's gregre or fetish, and according to their prejudice, regard as sacred."[226]

When "Bushrod Washington" came to Sierra Leone, he stayed in Regent. "His countrymen," Johnson wrote, "surrounded the son of their king, shook hands with him in the most affectionate manner, and enquired after their relatives."[227] David Noah and William Davis, also from Grand Bassa, were also able to get news of their families. "Some of the People were so struck when they saw Davis," Johnson wrote, "that they scarcely would believe that he was the same, as an instance of one returning, who had been sold out of the Country, had never occurred before."[228] It seemed possible that the American settlement might be connected from the outset to Sierra Leone through the agency of the Liberated Africans themselves. It is possible that the initiative of Davis and Tamba did not go unnoticed. Eli Ayers, the first officially appointed Agent of the ACS was deeply impressed with Regent and its communicants. Ayers remarked that the village presented the kind of scene "that caused a British Admiral to exclaim, 'See!! Behold what religion can do!' "[229] However, when Ayers came back to Sierra Leone in 1821, and Johnson again offered Davis's services as guide and translator, the Americans left Freetown without him. Perhaps the ACS had become uncomfortable with Davis and Tamba's independent missionary ambitions; the Americans may have intended to employ African converts as servants, and not as partners in colonization. Ayers made a deal for land at Cape Mesurado instead, the eventual site of Monrovia, the capital of Liberia. The connections between the Bassa-speaking missionaries from Regent and the American colony dissolved. The king's son died in Regent, a death that the ACS did not even bother to report to the king. "I think their conduct toward the Bassah King and people very reproachful," Johnson wrote. Johnson worried that the Bassa would take revenge on the Americans when they arrived at Mesurado, and mourned the low morale of his communicants at the failure of their first attempt at an independent mission.[230] He wrote that the Americans "are so whimsical, I think it most prudent to keep at a distance."[231] And yet Sierra Leone, and especially Regent, had made an impression on the minds of the founders of Liberia. Regent was a complex and interdependent society, but to the ACS it seemed like material proof that a small number of whites could "manage" black settlers.

In early 1822, the American settlers arrived at Cape Mesurado. In August, local chiefs attacked the new settlement. The armed schooner H.M.S. *Prince Regent,* sailing out of Freetown, intervened, and her captain helped to renegotiate a treaty to protect the American settlement.[232] In 1824, Liberia was again threatened with attack, but *Prince Regent* and another ship, H.M.S. *Driver,* happened to be in the area. According to Jehudi Ashmun, an early Governor of Liberia, "from this time, the colony has been considered as entirely invincible to any native force that may be brought against it."[233] The new Liberia, at least in 1823, was less intimidating than MacCarthy had feared. In 1823, a British officer, expressing more or less MacCarthy's opinion of American traders, noted with contempt that "Yankee honesty is well understood by the natives of this district, who to a man detest them, in fact in every African they have an enemy."[234] And perhaps the lessons the American Colonization Society learned about Sierra Leone filtered back to Britain as well. In the 1820s, as British abolitionists began to hope for the end of colonial slavery, the idea of hundreds of thousands of former slaves emancipated at a stroke, which had never really troubled a movement with a very gradual timeline for emancipation, suddenly gained gravity. In 1824 Thomas Clarkson wrote a new pamphlet on behalf of the newly founded Anti-Slavery Society. The abolition of the slave trade accomplished, he argued for the end of slavery. In his pamphlet he reflected on the Liberated Africans. "We find their present number, as compared with that of the whites in the same colony," he wrote, "nearly as *one hundred and fifty to one;* notwithstanding which superiority fresh emancipations are constantly taking place."[235] Colonization forced whites in both colonies to confront the everyday reality of mass emancipation, and to weigh "freedom" and the abdication of white supremacy against the desire to continue to control the economic and social lives of black people. On both sides of the Atlantic, and in both Anglo-American colonies in West Africa, the scales nearly always tipped toward control.

After the end of the war with France, Liberated Africans became the focus of the economic life of colonial Sierra Leone. In wartime, former slave ships were the stock-in-trade of British officials and European and settler merchants; in peacetime, former slaves themselves became the raw material for an ambitious civilizing mission. Not only was the civilizing mission organized for the "good" of former slaves; the Liberated African villages were essential to protecting and expanding the prestige and commerce of the colony. The village system under Charles MacCarthy had many uses—it was a means of organizing labour; a mechanism for encouraging Christian conversion; an elaborate performance of statistics and anecdotes of personal transformation put on to attract money from Whitehall and from ordinary, charitable Britons; a means of expanding the borders of the colony; and a model colony of former slaves in West Africa. From the very beginning of the movement in the mid-eighteenth century, the leaders of the British anti-slavery movement had emphasized the relationship between ending the slave trade and encouraging commerce. Those principles came ashore for the first time in Sierra Leone in the late eighteenth century, as the Sierra Leone Company tried to build new a trade network that would cut slavery out of West African commerce. The first Crown Governors hoped to use the Vice-Admiralty Court as an incentive to hunt slave ships and as an economic and military dynamo. But after 1815, under Charles MacCarthy, the practices of antislavery evolved. The Liberated African Department came into its own as the central mechanism of a sophisticated program of "civilizing" colonial rule and territorial expansion. British antislavery had come of age in the empire.

Epilogue

MacCarthy's Skull

Cape Coast Castle clung to the edge of West Africa like a barnacle, and like a barnacle it faced the sea, growing inland only enough to be anchored securely. The owners of the Castle, the Company of Merchants Trading to Africa, were interested in African politics only insofar as it might affect the supply of goods and enslaved people and the security of the fort. By 1822, the fort was in precipitous decline. Joseph Dupuis, a British ambassador to Asante, called it a "gangrened member of the empire, from which all communication was cut off, to prevent the contagion from spreading."[1] The abolition of the British slave trade had crippled an establishment crumbling due to neglect, incompetence, and souring relations with local allies.

By comparison, Sierra Leone was vital. *The British Review* commented in 1821 that the colony had become "a noble, and we trust an imperishable monument of British philanthropy, and perhaps the destined focus for the civilization and Christianizing of inland Africa."[2] Not all publications were as hyperbolic, but there was no doubt that Sierra Leone had outstripped the forts of the Gold Coast. In 1822 MacCarthy sent a copy of the *Sierra Leone Almanac*, in all likelihood the first bound book published in West Africa on a European-style printing press, back to London. The *Almanac* included a chart of Freetown weather; a timeline of notable events in British history; a list, with prices, of all of the goods for sale in the colony's markets; a census of the colonial population; and a ranking of colonial staff and army officers in both Sierra Leone and the colony's new island "possessions."[3] The *Almanac*, itself material proof of colonial progress, insisted on Sierra Leone's value and connection to Britain. The book also showed a colony with more ambition than the Gold Coast forts for British engagement in West Africa. Instead of clinging to the coast, Sierra Leone pushed inward, and made its own markets. Instead of accepting local politics as the price of doing business, Sierra Leone intended to transform Africans into Christians and consumers.

Colonial Sierra Leone began as an experiment, a place where the elite representatives of British antislavery could prove that their intuitions about the economics of slavery and the slave trade had been correct: that wage labour was not only more moral, but more profitable than slave labour; that plantation crops could be grown efficiently by wage workers; and that the "legitimate" products brought to market in Africa were more valuable than enslaved people. In the minds of many directors of the Sierra Leone Company, the clean lines of what we now call "classical" economics seemed almost divinely licensed: slavery was morally wrong *and* bad for business. However, the fiction that human beings can be property made a lot of people a lot of money, and spurred innovations in finance from long-range credit to sophisticated insurance. Moreover, slavery in Africa wasn't the same as slavery in the Americas. Enslaved people in Africa were subordinate kin, not chattel, and were sold as part of a wider system of trade and agriculture. Enslaved people in Africa produced and carried many of the goods prized by antislavery campaigners, and trade in slaves was a part of trade in many other commodities.

In Freetown, the Company and especially Zachary Macaulay discovered that they had been wrong about the horizon for the installation of free, wage labour in West Africa. The Company's staff soon learned how to buy and sell things according to routines established by slave traders without trading in slaves. When he returned to London, Macaulay had learned a few important lessons. He returned convinced that free labour could not sweep away the slave trade without being backed by capital and firepower. He also believed that his assumptions about the path from slavery to freedom were correct, and that enslaved and freedpeople from both the Americas and Africa would require extensive preparation in order to appreciate their "freedom." Above all, he learned that what the "friends of Africa" wanted to accomplish would require the kind of capacity that only a government, not a private company, could provide. Macaulay helped to arrange for the emigration of the Maroons and began to solicit the Crown to take over Sierra Leone by taking

on government contracts and recruiting Royal Navy officers as colonial officials, drawing Sierra Leone closer to the British armed forces.

In 1808, the 1807 Slave Trade Act came into force, and Sierra Leone
became a Crown Colony. The two events happened by coincidence: the Sierra Leone Company had been trying to pass its territory to the Crown since
1801. But the coincidence opened a new era in British antislavery. Instead of
ending the slave trade by transforming African commerce, the 1807 Slave
Trade Act proposed to stop it by force. Zachary Macaulay had learned in
Sierra Leone that antislavery required military support; James Stephen had
learned in the West Indies that naval officers responded with enthusiasm to
prize money. From 1808 until it lost its slave-trade mandate in 1817, the Vice-
Admiralty Court in Freetown made capturing slave ships profitable. The
benefits offered by the Court, including prizes and access to African soldiers,
who seemed more loyal and more resistant to disease than the white criminals usually consigned to West African service, made antislavery into a business. Wartime antislavery was expansionist, but it took little interest in
former slaves, except where they might fight or help to win prize money.

The practices of antislavery oriented around war-making and prize-
taking fell apart in the postwar diplomatic order. As more successful appeals
of prize cases were decided in the High Court of Admiralty, it became too
risky to seize slave ships belonging to other nations without clear, and re-
strictive, rules governing the distribution of prize money. In response, a civilizing mission directed at Liberated Africans replaced the Court as the
centrepiece of the colonial economy. For a while, Charles MacCarthy and
Sierra Leone prospered: the British government sent money and cheap supplies, the Liberated African Department helped to organize labour and trade,
and donations poured in to missionary societies. MacCarthy expanded the
colony, building a proprietary network of outposts from (present-day)
the Gambia to Ghana. Antislavery plans for West Africa in 1792 had been
commercial; in 1822 they were imperial.

MacCarthy's Last Stand

MacCarthy had eyed the Gold Coast for a long time. As early as 1818, MacCarthy complained that the Gold Coast forts "are all open to Foreigners without
any duty being raised on imports or exports in aid of the public expense, and
therefore Foreigners, and these only derive a bargain from our charges." The

Forts were flaccid and unpatriotic, he argued. The dissolute former slave traders' habit of "putting on a scarlet military dress after their morning avocation," MacCarthy wrote, "does not raise the dignity or importance of our Country."[4] MacCarthy argued the Company of Merchants had no ambition, no urge to "civilize" Africa, no desire to claim territory for Britain. Many British politicians agreed. In 1821, while he was on leave in Britain, MacCarthy learned that Parliament had dissolved the Company of Merchants and arranged for his knighthood. He, Sir Charles MacCarthy, would be Governor-in-Chief of Sierra Leone, the Gambia, the Isles-de-Los, and all of Britain's forts on the Gold Coast. By 1824, he was dead.

MacCarthy did not understand that different rules governed trade and diplomacy in the Gold Coast. In Sierra Leone, the village system, the slave-trade Courts, the English-speaking settler community, and the presence of British soldiers and sailors had established the colony as a significant player in regional politics, able to negotiate with local kings from a position of relative strength. Sierra Leone's neighbours were divided; Futa Djallon was the largest and most powerful empire near the colony, and it had only a foothold on the coast, maintained by its caravan trade. The coastal kingdoms were small and relatively weak, and Liberia was tiny, and dependent on British naval support for defense. In contrast, in the forts of the Gold Coast, Asante enjoyed unified and coherent power, and Europeans filled a niche as exporters and petty patrons in the Asante imperial order.[5] Charles MacCarthy imagined that he could easily supplant Asante on the coast, or at least redefine the relationship between the empires, and compel Asante to recognise and respect British prestige. "Sir Charles," Joseph Dupuis wrote, "was pleased to consider somewhat lightly, descriptions which tended to convey an adequate idea of the disposable force of Ashantee."[6]

When MacCarthy arrived on the Gold Coast to take command, the employees of the defunct Company of Merchants refused to continue in the service of the Government of Sierra Leone, leaving MacCarthy without any staff with local expertise. MacCarthy formed up the "native" troops remaining at the forts, along with soldiers from the West India Regiments and the Royal African Corps, into a new "Royal African Colonial Corps."[7] When Asante troops executed a black sergeant in the British service for committing lèse-majesté toward the Asantehene (or high king), MacCarthy proposed a punitive expedition. He did not consider a negotiated peace. As one of his successors, Governor Sir Neil Campbell, wrote, the coastal Fante people had been "the constant allies of the Ashantees until they were bribed, cajoled or frightened, by threats of destruction by Sir Charles MacCarthy (and even stronger measures) to join his alliance."[8] MacCarthy divided his forces into four divisions and took personal command of one group. However, the Asante war leaders mustered a detachment of a rumored 10,000 soldiers, who set a trap for MacCarthy's troops. "It will now be seen," a British official wrote, "that the Ashantees are a *people not to be utterly despised* . . . Sir Charles was overconfident, perhaps deluded."[9] On 21 January 1824, MacCarthy's division was surprised near the Pra River. MacCarthy struck up the regimental band to play "God Save the King." The Asante troops were not intimidated. The next morning, after a long night of gunfire and pounding drums, the Asante forded the river in a full assault on the British forces.[10] And so, at the end, back to the beginning: J. T. Williams, MacCarthy's private secretary, returned to consciousness beside the Governor's headless corpse.

When news of MacCarthy's death reached Freetown, the acting Governor, D. M. Hamilton, passed the command of the Gold Coast to one of the colony's leading military officers. Hamilton acknowledged, notwithstanding MacCarthy's efforts, that it was nearly impossible to govern Cape Coast from Freetown, "owing to the great distance and uncertainty of communications between this colony and those Possessions."[11] Hamilton conceded that when MacCarthy was out of the colony, "no control has been practically exercised over the different establishments" within Sierra Leone. When MacCarthy *was* in Freetown, he had "a very imperfect control over the Dependencies at the Gambia and on the Gold Coast."[12] MacCarthy's successor, Major-General Charles Turner, arrived in Sierra Leone in February 1825, just over a year after MacCarthy's death. He agreed with Hamilton's assessment of "greater Sierra Leone." "It would be easier for the General Officer at Cork to take charge of the Barbados," he wrote, "than for me to take charge of the Gold Coast."[13]

Turner found Sierra Leone in disarray. The Liberated African Department had a new building, "a magnificent brick edifice rising on three tiers of Italianate arches," but the town hall had collapsed. Without MacCarthy's secretive accounting, energy, and personal prestige, the bottom had fallen out of the colonial budget.[14] Turner continued many of MacCarthy's military policies. With Kenneth Macaulay's advice and approval, he launched attacks on the Gallinas and the Sherbro', and demanded of the Colonial Office the right to annex the entire coast of West Africa from Gorée to Cape Mount, forcing local chiefs to become British clients. The request was denied, and then Turner died of fever, barely more than year into his term as Governor, on 7 March 1826.[15] Under Turner, the village system was briefly under military command, but soon fell into neglect. From the perspective of the villagers, the neglect was a blessing. Freetown and the villages passed to local people, and especially to Liberated African teachers and traders, the seedbed of the Krio community in the Freetown Peninsula. In 1823, Zachary Macaulay formally retired from his partnership, leaving the business in the hands of his nephew, T. G. Babington. In 1827, Sierra Leone was stripped of control of the Gold Coast forts, which became independent British possessions once again. The decline of the village system and the shrinking footprint of the colony were reflected in shrinking grants from Parliament. The Liberated African Department's budget fell from more than £41,133 in 1823 to £18,201 in 1825.[16]

As Sierra Leone's most powerful patrons died or retired, and as the campaign to abolish slavery in the British empire began to grow, the attention of the public, and of lawmakers, turned overwhelmingly to the West Indies. Emancipation became, by and large, a West Indian problem. In 1827, D. M. Hamilton reflected on Sierra Leone's potential as a plantation. Hamilton had begun his career in West Africa as a clerk for Macaulay & Babington. He had survived long enough to hold nearly every office in the colonial government, from Collector of Customs to Acting Governor. He had eaten Sierra Leone rice, and had washed it down with excellent local coffee sweetened with coarse but high-quality local sugar. He had seen indigo, tobacco, ginger, Cayenne pepper, and arrowroot grow on colonial farmland. And yet, he reflected, "Capitalists, disposed to invest money in agriculture pursuits on a large scale, cannot rely with confidence upon a ready, efficient and continuous supply of labour."[17] More than 30 years of British attempts to create large-scale plantation agriculture in the colony had failed. Sierra Leone would never be a free-labour Jamaica. However, Hamilton concluded Sierra Leone could offer the British empire a lesson in "civilization." The colony was home, he reflected, to "liberated Africans of every gradation from those in a state of civilization equal to the Nova Scotian and Maroon Settlers to the Savage just landed from the Slave Ship."[18] Sierra Leone could not attract planters and capitalists, but it might prove the value of the British civilizing mission.

As free labour became a West Indian problem, "legitimate trade" and its civilizing effects became the great object of antislavery desire for West Africa. In his influential 1840 book, *The African Slave Trade and Its Remedy*, Thomas

Fowell Buxton, Wilberforce's successor as the leader of Parliamentary anti-slavery, proposed a plan very similar to the Sierra Leone Company's 50-year-old proposals for African trade. Buxton urged more vigorous military enforcement of the slave-trade law, written treaties with local rulers, the importing of European agricultural expertise and technology, and the encouragement of both legitimate trade in luxuries like ivory, and the cultivation of cash crops, especially cotton and palm oil. But unlike the Sierra Leone Company, Buxton was skeptical of African American settlers and unconvinced that Sierra Leone had been the right place to start an antislavery colony. "I admit," he wrote, "that Sierra Leone has failed to realize all the expectations which were at one time indulged." He explained that the colony was too prone to disease, too small, and too short of prime agricultural land. Moreover, he added, "there is wanting that, without which we can hardly expect to see commerce spring up and thrive in a barbarous country,—a river navigable far into the interior."[19] Buxton's book helped to launch the Niger Expedition of 1841, a disastrous attempt to plant "legitimate trade" in the African interior by sailing up the Niger.[20] After the failure of the Expedition, and until the floodgates broke in the 1870s, beginning the Scramble for Africa, the routine policies for British engagement with West Africa—interdiction, legitimate trade, and treaty making—were Victorian adaptations of the prospectus of the Sierra Leone Company.

As antislavery became routine for the Foreign Office, it lost some of its lustre in British popular politics. During the war with France, antislavery had unified Britons and offered a vision of British liberty and British virtue in ascendance.[21] In the uncertain postwar years, an ember of criticism of antislavery that had smoldered under patriotic support for the end of the slave trade rekindled. Robert Thorpe, the former Chief Justice of Sierra Leone, became one of many public critics of the Clapham Sect, which tried to defend the slave colonies of the West Indies by undermining the credibility of the "Saints." Newspapers like the wry, satirical *John Bull* and leading pamphleteers like James McQueen argued that the slave colonies were not as bad as advertised, that enslaved people were well fed and cared for, that emancipation would mean starvation, and that Africans would not know what to do with freedom even if they had it. However, because of lingering public pride regarding the end of the slave trade, critics had to be "anti-antislavery" instead of overtly pro-slavery. The elite antislavery lobby, critics charged, planned to maintain plantation slavery while claiming that they had abolished it. Consequently, many critics of antislavery insisted that the close relationship between the Clapham Sect and Sierra Leone was a smoking gun, and no Saint received more abuse than Zachary Macaulay. Sierra Leone, in the pages of *John Bull,* was the place "where sleep the bones of hundreds of brave and wise and honourable men, sacrifices to the hypocritical workings of Zackmackery."[22] In a typical cartoon from 1826, a rail-thin, black-clad Saint carries a sign urging Britons to "Buy only East India Sugar, 'Tis Sinful to buy any other," with invoices for "E. I. Sugar" tucked in his back pocket, in front of "Cantem Humbug & Co.'s Free Sugar Warehouse." On the wall of the warehouse is a poster advertising "Sierra Leone: A Farce as performed for the benefit of Signior Hum. Bamboozle." Meanwhile, to the left, children are cajoled into signing petitions to Parliament, and to the right another preacher holds a picture of the whipping of an enslaved person in front of the lens of a telescope, so that John Bull, the personification of the British public, is unable to see a beautiful, rustic West Indian village full of feasting, dancing slaves. The cartoon summarizes the argument: slaves were happy enough—certainly happier than the starving Irish beggars squatting in the foreground of the cartoon—and the dour piety of the leaders of the antislavery movement was a cover for a naked cash grab (fig. 10).

The critique of antislavery that grew out from West Indian fury at "Zackmackery" and contempt for the Clapham Sect's holier-than-thou reputation evolved after the abolition of colonial slavery. By the 1840s, as Buxton repackaged the Sierra Leone Company's original plans for a new generation of would-be merchants and civilizers, the factories of industrial England belched out what seemed like endless pollution, and numberless slums. To some Britons, the lives they imagined emancipated people living in the West Indies and in West Africa seemed easier and happier than the brutalized lives of industrial workers. The suffering of poor Britons in relentless wage work was projected against a vile fantasy of black freedom as ignorance and idleness. In his infamous but widely read pamphlet, *Occasional Discourse on the Nigger Question,* Thomas Carlyle snarled at his idea of an empire of lazy black subjects, eating "pumpkins cheap as grass . . . while the sugar-crops rot around them uncut, because labour cannot be hired, so cheap are the pumpkins."[23] To Carlyle, the antislavery of the age of revolution was a product not only of false piety and greed but also of Macaulay, Wilberforce, and their fellow travelers' naïve belief in human perfectibility. It was the "sad product of a sceptical Eighteenth Century . . . the Broad-brimmed

Figure 10. Robert Cruikshank, *John Bull taking a Clear View of the Negro Slavery Question!*, London, 1826. Cartoon satirizing British antislavery on the eve of emancipation, illustrating growing public suspicion of the movement. (Courtesy of the John Carter Brown Library at Brown University)

form of Christian Sentimentalism."[24] Antislavery, he argued, had never been a triumph of national virtue. Emancipation for African slaves was an insult to a white British world being torn apart by the centrifugal forces of industry and mass democracy. Most Britons did not share Carlyle's apocalyptic pessimism, but many shared his racism and his despair at a world that seemed to be changing faster than they could bear. Antislavery did not disappear in the face of these critiques, but it lost its grip on the public imagination and survived as one of many imperial ideologies, rather than as the object of public pride and national consensus.

Coda: Skulls

In 1824, a few miles inland from Cape Coast Castle, the commander and the surgeon of H.M.S. *Bann* were pulled along in their carriage by four Fante men. The officers were on their way to the site of a battle where, a few days earlier, a force under British command had defeated a detachment of Asante soldiers as the British regrouped after MacCarthy's death. The carriage's wheels pushed corpses "in various stages of decomposition" down into the mud. At the clearing where the battle had occurred, "the dead lay huddled together by thousands" in a macabre tableau, "laying and reclining in various attitudes, some even sitting with their backs against trees." Lieutenant Courtenay, the commander of the *Bann*, held a bag of camphor to his nose to keep from vomiting. The surgeon, to Courtenay's fascination and disgust, "snuffled up the air . . . as if it had been surcharged with all the spices of Arabia." The surgeon dabbled in phrenology, "and was delighted with the great variety of heads." Courtenay picked his way across the battlefield while the surgeon sawed off the skulls of choice dead Asante for his collection. The lieutenant found a better prize: the body of a chief, wrapped in cloth. "With a little difficulty and the aid of a stick," he reported proudly, "I contrived to roll the body off the bier, and to disengage it from the wrappers; I was rewarded for my trouble with a massive gold ring that remained on the fellow's forefinger of the right hand."[25]

As Courtenay gloated over his ring and the surgeon fussed with his sack of heads, the Asante may or may not have kept their own trophy, MacCarthy's skull. Well into the nineteenth century, the skull remained a powerful symbol of British heroism in the face of African savagery. Some British writers reported that the Asante swore oaths before battle on MacCarthy's "honoured skull and coat."[26] Others claimed that "on high festivals" the Asantehene drank "from a cup fashioned from the skull."[27] Henry Morton Stanley added that the "brave soldier's skull" was "gold rimmed and highly venerated."[28] In James Grant's bodice-ripping novel *Miss Cheyne of Essilmont*, murderous Asante warriors demand the return of "a famous fetish— famous even as the skull of the murdered Sir Charles MacCarthy."[29] MacCarthy's skull became a prop in the British theatre of "darkest Africa." But there is little evidence to suggest that the Asante particularly valued the skull, or that they kept it for very long, if at all. After MacCarthy's death, the forces under British command rallied and fought the Asante to a stalemate, establishing an unofficial border between Asante and British territory along the Pra River. According to one of MacCarthy's subaltern officers, the Governor's skull was recovered during this campaign, and returned to England.[30] The Welsh Wesleyan missionary William Davies wrote that the skull found its way to the British Museum, where it was put on display "as a token of national respect to the memory of that great man."[31] Davies seems to have been mistaken; his report is the only mention of the skull's appearance in the museum that I was able to find. The myth of a gold-rimmed goblet of bone was perhaps more appealing than the possibility that the skull simply disappeared.

So this book ends with MacCarthy's skull, and with the skulls of a group of anonymous Asante. MacCarthy's looked back at the difficult history of early colonial Sierra Leone. Sierra Leone, an imperial backwater, had been for a time the centre of British military and judicial antislavery and the headquarters of a remarkable system of military expansion, labour organization, naked acquisitiveness, and high-minded social engineering. Charles MacCarthy governed Sierra Leone longer than any other British official until Sierra Leone's independence in 1961, and he governed the colony when its influence was particularly wide. MacCarthy understood the logic of slave-trade interdiction in wartime and in peacetime, and tried to adapt the colonial political economy to the shock of the end of the Napoleonic wars. He grasped that the slave-trade Courts were most effective when they were free to act unilaterally, and that in order to sustain the profits of antislavery in peacetime, Sierra Leone would need to expand its footprint, as both a regional hub and as the headquarters of a civilizing mission.

The abolition of the slave trade was, to many Britons, irrefutable proof of the superiority of British civilization. But if Britain was declared the gold standard of civilization, where did the rest of the world rank? What was it about Britain in particular that made it so superior? Could British civilization be taught? In MacCarthy's time in Sierra Leone "civilization" came to mean obedience to the colonial government, some knowledge of English, nominal Christianity, and the willingness to work for and to spend wages. The Krio culture that emerged in Freetown thrived in the nineteenth century, and seemed to many missionaries to be a "success," since many Liberated Africans and their children were devout Christians, spoke English, admired Queen Victoria, and thought of themselves as British.

Roughly a century after MacCarthy's death, the arch-imperialist Frederick Lugard pronounced, "It was the task of civilization to put an end to slavery, to establish Courts of Law, to inculcate in the natives a sense of individual responsibility, of liberty, and of justice, and to teach their rulers how to apply these principles."[32] This model of "civilization" had similarities to one in place in MacCarthy's time. However, by the middle of the nineteenth century officials became suspicious of the idea of a "black Briton," a concept their grandfathers had imposed by force. To high-Victorian officials, the Krio seemed to be a parody of the white preserve of "Britishness." Lugard spoke for the generation that presided over, and profited from, the Scramble for Africa when he condemned the Krio as "Europeanised Africans" who "differ not merely in mental outlook from the other groups, but also in physique. Doctors and dentists tell us that he has become less fertile, more susceptible to lung-trouble and to other diseases, and to defective dentition . . . probably arisen from in-breeding among a very limited class, and to the adoption of European dress."[33] The Asante skulls, gathered for research into the capacities of Africans to be "civilized," looked forward with empty sockets to this revolting, exquisitely manicured racism.

In commemoration of the bicentenary of the 1807 Slave Trade Act, an official report from the Home Office affirmed that the Act was "a critical step into the modern world, and into a new and more just moral universe." Moreover, the Home Office declared that the Act was "not only the work of a few parliamentarians and members of the church. It was a grass-roots movement."[34] The report flattens into platitudes a history of the origins and legislative accomplishment of the abolition of the British slave trade focused, ultimately, on Britain. *Freedom's Debtors*, I hope, shows that approaching 1807 from the empire poses new questions about British antislavery. From Freetown the end of the British slave trade is a history of feverish, improvised policy as well as

a history of smooth domestic triumph; it is an Atlantic history of emancipation stunted by money, war, and white supremacy, as well as a history of the
symbolic affirmation of human freedom; it is a material history of everyday
commerce as well as a history of British popular politics. "The new and more
just moral universe" of the post-slave-trade British empire was, it turns out,
not particularly "new" or "just." Antislavery policies in West Africa adapted
the old routines of the transatlantic and coastal slave trades. Former slaves
were made subject to a regime of control rooted in the deep conservativism
and gradualism, commercial ambitions, and militarism of the powerful leaders
of elite antislavery in Britain.

So instead of rehearsing the history of *abolitionism*, of the transformation of British attitudes toward slavery, this books ends with what we can
scrape from Sierra Leone's colonial records about the life of one of freedom's debtors, one of the tens of thousands of people whose lives were defined by *abolition*, by the complicated translation of the 1807 Slave Trade Act
into everyday practice. Marquis Granby, a demobilized noncommissioned
officer from the West India Regiments, had, in all likelihood, originally been
shipped from Sierra Leone to the Caribbean via the recruiting depot at Bance
Island. His name, clearly chosen by recruiters, was likely a nod to John Manners, Marquess of Granby, a British general in the Seven Years' War who had
been especially popular with private soldiers. Granby was repatriated to Sierra Leone in 1819, and moved to the Liberated African Village of Wellington in 1822. By his own account, "a country man" taught him the craft of
shingle making, and he bartered his shingles with local "Mandingos" and
Temne for livestock and rice, which he sold in a small shop in Wellington.
With the profits he built a stone house, which he rented to a missionary for
£63 a year. He was given control of several apprentices by the Liberated African Department, and he also paid wages to several Liberated African saw-
yers to build him a spacious farmhouse, which he planned to open to the
public as a gin shop.[35]

The archival records of Marquis Granby's time in Sierra Leone map
onto the institutions built in the colony under the aegis of enforcing British
antislavery. It is likely that Granby was still enslaved when the arrival of the
Sierra Leone Company drove up demand for slave labour in the coastal kingdoms and caliphates of West Africa. The antislavery colony needed rice and
palm oil, timber and ivory—and enslaved workers did the harvesting and the
hunting. The Slave Trade Act then put in motion the chain of events that re-

leased Granby from slavery, and saved him from making the Middle Passage on a slave ship. However, British antislavery launched him across the Caribbean on a different Middle Passage. Through the Vice-Admiralty Court, Granby was conscripted by a system that made money for antislavery activists and military officers, and that connected London activism to imperial interdiction. As a black soldier in a British uniform, he represented the British military's anxieties about white soldiers' capacity to hold the West Indies against French and Haitian revolutionaries. At the end of the wars, he returned to Sierra Leone, where he was placed in the system of "civilization" maintained by the Liberated African Department. He prospered, and did business with Europeans and Africans according to commercial scripts that blended West African and British economic folkways with the pieties of Christian missionary work. He was respectable enough to be given apprentices, taking a share of a ubiquitous institution in the post-slavery British empire. Granby was just one out of thousands and thousands of people who lived through the implementation of the first two decades of the abolition of the slave trade, former slaves whose lives were defined by the debts Britons assumed they owed to the British empire in exchange for freedom. The history of the campaign to change British minds about slavery has been told before. Marquis Granby's life tells a different story.

Notes

ADM	Records of the Admiralty, The National Archives, Kew
BL Add. Ms.	Additional Manuscripts Collection, The British Library, London
CMS	Church Missionary Society Archives, University of Birmingham Library Special Collections, Birmingham
CO	Records of the Colonial Office, The National Archives, Kew
DTH	Papers of Thomas Perronet Thompson, Hull History Centre
FO	Records of the Foreign Office, The National Archives, Kew
HCA	Records of the High Court of Admiralty, The National Archives, Kew
MPG	Maps and Plans, Records of the Colonial Office, The National Archives, Kew
MPH	Maps and Plans, Records of the War Office, The National Archives, Kew
MY	Macaulay Papers, Huntington Library, San Marino
NAM	Templer Study Centre, National Army Museum, London
NSA	Nova Scotia Archives, Halifax
ODNB	*Oxford Dictionary of National Biography* (Online edition, 2004–2015)
OSB	James Marshall and Marie-Louise Osborn Collection, Beinecke Rare Book and Manuscript Library, Yale University, New Haven
SLPA	Sierra Leone Public Archives, Fourah Bay College, University of Sierra Leone, Freetown
TS	Records of the Treasury Solicitor and HM Procurator General, The National Archives, Kew
UICSL	Sierra Leone Collection, University of Illinois at Chicago (UIC), Richard J. Daley Library, Special Collections, Chicago
Wellcome MS	Archives and Special Collections, Wellcome Library, London
WO	Records of the War Office, The National Archives, Kew

Introduction

1. H. I. Ricketts, *Narrative of the Ashantee War: With a View of the Present State of the Colony of Sierra Leone* (London, 1831), 82–83.

2. Ibid., 122.

3. See data in "Voyages: The Trans-Atlantic Slave Trade Database," 2012, http://www.slavevoyages.org/tast/index.faces. Thanks to Richard Anderson for help with this figure.

4. Robert Ross, "The Last Years of the Slave Trade to the Cape Colony," *Slavery & Abolition* 9, no. 3 (1988): 209–19; Christopher Saunders, "Between Slavery and Freedom: The Importation of Prize Negroes to the Cape in the Aftermath of Emancipation," *Kronos* 9 (January 1, 1984): 36–43; Christopher Saunders, "Liberated Africans in Cape Colony in the First Half of the Nineteenth Century," *International Journal of African Historical Studies* 18, no. 2 (January 1, 1985): 223–39; Rosanne Marion Adderley, *"New Negroes from Africa": Slave Trade Abolition and Free African Settlement in the Nineteenth-Century Caribbean* (Bloomington, IN: Indiana University Press, 2006); Howard Johnson, "The Liberated Africans in the Bahamas, 1811–60," *Immigrants & Minorities* 7, no. 1 (March 1988): 16–40; Matthew S. Hopper, *Slaves of One Master: Globalization and Slavery in Arabia in the Age of Empire* (New Haven: Yale University Press, 2015), 142–80.

5. Thomas Clarkson, *The History of the Rise, Progress, and Accomplishment of the Abolition of the African Slave-Trade, by the British Parliament*, vol. 2 (London, 1808), 583.

6. See, among other notable books, Sven Beckert, *Empire of Cotton: A Global History* (New York: Knopf, 2014); Walter Johnson, *River of Dark Dreams: Slavery and Empire in the Cotton Kingdom* (Cambridge, MA: Belknap, 2013); Edward E. Baptist, *The Half Has Never Been Told: Slavery and the Making of American Capitalism* (New York: Basic Books, 2014). For earlier histories, see David Brion Davis, *The Problem of Slavery in the Age of Revolution, 1770–1823* (Ithaca, NY: Cornell University Press, 1975); David Brion Davis, "Reflections on Abolitionism and Ideological Hegemony," *American Historical Review* 92, no. 4 (October 1, 1987): 797–812; Thomas L. Haskell, "Capitalism and the Origins of the Humanitarian Sensibility, Part 1," *American Historical Review* 90, no. 2 (April 1, 1985): 339–61; Thomas L. Haskell, "Capitalism and the Origins of the Humanitarian Sensibility, Part 2," *American Historical Review* 90, no. 3 (June 1, 1985): 547–66.

7. See Alexander X. Byrd, *Captives and Voyagers: Black Migrants across the Eighteenth-Century British Atlantic World* (Baton Rouge, LA: Louisiana State

University Press, 2010), 33–45; Marcus Rediker, *The Slave Ship: A Human History* (New York: Penguin, 2007).

8. *An Address to the Dutchess of York, Against the Use of Sugar* (London, 1792), 10.

9. Vincent Brown, *The Reaper's Garden: Death and Power in the World of Atlantic Slavery* (Cambridge, MA: Harvard University Press, 2008); Emma Christopher, *Slave Ship Sailors and Their Captive Cargoes, 1730–1807* (New York: Cambridge University Press, 2006).

10. Christopher Leslie Brown, *Moral Capital: Foundations of British Abolitionism* (Chapel Hill, NC: Omohundro Institute of Early American History and Culture/University of North Carolina Press, 2006).

11. Mark Philp, "Vulgar Conservatism, 1792–3," *English Historical Review* 110, no. 435 (February 1, 1995): 42–69; Mark Philp, ed., *The French Revolution and British Popular Politics* (Cambridge: Cambridge University Press, 2004); Linda Colley, *Britons: Forging the Nation, 1707–1837* (New Haven: Yale University Press, 1992); Linda Colley, "The Apotheosis of George III: Loyalty, Royalty and the British Nation 1760–1820," *Past & Present*, no. 102 (February 1, 1984): 94–129.

12. Laurent Dubois, *Avengers of the New World: The Story of the Haitian Revolution* (Cambridge, MA: Harvard University Press, 2009); Laurent Dubois, *A Colony of Citizens: Revolution & Slave Emancipation in the French Caribbean, 1787–1804* (Chapel Hill: University of North Carolina Press, 2004); Robin Blackburn, "Haiti, Slavery, and the Age of the Democratic Revolution," *William and Mary Quarterly*, Third Series, 63, no. 4 (October 1, 2006): 643–74; Ada Ferrer, "Haiti, Free Soil, and Antislavery in the Revolutionary Atlantic," *American Historical Review* 117, no. 1 (February 1, 2012): 40–66.

13. Christopher L. Brown, "Empire without Slaves: British Concepts of Emancipation in the Age of the American Revolution," *The William and Mary Quarterly*, Third Series, 56, no. 2 (April 1, 1999): 273–306; Elsa V. Goveia, *Slave Society in the British Leeward Islands at the End of the Eighteenth Century* (New Haven: Yale University Press, 1965), 1–49.

14. Robert Charles Dallas, *The History of the Maroons: From Their Origin to the Establishment of Their Chief Tribe at Sierra Leone*, vol. 1 (London, 1803), i.

15. African Institution, *Ninth Report of the Directors of the African Institution: Read at the Annual General Meeting on the 12th of April, 1815* (London, 1815), 65; Robert Thorpe, *Postscript to the Reply "Point by Point": Containing an Exposure of the Misrepresentation of the Treatment of the Captured Negroes at Sierra Leone, and Other Matters Arising from the Ninth Report of the African Institution* (London, 1815), 35.

228 NOTES TO PAGES 10–12

16. "The Slave Trade—since the Treaty for Its General Abolition," *The Gentleman's Magazine*, August 1816, 119.

17. F. Harrison Rankin, *The White Man's Grave: A Visit to Sierra Leone, in 1834.*, vol. 1 (London, 1836), xiii.

18. Stephen J. Braidwood, *Black Poor and White Philanthropists: London's Blacks and the Foundation of the Sierra Leone Settlement, 1786–1791* (Liverpool: Liverpool University Press, 1994); Prince Hoare, ed., *Memoirs of Granville Sharp: With Observations on Mr. Sharp's Biblical Criticisms* (London, 1820).

19. Seymour Drescher, "Whose Abolition? Popular Pressure and the Ending of the British Slave Trade," *Past & Present*, no. 143 (May 1994): 136–66; John Brewer, "Commercialization and Politics," in *The Birth of a Consumer Society: The Commercialization of Eighteenth-Century England*, ed. Neil McKendrick, John Brewer, and J. H. Plumb (Bloomington, IN: Indiana University Press, 1982), 197–264.

20. James W. St. George Walker, *The Black Loyalists: The Search for a Promised Land in Nova Scotia and Sierra Leone, 1783–1870* (New York: Africana Publishing; Dalhousie University Press, 1976); Ellen Wilson, *The Loyal Blacks* (New York: Capricorn Books, 1976); Cassandra Pybus, *Epic Journeys of Freedom: Runaway Slaves of the American Revolution and Their Global Quest for Liberty* (Boston: Beacon Press, 2006); Maya Jasanoff, *Liberty's Exiles: American Loyalists in the Revolutionary World* (New York: Knopf, 2011); Gary B. Nash, "Thomas Peters: Millwright and Deliverer," in *Struggle and Survival in Colonial America*, ed. David Sweet and Gary B. Nash (Berkeley, CA: University of California Press, 1981), 69–85.

21. Brown, *Moral Capital*, 314–22; Deirdre Coleman, *Romantic Colonization and British Anti-Slavery* (New York: Cambridge University Press, 2004). Slave traders were especially aware of ethnic divisions in rice cultivation: See Daniel C. Littlefield, *Rice and Slaves: Ethnicity and the Slave Trade in Colonial South Carolina* (Baton Rouge, LA: Louisiana State University Press, 1981); Judith Carney, "Rice Milling, Gender and Slave Labour in Colonial South Carolina," *Past & Present*, no. 153 (November 1, 1996): 108–34; Judith Ann Carney, *Black Rice: The African Origins of Rice Cultivation in the Americas* (Cambridge, MA: Harvard University Press, 2001); Edda L. Fields-Black, *Deep Roots: Rice Farmers in West Africa and the African Diaspora* (Bloomington, IN: Indiana University Press, 2008). On the local knowledge of slave traders in West Africa, see V. R. Dorjahn and Christopher Fyfe, "Landlord and Stranger: Change in Tenancy Relations in Sierra Leone," *Journal of African History* 3, no. 3 (January 1, 1962): 391–97; George E. Brooks, *Western*

Africa and Cabo Verde, 1790s–1830s: Symbiosis of Slave and Legitimate Trades (Bloomington, IN: Authorhouse, 2010); Bruce L. Mouser, "Landlords-Strangers: A Process of Accommodation and Assimilation," *International Journal of African Historical Studies* 8, no. 3 (January 1, 1975): 425–40; Bruce L. Mouser, "Trade, Coasters, and Conflict in the Rio Pongo from 1790 to 1808," *Journal of African History* 14, no. 1 (January 1, 1973): 45–64.

22. *West-African Sketches* (London, 1824), 3. See also Ralph A. Austen and Woodruff D. Smith, "Images of Africa and British Slave-Trade Abolition: The Transition to an Imperialist Ideology, 1787–1807," *African Historical Studies* 2, no. 1 (January 1, 1969): 69–83; Philip D. Curtin, *The Image of Africa: British Ideas and Action, 1780–1850* (Madison, WI: University of Wisconsin Press, 1964).

23. See especially Boyd Hilton, *The Age of Atonement: The Influence of Evangelicalism on Social and Economic Thought, 1795–1865* (Oxford: Clarendon Press, 1988); Boyd Hilton, *A Mad, Bad, and Dangerous People?: England, 1783–1846* (Oxford: Clarendon Press, 2006), 183. See also James T. Campbell, *Middle Passages: African American Journeys to Africa, 1787–2005* (New York: Penguin, 2006), 24; Leonore Davidoff and Catherine Hall, *Family Fortunes: Men and Women of the English Middle Class, 1780–1850* (London: Hutchinson, 1987), 21.

24. Quoted in David Eltis, *Economic Growth and the Ending of the Transatlantic Slave Trade* (New York: Oxford University Press, 1987), 21.

25. Paul E. Lovejoy, *Transformations in Slavery: A History of Slavery in Africa*, 2d ed. (Cambridge: Cambridge University Press, 2000); Martin Lynn, *Commerce and Economic Change in West Africa: The Palm Oil Trade in the Nineteenth Century* (Cambridge: Cambridge University Press, 1997); David Northrup, "The Compatibility of the Slave and Palm Oil Trades in the Bight of Biafra," *Journal of African History* 17, no. 3 (January 1, 1976): 353–64; Brooks, *Western Africa and Cabo Verde;* Ibrahim K. Sundiata, *From Slaving to Neoslavery: The Bight of Biafra and Fernando Po in the Era of Abolition, 1827–1930* (Madison, WI: University of Wisconsin Press, 1996).

26. Eltis, *Economic Growth*, 108–9; John Dodson, *A Report of the Case of the Louis, Forest, Master: Appealed from the Vice-Admiralty Court at Sierra Leone and Determined in the High Court of Admiralty, on the 15th of December 1817: With an Appendix* (London, 1817).

27. Edward Bartlett Rugemer, *The Problem of Emancipation: The Caribbean Roots of the American Civil War* (Baton Rouge, LA: Louisiana State University Press, 2009), 5. See also Gregory E. O'Malley, *Final Passages: The Intercolonial Slave*

Trade of British America, 1619–1807 (Chapel Hill, NC: Omohundro Institute of Early American History and Culture/University of North Carolina Press, Chapel Hill, 2014).

28. Monica Schuler, *"Alas, Alas, Kongo": A Social History of Indentured African Immigration into Jamaica, 1841–1865* (Baltimore: Johns Hopkins University Press, 1980), 5. On "'palaver,'" see Thomas Masterman Winterbottom, *An Account of the Native Africans in the Neighbourhood of Sierra Leone: To Which Is Added, an Account of the Present State of Medicine among Them*, vol. 1 (London, 1803), 91.

29. Rankin, *White Man's Grave*, 1:165.

30. See Walter Rodney, *A History of the Upper Guinea Coast, 1545–1800* (Oxford: Clarendon Press, 1970); Philip Misevich, "The Sierra Leone Hinterland and the Provisioning of Early Freetown, 1792–1803," *Journal of Colonialism and Colonial History* 9, no. 3 (2008).

31. Winterbottom, *Account of the Native Africans*, 1:3–6.

32. See ibid., 1:7. See also Matt Schaffer, "Bound to Africa: The Mandinka Legacy in the New World," *History in Africa* 32 (2005): 321–69; Steven Thomson, "Revisiting 'Mandingization' in Coastal Gambia and Casamance (Senegal): Four Approaches to Ethnic Change," *African Studies Review* 54, no. 2 (September 2011): 95–121.

33. Winterbottom, *Account of the Native Africans*, 1:4. See also Bruce Mouser, "Rebellion, Marronage and Jihad: Strategies of Resistance to Slavery on the Sierra Leone Coast, c. 1783–1796," *Journal of African History* 48, no. 1 (2007): 27–44.

34. For Sierra Leone as a site of the American Revolution, see Jasanoff, *Liberty's Exiles;* Pybus, *Epic Journeys of Freedom*. For Sierra Leonean nationalist history, see Christopher Fyfe, *A History of Sierra Leone* (Oxford: Oxford University Press, 1962); John Peterson, *Province of Freedom: A History of Sierra Leone, 1787–1870* (London: Faber & Faber, 1969); Joe D. Alie, *A New History of Sierra Leone* (New York: St. Martin's Press, 1990); Arthur T. Porter, *Creoledom: A Study of the Development of Freetown Society* (Oxford: Oxford University Press, 1963); Akintola Wyse, *The Krio of Sierra Leone: An Interpretive History* (London: Hurst; The International African Institute, 1989).

35. See Jenny S. Martinez, "Antislavery Courts and the Dawn of International Human Rights Law," *Yale Law Journal* 117 (2008): 550–641; Jenny S. Martinez, *The Slave Trade and the Origins of International Human Rights Law* (New York: Oxford University Press, 2012); Tara Helfman, "The Court of Vice Admiralty at Sierra Leone and the Abolition of the West African Slave Trade," *Yale Law Journal* 115, no. 5 (March 1, 2006): 1122–56.

36. Laurent Dubois, *Haiti: The Aftershocks of History* (New York: Macmillan, 2012), 33.

37. Thomas C. Holt, *The Problem of Freedom: Race, Labour, and Politics in Jamaica and Britain, 1832–1938* (Baltimore: Johns Hopkins University Press, 1992), xxii.

38. Dubois, *Haiti,* 30.

39. See Holt, *Problem of Freedom;* Thomas C. Holt, "The Essence of the Contract: The Articulation of Race, Gender, and Political Economy in British Emancipation Policy, 1838–1866," in *Beyond Slavery: Explorations of Race, Labor and Citizenship in Postemancipation Societies,* by Frederick Cooper, Thomas C. Holt, and Rebecca J. Scott (Chapel Hill, NC: University of North Carolina Press, 2000), 33–59; Steven Hahn, *The Political Worlds of Slavery and Freedom* (Cambridge, MA: Harvard University Press, 2009); Rebecca J. Scott, *Slave Emancipation in Cuba: The Transition to Free Labor, 1860–1899* (Princeton, NJ: Princeton University Press, 1985); Rebecca J. Scott, *Degrees of Freedom: Louisiana and Cuba after Slavery* (Cambridge, MA: Harvard University Press, 2009); Rebecca J. Scott, "Paper Thin: Freedom and Re-Enslavement in the Diaspora of the Haitian Revolution," *Law and History Review* 29, no. 4 (2011): 1061–87; Dubois, *A Colony of Citizens;* Dubois, *Avengers of the New World.*

40. Ada Ferrer, *Freedom's Mirror: Cuba and Haiti in the Age of Revolution* (New York: Cambridge University Press, 2014), 338.

41. Kenneth Macaulay, *The Colony of Sierra Leone Vindicated from the Misrepresentations of Mr. Macqueen of Glasgow* (London, 1827), 5.

42. Rankin, *White Man's Grave,* 1:54–55.

43. Eric Williams, *Capitalism & Slavery* (New York: Russell & Russell, 1961); Lowell J. Ragatz, *The Fall of the Planter Class in the British Caribbean, 1763–1833: A Study in Social and Economic History,* 2d ed. (New York: Octagon Books, 1963); Davis, *Problem of Slavery.*

44. See J. R. Ward, *British West Indian Slavery, 1750–1834: The Process of Amelioration* (Oxford: Clarendon Press, 1988); Trevor Burnard, *Mastery, Tyranny, and Desire: Thomas Thistlewood and His Slaves in the Anglo-Jamaican World* (Chapel Hill, NC: University of North Carolina Press, 2004), 101–36; Justin Roberts, *Slavery and the Enlightenment in the British Atlantic, 1750–1807* (Cambridge: Cambridge University Press, 2013).

45. See especially Seymour Drescher, *Econocide: British Slavery in the Era of Abolition* (Pittsburgh: University of Pittsburgh Press, 1977); Roger Anstey, *The Atlantic Slave Trade and British Abolition, 1760–1810* (Atlantic

Highlands, NJ: Humanities Press, 1975). See also Eltis, *Economic Growth;* Holt, *Problem of Freedom*, 23; Brown, *Moral Capital*.

46. James J. Gigantino, *The Ragged Road to Abolition: Slavery and Freedom in New Jersey, 1775–1865* (Philadelphia: University of Pennsylvania Press, 2014), 5. See also Robert William Fogel and Stanley L. Engerman, "Philanthropy at Bargain Prices: Notes on the Economics of Gradual Emancipation," *Journal of Legal Studies* 3 (1974): 377–401; Arthur Zilversmit, *The First Emancipation: The Abolition of Slavery in the North* (Chicago: University of Chicago Press, 1969); Joanne Pope Melish, *Disowning Slavery: Gradual Emancipation and "Race" in New England, 1780–1860* (Ithaca, NY: Cornell University Press, 1998); Sarah Levine-Gronningsater, "Delivering Freedom: Gradual Emancipation, Black Legal Culture, and the Origins of Sectional Crisis in New York, 1759–1870" (Ph.D. diss., University of Chicago, 2014).

47. See especially Beckert, *Empire of Cotton*, 136–241; Sven Beckert, "Emancipation and Empire: Reconstructing the Worldwide Web of Cotton Production in the Age of the American Civil War," *American Historical Review* 109, no. 5 (December 1, 2004): 1405–38.

48. Byrd, *Captives and Voyagers*, 2.

49. Zachary Macaulay, *A Letter to William W. Whitmore, Esq., M.P. Pointing out Some of the Erroneous Statements Contained in a Pamphlet by Joseph Marryat, Esq., M.P., entitled "A Reply to the Arguments Contained in Various . . ."* (London, 1823), 19. Suzanne Miers and Richard L. Roberts, "Introduction: The End of Slavery in Africa," in *The End of Slavery in Africa*, ed. Suzanne Miers and Richard L. Roberts (Madison, WI: University of Wisconsin Press, 1988), 12–13.

50. Lovejoy, *Transformations in Slavery*, 254.

51. Siân Rees, *Sweet Water and Bitter: The Ships That Stopped the Slave Trade* (Durham, NH: University of New Hampshire Press, 2011); W. E. F. Ward, *The Royal Navy and the Slavers: The Suppression of the Atlantic Slave Trade* (New York: Pantheon, 1969); Christopher Lloyd, *The Navy and the Slave Trade: The Suppression of the African Slave Trade in the Nineteenth Century* (London: Cass, 1968).

52. Alan Lester and Fae Dussart, *Colonization and the Origins of Humanitarian Governance: Protecting Aborigines across the Nineteenth-Century British Empire* (Cambridge: Cambridge University Press, 2014), 13; Frederick Cooper, "Conditions Analogous to Slavery: Imperialism and Free Labor Ideology in Africa," in *Beyond Slavery: Explorations of Race, Labor, and Citizenship in*

Postemancipation Societies, by Frederick Cooper, Thomas C. Holt, and Rebecca J. Scott (Chapel Hill, NC: University of North Carolina Press, 2000), 107–50.

53. See C. A. Bayly, *Imperial Meridian: The British Empire and the World, 1780–1830* (London and New York: Longman, 1989), 194–95.

54. James Stephen, *The Crisis of the Sugar Colonies; Or, An Enquiry Into the Objects and Probable Effects of the French Expedition to the West Indies . . .* (London, 1802), 27.

55. Seth Rockman, *Scraping By: Wage Labor, Slavery, and Survival in Early Baltimore* (Baltimore: Johns Hopkins University Press, 2010), 5.

56. Davis, *Problem of Slavery*, 385; Catherine Hall, *Civilising Subjects: Colony and Metropole in the English Imagination, 1830–1867* (Chicago: University of Chicago Press, 2002), 157; Richard Drayton, *Nature's Government: Science, British Imperialism and the "Improvement" of the World* (New Haven and London: Yale University Press, 2000), 92.

57. Clarkson, *History*, 1808, 2:580.

1. *Antislavery on a Slave Coast*

1. Entry for 21 January, 1792, in John Clarkson, *Clarkson's Mission to America 1791–1792*, ed. Charles Bruce Fergusson (Halifax: Public Archives of Nova Scotia, 1971), 162.

2. Entry for 18 February 1792, ibid., 164–65.

3. Greg Dening, *The Death of William Gooch: A History's Anthropology* (Honolulu: University of Hawai'i Press, 1995), 21.

4. Christopher Tolley, *Domestic Biography: The Legacy of Evangelicalism in Four Nineteenth-Century Families* (Oxford: Clarendon Press, 1997), 56.

5. Entry for May 17 1792, "Diary of John Clarkson, 19 March–4 August 1792," UICSL II/4/p. 327.

6. Entry for March 25 1792, Clarkson's Diary, UICSL II/4/p. 40.

7. See Henry Thornton, *An Enquiry into the Nature and Effects of the Paper Credit of Great Britain* (London, 1802); Antoin Murphy, "Paper Credit and the Multi-Personae Mr. Henry Thornton," *European Journal of the History of Economic Thought* 10, no. 3 (October 1, 2003): 429–53; Neil Skaggs, "Thomas Tooke, Henry Thornton, and the Development of British Monetary Orthodoxy," *Journal of the History of Economic Thought* 25, no. 2 (June 1, 2003): 177–99.

8. "Orders and Regulations from the Directors of the Sierra Leone Company to the Superintendent and Council for the Settlement . . .," Autographs

(Manuscript Orders from the Directors of the Sierra Leone Company), SLPA.

9. See Nash, "Thomas Peters: Millwright and Deliverer"; Walker, *Black Loyalists;* Wilson, *Loyal Blacks;* Pybus, *Epic Journeys of Freedom;* Jasanoff, *Liberty's Exiles;* P. E. H. Hair, "Africanism: The Freetown Contribution," *Journal of Modern African Studies* 5, no. 4 (December 1, 1967): 521–39; A. P. Kup, "John Clarkson and the Sierra Leone Company," *International Journal of African Historical Studies* 5, no. 2 (January 1, 1972): 203–20. On the Maroons, see Mavis Campbell and George Ross, eds., *Back to Africa: George Ross and the Maroons from Nova Scotia to Sierra Leone* (Trenton, NJ: Africa World Press, 1993); Kenneth Bilby, *True-Born Maroons* (Gainesville: University Press of Florida, 2005); Robert Charles Dallas, *The History of the Maroons: From Their Origin to the Establishment of Their Chief Tribe at Sierra Leone,* vol. 2, 2 vols. (London, 1803).

10. "Letter addressed to the Chairman of the Sierra Leone Company by the Rev. Mr. Thomas Clarkson," BL Add. Ms. 12131, pp. 28–29; See also Suzanne Schwarz, "Commerce, Civilization and Christianity: The Development of the Sierra Leone Company," in *Liverpool and Transatlantic Slavery,* ed. David Richardson, Suzanne Schwarz, and Anthony Tibbles (Liverpool: Liverpool University Press, 2007), 256–57.

11. Rodney, *History of the Upper Guinea Coast,* 152; Coleman, *Romantic Colonization and British Anti-Slavery;* Pybus, *Epic Journeys of Freedom,* 170.

12. For contemporary accounts, see François Le Vaillant, *New Travels Into the Interior Parts of Africa . . .* (London, 1796); Mungo Park, *Travels in the Interior Districts of Africa . . .* (London, 1799); Joseph Hawkins, *A History of a Voyage to the Coast of Africa . . .* (Troy, NY, 1797); John Matthews, *A Voyage to the River Sierra-Leone, On the Coast of Africa . . .* (London, 1788); Jean Baptiste Léonard Durand, *A Voyage to Senegal . . .* (London, 1806). On slavery and economic integration, see David Hancock, *Citizens of the World: London Merchants and the Integration of the British Atlantic Community, 1735–1785* (Cambridge and New York: Cambridge University Press, 1995), 172, 172–220; Carl Wennerlind, *Casualties of Credit: The English Financial Revolution, 1620–1720* (Cambridge, MA: Harvard University Press, 2011), 224–30.

13. Jane I. Guyer, *Marginal Gains: Monetary Transactions in Atlantic Africa* (Chicago: University of Chicago Press, 2004), 4. See also Schwarz, "Commerce, Civilization and Christianity," 26.

14. Stephen, *Crisis of the Sugar Colonies,* 54.

15. Schwarz, "Commerce, Civilization and Christianity," 254; Seymour Dre-
    scher, *The Mighty Experiment: Free Labor vs. Slavery in British Emancipation*
    (New York: Oxford University Press, 2002), 90–94; Fyfe, *History of Sierra
    Leone*, 31.
16. Brown, *Moral Capital*, 261.
17. Holt, *Problem of Freedom*, 5.
18. Curtin, *Image of Africa*, 41.
19. Winterbottom, *Account of the Native Africans*, 1:87. See also Ismail Rashid,
    "'A Devotion to the Idea of Liberty at Any Price': Rebellion and Antislav-
    ery in the Upper Guinea Coast in the Eighteenth and Nineteenth Centuries,"
    in *Fighting the Slave Trade: West African Strategies*, ed. Sylviane A. Diouf
    (Athens, OH: Ohio University Press, 2003), 132–51.
20. Winterbottom, *Account of the Native Africans*, 1:v.
21. Ibid., 1:85–87.
22. Curtin, *Image of Africa*, 62, 106–7.
23. See ibid.; Lovejoy, *Transformations in Slavery;* Brooks, *Western Africa and
    Cabo Verde;* Lynn, *Commerce and Economic Change in West Africa;* Allen M.
    Howard, "Nineteenth-Century Coastal Slave Trading and the British Aboli-
    tion Campaign in Sierra Leone," *Slavery & Abolition* 27, no. 1 (April 2006):
    23–49.
24. Henry Smeathman to John Coakley Lettsom, Bance Island, 26 June 1773, in
    John Coakley Lettsom, *Memoirs of the Life and Writings of the Late John
    Coakley Lettsom . . .: With a Selection from His Correspondence*, ed. Thomas
    Joseph Pettigrew, vol. 2 (London, 1817), 266. See also Rodney, *History of the
    Upper Guinea Coast;* Walter Rodney, "A Reconsideration of the Mane Inva-
    sions of Sierra Leone," *Journal of African History* 8, no. 2 (1967): 219–46.
25. Igor Kopytoff and Suzanne Miers, "African 'Slavery' as an Institution of
    Marginality," in *Slavery in Africa: Historical and Anthropological Perspectives*,
    ed. Suzanne Miers and Igor Kopytoff (Madison, WI: University of Wiscon-
    sin Press, 1977), 7; John Thornton, *Warfare in Atlantic Africa, 1500–1800*
    (London: UCL Press, 1999), 16; Eltis, *Economic Growth*, 56.
26. Zilversmit, *First Emancipation*, 87; Dubois, *A Colony of Citizens*, 68–73.
27. Melish, *Disowning Slavery*, 64.
28. Ibid., 53; Gigantino, *Ragged Road to Abolition*, 98.
29. See Braidwood, *Black Poor and White Philanthropists;* Hoare, *Memoirs of
    Granville Sharp*.
30. "Treaty for 1788," Autographs (Manuscript Orders from the Directors of
    the Sierra Leone Company), SLPA.

31. Guyer, *Marginal Gains*, 52.

32. Joseph C. Miller, "The Dynamics of History in Africa and the Atlantic 'Age of Revolutions,'" in *The Age of Revolutions in Global Context, c. 1760–1840*, ed. David Armitage and Sanjay Subrahmanyam (New York: Palgrave Macmillan, 2010), 120.

33. For another historical use of "creole" and "pidgin," see Peter Galison, *Image and Logic: A Material Culture of Microphysics* (Chicago: University of Chicago Press, 1997), 831–32.

34. Dorjahn and Fyfe, "Landlord and Stranger"; Mouser, "Landlords-Strangers"; G. Ugo Nwokeji, *The Slave Trade and Culture in the Bight of Biafra: An African Society in the Atlantic World* (New York: Cambridge University Press, 2010), 117–43.

35. Winterbottom, *Account of the Native Africans*, 1:173.

36. "Orders and Regulations from the Directors of the Sierra Leone Company," SLPA. See also Rodney, *History of the Upper Guinea Coast*, 198. On iron, see Candice L. Goucher, "Iron Is Iron 'til It Is Rust: Trade and Ecology in the Decline of West African Iron-Smelting," *Journal of African History* 22, no. 2 (1981): 179–89. On currencies, weights, and measures see Karl Polanyi, "Sortings and 'Ounce Trade' in the West African Slave Trade," *Journal of African History* 5, no. 3 (1964): 381–93; Marion Johnson, "The Cowrie Currencies of West Africa Part I," *Journal of African History* 11, no. 1 (1970): 17–49; Marion Johnson, "The Cowrie Currencies of West Africa Part II," *Journal of African History* 11, no. 3 (1970): 331–53.

37. Winterbottom, *Account of the Native Africans*, 1:175, 174–77.

38. Entry for 15 February 1795, "Mr. Gray's Journal in January & February 1795 to & from Furry Cannaba," BL Add. Ms. 12131, p. 36/f59.

39. Austen and Smith, "Images of Africa and British Slave-Trade Abolition," 81.

40. See George E. Brooks, *Yankee Traders, Old Coasters & African Middlemen: A History of American Legitimate Trade with West Africa in the Nineteenth Century* (Brookline, MA: Boston University Press, 1970); Lovejoy, *Transformations in Slavery*, 166–69; Carney, *Black Rice*, 69–70.

41. "Orders and Regulations from the Directors of the Sierra Leone Company," SLPA.

42. 21 April 1792, Clarkson's Diary, UICSL II/4/p. 191.

43. Ibid.

44. Ibid.

45. 23 April 1792, ibid., p. 193.

46. "Strand's Journal of Occurrences," BL Add. Ms. 12131, p. 3/f35.
47. Ibid., p. 2/f35.
48. Ibid., p. 3/f35.
49. See Iain Whyte, *Zachary Macaulay 1768–1838: The Steadfast Scot in the British Anti-Slavery Movement* (Liverpool: Liverpool University Press, 2011); Catherine Hall, *Macaulay and Son: Architects of Imperial Britain* (New Haven: Yale University Press, 2012), 19–49; Sir George Otto Trevelyan, ed., *The Life and Letters of Lord Macaulay*, vol. 1 (London, 1880), 2–10.
50. Charles Booth, *Zachary Macaulay, His Part in the Movement for the Abolition of the Slave Trade and of Slavery: An Appreciation* (London: Longman, 1934), 4.
51. Viscountess Knutsford, ed., *Life and Letters of Zachary Macaulay* (London, 1900), 15.
52. Thomas Babington to Zachary Macaulay, 9 April 1793, ibid., 24.
53. Zachary Macaulay to Selina Millas, 12 February, 1796, ibid., 109.
54. Suzanne Miers and Martin Klein, "Introduction," in *Slavery and Colonial Rule in Africa*, ed. Suzanne Miers and Martin Klein (Portland, OR: Frank Cass, 1999), 5.
55. Entry for 26 August 1793, Suzanne Schwarz, ed., *Zachary Macaulay and the Development of the Sierra Leone Company, 1793–4: Journal, June–October 1793* (Leipzig: Institut für Afrikanistik, 2000), 51–52.
56. Entries for 1 September 1793 and 17 October 1793, Schwarz, *Journal, June–October 1793*. See also Booth, *Zachary Macaulay*, 41–45; Whyte, *Zachary Macaulay 1768–1838*, 40.
57. Entry for 11 September 1793, Schwarz, *Journal, June–October 1793*, 59.
58. Minute of Council, 29 October 1793, Sierra Leone Council Books, CO 270/2.
59. Minute of Council, 25 April 1794, CO 270/2.
60. Schwarz, "Commerce, Civilization and Christianity," 262. See also Rodney, *History of the Upper Guinea Coast*, 168–69.
61. Entry for 3 August 1793, Schwarz, *Journal, June–October 1793*, 41.
62. Brooks, *Yankee Traders*, 13, 53–54; Littlefield, *Rice and Slaves*, 38. On trade between West Africa and South Carolina in particular see Bruce L. Mouser, *American Colony on the Rio Pongo: The War of 1812, the Slave Trade, and the Proposed Settlement of African Americans, 1810–1830* (Trenton, NJ: Africa World Press, 2013), 63–65.
63. From John Gray and Thomas Ludham [Ludlam], to Robert Prescot and John Wentworth, Sierra Leone, June 24 1799, CO 217/70. See also Alison

Jones, "The Rhode Island Slave Trade: A Trading Advantage in Africa," *Slavery & Abolition* 2, no. 3 (1981): 227–44; Rachel Chernos Lin, "The Rhode Island Slave-Traders: Butchers, Bakers and Candlestick-Makers," *Slavery & Abolition* 23, no. 3 (2002): 21–38.

64. Winston McGowan, "The Establishment of Long-Distance Trade Between Sierra Leone and Its Hinterland, 1787–1821," *Journal of African History* 31, no. 1 (1990): 27.

65. Ibid., 28.

66. Bruce L. Mouser, ed., *Journal of James Watt: Expedition to Timbo, Capital of the Fula Empire in 1794* (Madison, WI: African Studies Program, University of Wisconsin-Madison, 1994), 25–26.

67. Ibid., 23–24.

68. Minute of Council, 5 May 1794, CO 270/2.

69. Fernard Gerbaux and Charles Schmidt, eds., *Proces-Vérbaux Des Comités D'agriculture et de Commerce de La Constituante, de La Législative et de La Convention*, vol. 3 (Paris, 1906), 651. I am grateful to Simon Macdonald for this reference.

70. Fyfe, *History of Sierra Leone*, 59–60; Sierra Leone Company, *Substance of the Report of the Court of Directors of the Sierra Leone Company, Delivered to the General Court of Proprietors, on Thursday the 26th February, 1795. Published by Order of the Directors.* (London, 1795), 18.

71. Minute of Council, 5 May 1795, CO 270/3.

72. Macaulay, *Colony of Sierra Leone Vindicated*, 30. See also Mouser, "Trade, Coasters, and Conflict in the Rio Pongo from 1790 to 1808"; Schwarz, "Commerce, Civilization and Christianity," 261.

73. Minute of Council, Letter from Cooper to Governor and Council, 1 September 1795, CO 270/3.

74. Minute of Council, 29 May 1795, CO 270/3.

75. Sierra Leone Company, *Substance of the Report: Delivered, by the Court of Directors of the Sierra Leone Company, to the General Court of Proprietors, on Thursday the 29th March, 1798. . . .* (London, 1798), 4–5.

76. Ibid., 6.

77. Entry for October 19 1793, Suzanne Schwarz, ed., *Zachary Macaulay and the Development of the Sierra Leone Company, 1793–4: Journal, October–December 1793* (Leipzig: Institut für Afrikanistik, 2002), 5–6.

78. Matthews, *A Voyage to the River Sierra-Leone*, 68–69.

79. Diary of Zachary Macaulay, Entry for 11 December 1798, Knutsford, *Life and Letters of Zachary Macaulay*, 213–14.

80. Richard Lovett, *The History of the London Missionary Society, 1795–1895,* vol. 1 (London, 1899), 479–80.

81. Bruce Mouser and Nancy Fox Mouser, *Case of the Reverend Peter Hartwig, Slave Trader or Misunderstood Idealist: Clash of Church Missionary Society Imperial Objectives in Sierra Leone, 1804–1815* (Madison, WI: African Studies Program, University of Wisconsin-Madison, 2003), 5.

82. Schwarz, "Commerce, Civilization and Christianity," 265; see also George E. Brooks, *Eurafricans in Western Africa: Commerce, Social Status, Gender, and Religious Observance from the Sixteenth to the Eighteenth Century* (Athens, OH: Ohio University Press, 2003), 308.

83. Anna Maria Falconbridge, Alexander Falconbridge, and Isaac DuBois, *Narrative of Two Voyages to the River Sierra Leone, During the Years 1791–1792–1793,* ed. Christopher Fyfe (Liverpool: Liverpool University Press, 2000), 45.

84. Entry for 7 February 1795, "Mr. Gray's Journal in January & February 1795 to & from Furry Cannaba," BL Add. Ms. 12131, p. 16.

85. Henry Brunton, *A Spelling-Book for the Susoos: And a Cathechism (I–IV) for Little Children* (Edinburgh, 1802); Henry Brunton, *Second Catechism for the Susoo Children* (Edinburgh, 1801).

86. Zachary Macaulay to Selina Mills, June 1, 1799, Knutsford, *Life and Letters of Zachary Macaulay,* 221. See also Society for the Education of Africans, *Meeting of the Committee of the Society for the Education of Africans, the 29th January, 1801* (London, 1801).

87. Sierra Leone Company, *Substance of the Report of the Court of Directors [1798],* 19.

88. Winterbottom, *Account of the Native Africans,* 1:133, 168–71.

89. James Rowan and Henry Wellington, "(312) Sierra Leone. Report of the Commissioners of Inquiry into the State of the Colony of Sierra Leone. First Part," House of Commons Papers; Reports of Commissioners, 1826, 11.

90. Entry for 6 August 1791, Clarkson, *Clarkson's Mission to America 1791–1792,* 31. See also Nash, "Thomas Peters: Millwright and Deliverer"; Andrew Jackson O'Shaughnessy, *The Men Who Lost America: British Command during the Revolutionary War and the Preservation of the Empire* (New Haven: Yale University Press, 2014), 244–45.

91. Brown, *The Reaper's Garden,* 43.

92. Entry for 25 July, 1792, "Mr. James Strands Journal of Occurrences from April 21st to September 10th, 1792," BL Add. Ms. 12131, p. 13/f40.

93. Entry for 27 March 1792, Clarkson's Diary, UICSL II/4/p. 54.

94. Entry for 3 May 1792, "Strand's Journal of Occurrences," BL Add. Ms. 12131, p. 6–7/f37.

95. Entry for 3 March 1788, Journal of Rev. William Jessop, 1 January to March 11, 1788, NSA MG/100/169.

96. Entry for 9 March 1788, Jessop's Journal, NSA MG/100/169.

97. 14 March 1787, Rough Memoranda of William Booth, Charles Bruce Fergusson Fonds, NSA MG/1/1911/file 16.

98. See Carney, *Black Rice.*

99. Winterbottom, *Account of the Native Africans,* 1:50–51.

100. Remarks, 1 April 1811, in Rosalind Cobb Wiggins, ed., *Captain Paul Cuffe's Logs and Letters, 1808–1817: A Black Quaker's "Voice from within the Veil"* (Washington, D.C.: Howard University Press, 1996), 182.

101. Rowan and Wellington, "Report of the Commissioners of Inquiry, Part 1," 72.

102. "Statement given to the Commissioner by Eli Aikin one of the Original Settlers from Nova Scotia," Appendix 6B, CO 267/92.

103. Rankin, *White Man's Grave,* 1:90.

104. "Evidence of John Kizell, March 1826," Appendix 5B, CO 267/92.

105. Sierra Leone Company, *Substance of the Report of the Court of Directors [1798],* 11.

106. "Evidence of John Kizell," Appendix 5B, CO 267/92.

107. Rowan and Wellington, "Report of the Commissioners of Inquiry, Part 1," 74.

108. Sierra Leone Company, *Substance of the Report of the Court of Directors [1798],* 11. See also "Queries proposed by Commodore Hallowell, with the Gov & Council's answer January 12 1803," WO 1/352.

109. Matthews, *A Voyage to the River Sierra-Leone,* 56–57.

110. "(24) Report of the Select Committee on Petition of Court of Directors of Sierra Leone Company," House of Commons Papers; Reports of Commissioners, 1804, 46.

111. Nathaniel Wansey to John Clarkson, 13 February 1800, in Christopher Fyfe, ed., *Our Children Free and Happy: Letters from Black Settlers in Africa in the 1790s* (Edinburgh: Edinburgh University Press, 1991), 60–62.

112. Luke Jordan and others to John Clarkson, 19 November 1794, in ibid., 43–44.

113. Luke Jordan and Isaac Anderson to John Clarkson, 28 June 1794, in ibid., 42–43.

114. Minute of Council, 20 June 1794 [Evening], CO 270/2.

115. Minute of Council, 4 March 1795, CO 270/3.

116. Fyfe, *History of Sierra Leone*, 89–91.

117. Zachary Macaulay to Selina Mills, 20 June 1799, Knutsford, *Life and Letters of Zachary Macaulay*, 226.

118. "Statement of the Chairman and Court of Directors . . . Respecting the Progress State and Prospect . . . of Sierra Leone," "(100) Report of the Select Committee on Petition of Court of Directors of Sierra Leone Company," House of Commons Papers; Reports of Commissioners, 1802.

119. Stephen Saunders Webb, *The Governors-General: The English Army and the Definition of the Empire, 1569–1681* (Chapel Hill, NC: University of North Carolina Press, 1987), xvi.

120. See Jerry Bannister, *The Rule of the Admirals: Law, Custom and Naval Government in Newfoundland, 1699–1832* (Toronto: Osgoode Society for Canadian Legal History/University of Toronto Press, 2003), 26–63.

121. Alan Frost, *Convicts and Empire: A Naval Question, 1776–1811* (Melbourne and New York: Oxford University Press, 1980), 170–71.

122. Sir Reginald Coupland, *The British Anti-Slavery Movement* (London: Frank Cass, 1964), 84–85. Whyte, *Zachary Macaulay 1768–1838*, 107.

123. Earl of Portland to John Wentworth, 13 June 1796, CO 217/67, see also Portland to Wentworth, Whitehall, 15 July 1796, CO 217/67.

124. Wentworth to Portland, Halifax, 29 June 1797, Commissioner of Public Records Collection, NSA RG/1/419.

125. Wentworth to Portland, 13 April 1799, CO 217/70.

126. Ibid.

127. "The Island of Jamaica (on account of Expenses incurred for the Subsistence and Removal of the Maroons up to 8th May, 1804) in Account with Sir John Wentworth," NSA RG/1/419.

128. Anonymous to Portland, 24 February, [1799?], CO 217/70.

129. Portland to Wentworth, 30 May 1799, CO 217/70; see also Wentworth to Portland, 29 May 1799, CO 217/70.

130. Portland to Wentworth, 18 June 1799, CO 217/70.

131. Portland to Wentworth, 8 October 1799, CO 217/70.

132. Henry Thornton to John King, 11 March 1799, CO 217/70.

133. Extract from the Minutes of the Court of Directors of the Sierra Leone Company, March 1799, CO 217/70.

134. Portland to Court of Directors, Whitehall, 5 March 1799, CO 217/70.

135. Rowan and Wellington, "Report of the Commissioners of Inquiry, Part 1," 14.

136. Wentworth to John Gray and Thomas Ludlam, 5 August 1800, CO 217/74.

137. Thornton to King, 11 March 1799, CO 217/70.

138. Zachary Macaulay to Portland, 9 November 1799, CO 217/70.

139. Macaulay to Lord Castlereagh, 6 October 1802, WO 1/352.

140. Hoare, *Memoirs of Granville Sharp*, 257–77.

141. Fyfe, *History of Sierra Leone*, 82–87.

142. Thornton to King, 12 Feb 1800, CO 217/74; See also "Account of Monies Paid to Sierra Leone Company, 1801–04," House of Commons Papers; Accounts and Papers (1806).

143. Fyfe, *History of Sierra Leone*, 86.

144. "Statement of the Court of Directors of the Sierra Leone Company of the Present State of the Colony," WO 1/352.

145. *House of Commons Debates*, 29 July 1807, vol. 9 cc. 1002–5, 1003.

146. [Remarks of D. M. Hamilton], Appendix C9, CO 267/92.

147. Winterbottom, *Account of the Native Africans*, 1:154.

148. "Military Memorandums kept by J. Kingsley, Lt. African Corps commencing at Sierra Leone, 29 May 1803," Kingsley Papers, NAM 8011/10/1.

149. Diary of Melchior Renner, March 1805, CMS C/A/1/E/115b.

150. Ibid.

151. Joseph Corry, *Observations Upon the Windward Coast of Africa: The Religion, Character, Customs &c., of the Natives . . . Made in the Years 1805 and 1806* (London, 1807), 6–7.

152. Macaulay to James Sullivan, 19 March 1802; Macaulay to Sullivan, 27 July 1802; Macaulay to Sullivan, 4 April 1803, WO 1/352.

153. "Extract from a Memoir presented to Lord Hobart . . . by Mr. Zachary Macaulay, Secretary to the SLC, on the Means of Establishing a Commercial Intercourse between the Western Coast of Africa and the River Niger. August 1802," WO 1/352.

154. Thornton to Lord Castlereagh, 3 April 1807, WO 1/352.

155. Macaulay to Castlereagh, Sierra Leone Office [London], 8 May 1807, WO 1/352.

156. Macaulay to Castlereagh, 8 May 1807, WO 1/352.

157. Macaulay to Ludlam, 4 November 1807, CO 267/27.

158. William Wilberforce to Castlereagh, 7 December 1808, CO 267/24.

159. Fyfe, *History of Sierra Leone*, 87.

160. House of Commons Debates, 29 July 1807, vol. 9, cc. 1002–5, 1002.

2. *Let That Heart Be English*

1. Descriptions of Freetown from "Original Journal of a Voyage to the Coast of Africa in 1805, in His Majesty's Ship Success, by J. Strang, Surgeon," in *La Belle Assemblée: Or, Bell's Court and Fashionable Magazine, Addressed Particularly to the Ladies,* vol. 4 (London, 1811), 291; Winterbottom, *Account of the Native Africans,* 1:47–49; Fyfe, *History of Sierra Leone,* 98–101. See also MPG 1/1132 and MPH 1/872; Thomas Perronet Thompson to Nancy Barker, 18 June 1809, DTH 1/74; Thomas Ludlam to D. M. Hamilton, 10 May 1808, Local Letters: Governor's Letter Book, 1808–1811, SLPA.

2. Macaulay to Ludlam, 24 February 1804, DTH 1/2; Court of Directors of the Sierra Leone Company to Governor and Council of Sierra Leone, 13 January 1806, DTH 1/2.

3. Macaulay to Ludlam, London, August 1806, DTH 1/2.

4. Lamin Sanneh, *Abolitionists Abroad: American Blacks and the Making of Modern West Africa* (Cambridge, MA: Harvard University Press, 1999), 4.

5. Rees, *Sweet Water and Bitter,* 18.

6. Ludlam to Hamilton, 10 May 1808, Local Letters: Governor's Letter Book, 1808–1811, SLPA.

7. Thomas Clarkson, *The History of the Rise, Progress, and Accomplishment of the Abolition of the African Slave-Trade by the British Parliament,* vol. 1 (London, 1808), 259.

8. Ibid., 1:266.

9. Ludlam to *Alimami* Amrah, 1 February 1808, Local Letters: Governor's Letter Book, 1808–1811, SLPA.

10. Testimony of John Prime, Court of Vice-Admiralty, 6 September 1809, CO 267/27.

11. Testimony of Frederick Forbes, Court of Vice-Admiralty, 6 September 1809, CO 267/27.

12. Testimony of John Leedam Morgan, Court of Vice-Admiralty, 6 September 1809, CO 267/27.

13. Testimony of John Prime, Court of Vice-Admiralty, 6 September 1809, CO 267/27.

14. Ludlam to Macaulay, 13 April 1808, CO 267/24.

15. Ludlam to Hamilton, 10 May 1808, Local Letters: Governor's Letter Book, 1808–1811, SLPA.

16. Macaulay to Ludlam, 7 November 1807, DTH 1/2.

17. Published by Parliament as *At the Court at the Queen's Palace, the 16th Day of March, 1808, Present, the King's Most Excellent Majesty in Council* (London, 1808).

18. Beckert, *Empire of Cotton*, 188.
19. See Catherine Hall, "'From Greenland's Icy Mountains . . . to Afric's Golden Sand': Ethnicity, Race and Nation in Mid-Nineteenth-Century England," *Gender and History* 5, no. 2 (June 1, 1993): 212–30.
20. Evidence of Joseph Reffell, Appendix 10B, CO 267/92.
21. Joan Lane, *Apprenticeship in England, 1600–1914* (London: UCL Press, 1996); Douglas Hay and Paul Craven, "Introduction," in *Masters, Servants, and Magistrates in Britain and the Empire, 1562–1955*, ed. Douglas Hay and Paul Craven (Chapel Hill, NC: University of North Carolina Press, 2004), 1–58.
22. Kenneth Macaulay, Comments on Apprenticeship, Appendix C8, CO 267/92.
23. John Clarkson to Isaac Dubois, 4 October 1792, Manuscript Journal of John Clarkson, SLPA.
24. Census of Nova Scotian Settlers [ca. 1801?], WO 1/352.
25. Diary of Peter Hartwig, 25 November to 29 December 1805, CMS C/A/1/E/116b.
26. Census of Nova Scotian Settlers [ca. 1801?], WO 1/352.
27. Paul Cuffe to William Allen, 22 April 1811, in Wiggins, *Paul Cuffe's Logs*, 119.
28. Census of Nova Scotian Settlers [ca. 1801?], WO 1/352.
29. Ibid.
30. Thompson to Lord Castlereagh, 8 August 1808, CO 267/24.
31. The King v. Susanna Caulker, Deposition of Nancy, Minutes of the Council, 8 July 1809, CO 270/11.
32. Testimony of John Leedam Morgan, Court of Vice-Admiralty, Sierra Leone, 6 September 1809, CO 267/27.
33. Excerpts from the Minutes of the Council, 19 March 1808, DTH 1/51.
34. Testimony of John Leedam Morgan, Court of Vice-Admiralty, Sierra Leone, 6 September 1809, CO 267/27.
35. Testimony of John Prime, Court of Vice-Admiralty, Sierra Leone, 6 September 1809, CO 267/27.
36. Testimony of George Steven Caulker, Court of Vice-Admiralty, Sierra Leone, 6 September 1809, CO 267/27.
37. George Rickards to D. M. Hamilton, 27 April 1808, Local Letters: Governor's Letter Book, 1808–1811, SLPA.
38. Testimony of George Steven Caulker, Court of Vice-Admiralty, Sierra Leone, 6 September 1809, CO 267/27.

39. Ibid.

40. *Sierra Leone Gazette* [Freetown], January 1808. Letters from Ludlam to W. A. Leedam; to Abraham Vanneck; to J. M. Wilson; to James Wise; to George Nichol; to John Leedam Morgan, all dated 1 January 1808, Local Letters: Governor's Letter Book, 1808–1811, SLPA.

41. Ludlam to Stephen Caulker, Sierra Leone, 5 February 1808, Local Letters: Governor's Letter Book, 1808–1811, SLPA.

42. Eltis, *Economic Growth*, 105. See also Wayne Ackerson, *The African Institution (1807–1827) and the Antislavery Movement in Great Britain* (Lewiston, NY: Edward Mellen, 2005); Porter, *Creoledom*, 110.

43. Statement of Eli Aikin, Appendix 6B, CO 267/92.

44. John Darwin, *Unfinished Empire: The Global Expansion of Britain* (New York: Bloomsbury, 2013), 214–15.

45. Decision of Thomas Perronet Thompson, in the Vice-Admiralty Court, November 1809, CO 267/27.

46. Fyfe, *History of Sierra Leone*, 100; Michael J. Turner, "The Limits of Abolition: Government, Saints and the 'African Question,' c. 1780–1820," *English Historical Review* 112, no. 446 (April 1, 1997): 357.

47. Thompson to Castlereagh, 2 November 1808, CO 267/24.

48. Leonard Johnson, *General T. Perronet Thompson, 1783–1869: His Military, Literary, and Political Campaigns.* (London: G. Allen and Unwin, 1957), 1–25.

49. Thompson to Castlereagh, 2 November 1808, CO 267/24.

50. "A Narrative of Facts Connected with the Colony of Sierra Leone," DTH 1/102.

51. Ibid.

52. Quoted in Johnson, *General T. Perronet Thompson*, 26.

53. Ibid., 39.

54. Wilberforce to Castlereagh, 19 January 1809, CO 267/25. See also David Turley, *The Culture of English Antislavery, 1780–1860* (London, New York: Routledge, 1991), 83–84; Adam Kuper, *Incest and Influence: The Private Life of Bourgeois England* (Cambridge, MA: Harvard University Press, 2009), 145–47.

55. Thornton to Ludlam, 7 February 1807, DTH 1/2.

56. "A Narrative of Facts Connected with the Colony of Sierra Leone," DTH 1/102.

57. Ibid.

58. Quoted in Johnson, *General T. Perronet Thompson*, 29.

59. Thompson to Nancy Barker, 27 May 1808, quoted in ibid., 52.

60. "A Narrative of Facts Connected with the Colony of Sierra Leone," DTH 1/102.

61. Diary of Thomas Perronet Thompson, 8 June 1808, quoted in Johnson, *General T. Perronet Thompson*, 34.

62. "A Narrative of Facts Connected with the Colony of Sierra Leone," DTH 1/102.

63. Castlereagh to Thompson, 11 April 1809, DTH 1/19.

64. Diary of Thomas Perronet Thompson, 6 June 1808, quoted in Johnson, *General T. Perronet Thompson*, 33.

65. Adam Smith, *An Inquiry into the Nature and Causes of the Wealth of Nations*, ed. R. A. Seligman, vol. 1 (London: Everyman, 1957), 401.

66. "A Narrative of Facts Connected with the Colony of Sierra Leone," DTH 1/102.

67. Rough Journal of Thomas Perronet Thompson, 21 July 1808, DTH 1/21.

68. Ibid.

69. Ibid.

70. Deposition of William Dawes, taken by Edward Columbine, Sierra Leone, 15 April 1810, CO 267/27.

71. Ludlam to Thompson, 7 July 1809, CO 270/11.

72. Thompson to Castlereagh, 2 August 1808, CO 267/24; Thompson to Castlereagh, 4 February 1810, CO 267/27.

73. Thompson, Reply to the Address from the Commercial Residents of the Rio Pongo, 5 March 1810, DTH 1/30.

74. Thompson to the Directors of the African Institution, 31 July 1809, DTH 1/27.

75. Rough Journal of Thomas Perronet Thompson, 30 July 1808, DTH 1/21.

76. *Sierra Leone Gazette* [Freetown], 1 August 1808.

77. Rough Journal of Thomas Perronet Thompson, 30 July 1808, DTH 1/21; Order signed by Thomas Perronet Thompson and Frederick Forbes, 17 October 1809, Local Letters: Governor's Letter Book, 1808–1811, SLPA.

78. "A Narrative of Facts Connected with the Colony of Sierra Leone," DTH 1/102.

79. Rough Journal of Thomas Perronet Thompson, 2 August 1808, DTH 1/21.

80. Rankin, *White Man's Grave*, 1:106.

81. Minutes of the Council, 25 October 1809, CO 270/11.

82. Thompson to Castlereagh, 17 February 1809, CO 267/25.

83. 13 July 1810, Memoranda of Edward Columbine, 1809–1811, UICSL III/10/p. 147–48.

84. Thompson to Castlereagh, accompanying return of people freed under the 1807 Slave Trade Act, Minutes of Council, 31 December 1808, CO 270/11.

85. Thompson to African Institution, November 1808, DTH 1/27.

86. Thompson to Castlereagh, 2 November 1808, CO 267/24.

87. Ibid.

88. Thompson to the "Captain of a Merchant Vessel," 3 August 1809, DTH 1/41.

89. Thompson to Nancy Barker, 8 March 1809, DTH 1/74.

90. Thompson to Castlereagh, 15 August 1809, CO 267/25.

91. Thompson to Ludlam, 1 September 1808, CO 267/25.

92. Thompson to the Directors of the African Institution, 3 August 1809, DTH 1/41.

93. Thompson to Wilberforce, 23 August 1808, DTH 1/41.

94. Minutes of the Council, 1 November 1808, CO 270/11.

95. *Sierra Leone Gazette* [Freetown], 17 December 1808.

96. Minutes of the Council, 1 November 1808, CO 270/11.

97. *Sierra Leone Gazette* [Freetown], 17 December 1808.

98. Minutes of the Council, 25 October 1809, CO 270/11.

99. *African Herald* [Freetown], 25 February 1808.

100. Ibid.

101. *African Herald* [Freetown], 27 May 1809.

102. Minutes of the Council, 3 April 1809, CO 270/11. E 8 March 1810, Memoranda of Edward Columbine, 1809–1811, UICSL III/10/p. 53–55.

103. Minutes of the Council, 29 July 1809, CO 270/11.

104. Thompson to the "Captain of a Merchant Vessel," 3 August 1809, DTH 1/41.

105. Thompson to Nancy Barker, 15 August 1809, DTH 1/74.

106. Thompson to Castlereagh, Minutes of the Council, 25 January 1810, CO 270/11.

107. Zachary Macaulay, *A Letter to the Duke of Gloucester . . . Occasioned by a Pamphlet Lately Published by Dr. Thorpe . . . Entitled "A Letter to William Wilberforce"* (London, 1815), 2.

108. Thompson to Nancy Barker, 15 August 1809 DTH 1/74.

109. Extracts from Macaulay to Ludlam, 1 May 1807, CO 267/27.

110. Extracts from Macaulay to Ludlam, 4 November 1807, CO 267/27.

111. Thompson to Nancy Barker, 30 September 1809, DTH 1/74.

112. Decision of the Court of Vice-Admiralty, 6 November 1809 CO 267/27.

113. Thompson to Castlereagh, Minutes of the Council, 31 December 1808, CO 270/11.

114. "Estimate of Price for Each Day's Labour of Slaves Employed in the Colony Until Their Distribution among the Inhabitants," DTH/1/18.

115. Marginal note, Return of People Freed under the 1807 Act, Minutes of the Council, 31 December 1808, CO 270/11.

116. Minutes of the Council, 11 November 1808, CO 270/11.

117. Thompson to the Directors of the African Institution, 2 November 1808, DTH 1/27.

118. "An Englishman" to Columbine, 19 December 1810, Public Papers on Africa, UICSL III/11/vol. 2/ p. 233–35.

119. Fyfe, *History of Sierra Leone,* 108.

120. Joseph Davies to Thompson, Minutes of the Council, 15 October 1809, CO 270/11.

121. 19 January 1809, Memoranda of Edward Columbine, 1809–1811, UICSL III/10/p. 6.

122. 13 February 1810, in ibid., p. 24.

123. 31 March 1810, in ibid., p. 85.

124. 6 April 1810, in ibid., pp. 98–99.

125. 1st Letter, "Letters from the Imam of Futa Jallon," CO 268/8.

126. "A Narrative of Facts Connected with the Colony of Sierra Leone," DTH 1/102.

127. Thompson to the Directors of the African Institution, 2 November 1808, DTH 1/27.

128. Robert René Kuczynski, *Demographic Survey of the British Colonial Empire,* vol. 1 (London: Oxford University Press, 1948), 96, 162.

129. Fyfe, *History of Sierra Leone,* 109.

130. Quoted in Johnson, *General T. Perronet Thompson,* 45.

131. Evidence of John Kizell, Appendix 5B, CO 267/92. See also Rankin, *White Man's Grave,* 1:95–96.

132. Thompson to the Directors of the African Institution, 2 November 1808, DTH 1/27.

133. Thompson to Castlereagh, 17 February 1809, CO 267/25.

134. Samuel Curry to Frederick Forbes, 12 April 1810, Local Letters: Governor's Letter Book, 1808–1811, SLPA. On Columbine's struggle with Forbes, see 3 March 1810, Memoranda of Edward Columbine, UICSL, III/10/p. 42; 1 April 1810, Memoranda of Edward Columbine, UICSL, III/10/p. 87.

135. James Stephen to the Office of the Secretary of State for War and the Colonies, 23 November 1809, CO 267/25. See also 19 January 1809, Memoranda of Edward Columbine, 1809–1811, UICSL III/10/p. 5.

136. "A Narrative of Facts Connected with the Colony of Sierra Leone," DTH 1/102.

137. Decision of the Court of Vice-Admiralty, 6 November 1809, CO 267/27.

138. Thompson to Castlereagh, 17 February 1809, CO 267/25.

139. Testimony of Dalu Mohammed, Court of Vice-Admiralty, September 1809, CO 267/27.

140. "Memoir Respecting the Best Means of Promoting Improvement in Africa," DTH 1/6.

141. Thompson to Castlereagh, 17 February 1809, CO 267/25.

142. Rough Journal of Thomas Perronet Thompson, 29 July 1808, DTH 1/21.

143. Wilberforce to Castlereagh [Private], 7 December 1808, CO 267/24.

144. James Stephen to [Henry Thornton?], 28 January 1809, CO 267/25.

145. Wilberforce to Thompson, 22 December 1808, DTH /61.

146. Extracts from the Minutes of the Court of Directors, Letter from Sierra Leone Office, 20 October 1808, CO 267/27.

147. Thornton to Thompson, 22 October 1808, DTH 1/61; see also Wilberforce to Thompson, 19 October 1808, DTH 1/61; extracts from the Minutes of the Court of Directors, Letter from Sierra Leone Office, 20 October 1808, CO 267/27.

148. Thompson to Nancy Barker, 6 March 1809, DTH 1/74.

149. Thompson to Nancy Barker, 16 September 1809, DTH 1/74.

150. Thompson to the "Captain of a Merchant Vessel," 3 August 1809, DTH 1/41.

151. Thompson to Columbine, 11 February 1810, DTH 1/47.

152. Columbine to Macaulay, 11 August 1810, Public Papers on Africa III/11/vol. 2/p. 185.

153. Pardon of Anne Morgan, Minutes of the Council, 8 March 1810, CO 270/11.

154. 8 March 1810, Memoranda of Edward Columbine, 1809–1811, UICSL III/10/p. 53.

155. Minutes of the Council, 26 March 1810, CO 270/11.

156. 21 February 1810, Memoranda of Edward Columbine, 1809–1811, UICSL III/10/p. 36.

157. 8 March 1810, in ibid., p. 53.

158. Thompson to Lord Liverpool, 9 January 1811, CO 267/30.

159. African Institution, *Third Report of the Directors of the African Institution: Read at the Annual General Meeting on the 25th of March, 1809* (London, 1809), 16. This practice continues in later reports; see, for example, African Institution, *Fourth Report of the Directors of the African Institution: Read at the Annual General Meeting on the 28th of March, 1810* (London, 1810), 21–23.

160. Wilberforce to Thompson, 22 December 1808, DTH 1/61.

161. Wilberforce to Liverpool, 30 June 1810, CO 267/28.

162. See Michael J. Turner, "Radical Opinion in an Age of Reform: Thomas Perronet Thompson and the Westminster Review," *History* 86, no. 281 (January 1, 2001): 18–40; Michael J. Turner, "Thomas Perronet Thompson, 'Sensible Chartism' and the Chimera of Radical Unity," *Albion: A Quarterly Journal Concerned with British Studies* 33, no. 1 (April 1, 2001): 51–74.

163. Mary Botham Howitt and William Howitt, *Howitt's Journal of Literature and Popular Progress*, vol. 2 (London, 1847), 67.

164. Robert Thorpe, *A Letter to William Wilberforce . . .: Containing Remarks on the Reports of the Sierra Leone Company, and African Institution: With Hints Respecting the Means by Which an Universal Abolition of the Slave Trade Might Be Carried into Effect* (London, 1815), 16.

165. Robert Thorpe, *A Reply "Point by Point" to the Special Report of the Directors of the African Institution* (London, 1815), 72–73.

166. See the appendices of Macaulay, *Letter to the Duke of Gloucester.*

167. Thompson to Nancy Barker, 28 March 1809, DTH 1/74.

3. *The Vice-Admiralty Court*

1. African Institution, *Fourth Report [1810]*, 57–58. See also William Gray, *Travels in Western Africa: In the Years 1818, 19, 20, and 21, from the River Gambia through Woolli, Bondoo, Galam, Kasson, Kaarta, and Foolidoo, to the River Niger* (London, 1825), 335–36.

2. Register of Liberated Africans 1814–1815, no. 7367, SLPA.

3. Proceedings of the Vice-Admiralty Court of Sierra Leone, HCA 49/97; Condemnation of the *Intrepida*, HCA 49/10; Receipts related to prize agency for seven ships captured by the *Comus* in 1815, HCA 49/101; Evidence of Kenneth Macaulay, CO 267/92.

4. Charles MacCarthy to Earl Bathurst, 14 August 1815, Governor's Despatches to Secretary of State, 1813–1818, SLPA.

5. MacCarthy to Bathurst, 18 June 1815, CO 267/40.

6. Receipts for the *Intrepida*, HCA 49/101.

7. Charles MacCarthy to Earl Bathurst, 31 December 1815, Governor's Despatches to Secretary of State, 1813–1818, SLPA.

8. Case of the *Intrepida*, HCA 49/101.

9. Thomas Coke, *An Interesting Narrative of a Mission, Sent to Sierra Leone, in Africa: By the Methodists, in 1811: To Which Is Prefixed, an Account of the Rise, Progress, Disasters, and Present State of That Colony: The Whole Interspersed with a Variety of Remarkable Particulars* (London, 1812), 30.

10. Kuczynski, *Demographic Survey of the British Colonial Empire*, 1:99–100.

11. Case of the *Intrepida*, HCA 49/101. See also Joseph Marryat, *Thoughts on the Abolition of the Slave Trade and Civilization of Africa* (London, 1816), 57.

12. Stephanie E. Smallwood, *Saltwater Slavery: A Middle Passage from Africa to American Diaspora* (Cambridge, MA: Harvard University Press, 2007), 35.

13. Helfman, "The Court of Vice Admiralty at Sierra Leone and the Abolition of the West African Slave Trade," 1122. See also Martinez, "Antislavery Courts and the Dawn of International Human Rights Law"; Martinez, *The Slave Trade and the Origins of International Human Rights Law*.

14. See Lauren Benton and Lisa Ford, *Rage for Order: The British Empire and the Origins of International Law, 1800–1850* (Cambridge, MA: Harvard University Press, 2016), 117–47.

15. Lauren Benton, "Abolition and Imperial Law, 1790–1820," *Journal of Imperial and Commonwealth History* 39 (September 2011): 369; see also Lauren Benton, " 'This Melancholy Labyrinth': The Trial of Arthur Hodge and the Boundaries of Imperial Law," *Alabama Law Review* 64 (2012): 91–122.

16. Kate Masur, " 'A Rare Phenomenon of Philological Vegetation': The Word 'Contraband' and the Meanings of Emancipation in the United States," *Journal of American History* 93, no. 4 (March 1, 2007): 1050–84; Davis, *Problem of Slavery*, 470.

17. Scott, "Paper Thin," 1086.

18. Calculated based on data in HCA 49/97 and in the Liberated African Department Statement of Disposals, 1821–33, SLPA.

19. William Blackstone, *Commentaries on the Laws of England: In Four Books*, 13th ed., vol. 3 (London, 1800), 32.

20. Clarkson, *History*, 1808, 1:568.

21. Rowan and Wellington, "Report of the Commissioners of Inquiry, Part 1," 25.

22. Quoted in Knutsford, *Life and Letters of Zachary Macaulay*, 401.

23. Richard W. Van Alstyne, "The British Right of Search and the African Slave Trade," *Journal of Modern History* 2, no. 1 (March 1, 1930): 37–47.

24. Alan Taylor, *The Civil War of 1812: American Citizens, British Subjects, Irish Rebels, & Indian Allies* (New York: Vintage, 2011), 123.

25. Goveia, *Slave Society*, 61–63.

26. Patrick C. Lipscomb, III, "Stephen, James (1758–1832)," *ODNB*.

27. Macaulay to Castlereagh, 8 May 1807, WO 1/352; Wilberforce to Castlereagh, 26 October 1807, WO 1/352; Wilberforce to Edward Cooke, 30 October 1807, WO 1/352.

28. Macaulay to Thomas Ludlam, 7 November 1807, DTH 1/2.

29. George Gosling to W. W. Pole, 7 May 1808, ADM 1/3898.

30. Benton, "Abolition and Imperial Law, 1790–1820," 357.

31. Edward Stanley Roscoe, *A History of the English Prize Court* (London: Lloyd's, 1924), 39–40. See also J. R. Hill, *The Prizes of War: The Naval Prize System in the Napoleonic Wars, 1793–1815* (Portsmouth: Royal Naval Museum Publications, 1998), 11, 95; J. M. Fewster, "Prize-Money and the British Expedition to the West Indies of 1793–4," *Journal of Imperial and Commonwealth History* 12, no. 1 (1983): 1–28.

32. Dodson, *Case of the Louis*, 31.

33. Hill, *Prizes of War*, 246–47. Conversions to 2015 currency made using www.measuringworth.com.

34. Hay and Craven, "Introduction," 55–56.

35. Thomas Cochrane, *The Autobiography of a Seaman*, vol. 2 (London, 1860), 167.

36. "Respecting a Claim for Head Money under the Act of 47th Geo. 3rd c. 36 for the Abolition of the Slave Trade," [17 December 1810], TS 25/4.

37. J. C. Beaglehole, "The Colonial Office, 1782–1854," *Historical Studies: Australia and New Zealand* 1, no. 3 (1941): 170–89; D. M. Young, *The Colonial Office in the Early Nineteenth Century* (London: Longmans, 1961), 1–12; Henry Roseveare, *The Treasury, 1660–1870: The Foundations of Control* (London: Allen and Unwin, 1973), 65–70.

38. Henry Goulburn to James Stephen, 7 April 1813, CO 138/45.

39. N. A. M. Rodger, *The Command of the Ocean: A Naval History of Britain, 1649–1815* (New York: W. W. Norton, 2005), 522–27; Hill, *Prizes of War*, 155. Anthony Gutridge, "Aspects of Naval Prize Agency, 1793–1815," *Mariner's Mirror* 80, no. 1 (1994): 46; N. A. M. Rodger, *The Command of the Ocean: A Naval History of Britain, 1649–1815* (New York: W. W. Norton, 2005), 522–27; Hill, *Prizes of War*, 155; Anthony Gutridge, "George Redmond Hubert: Prize Agent at Halifax, Nova Scotia, 1812–1814," *Mariner's Mirror* 87, no. 1 (2001): 30–42.

40. Thorpe, *A Letter to William Wilberforce . . .*, 8. See also James MacQueen, "Sierra Leone—Civilization of Africa—To R. W. Hay, Esq. Letter III," *Blackwood's Edinburgh Magazine* 21 (May 1827): 622; Macaulay, *Letter to the Duke of Gloucester*, 31; David Lambert, *Mastering the Niger: James Mac-Queen's African Geography and the Struggle over Atlantic Slavery* (Chicago: University of Chicago Press, 2013), 148–75; David Lambert, "Sierra Leone and Other Sites in the War of Representation over Slavery," *History Workshop Journal* 64, no. 1 (September 21, 2007): 103–32.

41. Ackerson, *African Institution*, 225.

42. African Institution, *Fourth Report [1810]*, 3–4. See also African Institution, *Sixth Report of the Directors of the African Institution: Read at the Annual General Meeting on the 25th of March, 1812* (London, 1812), 9; August 1810, *The Edinburgh Review: Or Critical Journal* (London, 1810), 438.

43. James Chisholm to Charles Maxwell, Gorée, 10 July 1810, Chisholm Papers, NAM 9301/2/8. See also James Chisholm to Zachary Macaulay, Gorée, 19 July 1811, Chisholm Papers, NAM 9301/2/8; Rees, *Sweet Water and Bitter*, 169.

44. Hill, *Prizes of War*, 14.

45. Based on data in HCA 49/97.

46. Calculated based on tables in HCA 49/97.

47. On Ommaney & Druce, see *The Picture of London, Enlarged and Improved, Being a Correct Guide for the Stranger, and Useful Compendium for the Inhabitant* (London, 1825), 415. On Bouverie & Antrobus see British and Foreign Bible Society, *Ninth Report of the British & Foreign Bible Society* (London, 1813), 107.

48. Records of the Vice-Admiralty Court, HCA 49/97.

49. MacQueen, "Sierra Leone—Civilization of Africa—To R. W. Hay, Esq. Letter III," 623.

50. Calculated based on data in HCA 49/97.

51. George Stephen, *Anti-Slavery Recollections: In a Series of Letters Addressed to Mrs. Beecher-Stowe* (London, 1854), 51–52. See also Fyfe, *History of Sierra Leone*, 49; Coupland, *British Anti-Slavery Movement*, 79; Catherine Hall, "Macaulay's Nation," *Victorian Studies* 51, no. 3 (April 1, 2009): 508.

52. Whyte, *Zachary Macaulay 1768–1838*, 194.

53. Rowan and Wellington, "Report of the Commissioners of Inquiry, Part 1," 22.

54. James Stephen to Robert Peel, London, 23 August 1811, CO 267/31.

55. Fyfe, *History of Sierra Leone*, 136–37.

56. Lloyd, *The Navy and the Slave Trade*, 80.

57. Based on data in HCA 49/97.

58. Macaulay, *Letter to the Duke of Gloucester*, 38–39.

59. See receipts in HCA 49/101.

60. Joseph Marryat, *More Thoughts, Occasioned by Two Publications Which the Authors Call "An Exposure of Some of the Numerous Misstatements and Misrepresentations Contained in a Pamphlet, Commonly Known by the Name of Mr. Marryat's Pamphlet, Entitled Thoughts, &c.," and "A Defence of the Bill for the Registration of Slaves"* (London, 1816), 60–65.

61. Ibid., 66.

62. See Powers-of-Attorney, HCA 49/101.

63. See Records of the Vice-Admiralty Court, HCA 49/101.

64. See receipts enclosed with the cases of *Abismo, Bon Sorte, Carmen, Catalina, Estrella, Intrepida* and *Santa Anna*, HCA 49/101.

65. Entry for 7 January 1812, in Wiggins, *Paul Cuffe's Logs*, 183.

66. Account of the Stores Cellars . . . Hired . . . for the Service of the Navy [31 March 1826], Appendix 23A, CO 267/91.

67. Paul Cuffe to William Allen, 22 April 1811, in Wiggins, *Paul Cuffe's Logs*, 119.

68. Report of Messrs. Carew, Reffell & Nelson on the State of the Licensed Public Houses in Freetown, Minute in Council, 3 October 1818, CO 270/15.

69. Henry William Macaulay to Zachary Macaulay, 16 August 1830, MY 369.

70. Robert Thorpe to J. Croker, 1 August 1814, ADM 1/3902.

71. William Scott to John W. Cromer, 5 August 1812, ADM 1/3900; See also Report of the Commissioners to the Office of the Lord High Admiral, 27 February 1812, ADM 1/3900.

72. James Bush to J. Croker, 18 February 1813, ADM 1/3901.

73. Fyfe, *History of Sierra Leone*, 166.

74. Rockman, *Scraping By*, 185.

75. Protest from Kenneth Macaulay, Enclosed in MacCarthy to Bathurst, 21 June 1822, CO 267/56; MacQueen, "Sierra Leone—Civilization of Africa—To R. W. Hay, Esq. Letter III," 622.

76. Henry William Macaulay to Zachary Macaulay, 16 August 1830, MY 369.

77. Ibid.

78. Claude George, *The Rise of British West Africa: Comprising the Early History of the Colony of Sierra Leone, the Gambia, Lagos, Gold Coast, Etc., Etc. with a Brief Account of Climate, the Growth of Education, Commerce and Religion and a Comprehensive History of the Bananas and Bance Islands and Sketches of the Constitution* (London, 1904), 76–79.

79. *The Royal Gazette and Sierra Leone Advertiser* [Freetown], 23 August, 1817.

80. Brown, *The Reaper's Garden,* 102.

81. Emma Rothschild, *The Inner Life of Empires: An Eighteenth-Century History* (Princeton, NJ: Princeton University Press, 2011), 171. See also Beckert, *Empire of Cotton,* 227.

82. *The Royal Gazette and Sierra Leone Advertiser* [Freetown], 2 August 1817.

83. Ibid.

84. Henry William Macaulay to Zachary Macaulay, 16 August 1830, MY 369.

85. Rankin, *White Man's Grave,* 1:68–69.

86. *The Royal Gazette and Sierra Leone Advertiser* [Freetown], 3 January 1818. In another advertisement, Sutherland offered retail goods "*On the most reasonable Terms—for Cash, Camwood, Palm oil, or White and Red Rice,*" *The Royal Gazette and Sierra Leone Advertiser* [Freetown], 31 January 1818. See also William Allen to Paul Cuffe, [?] 1 November 1815, in Wiggins, *Paul Cuffe's Logs,* 406. See also Rodney, *History of the Upper Guinea Coast,* 172.

87. African Institution, *Ninth Report [1815],* 64.

88. Church Missionary Society Central Committee Minutes, 4 August 1800, CMS G/C/1/Volume 1.

89. Macaulay to the Freetown Corresponding Committee of the Mission Society to Africa and the East, 10 June 1803 CMS C/A/1/E/1/1.

90. Gustavus Nyländer to Josiah Pratt, Sierra Leone, 22 January 1807, CMS C/A/1/E/1/94.

91. Leopold Butscher to Josiah Pratt, Sierra Leone, 16 June 1813, CMS C/A/1/E/3/83.

92. Northrup, "The Compatibility of the Slave and Palm Oil Trades in the Bight of Biafra," 358–59; Alexander Gordon Laing, *Travels in the Timannee, Kooranko, and Soolima Countries, in Western Africa* (London, 1825), 223–24; Peter H. Wood, *Black Majority: Negroes in South Carolina from 1670 through the Stono Rebellion* (New York: W. W. Norton & Company, 1996), 58–61; D. C. Dorward and A. I. Payne, "Deforestation, the Decline of the Horse, and the Spread of the Tsetse Fly and Trypanosomiasis (Nagana) in Nineteenth Century Sierra Leone," *Journal of African History* 16, no. 2 (1975): 247.

93. Coke, *Interesting Narrative of a Mission,* 40.

94. See the cases listed as "48 slaves part of the cargo of the Venganza," and "20 slaves seized in the Rio Dembia," co-managed by Zachary Macaulay and Michael Macmillan; Macaulay was sole agent in the cases listed as "17 slaves Natives of Africa," "3 Natives of Africa in an illegal state of slavery," "55 Slaves," "11 Slaves," "1 Person held in an illegal state of slavery," "4 persons," and the case of the *San Jose,* HCA 49/97.

95. Zachary Macaulay to Selina Macaulay, 20 September 1821, in Knutsford, *Life and Letters of Zachary Macaulay*, 368.

96. Army Medical Board Certificate for James Chisholm, 19 July 1816, Chisholm Papers, NAM 9301/2/3.

97. Statement of Service, James Chisholm, NAM 9301/2/1; Army Medical Board Certificate for James Chisholm, 19 July 1816, NAM 9301/2/1.

98. *The Gentleman's Magazine*, vol. 92 (London, 1822), 182.

99. Chisholm to Assistant Surgeon W. Bean, Guernsey, 3 April 1809, NAM 9301/2/7.

100. Chisholm to Lt. Ronald MacDonald, Guernsey, 24 March 1809, NAM 9301/2/7; Chisholm to Messrs. McLean and Co., Guernsey, 24 March 1809, NAM 9301/2/7.

101. Charles Maxwell to Thomas Perronet Thompson, Gorée, 16 December 1808, DTH 1/67.

102. Chisholm to Charles Maxwell, Gorée, 10 July 1810, NAM 9301/2/8.

103. Chisholm to Macaulay, 19 July 1811, NAM 9301/2/8.

104. See case of the *Dona Luzia,* the *Dos Hermanos,* and the *San Antonia* alias *Empecinador,* in the register of cases heard at the Vice-Admiralty Court at Freetown, HCA 49/97.

105. There is no record of this case in the files of the Vice-Admiralty Court held at Kew (HCA 49/97). See receipt from Zachary Macaulay to James Chisholm, London, 22 March 1815, NAM 9308/307/7.

106. James Chisholm copied out this advertisement by hand for his records, see NAM 9301/2/122. See also *Royal Gazette and Sierra Leone Advertiser* [Freetown], 22 November 1817.

107. *Tentativa,* see HCA 49/97. Memorandum of Kenneth Macaulay 9301/2/150; see also NAM 9301/2/154, a calculation of prize monies owed, in Chisholm's hand.

108. Memorandum for Lt. Col. Chisholm, Sierra Leone, 25 August 1818, 9301/2/156. This document is signed "James Chisholm"—Lt. Col. James Chisholm's nephew, also an officer in the Royal African Corps.

109. Henry Stuart to Dr. Stoddart, Esq., Mansion House, London, 9 January 1823, NAM 9301/2/179; Henry Stuart to Dr. Stoddart, Esq., Mansion House, London, 10 July 1822, NAM 9301/2/180.

110. Henry Stuart to Dr. Stoddart, Esq., Mansion House, London, 22 November 1825, NAM 9301/2/182.

111. Zachary Macaulay to the Office of the Horse Guards, 11 October 1811, CO 267/31.

112. Leopold Butscher to Josiah Pratt, 27 February 1813, CMS C/A/1/E/3/57.

113. Ninian Bruce to James Chisholm, 30 August 1819, Wellcome MS 7027/2.

114. Receipt from Macaulay to Chisholm, 22 March 1815, NAM 9308/307/7.

115. James MacQueen, *The Colonial Controversy: Containing a Refutation of the Calumnies of the Anticolonists . . . with a Supplementary Letter to Mr. Macaulay* (Glasgow, 1825), 100.

116. Macaulay to Chisholm, 27 April 1814, NAM 9308/307/4.

117. Chisholm to Macaulay, 11 March 1812, NAM 9301/2/10. See also Chisholm to Macaulay, 18 April 1814, NAM 9301/2/11; African Institution, *Ninth Report [1815]*, 68.

118. Chisholm to Macaulay, Gorée, 18 April 1814, NAM 9301/2/11.

119. Chisholm to Maxwell, 8 October 1812, NAM 9301/2/10. See also Alexander Mackenzie, *History of the Chisholms: With Genealogies of the Principal Families of the Name* (Inverness, 1891), 155.

120. Chisholm to Maxwell, 26 March 1810, NAM 9301/2/8.

121. Edward Lloyd to Macaulay, 7 January 1812, CO 267/34.

122. Wilberforce to [Earl Bathurst?], 24 [April?] 1812, CO 267/35.

123. Colonel Torrens to Robert Peel, 29 July 1812, CO 267/35.

124. Wilberforce to Rev. James Jowers, 1 March 1817, NAM 9301/2/76.

125. *The Royal Military Chronicle: Or, the British Officer's Monthly Register, Chronicle, and Military Mentor*, vol. 2 (London, 1811), 40–41.

126. Proceedings of Garrison Courts Martial, Gorée, 12 November 1810, NAM 9301/2/15.

127. Leopold Butscher to Josiah Pratt, 27 February 1813, CMS C/A/1/E/3/57.

128. See *The Trial of Governor Wall: Executed at the Old Bailey, Jan. 28th, 1802, for the Murder of Benjamin Armstrong, in the Garrison at Goree, upon the Coast of Africa, July, 1782; with the Extraordinary Particulars of His Escape at Reading, after Being Captured under a Warrant from the Privy Council in 1784, and His Subsequent Surrender in 1802, Having Lived Twenty Years in Exile* (London, 1802).

129. Ebenezer Rogers, *Campaigning in Western Africa and the Ashantee Invasion of 1874* (London, 1874), 173.

130. J. J. Crooks, ed., *Historical Records of the Royal African Corps* (Dublin: Browne and Nolan, 1925), 2.

131. See Philip Harling, "The Duke of York Affair (1809) and the Complexities of War-Time Patriotism," *The Historical Journal* 39, no. 4 (December 1, 1996): 963–84.

132. Crooks, ed., *Historical Records of the Royal African Corps*, 2.

133. George Fraser to Lord Hobart, 23 January 1801, in ibid., 13.

134. Quoted in Roger Norman Buckley, *Slaves in Red Coats: The British West India Regiments, 1795–1815* (New Haven: Yale University Press, 1979), 26.

135. Brian Dyde, *The Empty Sleeve: The Story of the West India Regiments of the British Army* (Hertford: Hansib Caribbean, 1997), 122.

136. "Memorandums kept by J. Kingsley," Kingsley Papers, NAM 8011/10/2.

137. Ibid.

138. Ibid.

139. Monthly Returns for 1807, Crooks, *Records of the Royal African Corps*, 49.

140. Report from 1 June 1808, in ibid., 50.

141. Report from 27 July 1808, in ibid., 52.

142. William Cobbett, ed., *Cobbett's Weekly Political Register* (London, 1802), 255. See also Scott Hughes Myerly, *British Military Spectacle: From the Napoleonic Wars through the Crimea* (Cambridge, MA: Harvard University Press, 1996), 75.

143. Myerly, *British Military Spectacle*, 28.

144. James Belich, *The New Zealand Wars and the Victorian Interpretation of Racial Conflict* (Auckland: Auckland University Press, 1986), 23.

145. Myerly, *British Military Spectacle*, 54–55.

146. Philip D. Curtin, *Disease and Empire: The Health of European Troops in the Conquest of Africa* (Cambridge: Cambridge University Press, 1998), 4.

147. Dispatch from Charles Maxwell, Senegal, 11 December, 1810, Crooks, *Records of the Royal African Corps*, 80.

148. Chisholm to Maxwell, April 1812, NAM 9301/2/10; 14 March 1810, Memoranda of Edward Columbine, UICSL III/10/p.63.

149. Proceedings of Garrison Courts Martial, Gorée, 12 November 1810, NAM 9301/2/15.

150. Chisholm to Maxwell, Gorée, 2 July 1812, NAM 9301/2/10.

151. Roger Norman Buckley, *The British Army in the West Indies: Society and the Military in the Revolutionary Age* (Gainesville, FL; Barbados: University Press of Florida; The Press, University of the West Indies, 1998), 57–58.

152. Ibid., 60.

153. See Earl of Balcarres Papers, NAM 7508/55/3; Buckley, *Slaves in Red Coats;* Buckley, *The British Army in the West Indies;* Claudius Fergus, "'Dread of Insurrection': Abolitionism, Security, and Labor in Britain's West Indian Colonies, 1760–1823," *William and Mary Quarterly,* Third Series, 66, no. 4 (October 1, 2009): 766; Philip D. Morgan and Andrew Jackson O'Shaughnessy, "Arming Slaves in the American Revolution," in

Arming Slaves: From Classical Times to the Modern Age, ed. Christopher Leslie Brown and Philip D. Morgan (New Haven: Yale University Press, 2006), 180–208; Peter Voelz, *Slave and Soldier: The Military Impact of Blacks in the Colonial Americas* (New York: Garland, 1993); O'Shaughnessy, *The Men Who Lost America,* 277.

154. Goveia, *Slave Society,* 147–49.

155. Buckley, *The British Army in the West Indies,* 137.

156. Dyde, *Empty Sleeve,* 23.

157. Dubois, *Avengers of the New World,* 215–17.

158. Quoted in Buckley, *Slaves in Red Coats,* 60.

159. Quoted in Voelz, *Slave and Soldier,* 200.

160. Duke of York to Lord Liverpool, Horse Guards, 11 August 1811, CO 267/31.

161. Wilberforce to Edward Cooke, 30 October 1807, WO 1/352.

162. Wilberforce to Castlereagh, 26 October 1807, WO 1/352.

163. Voelz, *Slave and Soldier,* 200.

164. Quoted in Buckley, *Slaves in Red Coats,* 60. See also H. M. Chichester, Roger T. Stearn, "Gordon, Sir James Willoughby, first baronet (1772–1851)," rev. Roger T. Stearn; W. P. Courtney, "Wardle, Gwyllym Lloyd (1761/2–1833)," rev. H. C. G. Matthew, *ODNB;* Philip Harling, "The Duke of York Affair (1809) and the Complexities of War-Time Patriotism," *Historical Journal* 39, no. 4 (December 1, 1996): 963–84.

165. 9 November 1810, Memoranda of Edward Columbine, UICSL, III/10/p. 198.

166. Crooks, *Records of the Royal African Corps,* 48.

167. A. B. Ellis, *History of the First West India Regiment* (London, 1885), 16.

168. Buckley, *Slaves in Red Coats,* 2.

169. Linda Colley, *Captives: Britain, Empire and the World, 1600–1850* (New York: Anchor Books, 2004), 314.

170. Return for 25th February 1810, Crooks, *Records of the Royal African Corps,* 68.

171. James Higgins to the Office of the Secretary of State for War and the Colonies, 10 August 1811, CO 267/31.

172. Colonial Surgeon Stormouth to Charles MacCarthy, 4 April 1816, CO 267/42.

173. Samuel Curry to the Office of the Secretary of State for War and the Colonies, 30 July 1811, CO 267/31.

174. Dyde, *Empty Sleeve,* 37.

260 NOTES TO PAGES 126–128

175. "General Statement of the Disposal of the Captured Negroes received into the colony of Sierra Leone to the 9th of July 1814," CO 267/38. See also ibid., 30; Kuczynski, *Demographic Survey of the British Colonial Empire,* 1:100.

176. MacCarthy to Bathurst, 21 July 1816, Governor's Despatches to Secretary of State, SLPA.

177. E. P. Thompson, *The Making of the English Working Class* (New York: Vintage Books, 1966), 59.

178. *The Missionary Magazine* (Edinburgh, Scotland), Monday, July 15, 1811, p. 262, Issue 7. On devotional literature in military life, see Graham Shaw, "The British Book in India," in *The Cambridge History of the Book in Britain,* ed. Michael Suarez and Michael F. Turner (Cambridge: Cambridge University Press, 2009), 564; Scott Mandelbrote, "The Publishing and Distribution of Religious Books by Voluntary Associations: From the SPCK to the British and Foreign Bible Society," in *The Cambridge History of the Book in Britain,* ed. Michael Suarez and Michael F. Turner (Cambridge: Cambridge University Press, 2009), 613–30.

179. Richard D. Altick, *The English Common Reader: A Social History of the Mass Reading Public, 1800–1900,* 2d ed. (Columbus: Ohio State University Press, 1998), 26–27. See also Leah Price, *How to Do Things with Books in Victorian Britain* (Princeton, NJ: Princeton University Press, 2012), 139–74.

180. Altick, *English Common Reader,* 27–28.

181. See Maeve Ryan, "The Price of Legitimacy in Humanitarian Intervention: Britain, the Right of Search, and the Abolition of the West African Slave Trade, 1807–1867," in *Humanitarian Intervention: A History,* ed. Brendan Simms and D. J. B. Trim (Cambridge: Cambridge University Press, 2011), 232.

182. Journals of the House of Commons, vol. 69, 424–25.

183. Quoted in Eltis, *Economic Growth,* 109. See also Case of *San Juan Nepomuceno,* 6 July 1824, reported in John Haggard, *Reports of Cases Argued and Determined in the High Court of Admiralty* (London, 1825), 267.

184. 1&2 Geo. IV, Cap. 99, *An Act for the Appropriation of certain Proceeds arising from the Capture of Vessels and Cargoes . . . in Violation of the Conventions made with those States.*

185. Zachary Macaulay to T. B. Macaulay, 5 April 1813, in Knutsford, *Life and Letters of Zachary Macaulay,* 297.

186. See *Railway Times and Joint-Stock Chronicle,* vol. 61 (London, 1892), 219; East India Company, *Asiatic Journal and Monthly Register for British India*

and Its Dependencies, vol. 27 (London, 1829), 68–69; Knutsford, *Life and Letters of Zachary Macaulay,* 402.

187. Knutsford, *Life and Letters of Zachary Macaulay,* 398. See also J. R. Oldfield, "Macaulay, Zachary (1768–1838)," *ODNB.*

188. Zachary Macaulay to Colin Macaulay, 28 January 1829, in ibid., 405.

189. Henry William Macaulay to Zachary Macaulay, 16 August 1830, MY 369.

190. Christopher Fyfe, "Four Sierra Leone Recaptives," *Journal of African History* 2, no. 1 (January 1, 1961): 79.

191. African Institution, *Report of the Committee of the African Institution: Read to the General Meeting on the 15th July, 1807* (London, 1807), 9, 28.

4. *The Absolute Disposal of the Crown*

1. Brevet-Major Wingfield to Lt. Col. Torrens, Windsor, 18 November 1811, CO 267/35.

2. Ibid.

3. See Douglas M. Peers, "'The Habitual Nobility of Being': British Officers and the Social Construction of the Bengal Army in the Early Nineteenth Century," *Modern Asian Studies* 25, no. 3 (July 1, 1991): 546; Douglas M. Peers, "Colonial Knowledge and the Military in India, 1780–1860," *Journal of Imperial and Commonwealth History* 33, no. 2 (May 2005): 157–80. On African "martial races," see S. C. Ukpabi, "West Indian Troops and the Defence of British West Africa in the Nineteenth Century," *African Studies Review* 17, no. 1 (April 1, 1974): 133–50; David Killingray, "Imagined Martial Communities: Recruiting for the Military and Police in Colonial Ghana, 1860–1960," in *Ethnicity in Ghana,* ed. Carola Lentz and Paul Nugent (Basingstoke, Hampshire: Palgrave Macmillan, 2000), 119–36.

4. Zachary Macaulay to Thomas Ludlam, London, 26 February 1807, published in the appendix to Macaulay, *Letter to the Duke of Gloucester,* 17.

5. See Douglas Peers, *Between Mars and Mammon: Colonial Armies and the Garrison State in India, 1819–1835* (London: Tauris, 1995).

6. Colley, *Captives,* 312–13.

7. Entry dated "1808," [written 4 February 1809?], Daily Journal of Edward Columbine, 1808, UICSL III/9/p. 2.

8. Ibid., p. 4.

9. 23 June 1809, Daily Journal of Edward Columbine, UICSL III/9/pp. 14–15.

10. Columbine to the Lords Commissioners of the Admiralty, Senegal, 20 July 1809, Daily Journal of Edward Columbine, UICSL III/9/p. 18.

11. Ibid.

12. 28 August 1809, Daily Journal of Edward Columbine, UICSL III/9/p. 42; 3 April 1809, Daily Journal of Edward Columbine, UICSL III/9/p. 7.

13. 12 February 1810, Memoranda of Edward Columbine, UICSL, III/10/ p. 21. See also 12 February 1810, in ibid., p. 19; Columbine to Macaulay, 7 September 1810, Public Papers on Africa, UICSL III/11/vol. 2/p. 158.

14. Edward Columbine to "D," 28 February 1810, Public Papers on Africa, UICSL III/11/vol. 1/ pp. 176–77.

15. Columbine to Macaulay, 7 September 1810, Public Papers on Africa, UICSL III/11/vol. 2/p. 159.

16. Ibid.; see also 26 May 1810, Memoranda of Edward Columbine, UICSL, III/10/p.129.

17. Entry for 2 April 1811 [?], in Wiggins, *Paul Cuffe's Logs,* 106.

18. Sir John William Fortescue, *The British Army, 1783–1802: Four Lectures Delivered at the Staff College and Cavalry School* (London: Macmillan, 1905), 7.

19. *Treatise on Military Finance Containing the Pay and Allowances in Camp, Garrison and Quarters of the British Army with . . .: Official Documents for the Guidance of Officers in Every Military Department* (London, 1809), 203.

20. African Institution, *Fifth Report of the Directors of the African Institution: Read at the Annual General Meeting on the 27th of March, 1811* (London, 1811), 38.

21. Columbine to Macaulay, 11 August 1810, Public Papers on Africa, UICSL III/11/vol. 2/pp. 185–87.

22. Ibid., pp. 188–89.

23. 13 September 1810, Memoranda of Edward Columbine, UICSL, III/10/p.184.

24. 1 August 1810, in ibid., pp. 156–57. See also entries for 8 September/15 October 1810, in ibid., pp. 187–88.

25. Including the cases of the *Diana, Emprenadadora, Los Dos Amigos, Doris, Polly, Esperanza, Marianna, Zaragozana, Donna Mariana, St. Jago,* and *Vivillia,* HCA 49/97.

26. Stephen Cottrell to Edward Cooke, Office of Committee of the Privy Council for Trade, 6 September 1809, Secretary of State Despatches, 3rd April 1809–24th November 1812, SLPA.

27. Extract, conveyed to Robert Peel, of Maxwell to Colonel Torrens, 29 August 1810, CO 267/33.

28. In August 1810, the Court condemned the *San Carlos, Floridiana, Merced,* and *Vincedor.* The Court condemned the *Catalina, Pearla, Maria Dolores,* and *Santa Barbara* in December. See HCA 49/97.

29. Taylor, *Civil War of 1812*, 102. See also Rodger, *The Command of the Ocean*, 397.

30. 2 February 1810, Memoranda of Edward Columbine, UICSL, III/10/p. 13.

31. 10 July 1810, Memoranda of Edward Columbine, UICSL, III/10/p. 144.

32. Ibid.

33. Richard Anderson, "The Diaspora of Sierra Leone's Liberated Africans: Enlistment, Forced Migration, and 'Liberation' at Freetown, 1808–1863," *African Economic History* 41, no. 1 (2013): 101–38.

34. 10 July 1810, Memoranda of Edward Columbine, UICSL, III/10/p. 144.

35. Memorial of the *Solebay* and *Derwent* Sailors, August 1810, Public Papers on Africa, UICSL III/11/vol. 2/p. 191.

36. Columbine to Charles Moore, 10 August 1810; see also Columbine to Macaulay, 11 August 1810, Public Papers on Africa, UICSL III/11/vol. 2/pp. 197–200.

37. Moore to Columbine, 3 August 1810, Public Papers on Africa, UICSL III/11/vol. 2/p. 193.

38. 9 August 1810, Memoranda of Edward Columbine, UICSL, III/10/pp. 164–65.

39. 6 August 1810, in ibid., p. 161.

40. 6 August 1810, Memoranda of Edward Columbine, UICSL, III/10/pp. 161–62.

41. 3 April 1810, Memoranda of Edward Columbine, UICSL, III/10/pp. 91–92.

42. These figures are calculated based on data from HCA 49/97.

43. Paul Cuffe to William Allen, 22 April 1811, in Wiggins, *Paul Cuffe's Logs*, 119.

44. See *A Brief Account of the Settlement and Present Situation of the Colony of Sierra Leone, in Africa* (New York: Samuel Wood, 1812), 4; Extract of Paul Cuffe to Samuel Mills, 6 January 1817, American Colonization Society, *The First Annual Report of the American Society for Colonizing the Free People of Color of the United States and the Proceedings of the Society at Their Annual Meeting in the City of Washington, on the First Day of January, 1818.* (Washington, D.C., 1818), 27.

45. Remarks, April 1811, in Wiggins, *Paul Cuffe's Logs*, 182.

46. Coke, *Interesting Narrative of a Mission*, 57–58.

47. 10 April 1810, Memoranda of Edward Columbine, UICSL, III/10/p. 103.

48. 11 April 1810, in ibid., p. 105.

49. Ludlam to Forbes, 16 February 1808, Local Letters: Governor's Letter Book, 1808–1811, SLPA.

50. Maxwell to Castlereagh, 9 March 1810, Crooks, *Records of the Royal African Corps*, 74.

51. Samuel Curry to the Commanding Officer of the Royal African Corps, 9 April 1810, Local Letters: Governor's Letter Book, 1808–1811, SLPA.

52. Columbine to Moore, 10 August 1810, Public Papers on Africa, UICSL III/11/vol. 2/p. 197–200.

53. 12 April 1810, Memoranda of Edward Columbine, UICSL, III/10/p. 106.

54. Moore to Columbine, 10 August 1810, Public Papers on Africa, UICSL III/11/vol. 2/p. 201; 17 May 1810, Memoranda of Edward Columbine, UICSL, III/10/p. 124. When the Honourable Frederick returned to Guernsey in 1811, he was cashiered for, among other offenses, "presuming, repeatedly, to go to town in coloured clothes." Charles James, *A Collection of the Charges, Opinions, and Sentences of General Courts Martial: As Published by Authority; from the Year 1795 to the Present Time; Intended to Serve as an Appendix to Tytler's Treatise on Military Law, and Forming a Book of Cases and References; with a Copious Index* (London, 1820), 282–83.

55. Maxwell to Castlereagh, 30 September 1810, Crooks, *Records of the Royal African Corps*, 75.

56. Maxwell to Castlereagh, 11 December 1810, in ibid., 79.

57. Chisholm to Maxwell, 27 October 1810, NAM 9301/2/9.

58. Maxwell to Castlereagh, 1 November 1810, Crooks, *Records of the Royal African Corps*, 77.

59. 9 October 1810, Memoranda of Edward Columbine, UICSL, III/10/p. 190–91.

60. Ibid.; Samuel Curry to Lt. Christie, 8 October 1810, Local Letters: Governor's Letter Book, 1808–1811, SLPA.

61. 9 October 1810, Memoranda of Edward Columbine, UICSL, III/10/p. 190–91.

62. Ibid.; Columbine to Lord Liverpool, 8 October 1810, Public Papers on Africa, UICSL III/11/vol. 2/p. 176–77.

63. "Authentic Account of Sierra Leone," *The African Repository and Colonial Journal*, vol. 7 (Washington D.C., 1832), 364.

64. Rodger, *The Command of the Ocean*, 397.

65. Macaulay to Robert Peel, 22 August 1811, CO 267/31.

66. Maxwell to Liverpool, Sierra Leone, 29 July 1811, CO 267/30.

67. Ibid.

68. Ibid.

69. Maxwell to Bathurst, 3 March 1813, CO 267/36.

70. Maxwell to Bathurst, 16 March 1813, CO 267/36.

71. *The Trials of the Slave Traders, Samuel Samo, Joseph Peters, and William Tufft, Tried in April and June, 1812, before the Hon. Robert Thorpe . . . with Two Letters on the Slave Trade, from a Gentleman* (London, 1813), 54.

72. African Institution, *Ninth Report [1815],* 55.

73. Minutes of the Council, Sierra Leone, 11 June 1811, CO 270/12.

74. Coke, *Interesting Narrative of a Mission,* 40.

75. "Answer of Lt. Col. Charles Wm. Maxwell . . . to the charges preferred against him," CO 267/88.

76. Ibid.

77. Kenneth Macaulay to George Stephen Caulker, 15 June 1811, Local Letters: Governor's Letter Book, 1808–1811, SLPA.

78. George Stephen Caulker to Kenneth Macaulay, 18 June 1811, Local Letters: Governor's Letter Book, 1808–1811, SLPA.

79. Coke, *Interesting Narrative of a Mission,* 41.

80. See Evidence of Eli Akin, Appendix 6B, CO 267/92; Remarks, 30 December 1811, in Wiggins, *Paul Cuffe's Logs,* 179.

81. Petition of the Maroons of Sierra Leone, 27 June 1812, CO 267/34.

82. Maxwell to Bathurst, 24 November 1812, CO 267/34.

83. Ibid.

84. Maxwell to Henry Golbourn, n.d., CO 267/40.

85. Ibid.

86. "Petition read at a Colonial Meeting held at the Court House in Freetown on Monday the 17th day of December, 1814," CO 267/40.

87. Ibid. See also James Carr to Captain Maling, 20 December 1814, CO 267/40.

88. See Roger N. Buckley, "Slave or Freedman: The Question of the Legal Status of the British West India Soldier, 1795–1807," *Caribbean Studies* 17, no. 3/4 (October 1, 1977): 83–113; Buckley, *Slaves in Red Coats;* David Brion Davis, "Introduction," in *Arming Slaves: From Classical Times to the Modern Age,* ed. Christopher Leslie Brown and Philip D. Morgan (New Haven: Yale University Press, 2006), 1–13.

89. Wilberforce to Edward Cooke, 30 October 1807, WO 1/352; Macaulay to Castlereagh, 6 October 1802, WO 1/352; Castlereagh to Columbine, 3 April 1809, Secretary of State Despatches, 3rd April 1809–24th November 1812, SLPA.

90. Maxwell to Liverpool, 24 September 1812, CO 267/34.

91. Wilberforce to Liverpool, 20 September 1811, CO 267/31. See also Dyde, *Empty Sleeve,* 30–33.

92. Duke of York to Liverpool, Horse Guards, 4 October 1811, CO 267/31.

93. James Stephen to the Office of the Secretary of State for War and the Colonies, 20 August 1811, CO 267/31.

94. Quoted in Macaulay to Peel, 22 August 1811, CO 267/31.

95. Zachary Macaulay, Comment on Major Wingfield's Plan, 13 November 1811, CO 267/31; see also Wilberforce to Liverpool [Private], 14 November 1811, CO 267/31.

96. Robert Peel to Lt. Colonel Torrens, Downing Street, 13 December 1811, CO 267/35.

97. Paul Cuffe to Thomas Wainer, 27 July 1811, in Wiggins, *Paul Cuffe's Logs*, 139.

98. Copy of Orders to Brevet Major Wingfield, 8th West India Regiment, CO 267/31.

99. *The Royal Military Chronicle: Or, the British Officer's Monthly Register, Chronicle, and Military Mentor*, vol. 4, 1811, 49–50.

100. Maxwell to Liverpool, 24 September 1812, CO 267/34.

101. Maxwell to Liverpool, 2 May 1812, CO 267/34.

102. Bathurst to Maxwell, 1 July 1812, Secretary of State Despatches, 3rd April 1809–24th November 1812, SLPA.

103. Maxwell to Liverpool, 2 May 1812, CO 267/34; Maxwell to Liverpool, 26 October 1812, CO 267/34; Charles Maxwell to Lord Liverpool, 9 March 1813, CO 267/36; Alexander Anderson to George Harrison, 10 February 1813, CO 267/36; Alexander Anderson to George Harrison, 15 June 1814, CO 267/39. On the history of Bance Island, see Hancock, *Citizens of the World*, 172–220.

104. Maxwell to Liverpool, 13 September 1812, CO 267/34.

105. Ibid.

106. Maxwell to Liverpool, 24 November 1812, CO 267/34.

107. Maxwell to Liverpool, 13 September 1812, CO 267/34.

108. Ibid. See also Brevet-Major Wingfield to Lt. Col. Torrens, Windsor, 18 November 1811, CO 267/35.

109. Kenneth Macaulay, "Report of Conversation with several Chiefs of the Rokele River respecting some Recruits sent to Major Wingfield, November 2nd, 1812," CO 267/34.

110. Robert Thorpe to Maxwell, 6 November 1812, CO 267/34.

111. Maxwell to Bathurst, 25 November 1812, CO 267/34.

112. "Account of Bance Island, in Sierra-Leone River," *The Monthly Magazine*, vol. 39 (London, 1815), 387.

113. Peter Wenzell to Josiah Pratt, 3 October 1812, CMS C/A/1/E/3/17.

114. Kuczynski, *Demographic Survey of the British Colonial Empire*, 1:169.

115. African Institution, *Ninth Report [1815]*, 54–55.

116. Thorpe, *A Letter to William Wilberforce . . .*, 24.

117. African Institution, *Ninth Report [1815]*, 54.

118. Jane Wingfield to Lt. Col. Torrens, Falmouth, 2 August 1813, CO 267/37; See also an extract from one of Jane Wingfield's letters in the Colonial Office files, Jane Wingfield to Lt. Col. Torrens, 9 August 1813, CO 267/37.

119. Jane Wingfield to Bathurst, 8 September 1813, CO 267/37.

120. On the flyleaf of a letter from Lt. Col. Torrens to Henry Goulbourn, 11 March 1813, CO 267/36; see also Duke of York to Bathurst, 24 May 1813, CO 267/37.

121. "House of Commons—Army Extraordinaries, 23 June 1813," Thomas Hansard and William Cobbett, eds., *The Parliamentary Debates from the Year 1803 to the Present Time Forming a Continuation of the Work entitled "The Parliamentary History of England from the Earliest Period to the Year 1803"* (London, n.d.), vol. 26, 886.

122. MacCarthy to Bathurst, 26 August 1814, CO 267/38.

123. MacCarthy to Bathurst, 22 July 1815, CO 267/40.

124. Quoted in Sir John Eardley-Wilmot, *Lord Brougham's Law Reforms: Comprising the Acts and Bills Introduced or Carried by Him through the Legislature since 1811, with an Analytical Review of Them* (London, 1860), 6.

125. 51 George III. Cap. 23, *Slave Trade Felony Act.*

126. Mouser, *American Colony on the Rio Pongo*, 3.

127. 1 Acton 240 Amedie, Johnson, Master, 17 March 1810, reported in George Minot, ed., *Reports of Cases Argued and Determined before the Most Noble and Right Honorable the Lords Commissioners of Appeals in Prize Causes*, vol. 1 (Boston: Little, Brown, 1853), 241–52, 251.

128. Report quoted in African Institution, *Fifth Report [1811]*, 40.

129. April 1817, *The Christian Observer*, vol. 16 (London, 1817), 274.

130. Mary Louise Pratt, *Imperial Eyes: Travel Writing and Transculturation* (London; New York: Routledge, 1992), 7.

131. Taylor, *Civil War of 1812*, 4.

132. Mouser, *American Colony on the Rio Pongo*, 19–62.

133. Ibid., 1–18.

134. *Trials of the Slave Traders*, 21–22.

135. Ibid., 22.

136. African Institution, *Seventh Report of the Directors of the African Institution: Read at the Annual General Meeting on the 24th of March, 1813* (London, 1813), 4. See also *Trials of the Slave Traders,* 36–37.

137. Bathurst to Maxwell, 26 October 1812, Secretary of State Despatches, 3rd April 1809–24th November 1812, SLPA.

138. *Trials of the Slave Traders,* 31–32.

139. Ibid., 42–45.

140. Review of "Trials of the Slave Traders," *The Edinburgh Review, or Critical Journal,* vol. 21 (London, 1813), 82. See also *Trials of the Slave Traders,* 41.

141. Maxwell to Bathurst, 30 September 1814, CO 267/38.

142. Robert Purdie to Maxwell, 1 July 1813, CO 267/36. Bostock was a well-established figure in the local slave trade. See Denise Jones, "Robert Bostock of Liverpool and the British Slave Trade on the Upper Guinea Coast, 1769–93," in *Slavery, Abolition and the Transition to Colonisation in Sierra Leone,* ed. Paul Lovejoy and Suzanne Schwarz (Trenton, NJ: Africa World Press, 2015), 69–87.

143. Fyfe, *History of Sierra Leone,* 120–21; Mouser, *American Colony on the Rio Pongo,* 67–68.

144. Attestation of "Mrs. Boy," OSB MSS 19662.

145. Attestation and Confession of John Sterling Mills and Phillipa Hayes, 1 July 1813, OSB 19662.

146. Malcolm Brodie to W. H. Leigh, 17 July 1817, Governor's Despatches to Secretary of State, 1813–1818, SLPA.

147. *Trials of the Slave Traders,* 23.

148. Melchior Renner to Josiah Pratt, 24 March 1812, CMS C/A/1/E/2/140.

149. *Trials of the Slave Traders,* 16. Mouser, "Trade, Coasters, and Conflict in the Rio Pongo from 1790 to 1808," 45–47, 64.

150. Mouser, *American Colony on the Rio Pongo,* 69–70.

151. Bruce Mouser, "Amara, Alimamy of Moria from 1802 to 1826," unpublished working paper, written 1975, revised 2008, available online from the Harriett Tubman Centre, York University, at http://www.tubmaninstitute.ca/sites/default/files/file/amara%2070s.pdf.

152. Alimami Amrah and Wili Solyman to Maxwell, 2 March 1814, CO 267/38.

153. John Thornton, *Africa and Africans in the Making of the Atlantic World, 1400–1800,* 2d ed. (Cambridge: Cambridge University Press, 1998), 105.

154. See Mouser and Mouser, *Case of the Reverend Peter Hartwig.*

155. Maxwell to Bathurst, 1 May 1814, CO 267/38.

156. Mouser, *American Colony on the Rio Pongo,* 63–65.

157. Maxwell to Bathurst, 1 May 1814, CO 267/38.

158. Ibid.

159. Ibid.

160. Thorpe, *A Reply "point by Point" to the Special Report of the Directors of the African Institution*, 60.

161. The pamphlets published in the controversy include Thorpe, *A Letter to William Wilberforce . . . &c. By R. Thorpe, Esq. &c."* (London, 1815). See also, See Statement of Dr. Thorpe's Case, In Mr. Hutchinson's 16 May 1823, CO 267/88. On Thorpe's checkered legal career before Sierra Leone, see John McLaren, *Dewigged, Bothered, and Bewildered: British Colonial Judges on Trial, 1800–1900* (Toronto: Osgoode Society for Canadian Legal History/University of Toronto Press, 2011), 56–71, 229–31; Taylor, *Civil War of 1812*, 95.

162. Robert Thorpe to Charles Maxwell, 16 March 1813, CO 267/88; see also Review of "Trials of the Slave Traders," *The Edinburgh Review, or Critical Journal*, 21:79.

163. Thorpe, *A Letter to William Wilberforce . . .*, 21.

164. Ibid., 20.

165. "Answer of Lt. Col. Charles Wm. Maxwell . . . to the charges preferred against him," CO 267/88.

166. Macaulay to J. Chapman, 17 June 1811, CO 267/31.

167. African Institution, *Seventh Report [1813]*, 21–22.

168. Thorpe, *A Letter to William Wilberforce . . .*, 89–90.

169. 2 Starkie, Cooke v. Maxwell, N.P. 1817, reported in Thomas Starkie, ed., *Reports of Cases, Determined at Nisi Prius, in the Courts of King's Bench and Common Pleas, and on the Circuit, from the Sittings after Michaelmas Term. 57 Geo. III. 1816. to the Sittings after Michaelmas Term, 60 Geo. III, 1819*, vol. 2 (London, 1820), 185.

170. *The Annual Register, or a View of the History, Politics, and Literature, for the Year 1817* (London, 1818), 181–82.

171. Ibid., 182.

172. Taylor, *Civil War of 1812*, 102, 123.

173. Brooks, *Western Africa and Cabo Verde*, 26.

174. Malcolm Brodie to W. H. Leigh, 17 July 1817, Governor's Despatches to Secretary of State, 1813–1818, SLPA; see also Mouser, *American Colony on the Rio Pongo*, 70–76.

175. *Annual Register, 1818*, 183.

176. Georges Cuvier et al., *The Animal Kingdom: The Class Mammalia, Arranged by the Baron Cuvier, with Specific Descriptions*, vol. 4 (London, 1827), 267.

177. *The Gentleman's Magazine*, vol. 30, New Series (London, 1848), 544.

178. 9 July 1893, William White, *Notes and Queries: A Medium of Intercommunication for Literary Men, General Readers, Etc.*, vol. 2 (London, 1892), 25.

5. The Liberated African Department

1. Ephraim Bacon, *Abstract of a Journal of E. Bacon, Assistant Agent of the United States, to Africa* (Philadelphia, 1821), 6, 37; Letter from Rev. Daniel Coker, 25 September 1820, in American Colonization Society, *The Fourth Annual Report of the American Society for Colonizing the Free People of Colour of the United States, with an Appendix* (Washington D.C., 1821), 18.

2. Bacon, *Abstract of a Journal*, 24. See also Capt. Edward Trenchard to the Secretary of the Navy, 25 December 1820, American Colonization Society, *Fourth Annual Report*, 55.

3. Johnson to Pratt, 2 May 1818, CMS C/A/1/E7/6.

4. Minutes of First Missionary Meeting at Regent's Town, 7 December 1819, CMS C/A/1/E7/80.

5. G. S. Bull's Report on the Seminary Students, 30 June 1820, Mission Book, 21st Year, CMS C/A/1/M1/48.

6. Johnson, journal entry, 17 December 1817, CMS C/A/1/E7A/47.

7. See Johnson to the Secretaries, 12 February 1820, CMS C/A/1/E8/119; J. B. Cates to the Secretaries, 20 January 1820, CMS C/A/1/E7A/24; Johnson, journal entry for 6 October 1818, CMS C/A/1/E7A/47.

8. As late as 1822, in a dispatch to Earl Bathurst, MacCarthy asked for "articles for the service of sick Liberated Africans" and for "clothing for the service of the Captured Negroes." Charles MacCarthy to Earl Bathurst, Government House, Sierra Leone, 12 January 1822, Governor Despatches 1818–1822, SLPA.

9. Rowan and Wellington, "Report of the Commissioners of Inquiry, Part 1," 92.

10. *The Royal Gazette and Sierra Leone Advertiser* [Freetown], 10 August 1822. See also Jean Herskovits Kopytoff, *A Preface to Modern Nigeria: The "Sierra Leonians" in Yoruba, 1830–1890* (Madison, WI: University of Wisconsin Press, 1965), 25.

11. Charles MacCarthy, Memorandum Relating to the Constitution of Sierra Leone, Shewing the Necessity of Making Alterations in the Same [ca. 1816], CO 267/42.

12. See, among many others, Andrew Porter, "An Overview, 1700–1914," in *Missions and Empire*, ed. Norman Etherington (Oxford: Oxford University Press, 2005), 40–63; Alan Lester, "British Settler Discourse and the Circuits

of Empire," *History Workshop Journal* 54, no. 1 (January 1, 2002): 24–48; Lester and Dussart, *Colonization and the Origins of Humanitarian Governance;* David Hempton, *Methodism: Empire of the Spirit* (New Haven: Yale University Press, 2005).

13. See Bronwen Everill, *Abolition and Empire in Sierra Leone and Liberia* (Houndmills, Basingstoke, Hampshire: Palgrave Macmillan, 2013); Monday B. Abasiattai, "The Search for Independence: New World Blacks in Sierra Leone and Liberia, 1787–1847," *Journal of Black Studies* 23, no. 1 (1992): 107–16; Richard West, *Back to Africa: A History of Sierra Leone and Liberia* (New York: Holt, Rinehart and Winston, 1971).

14. American Colonization Society, *The Second Annual Report of the American Society for Colonizing the Free People of Colour in the United States, With an Appendix* (Washington, D.C., 1819), 7. See also Eric Burin, *Slavery and the Peculiar Solution: A History of the American Colonization Society* (Gainesville, FL: University Press of Florida, 2008); Claude Andrew Clegg, *The Price of Liberty: African Americans and the Making of Liberia* (Chapel Hill, NC: University of North Carolina Press, 2004); Rugemer, *The Problem of Emancipation,* 73–101.

15. See especially Davis, *Problem of Slavery.*

16. On the ecological and political processes of the expansion of slavery, see Johnson, *River of Dark Dreams.*

17. Linda Colley, *Britons: Forging the Nation, 1707–1837* (New Haven: Yale University Press, 1992), 322.

18. Speech of Lord Castlereagh, "Treaty with Spain for Preventing the Slave Trade," House of Commons Debates, HC Deb., 9 February 1818, vol. 37, cc. 234; see also Drescher, "Whose Abolition? Popular Pressure and the Ending of the British Slave Trade."

19. Christopher Robinson to Bathurst, 18 July 1816, CO 267/44; see also Copy of confidential orders, J. W. Ordmer to Admiral [redacted], 24 July 1816, CO 267/44; Lloyd, *The Navy and the Slave Trade,* 80.

20. Dodson, *Case of the Louis,* 23, 31.

21. *San Juan Nepomuceno,* Haggard, *Reports of Cases Argued and Determined in the High Court of Admiralty,* 270.

22. See David R. Murray, *Odious Commerce: Britain, Spain, and the Abolition of the Cuban Slave Trade* (Cambridge: Cambridge University Press, 1980); Leslie Bethell, *The Abolition of the Brazilian Slave Trade: Britain, Brazil and the Slave Trade Question* (Cambridge: Cambridge University Press, 2009).

23. Leslie Bethell, "The Mixed Commissions for the Suppression of the Trans-atlantic Slave Trade in the Nineteenth Century," *Journal of African History* 7, no. 1 (January 1, 1966): 84.

24. Castlereagh to Thomas Gregory, Esq., 20 February 1819, FO 84/3.

25. Evidence of D. M. Hamilton, Appendix C17, CO 267/92.

26. MacCarthy to Lt. Colonel Burke, 2nd West India Regiment, 27 November 1820, Colonial Secretary's Letterbook, 6 June 1820–2 December 1824, SLPA.

27. MacCarthy to Bathurst, 8 February 1817, CO 267/45.

28. Thomas Gregory and Edward Fitzgerald to Castlereagh, 20 November 1819, FO 84/3.

29. Statement of Sums, the Proceeds of Prizes, paid into the Registry of the Mixed Courts by James Woods, Commissioner of Appraisement and Sale, 9 August 1820, FO 84/4.

30. Fitzgerald and Gregory to Castlereagh, 20 March 1820, FO 84/4.

31. R. B. Fitzgerald, Acting Registrar, to D. M. Hamilton, 23 November 1821, FO 84/9; Thomas Gregory and Edward Fitzgerald to Castlereagh, Sierra Leone, 20 November 1819, FO 84/3.

32. George, *The Rise of British West Africa*, 232.

33. Gregory and Fitzgerald to Castlereagh, 4 March 1820, FO 84/4.

34. Gregory and Fitzgerald to T. R. Lushington, 22 November 1821, FO 84/9; Thomas Carew to R. B. Fitzgerald, Registrar to the Mixed Commissions, 4 December 1821, FO 84/9.

35. George Collier to Registrar of the Court of Mixed Commission, H.M.S. *Tartar*, 19 February 1820, FO 84/4; Edward Gregory and Edward Fitzgerald to the Marquis of Londonderry, 20 June 1821, FO 84/9; George Collier to the Registrar of the Courts of the British and Portuguese and British and Spanish Mixed Commissions, 6 June 1821, FO 84/9.

36. See Rowan and Wellington, "Report of the Commissioners of Inquiry, Part 1," 22. See also Robert T. Brown, "Fernando Po and the Anti-Sierra Leonean Campaign: 1826–1834," *International Journal of African Historical Studies* 6, no. 2 (January 1, 1973): 250; Lovejoy, *Transformations in Slavery,* 165; David Northrup, "West Africans and the Atlantic, 1550–1800," in *Black Experience and the Empire*, ed. Philip D. Morgan and Sean Hawkins (Oxford: Oxford University Press, 2004), 41–44.

37. Report on the Slave Trade, James Yeo to John Wilson Croker, London, 6 November 1816, CO 267/44; see also *Royal Gazette and Sierra Leone Advertiser* [Freetown], 1 April 1820.

38. West African Journal of Lt. George W. Courtenay, Commander of H.M.S. *Bann*, UICSL V/16/p. 113.

39. Speech of Joseph Marryat, "Netherlands Slave Trade Bill—Sierra Leone," House of Commons Debates, 19 March 1819, vol. 39, cc. 1106; see also Speech of Joseph Marryat, "Treaty with Spain for Preventing the Slave Trade," House of Commons Debates, 9 February 1818, vol. 37, cc. 259. See also Joseph Marryat, *More Thoughts Still on the State of the West India Colonies, and the Proceedings of the African Institution with Observations on the Speech of James Stephen* (London, 1818).

40. David Lambert, "Sierra Leone and Other Sites in the War of Representation Over Slavery," *History Workshop Journal* 64, no. 1 (September 21, 2007): 103–32.

41. Lambert, *Mastering the Niger*, 58.

42. Speech of William Wilberforce, "Treaty with Spain for Preventing the Slave Trade," House of Commons Debates, 9 February 1818, vol. 37, cc. 260.

43. MacCarthy to Bathurst, Government House, Sierra Leone, 31 May 1816, CO 267/42.

44. Paul Cuffe to Nathan Lord [Andover Theological Seminary], 19 April 1815, in Wiggins, *Paul Cuffe's Logs*, 342.

45. *Royal Gazette and Sierra Leone Advertiser* [Freetown], 4 April 1818.

46. MacCarthy to Bathurst, Government House, Sierra Leone, 31 May 1816, CO 267/42.

47. See S. T. McCarthy, "The Clann Carthaigh," *Kerry Archaeological Magazine* 2, no. 12 (March 1, 1914): 195–99; Peterson, *Province of Freedom*, 81.

48. McCarthy, "The Clann Carthaigh," 197. See also Letters and Documents Connected with Sir Charles McCarthy and the McCarthy Family, 1695–1824, NAM 6612/10/3; Edward O'Shill to Colonel Robert Brownrigg, 22 September 1798, NAM 6612/10/8/1; John Haig to Army Medical Department, 12 January 1799, NAM 6612/10/8/5.

49. MacCarthy to Bathurst, Separate, 7 January 1818, CO 267/47.

50. MacCarthy to Bathurst, 31 May 1816, CO 267/42.

51. Paul Cuffe to William Allen, 22 April 1811, in Wiggins, *Paul Cuffe's Logs*, 118.

52. Edward Fitzgerald to Josiah Pratt, 3 May 1821, Mission Book, 22nd Year (1820–1821), CMS C/A/1/M1/44; on religion in Freetown, see also Paul Cuffe to William Allen, 22 April 1811, in ibid.

53. See Elizabeth Elbourne, "Early Khoisan Uses of Missionary Christianity," *Kronos*, no. 19 (November 1, 1992): 3–27; Elizabeth Elbourne and Robert

Ross, "Combating Spiritual and Social Bondage: Early Missions in the Cape Colony," in *Christianity in South Africa*, ed. Richard Elphick, and T. R. H. Davenport (Berkeley, CA: University of California Press, 1997), 31–50; Elizabeth Elbourne, *Blood Ground: Colonialism, Missions, and the Contest for Christianity in the Cape Colony and Britain, 1799–1853* (Montreal: McGill-Queen's University Press, 2002); Jean Comaroff and John Comaroff, *Of Revelation and Revolution, Volume 1: Christianity, Colonialism, and Consciousness in South Africa* (Chicago: University of Chicago Press, 1991); V. Y. Mudimbe, *The Invention of Africa: Gnosis, Philosophy, and the Order of Knowledge* (Bloomington, IN: Indiana University Press, 1988), 44–97; John David Yeadon Peel, *Religious Encounter and the Making of the Yoruba* (Bloomington, IN: Indiana University Press, 2003), 215–47; Jehu Hanciles, *Euthanasia of a Mission: African Church Autonomy in a Colonial Context* (Westport, CT: Praeger, 2002); Hair, "Africanism"; Kopytoff, *A Preface to Modern Nigeria*.

54. Rowan and Wellington, "Report of the Commissioners of Inquiry, Part 1," 18.

55. Fitzgerald to Pratt, 3 May 1821, Mission Book, 22nd Year, CMS C/A/1/M1/44.

56. Ibid.

57. Central Committee Minutes, G C 1, Vol. 2: 27 February 1815–10 March 1817, 15 July 1815, 23 October 1815, pp. 394–98.

58. MacCarthy to Pratt, 7 February 1816, in Walker, *Missions in Western Africa*, 465–66. See also MacCarthy to Pratt, 29 June 1817, CMS C/A/1/E6/102; MacCarthy to Bickersteth, 20 June 1818, CMS C/A/1/E7/22.

59. Josiah Pratt to Edward Bickersteth, 12 August 1815, in Thomas Rawson Birks, ed., *Memoir of the Rev. Edward Bickersteth, Late Rector of Watton, Herts*, vol. 1 (New York, 1851), 223–24. See also Eugene Stock, *The History of the Church Missionary Society, Its Environment, Its Men and Its Work*, vol. 1 (London, 1899), 45, 80, 107, 122; Bruce L. Mouser, "Origins of Church Missionary Society Accommodation to Imperial Policy: The Sierra Leone Quagmire and the Closing of the Susu Mission, 1804–17," *Journal of Religion in Africa* 39, no. 4 (2009): 375–402; Bruce L. Mouser, "Continuing British Interest in Coastal Guinea-Conakry and Fuuta Jaloo Highlands (1750 to 1850)," *Cahiers d'Études Africaines* 43, no. 172 (January 1, 2003): 771; Mouser and Mouser, *Case of the Reverend Peter Hartwig*; Hanciles, *Euthanasia of a Mission*, 13.

60. Birks, *Memoir of the Rev. Edward Bickersteth*, 1:250–51. See also Kristina Bross, "'Come Over and Help Us': Reading Mission Literature," *Early American Literature* 38, no. 3 (January 1, 2003): 395–400.

61. Central Committee Minutes, 15 November 181, CMS G/C/1/Vol. 2; see also Stock, *History of the CMS*, 1:125–26; Silke Strickrodt, "African Girls' Samplers from Mission Schools in Sierra Leone (1820s to 1840s)," *History in Africa* 37, no. 1 (2010): 189–245.

62. Journal entry ca. 1816, in Birks, *Memoir of the Rev. Edward Bickersteth*, 1:259.

63. MacCarthy to Bathurst, 31 May 1816, CO 267/42.

64. See Suzanne Schwarz, "Extending the African Names Database: New Evidence from Sierra Leone," *African Economic History* 38, no. 1 (2009): 137–63; Suzanne Schwarz, "Reconstructing the Life Histories of Liberated Africans: Sierra Leone in the Early Nineteenth Century," *History in Africa* 39, no. 1 (2012): 175–207; G. Ugo Nwokeji and David Eltis, "The Roots of the African Diaspora: Methodological Considerations in the Analysis of Names in the Liberated African Registers of Sierra Leone and Havana," *History in Africa* 29 (January 1, 2002): 365–79; Adam Jones, "Recaptive Nations: Evidence Concerning the Demographic Impact of the Atlantic Slave Trade in the Early Nineteenth Century," *Slavery & Abolition* 11, no. 1 (1990): 42–57; Adam Jones, "New Light on the Liberated Africans and Their Origins: A List of Children Named after Benefactors," in *Sierra Leone Studies at Birmingham 1988*, ed. Adam Jones, Peter K. Mitchell, and Margaret Peil (Birmingham: University of Birmingham Press, 1990), 32–42.

65. Ricketts, *Narrative of the Ashantee War*, 197.

66. Liberated African Department, Statement of Disposals 1821–1833, SLPA.

67. Evidence of Joseph Reffell [Former Chief Superintendent, Liberated African Department], Appendix 10B, CO 267/92.

68. Evidence of Mr. Cole [Chief Superintendent, Liberated African Department], Appendices 9B & 10B, CO 267/92; see also Johnson, Journal entry for 19 December 1818, CMS C/A/1/E7A/66.

69. Johnson to Bickersteth, 21 May 1820, published in *Memoir of the Rev. Edward Bickersteth*, 1:268; Evidence of Mr. Cole, Appendices 9B & 10B, CO 267/92.

70. Evidence of Joseph Reffell, Appendix 10B, CO 267/92.

71. *West-African Sketches*, 174.

72. MacCarthy to Bathurst, Government House, Sierra Leone, 22 April 1819, CO 267/49; Evidence of Mr. Cole, Appendices 9B & 10B, CO 267/92.

73. MacCarthy to Henry Goulburn, 22 April 1819, CO 267/49.

74. Evidence of Mr. Cole, Appendices 9B & 10B, CO 267/92.

75. Rowan and Wellington, "Report of the Commissioners of Inquiry, Part 1," 87.

76. Peterson, *Province of Freedom*, 83.

77. Total Colonial Expenditures, Appendix 16A, CO 267/91.

78. D. M. Hamilton to Captain Findlay, Commandant, Bathurst, Saint Mary, River Gambia, 28 June 1824, Local Letters: D. M. Hamilton's Letter Book, April 1824 to February 1825, SLPA.

79. Hamilton to William Sutherland, 28 April 1824, Local Letters: D. M. Hamilton's Letter Book, April 1824 to February 1825, SLPA. See also Fyfe, *History of Sierra Leone*, 155.

80. These 71 inquiries are spread across three boxes of files in the National Archives, Kew. They include memoranda sent from the Office of the Treasury to the Office of the Secretary of State for War and the Colonies on 15 January, 16 February, 1 April, 8 April, 21 April, 8 May, 22 May, 8 June, 11 June, 23 July, 27 July, 1 August, and 10 December 1818 (CO 267/48); on 4 January, 27 April, 26 May, 27 May, 1 June, and 10 July 1820 (CO 267/52); and on 24 January, 9 March, 16 March, 30 March, 26 April, 10 May, and 29 May 1821 (CO 267/55).

81. Rowan and Wellington, "Report of the Commissioners of Inquiry, Part 1," 61. Conversion made with www.measuringworth.com.

82. "[List of Articles] Required for the Service of Captured Negroes in this colony of Sierra Leone," 11 January 1822, Governor Despatches 1818-1822, SLPA. See also MacCarthy to Bathurst, February 1817, CO 267/45; see also Fyfe, *History of Sierra Leone*, 128-31.

83. "Request for Service of Captured Negroes &c. in the colony of Sierra Leone, Sierra Leone," 19 May 1818, CO 267/47; "[List of articles] Required for serving of Captured Negroes in the colony of Sierra Leone and for furnishing the Churches and Build Stores and Superintendents' Houses," CO 267/47.

84. Reffell received 3,000 yards of cloth for jackets and another 30,000 yards of fabric for trousers and shirts, or almost 19 miles. See "[List of articles] Required for the Service of Captured Negroes in this colony of Sierra Leone," 11 January 1822, Governor Despatches 1818-1822, SLPA.

85. MacCarthy to Bathurst, 14 January 1819, CO 267/49.

86. Rowan and Wellington, "Report of the Commissioners of Inquiry, Part 1," 27.

87. Ibid., 28.

88. Evidence of Mr. Cole, Appendices 9B & 10B, CO 267/92; Rowan and Wellington, "Report of the Commissioners of Inquiry, Part 1," 75-76.

89. Table of Rice Contracts and Tenders, Appendix 15A, CO 267/91.

90. This is clear from the records, and from contemporary descriptions of, for example, plantations in the colony of "orange, lime, coffee, cotton, acacia, cocoa-nut, banana, palm and other trees in wonderful variety." See *Transactions of the Geological Society, Established November 13th 1807*, vol. 1 (London, 1824), 417.

91. Rowan and Wellington, "Report of the Commissioners of Inquiry, Part 1," 29, 32.

92. Ibid., 75.

93. Evidence of Joseph Reffell, 10B, CO 267/92.

94. Rowan and Wellington, "Report of the Commissioners of Inquiry, Part 1," 28.

95. Ibid., 29.

96. Evidence of Mr. Cole, Appendices 9B & 10B, CO 267/92.

97. Evidence of Mr. Myrton, [Clerk of Works, Ordnance Department], Appendix 16B, CO 267/92.

98. Ibid.

99. Reports on Liberated Africans, Appendix 11A, CO 267/91.

100. Ibid.

101. Rowan and Wellington, "Report of the Commissioners of Inquiry, Part 1," 30.

102. Ibid.

103. See E. P. Thompson, "Time, Work-Discipline, and Industrial Capitalism," *Past & Present*, no. 38 (December 1, 1967): 56–97; Frederick Cooper, "Colonizing Time: Work Rhythms and Labor Conflict," in *Colonialism and Culture*, ed. Nicholas B. Dirks (Ann Arbor, MI: University of Michigan Press, 1992), 209–46.

104. Rankin, *White Man's Grave*, 1:57.

105. Evidence of Mr. Myrton, Appendix 16B, CO 267/92.

106. Rowan and Wellington, "Report of the Commissioners of Inquiry, Part 1," 28–29.

107. Ibid., 29.

108. Evidence of Mr. Cole, Appendices 9B & 10B, CO 267/92.

109. Johnson to Pratt and Bickersteth, 7 February 1820, CMS C/A/1/E8/117.

110. Winterbottom, *Account of the Native Africans*, 1:89. See also Kopytoff, *A Preface to Modern Nigeria*, 30.

111. Johnson, journal entry for 8 October 1816, in Seeley, ed., *A Memoir of the Rev. W. A. B. Johnson . . .* (New York, 1853), 46.

112. *Royal Gazette and Sierra Leone Advertiser* [Freetown], 1 January 1820.

113. Thomas Sylvester Johnson, *The Story of a Mission: The Sierra Leone Church, First Daughter of C. M. S.* (London: S.P.C.K., 1953). See also John Peterson, "The Sierra Leone Creole: A Reappraisal," in *Freetown: A Symposium,* ed. Christopher Fyfe (Freetown: Sierra Leone University Press, 1968), 100–17; Porter, *Creoledom;* Akintola Wyse, "The Sierra Leone Krios: A Reappraisal from the Perspective of the African Diaspora," in *Global Dimensions of the African Diaspora,* ed. Joseph Harris (Washington D.C.: Howard University Press, 1982), 309–37.

114. Lester and Dussart, *Colonization and the Origins of Humanitarian Governance,* 11.

115. Pratt to Johnson, 8 October 1817, CMS C/A/1/E6/73.

116. Andrew Porter, *Religion versus Empire?: British Protestant Missionaries and Overseas Expansion, 1700–1914* (Manchester, New York: Manchester University Press, 2004), 9. See also Anna Johnston, *Missionary Writing and Empire, 1800–1860* (Cambridge, New York: Cambridge University Press, 2003).

117. Johnson, journal entries from March 1816 to June 1819, CMS C/A/1/E7A/66.

118. William Garnon to Pratt, 27 June 1817, CMS C/A/1/E6/58.

119. Johnson, journal entry for 2 August 1818, in Seeley, *Memoir of the Rev. W. A. B. Johnson,* 105.

120. Johnson to Pratt, 18 June 1816, in ibid., 37.

121. Johnson, journal entry for 18 June 1816, C/A/1/E7A/66; Johnson, journal entry for 20 June 1816, CMS C/A/1/E7A/66.

122. Johnson, journal entry for 15 July 1816, CMS C/A/1/E7A/66.

123. William Tamba, journal entry for 24 May 1821, Mission Book, 22nd Year, CMS C/A/1/M1/36.

124. Johnson, journal entry for 15 July 1816, CMS C/A/1/E7A/66.

125. MacCarthy to Pratt and Bickersteth, 20 November 1819, CMS C/A/1/E8/74.

126. Johnson, journal entry for 15 July 1816, C/A/1/E7A/66. See also Peterson, Peterson, *Province of Freedom,* 116–17.

127. Johnson, journal entry for 21 February 1820, Mission Book, 21st Year, CMS C/A/1/M1/21/9; see also Sir George Collier to Pratt, 11 February 1819, C/A/1/E7/63.

128. In one six-month period, the society collected £6, 14s, 1d and spent £6, 11d, 5d. Johnson, journal entry for 11 July 1818, C/A/1/E7/47.

129. Johnson, journal entry for 18 May 1822, Mission Book, 23rd Year (1821–1822), C/A/1/M1/14.

130. Johnson, journal entry for 5 August 1820, Mission Book, 21st Year, CMS C/A/1/M1/94.

131. Cates to Pratt, 7 November 1818, CMS C/A/1/E7/62.

132. Johnson, journal entry for Mission Book, 4 April 1821, 21st Year, CMS C/A/1/M1/34; see also Committee Managing a Fund Raised by Some Friends, for the Purpose of Promoting African Instruction, *Report of the Committee Managing a Fund Raised by Some Friends, for the Purpose of Promoting African Instruction; with an Account of a Visit to the Gambia and Sierra Leone. (Second Report . . . With an Appendix.—Continuation of the Appendix to the Second Report.)* (London, 1822), 58–59.

133. Samuel Abraham Walker, *The Church of England Mission in Sierra Leone: Including an Introductory Account of That Colony, and a Comprehensive Sketch of the Niger Expedition in the Year 1841* (London, 1847), 104.

134. Maria Louisa Charlesworth, *Africa's Mountain Valley; Or, The Church in Regent's Town, West Africa* (London, 1856), 160.

135. Walker, *Church of England Mission in Sierra Leone*, 134–35. For other examples, see Johnson, journal entry for 12 September 1818, C/A/1/E7/47; David Noah and William Davies to Pratt and Bickersteth, [received] 30 October 1818, CMS C/A/1/E7/38.

136. Johnson, journal entry for 23 April 1818, C/A/1/E7/47.

137. Johnson, journal entry for 13 July 1818 C/A/1/E7/47.

138. "Memoir of George Paul," 26 March 1820, Mission Book, 21st Year, CMS C/A/1/M1/21/46.

139. Johnson, journal entry for 7 September 1818, CMS C/A/1/E7/47.

140. Johnson, journal entry for 9 September 1818, CMS C/A/1/E7/47.

141. Johnson, journal entry for 27 July 1820, Mission Book, 21st Year, CMS C/A/1/M1/21/94.

142. Johnson, journal entry for 3 September 1820, Mission Book, 21st Year, CMS C/A/1/M1/21/94.

143. Johnson to Pratt and Bickersteth, 29 December 1821, Mission Book, 23rd Year, C/A/1/M1/2.

144. Committee Managing a Fund Raised by Some Friends, for the Purpose of Promoting African Instruction, *Report of the Committee Managing a Fund Raised by Some Friends*, 56.

145. Accounts of Produce Purchased the Liberated African Department, 1819–1825, Appendix 27A, CO 267/91; Excerpt from the *Sierra Leone Gazette* in American Colonization Society, *The Third Annual Report of the American Society for Colonizing the Free People of Colour of the United States*

with an Appendix (Washington, D.C., 1820), 108. See also Johnson, journal entry for 11 March 1817, in Seeley, *Memoir of the Rev. W. A. B. Johnson,* 56.

146. Charlesworth, *Africa's Mountain Valley,* 101.

147. Ibid., 234–35.

148. Peterson, *Province of Freedom,* 113.

149. MacCarthy to Pratt and Bickersteth, 21 September 1819, CMS C/A/1/ E8/58. See also Travis Glasson, *Mastering Christianity: Missionary Anglicanism and Slavery in the Atlantic World* (New York: Oxford University Press, 2011), 157.

150. Johnson, journal entry for 19 December 1818, C/A/1/E7A/66.

151. Bickersteth to Johnson, 25 May 1821, CMS C/A/1/L1/167; see also Johnson to Pratt, 6 February 1821, Mission Book, 21st Year, CMS C/A/1/ M1/131; Johnson to Pratt, 6 February 1821, CMS C/A/1/E8/117.

152. MacCarthy to Pratt, 8 June 1819, CMS C/A/1/E7A/72.

153. Ibid.

154. Melchior Renner to Pratt and Bickersteth, 21 September 1819, CMS C/A/1/E8/59.

155. Johnson, journal entry for 18 September 1818, CMS C/A/1/E7/47.

156. Johnson, journal entry for 11 April 1820, Mission Book, 21st Year, CMS C/A/1/M1/45.

157. Johnson, journal entry for 23 February 1818, CMS C/A/1/E7/47.

158. Johnson, journal entry for 5 August 1818, CMS C/A/1/E7/47.

159. Johnson, journal entry for 13 August 1820, Mission Book, 21st Year, CMS C/A/1/M1/94.

160. Johnson, journal entry for 21 April 1821, Mission Book, 22nd Year, CMS C/A/1/M1/34.

161. Artificers & Mechanics Named After the Benefactors and who Attend Evening School, December 1822, CMS C/A/1/O/13/Nos. 7 & 31.

162. Bickersteth to Johnson, 29 August 1822, CMS C/A/1/L1/115.

163. William Tamba was a butcher, William Davis a master shingle maker, Peter Hughes a master mason, David Noah a clerk—see Johnson, journal entry for 11 April 1820, Mission Book, 21st Year, CMS C/A/1/M1/45.

164. G. S. Bull's Report on the Seminary Students, 30 June 1820, Mission Book, 21st Year, CMS C/A/1/M1/48.

165. Johnson to Pratt and Bickersteth, 12 July 1820, Mission Book, 21st Year, C/A/1/M1/63.

166. Johnson to Pratt and Bickersteth, 18 October 1822, Mission Book, 23rd Year, CMS C/A/1/M2/51.

167. McGowan, "Establishment of Long-Distance Trade," 38.

168. James Reffell to Alfred W. J. Percival, Esq., Collector of Duties, Secretary's Office, 20 April 1824, Colonial Secretary's Letter Book, 6 June 1820–2 December 1824, SLPA; see also James Reffell to Alimamy Amarah, Fouricaria, 2 November 1824; Reffell to Alimamy Amarah, 3 December 1824, Colonial Secretary's Letter Book, 6 June 1820–2 December 1824, SLPA; Patrick S. Caulker, "Legitimate Commerce and Statecraft: A Study of the Hinterland Adjacent to Nineteenth-Century Sierra Leone," *Journal of Black Studies* 11, no. 4 (June 1, 1981): 405; McGowan, "Establishment of Long-Distance Trade," 38.

169. John Milner Gray, *A History of the Gambia* (London: Frank Cass, 1966), 286–97; Martin Lynn, "Britain's West African Policy and the Island of Fernando Po, 1821–43," *Journal of Imperial and Commonwealth History* 18, no. 2 (1990): 191–207.

170. MacCarthy to Bathurst, 16 April 1816, CO 267/42.

171. *West-African Sketches*, 251. See also Corry, *Observations Upon the Windward Coast of Africa*, 107–8; H. R. Jarrett, "Bathurst: Port of the Gambia River," *Geography* 36, no. 2 (May 1, 1951): 98–107.

172. MacCarthy to Bathurst, 2 November 1817, CO 267/45.

173. See Mouser, "Continuing British Interest in Coastal Guinea-Conakry and Fuuta Jaloo Highlands (1750 to 1850)"; Brooks, *Eurafricans in Western Africa;* Mouser, "Trade, Coasters, and Conflict in the Rio Pongo from 1790 to 1808"; Mouser, "Landlords-Strangers"; Mouser, *American Colony on the Rio Pongo*, 81.

174. MacCarthy to Henry Goulbourn, 20 May 1817, CO 267/45.

175. MacCarthy to Bathurst, 2 January 1818, CO 267/47. See also Pratt to J. S. Klein, received 7 October 1817 CMS C/A/1/E6/66.

176. MacCarthy to Henry Goulbourn, 20 May 1817, CO 267/44; George, *The Rise of British West Africa*, 76.

177. MacCarthy to Bathurst, 20 July 1818, CO 267/47.

178. Ibid.; see also MacCarthy to Bathurst, 22 April 1819, CO 267/49.

179. Nicholas Guyatt, " 'The Outskirts of Our Happiness': Race and the Lure of Colonization in the Early Republic," *Journal of American History* 95, no. 4 (March 1, 2009): 991.

180. See Nicholas Guyatt, *Bind Us Apart: How Enlightened Americans Invented Racial Segregation* (New York: Basic Books, 2016), 263–69.

181. Quoted in Campbell, *Middle Passages*, 29.

182. George E. Brooks, "The Providence African Society's Sierra Leone Emigration Scheme, 1794–1795: Prologue to the African Colonization

Movement," *International Journal of African Historical Studies* 7, no. 2 (January 1, 1974): 183–202.

183. Thomas Jefferson to John Lynd, 21 January 1811, published in American Colonization Society, *First Annual Report*, 14.

184. On Cuffe, see Sheldon H. Harris, *Paul Cuffe: Black America and the African Return* (New York: Simon and Schuster, 1972); Lamont D. Thomas, *Rise to Be a People: A Biography of Paul Cuffe* (Urbana, IL: University of Illinois Press, 1986).

185. American Colonization Society, *A View of Exertions Lately Made for the Purpose of Colonizing the Free People of Colour, in the United States, in Africa, or Elsewhere* (Washington D.C., 1817), 17.

186. *A Brief Account of the Settlement and Present Situation of the Colony of Sierra Leone, in Africa*, 11–12.

187. For examples of Cuffe in anachronistic poses, see Lamont D. Thomas, *Paul Cuffe: Black Entrepreneur and Pan-Africanist* (Urbana, IL: University of Illinois Press, 1988); Michael Westgate, *Captain Paul Cuffe (1759–1817): A One-Man Civil Rights Movement* (Museum of the National Center of Afro-American Artists and Education and Resources Group [ERG], 1989).

188. Levine-Gronningsater, "Delivering Freedom," 21.

189. Cuffe to Samuel Mills, 6 August 1816, published in American Colonization Society, *First Annual Report*, 27.

190. 19 March 1811 [?], in Wiggins, *Paul Cuffe's Logs*, 109.

191. Paul Cuffe to William Allen, 22 April 1811, in ibid., 119.

192. Remarks, 6 March 1811, 14 March 1811, 18 March 1811, 9 July 1811, in ibid., 107–9.

193. Copy of a Petition by the Inhabitants of Sierra Leone; Paul Cuffe to William Allen, 22 April 1811, in Wiggins, *Paul Cuffe's Logs*, 115–16.

194. Paul Cuffe to William Allen, 22 April 1811, in Wiggins, *Paul Cuffe's Logs*, 119.

195. Rankin, *White Man's Grave*, 1:97.

196. Paul Cuffe to Daniel Coker, 13 March 1815, in Wiggins, *Paul Cuffe's Logs*, 322.

197. Paul Cuffe to Nathan Lord [Andover Theological Seminary], 19 April 1815, in ibid., 342.

198. Letter from the Philadelphia African Institution, 15 November 1815, Church Missionary Society, *Missionary Register* (London, 1816), 10.

199. Paul Cuffe to William Allen, February 1816, in Wiggins, *Paul Cuffe's Logs*, 404.

200. American Colonization Society, *First Annual Report*, 11.

201. Peter Williams, *A Discourse Delivered on the Death of Capt. P. Cuffee, before the New-York African Institution, . . . October 21, 1817, Etc* (New York, 1818), 28.

202. *West-African Sketches*, 33–34.

203. African Institution, *Special Report [1815]*, 33–34.

204. In manuscript in Columbine's Public Papers on Africa, UICSL III/11. Also excerpted in African Institution, *Sixth Report [1812]*, 113–53.

205. Remarks, 23 December 1811, in Wiggins, *Paul Cuffe's Logs*, 176.

206. Extract, Cuffe to Mills, 6 January 1817, published in American Colonization Society, *First Annual Report*, 27.

207. Journal entry, 27 March 1818, Gardiner Spring, ed., *Memoirs of the Rev. Samuel J. Mills: Late Missionary to the South Western Section of the United States and Agent of the American Colonization Society Deputed to Explore the Coast of Africa* (New York, 1820), 165–66.

208. Ibid., 182–83.

209. Ibid.

210. John Kizell to Bushrod Washington, 22 March 1820, published in American Colonization Society, *Address of the Board of Managers of the American Colonization Society, to the Auxiliary Societies and the People of the United States* (Washington, D.C., 1820), 17.

211. Spring, *Memoirs of the Rev. Samuel J. Mills*, 157.

212. *Africa Redeemed: Or, The Means of Her Relief Illustrated by the Growth and Prospects of Liberia* (London, 1851), 16–18.

213. Archibald Alexander, *A History of Colonization on the Western Coast of Africa* (Philadelphia, 1846), 101.

214. Spring, *Memoirs of the Rev. Samuel J. Mills*, 167.

215. Alexander, *History of Colonization*, 101.

216. Samuel A. Crozer to E. B. Caldwell, 31 March 1820, Society, *Address of the Board of Managers of the American Colonization Society, to the Auxiliary Societies and the People of the United States*, 13.

217. MacCarthy to Bathurst, 12 March 1820, Governor Despatches 1818–1822, SLPA.

218. Diary of Lt. George Courtenay, UICSL V/16/pp. 17–18.

219. *Royal Gazette and Sierra Leone Advertiser* [Freetown], 2 September 1820.

220. MacCarthy to Bathurst, 9 May 1818, CO 267/47. See also *Royal Gazette and Sierra Leone Advertiser* [Freetown], 25 April 1818; MacCarthy to Bathurst, 2 January 1818, CO 267/47; Mouser, *American Colony on the Rio Pongo*, 83.

221. Letter from Daniel Coker, 25 September 1820, published in American Colonization Society, *Fourth Annual Report*, 18.

222. Edward Trenchard to the Secretary of the Navy, 25 December 1820, published in ibid., 55.

223. Johnson to the Secretaries, 20 March 1821, CMS C/A/1/M1/22nd Year/3.

224. Entry for 3 April 1821, Bacon, *Abstract of a Journal*, 18–19.

225. Entry for 5 April 1821, in ibid., 21.

226. Entry for 10 April 1821, in ibid., 27.

227. Johnson, journal entry, 28 April 1821, CMS C/A/1/M1/22/34.

228. Ibid.

229. American Colonization Society, *The Sixth Annual Report of the American Society for Colonizing the Free People of Colour of the United States with an Appendix* (Washington, D.C., 1823), 43.

230. Johnson, journal entry, 15 March 1822, CMS C/A/1/M1/23/14.

231. Johnson to the Secretaries, 29 December 1821, CMS C/A/1/M1/23rd Year/2.

232. Diary of Lt. George Courtenay, UICSL V/16/p. 6; see also Caulker, "Legitimate Commerce and Statecraft," 405.

233. Jehudi Ashmun, *History of the American Colony in Liberia, from December 1821 to 1823* (Washington, D.C., 1826), 37–38.

234. Diary of Lt. George Courtenay, UICSL V/16/pp. 6–7.

235. Thomas Clarkson, *Thoughts on the Necessity of Improving the Condition of the Slaves in the British Colonies, with a View to Their Ultimate Emancipation: And on the Practicability, the Safety, and the Advantages of the Latter Measure* (London, 1824), 18.

Epilogue

1. Joseph Dupuis, *Journal of a Residence in Ashantee* (London, 1824), 210.

2. *The British Review and London Critical Journal*, vol. 18 (London, 1821), 488.

3. *The Sierra Leone Almanac, for the Year of Our Lord 1822, Being the Second after Bissextile, Calculated for the Meridian of Freetown, to Which Are Added Lists of Civil and Army Departments* (Freetown, 1822), 28.

4. MacCarthy to Bathurst, 9 October 1818, CO 267/47. See also Lynn, "Britain's West African Policy and the Island of Fernando Po, 1821–43," 193.

5. Ty M. Reese, "Controlling the Company: The Structures of Fante-British Relations on the Gold Coast, 1750–1821," *Journal of Imperial and Commonwealth History* 41, no. 1 (2013): 105.

6. Dupuis, *Journal of a Residence in Ashantee*, 209. See also Kwame Arhin, "The Structure of Greater Ashanti (1700–1824)," *Journal of African History* 8, no. 1 (January 1, 1967): 65–85; Ivor Wilks, *Asante in the Nineteenth Century: The Structure and Evolution of a Political Order* (London, New York: Cambridge University Press, 1975).

7. MacCarthy to Bathurst, 24 April 1822, Governor Despatches 1818–1822, SLPA.

8. Wilks, *Asante in the Nineteenth Century*, 170.

9. "From Private Correspondence," Accra, 31 January 1824, published in Dupuis, *Journal of a Residence in Ashantee*, 218.

10. Ricketts, *Narrative of the Ashantee War*, 56.

11. "Proclamation, signed by James Reffell, Given at Government House, Freetown, Sierra Leone, under the Seal now used as the Great Seal of the colony, this [28th] day of April, [1824]," Colonial Secretary's Letter Book, 6 June 1820–2 December 1824, SLPA.

12. Evidence of D. M. Hamilton, Appendix C17, CO 267/92.

13. Fyfe, *History of Sierra Leone*, 165.

14. Ibid., 155.

15. Ibid., 154–58.

16. Rowan and Wellington, "Report of the Commissioners of Inquiry, Part 1," 87.

17. Evidence of D. M. Hamilton, Appendix C17, CO 267/92.

18. Ibid.

19. Thomas Fowell Buxton, *The African Slave Trade and Its Remedy* (London, 1840), 363.

20. For the history of the Niger Expedition, see William Allen and Thomas Richard Heywood Thomson, *A Narrative of the Expedition Sent by Her Majesty's Government to the River Niger, in 1841: Under the Command of Captain H. D. Trotter, R.N.*, 2 vols. (London, 1848); Lambert, *Mastering the Niger;* Howard Temperley, *White Dreams, Black Africa: The Antislavery Expedition to the River Niger 1841–1842* (New Haven: Yale University Press, 1991).

21. Colley, *Britons*, 350–60.

22. 10 April 1835, *John Bull* [London], vol. 15, no. 773. See also Lambert, "Sierra Leone and Other Sites in the War of Representation Over Slavery"; Lambert, *Mastering the Niger;* Hall, *Macaulay and Son*, 72; Fyfe, *History of Sierra Leone*, 187.

23. Thomas Carlyle, *Occasional Discourse on the Nigger Question. [Reprinted, with Additions, from Fraser's Magazine.]* (London, 1853), 5. For an important gloss on Carlyle, see Hall, *Civilising Subjects*, 338–79.

24. Carlyle, *Occasional Discourse on the Nigger Question. [Reprinted, with Additions, from Fraser's Magazine.]*, 6.

25. Lt. George W. Courtenay, "West African Journal of HMS Bann," UICSL V/16, p. 88–90.

26. G. A. Lethbridge Banbury, *Sierra Leone: Or the White Man's Grave* (London, 1889), 74.

27. *The Annual Register*, vol. 115 (London, 1874), 100.

28. Henry Morton Stanley, *Coomassie and Magdala: The Story of Two British Campaigns in Africa* (London, 1891), 14.

29. James Grant, *Miss Cheyne of Essilmont* (London, 1884), 265.

30. Ricketts, *Narrative of the Ashantee War*, 122.

31. William Davies, *Extracts from the Journal Of . . . William Davies . . . When a Missionary at Sierra Leone* (Llandiloes, 1835), 77.

32. Frederick John Dealtry Lugard, *The Dual Mandate in British Tropical Africa*, 5th ed., vol. 1 (London: Archon, 1965), 5.

33. Ibid., 1:79–80.

34. Great Britain, Home Office, Department for Culture, Media and Sport, "Reflecting on the Past and Looking to the Future: The 2007 Bicentenary of the Abolition of the Slave Trade in the British Empire" (London: Department for Culture, Media and Sport, 2006), 7–8.

35. Reports on Liberated Africans, Appendix 11A, CO 267/91; Disposals from HMS *Maidstone* and HMS *Brazen*, Liberated African Department Statement of Disposals, 1821–33, SLPA.

Index

Page numbers in *italics* refer to illustrations.